D1065139

Airplanes of the World

1490 to 1976

REVISED AND ENLARGED EDITION

Drawings and Descriptions of Planes by
DOUGLAS ROLFE

Historical Introductions by
ALEXIS DAWYDOFF

Revised by
William Winter, William Byshyn, Hank Clark

Additional Descriptions by Don Berliner
and Drawings by Mel Klapholz

SIMON AND SCHUSTER • NEW YORK

TEXAS STATE TECHNICAL INSTITUTE
ROLLING PLAINS CAMPUS – LIBRARY
SWEETWATER, TEXAS 79556

COPYRIGHT © 1954, 1962, 1969, 1978 BY THE CONDÉ NAST PUBLICATIONS INC.
ALL RIGHTS RESERVED
INCLUDING THE RIGHT OF REPRODUCTION
IN WHOLE OR IN PART IN ANY FORM
PUBLISHED BY SIMON AND SCHUSTER
A DIVISION OF GULF & WESTERN CORPORATION
SIMON & SCHUSTER BUILDING
ROCKEFELLER CENTER
1230 AVENUE OF THE AMERICAS
NEW YORK, NEW YORK 10020
FOURTH REVISED EDITION
MANUFACTURED IN THE UNITED STATES OF AMERICA

MOST OF THE DRAWINGS IN THIS BOOK APPEARED ORIGINALLY IN AIR PROGRESS MAGAZINE.

LIBRARY OF CONGRESS CATALOGING IN PUBLICATION DATA

Rolfe, Douglas.

Airplanes of the world, 1490–1976
Includes index.
1. Airplanes—History. I. Title.
TL670.3.R64 1978 629.133'34'09 77-16105

ISBN 0-671-22684-3

2 3 4 5 6 7 8 9 10

CONTENTS

9.32

791233

PART ONE

To Fly Like a Bird

1490-1898

THE DREAM was always there. Watching birds wing their way aloft, man too longed to be able to fly. His earliest myths and legends reflect this wishful thinking. The Chinese emperor Shun was supposed to have built himself an air chariot in 2500 B.C. An "aerial chariot" was presented to the Queen of Sheba by King Solomon. In Greece, they told about Icarus, who along with his father made wings of feathers and wax to stage a successful escape from imprisonment on Crete. As all good fifth-grade pupils can tell you, Icarus' wings melted when he tried for altitude near the sun, plunging him into the sea.

Serious thinkers began to ask: What is air and how can you fly in it? The Greek philosopher Aristotle conceived the idea that air has weight, and Archimedes discovered the law of floating bodies—eventual basis of the principle of lighter-than-air craft. Later, in the thirteenth century, these probings into the mysteries of the atmosphere became more specific when research by men of science like Galileo, Roger Bacon, and Pascal proved that air is a gas, elastic, that the higher you go, the less its pressure, that hot air rises while cool air descends.

It was the Italian painter Leonardo da Vinci who made the biggest contribution. Around 1490 he invented the "air screw," ancestor of the propeller and helicopter rotor. Using a crude form of it containing feathers, he fashioned a little model helicopter which actually flew. And as an avid student of bird flight, he correctly deduced that it is the flow of air over the bird's wing that gives it lift—and the faster such flow of air, the greater the lift. As a result of these studies he built a couple of flying machines with flapping wings intended to be capable of supporting a man.

These ornithopters did not fly. Though Da Vinci had determined the fundamental principle of how a bird does it, he did not understand the complexity of its wing which, to obtain the various effects desired in flight, can infinitely alter its camber, or curve, the angle of incidence (angle at which the wing sets into the body or "fuselage"), its dihedral, and even its area.

The first actual flying machine did not copy the birds. It was a hot-air balloon constructed in 1783 by two French brothers, Jacques and Joseph Montgolfier. After a test flight during which the only passengers were a sheep, a rooster, and a goose, a daring French nobleman named François Pilatre de Rozier climbed into the basket to become the first man in the world to rise into the air. With hydrogen proving a better lifting medium than hot air, ballooning went on to enjoy a run of popularity lasting over a hundred years.

The Montgolfiers' accomplishment was still not the answer. A balloon was not controllable except up or down and was subject to the vagaries of the wind. The invention of the steam engine by James Watt of England in 1769 opened the way for aerial navigation. A Frenchman, Henri Giffard, first proved the practicability of a mechanical power plant by building a dirigible driven by a steam engine. In this, in 1852, he cruised over Paris at a leisurely 6 m.p.h. (Of course, the invention of the internal-combustion engine by Germany's Nicholas Otto in 1876 was destined really to show air navigation the way—but not till years after its debut.)

In the meantime, the advocates of the "airplane" were hard at work. To them, a mere balloon fitted with an engine was not the answer either. A dirigible had no resemblance to a bird, still man's ideal for conquest of the air. As early as 1810 Sir George Cayley of England wrote a treatise on basic aerodynamics laying down the fundamentals of both fixed- and rotary-wing aircraft. During his lifetime he built and experimented with gliders and a steam-powered helicopter with laterally disposed, contrarotating rotors.

In Italy, Vittorio Sarti also experimented with a helicopter equipped with oppositely turning sail-like rotors mounted one above the other and driven by jets of steam impinging on blades attached to the shafts. As a matter of fact, in these early struggles with the idea of heavier-than-air craft, there were probably more inventors working on direct-lift machines than the fixed-wing airplane. The helicopter had several advantages over the airplane, the chief one undoubtedly being concerned with the excessive weight and low power of available engines.

In order to develop a lifting force, the wing had to be pushed through the air. In the fixed-wing airplane, the entire machine must be pushed forward with sufficient speed to rise. However, the low engine power at hand couldn't cope with the large weight factors involved, making a take-off impossible. Then why not, asked the early aeronautical engineers, give the wing forward motion independent of the rest of the craft?

The obvious solution was to make the wing in the form of a propeller and rotate it with an engine. The forward-swinging blades would generate sufficient lift to carry the machine directly upward, minus the long ground run. All of which was sound, excellent theory . . . but so complex was the rotor system that it took more than 200 years to perfect the helicopter.

Thus, after many unsuccessful ventures with helicopters, men returned to the airplane. By now, the engine situation was a bit brighter. Improving on Nicholas Otto's internal-combustion job that had ordinary house gas as fuel, Gottlieb Daimler of Germany perfected a gasoline-burning engine in 1880. Its use for airplanes was still in the future—but the fact had been established that it could be mounted in moving vehicles.

Men like Samuel Henson, John Stringfellow, and Thomas Moy of England built successful scale models, powered either by springs or compressed air, that definitely flew. Henson actually patented the design for a giant 150-foot wingspan passenger air liner with a 30-h.p. steam engine. He visualized the possibilities of air travel and, in partnership with Stringfellow, formed the Aerial Transit Company in 1842.

Sticking to birds as their pattern, these pioneer designers of the airplane naturally enough thought only in terms of the monoplane as to shape. (In some cases they even fastened reasonable facsimiles of the bird's head and beak in front.) However, in 1860 an English scientist, Francis Wenham, advanced the idea of the double wing or biplane as a way of increasing wing area without increase in span. He also proved a curved wing surface is greatly superior to a flat one. Practical research in wing contours, or airfoils, was conducted by a Canadian, Horatio Phillips, with a crude type of wind tunnel and his "Venetian Blind" tethered airplane. With the data thus obtained he patented the "undercambered" airfoil, capable of generating substantially more lift than those in use.

Wenham, incidentally, received credit for adapting the gasoline engine to the airplane. His efforts in this respect were mostly theoretical; there is no record of his engine ever taking to the air.

And so at the three-quarter mark of the nineteenth century the jackpot question was still the power plant. Groundling man had a fairly good idea of how to build a plane that would fly. Yet the steam engine, the only practical form of propelling energy developed thus far, weighed, with boiler and fuel, more than the airplane itself. Nevertheless, many brave attempts incorporating it were made. France's Clement Ader constructed two steam-powered full-size airplanes, the Eole and the Avion, the latter of which is claimed to have risen several feet.

In England, American-born Sir Hiram Maxim, inventor of the machine gun, built a huge 110-foot-wingspan flying machine weighing over 7,000 pounds and driven by a 350-h.p. engine. Pilotless, without adequate controls, it was intended mainly to test power required for flight and was not expected to fly. However, so powerful did the engine prove to be that the craft tore loose from the restraining rails mounted above the railroad-like track on which it was being run and crashed.

At this stage the dirigible boys were cutting fancy capers.

All they had to do, if bigger engines were desired, was to attach a bigger gas bag to the gondola. A number of dirigibles, such as the French military type "La France," were powered by electric motors. The behemoth "La France" measured 165 feet in length, had a 9-h.p. motor operating from a battery weighing close to 1,200 pounds. Its top speed was 14 m.p.h.

Toward the end of the nineteenth century success for the airplane arrived at long-deserved last. A German, Otto Lilienthal, became the first man to fly in a heavier-than-air craft—though without an engine. He and his brother Gustave had spent their youth in the province of Pomerania studying birds and bird flight. This eventually led to the construction of a man-carrying glider that copied the winged creatures in deed as well as in form.

Glider experiment had been going on for years. Logically, man had tried to imitate the ability of birds to soar—to utilize the energy of rising warm air in place of muscle power. Why not let this invisible h.p. serve an air frame to navigate on high? In 1857, for instance, a French sailor named Jean-Marie La Bris built a large glider, faithfully following the lines of his occupational friend the albatross, and had himself towed aloft in it by a team of horses. Though the craft rose, it crashed immediately, as was true of a second attempt.

The Lilienthals' study of birds had been more scientific. Where predecessors had merely pointed out general fundamentals, these two discovered the definite factors and relationships. They learned exactly what a bird does with its wing in flight—how it alters the dihedral for greater stability, or the camber to get more lift; and just how much lift, for example, is needed to overcome a known amount of weight. From their observations and experiments the Lilienthals evolved the theory of flight which is still the basis of our present science of aerodynamics.

Deciding that the only way to learn to fly was to do so himself, Otto built numerous man-carrying hang gliders—the kind in which most of the pilot's body is suspended underneath the craft—both of the monoplane and biplane type. Laboriously he taught himself to fly by jumping off various elevations. In all he made a total of 2,000 successful flights, some with 180-degree turns. His gliders were crude and had to be controlled by shifting the weight of the body—but they were the first workable airplanes. Lilienthal was killed during a flight in 1896, and his brother Gustave gave up further experiments.

With the thing finally accomplished, a frenzy of glider building and flying spread throughout the world. In England Percy Pilcher duplicated Lilienthal's feats, towed aloft by horse team—and died in one of his gliders when a wing guy wire broke. In the United States, 60-year-old Octave Chanute conducted a number of experiments at a camp established by him among the tall dunes of Lake Michigan. His purpose was to devise means of control other than the shifting of body weight. His first craft was a multiplane whose wings could move forward and backward to adjust the center of lift. This was followed by a biplane hang glider with a flexible tail.

All told, 1,000 flights were made between 1896 and 1897 in Chanute gliders—all by assistants as pilots, since Chanute himself was too old for the effort and risk. In 1898 one of his assistants, A. M. Herring, built a biplane with a compressed-air motor, with the glider as its basis.

And meanwhile, at the Smithsonian Institution in the nation's capital, Dr. Samuel P. Langley was toying with powered airplanes. He put together many models propelled by rubber motors and tiny steam engines, the most successful being a 17-foot-span tandem biplane, the "Aerodrome," fitted with a steam engine driving two propellers, which flew a distance of 420 feet at a speed of 30 m.p.h.

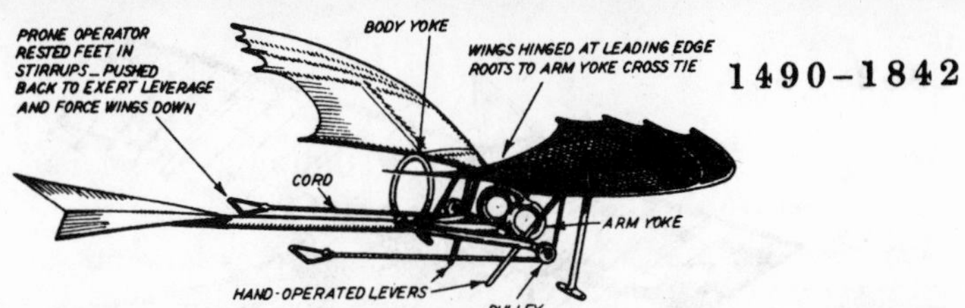

LEONARDO DA VINCI First scientific approach to the problem of heavier-than-air flight was this man-powered ornithopter devised by this brilliant fifteenth-century master craftsman, artist, and engineer. It failed to fly but was nonetheless a noteworthy effort toward flight. –1490

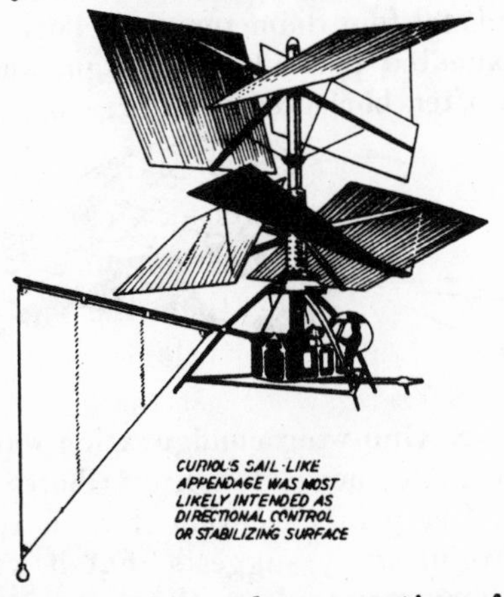

VITTORIO SARTI This early conception of the coaxial, contra-rotating helicopter was also of Italian origin. Details of the intended power plant and drive gear are not known. –1825

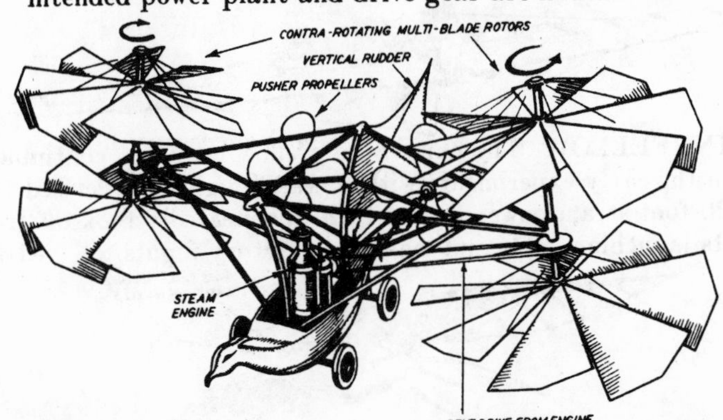

GEORGE CAYLEY First practical helicopter design which might well have flown had an efficient power plant been available. Sir George Cayley, noted British pioneer in aeronautics, correctly anticipated the laterally displaced twin-rotor system by 100 years. –1842

WILLIAM SAMUEL HENSON Huge air liners were anticipated in this extraordinary and historic design which was patented by Henson in 1842. Specifications included 150-foot wingspread, 20-foot-diameter propellers. Configuration crudely approximated present-day design, and the Henson wing truss was often borrowed in later, more successful, designs. –1842

NOTE CRUCIFORM TAIL ASSEMBLY

WERNER SIEMENS Gull-wing configuration was a feature of this curious and little-known design attributed to a German ex-army officer. Old prints mention it as a rocket-powered plant, but a careful study suggests that it was in fact intended to be a steam-powered ornithopter. –1847

STRINGFELLOW The name Stringfellow crops up continually in the early experiments with powered flight. He devised this 20-foot steam-powered model which repeatedly took off from its launching cable and made satisfactory flights. –1848

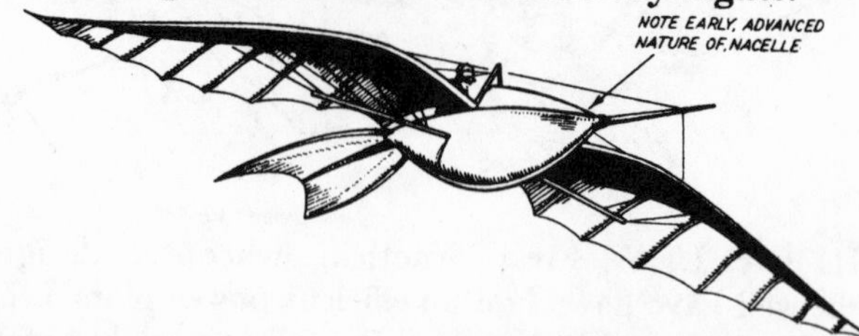

LA BRIS Jean-Marie La Bris built this unusually clean soaring plane almost 100 years ago. Launched from a horse-drawn cart, it is said actually to have lifted from its cradle. –1857

DU TEMPLE A very early conception of the tractor monoplane. This French design had steam power, anticipated delta-wing configuration. –1857

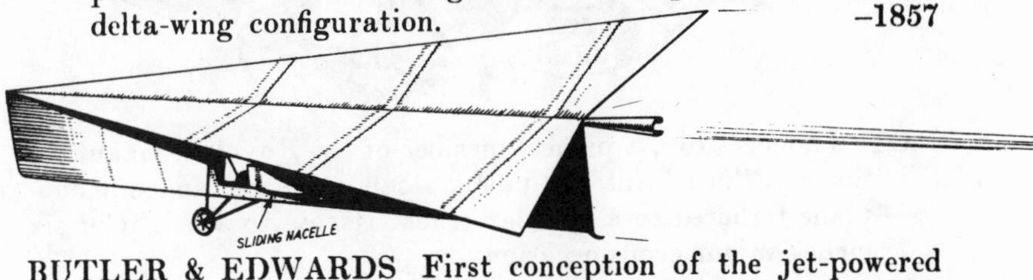

BUTLER & EDWARDS First conception of the jet-powered delta-wing airplane. A solid fuel propellant was intended. Longitudinal control was to be effected by changing the center of gravity by moving the nacelle back and forth. –1867

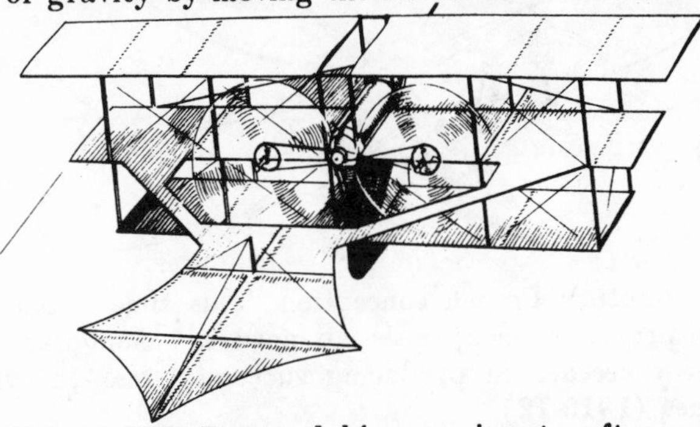

STRINGFELLOW Resumed his experiments after a lapse of twenty years and produced this triplane which clearly anticipated the early box-kite airplanes. –1869

POMES-DE LA PAUZE Introduced this design which anticipated the present-day McDonnell "Little Henry" type helicopter. Provision was made for varying the pitch of the two-bladed rotor, but details of the mechanism and power plant are not known. –1871

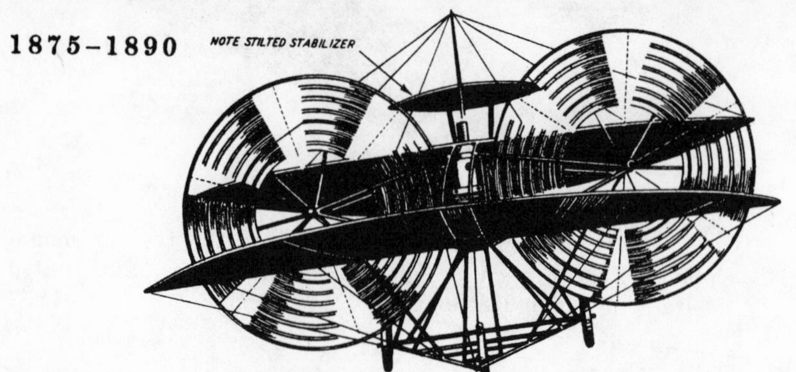

MOY Thomas Moy, a pioneer member of the Royal Aeronautical Society, "flew" this 120-pound steam-powered tandem monoplane tethered to a circular track. It rose to a height of six inches on numerous occasions. –1875

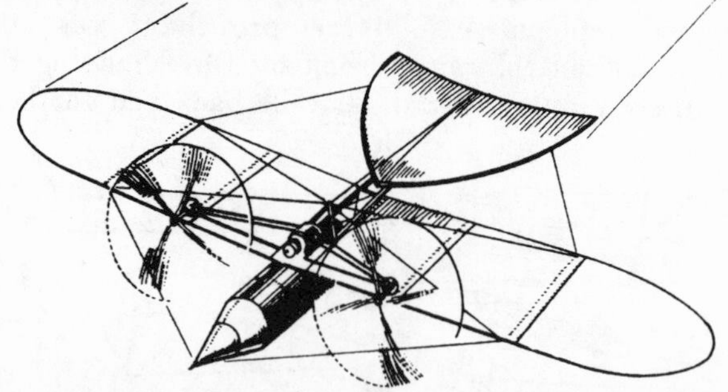

TATIN Another French conception. This time anticipating a twin-propeller compressed-air-powered monoplane. Tatin later succeeded in producing successful man-carrying airplanes (1910-12). –1875

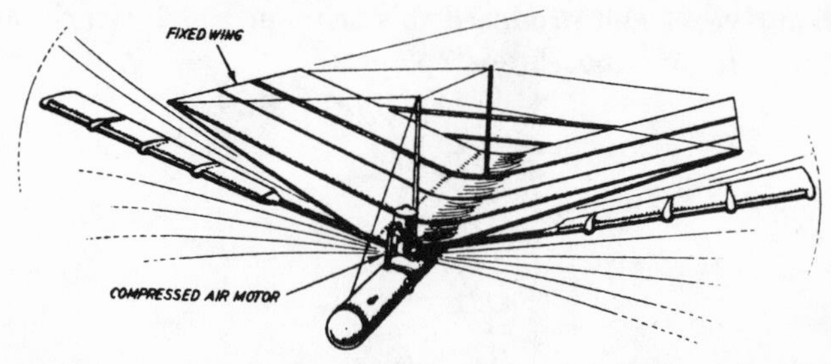

HARGRAVE Lawrence Hargrave, noted Australian pioneer, perfected flapping flight with this compressed-air-powered model. He later directed his talents to developing box-kite-type gliders. –1890

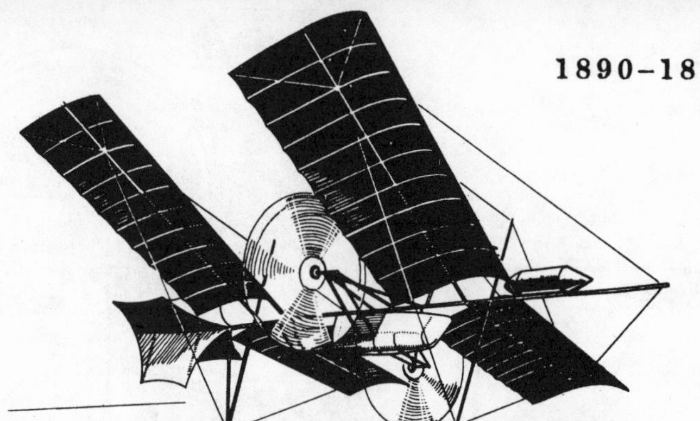

LANGLEY The great American pioneer, Samuel Pierpont Langley, established the possibility of free flight with this, his No. 5 model. Launched from a catapault, it made flights up to 420 feet. –1890

PHILLIPS Horatio Phillips, generally regarded today as the father of the science of aerodynamics, used this curious multiplane in captive flight to demonstrate his theories on the properties of curved airfoils. –1893

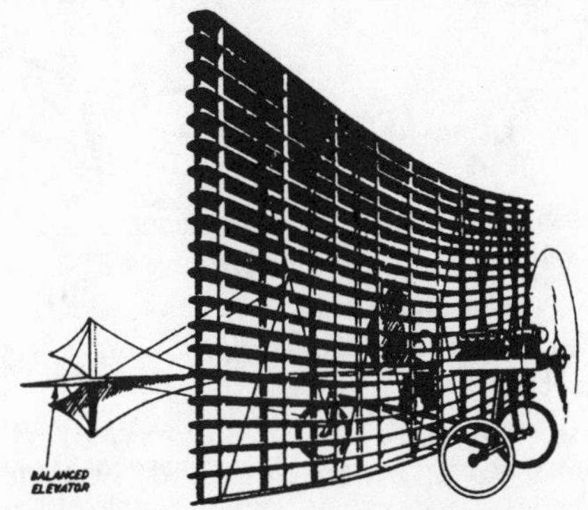

PHILLIPS Full-scale gas-powered Phillips multiplane was a much later production and is said to have made short hops.

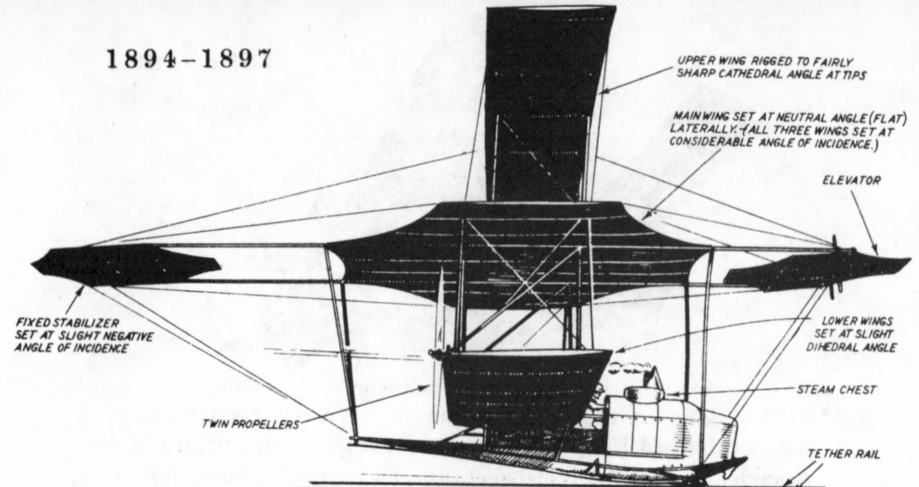

HIRAM MAXIM U.S.-born English inventor and scientist conducted experiments with this huge (350 h.p., 110 feet long, $3\frac{1}{2}$ tons) multiplane. –1894

LILIENTHAL Otto Lilienthal, noted German pioneer master of the art of gliding flight, evolved the elementiry hang-type glider. He accomplished more than 2,000 flights before he fell to his death in 1896. –1890-96

CHANUTE Octave Chanute, U.S. pioneer in gliding flight, experimented with many types of gliders. These are but two of his many successful designs. It is of interest to learn that this brilliant engineer and scientist was over sixty when he essayed his first flight.

Another design by this great pioneer, noteworthy for the introduction of a regular fuselage and the rigid X-type wing truss. –1896-97

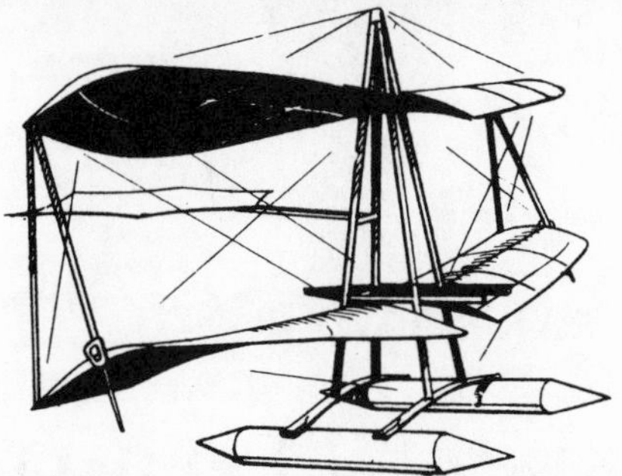

GALLAUDET This American pioneer continued experiments with the properties of the curved, or "cambered," airfoil. This is one of his early amphibious gliders. Much later Galaudet designed and built a successful airplane which had a centrally located propeller which revolved about the fuselage. –1897

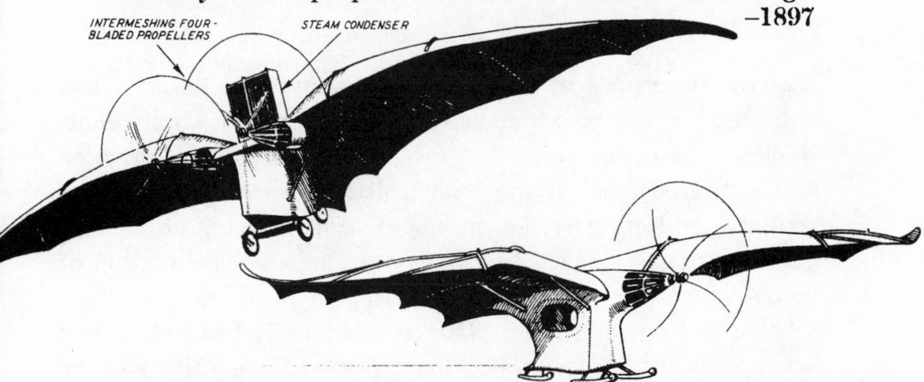

ADER Clement Ader, noted French engineer, is one of the most controversial characters in the story of the airplane. Even today there are some who claim that he was the first human being to make a powered flight. The single-engine Eole and the twin-motor Avion are shown here. Both utilized steam power. The Avion actually got off the ground but, lacking any means of control, soon crashed. –1890-97

HERRING. Augustus Herring, one-time associate of the great Chanute, split with him on the timeliness of introducing power and built this full-scale Chanute-type biplane powered with a compressed-air engine. It did not fly but was clearly the inspiration for the later-successful early Curtiss designs. –1898

PART TWO

The Wrights Lead the Way

1900-1913

At the beginning of the twentieth century Dr. Langley was well ahead in the race to achieve powered flight in an airplane. Backed by a grant from Congress, he built a full-scale version of his "Aerodrome" flying model, fitted with a specially constructed 50-h.p. gasoline engine. Unfortunately, launching-gear or wing structure failure (or perhaps a combination of both) caused this plane to crash during its initial take-off from a houseboat on the Potomac River, October 7, 1903. A second attempt in early December had the same negative watery ending.

Hardly more than a week later, two brothers named Wright reached the coveted goal by making the first sustained flights in an engine-driven airplane at Kitty Hawk, N. C. The historic day was December 17, 1903.

Orville and Wilbur Wright, owners of a bicycle shop in Dayton, Ohio, had studiously concerned themselves with the question of flight since 1896. Very soon they concluded that the vital remaining problem—that of how to control the airplane—must be solved by mechanical means serving the aerodynamic factors involved. There must be a rudder, elevators, and the like. After several seasons of testing this idea in man-carrying gliders over the sand dunes of Kitty Hawk, they were ready for the trial-by-engine. With no engine on the market, the brothers had their mechanic, Charles Taylor, build one developing around 12 h.p. and weighing 170 pounds.

On its first flight that cold, gusty December 17, the Wright machine rose and stayed in the air for 12 seconds, piloted by Orville. On the fourth try of the day it remained airborne for 59 seconds and traveled a distance of 852 feet. And by the end of the following year the brothers were making regular flights which included complete turns around a circular course.

The "Wright Flyer" itself was a conventional biplane whose single-engine chain-driven two pusher propellers were located on either side of the pilot's position. The real genius of the Wrights, however, was expressed in their control system, and this was their greatest contribution to aviation. Whereas Lilienthal had to shift his body weight, the Flyer's pilot warped the entire wing tips by mechanical arrangement (a job later done by ailerons). Climb and dive control came from double or biplane-type elevators mounted in front and operated by lever; the twin rudders were interconnected with the wing-warp mechanism and set behind the pilot. All the chief components for turning and maneuvering today's airplane were to be found in that first craft, primitive though it was.

They were the first to perceive the true function of an aerial rudder, which does not, as in the case of a boat, cause the plane to turn. The function of their rudders was simply to hold the plane straight—that is, to prevent yawing—while the plane was being caused to bank by means of the wing warp. Once the bank was established, the controls were returned to neutral, and the plane flew on a curved course until opposite control was applied to straighten it up again.

With the brothers from Ohio having struck gold in the sky, a general "rush" followed the world over. This time, men were humble as well as anxious, and aeronautical research laboratories grew up everywhere. Most significant was the Eiffel laboratory in France, established by the builder of the Tower and the first to have a full-fledged wind tunnel for experimentation. In Russia the Aerodynamic Institute of Kotchino near Moscow was organized as early as 1904, and in Germany the University of Göttingen, under Professor Ludwig Prandtl, began probing into the mysteries of flight and solving aerodynamic and structural requirements of aircraft.

The first airplane flight in France (and Europe as well) was made in 1906 by Alberto Santos-Dumont, the wealthy Brazilian who had earlier thrilled Paris by his nonchalant cruising over the city in his powered dirigible. His pioneer plane was a boxlike contraption with the tail surfaces out in front; the pilot rode standing erect in a deep wicker basket. Far better known became his later tiny "Demoiselle" monoplane with pilot located below the wing. Right after Santos-Dumont came such luminaries as Blériot, Farman, Voisin. Blériot, first to build a successful mid-wing monoplane, is best remembered as the first man to fly over the English Channel, from Calais to Dover.

In sum, France poured so much energy into aviation that in a few years it held the title of world leader; by 1910 it was the only country with almost a dozen different airplane engines available and had by far the most streamlined craft. At the same time, England, Russia, Holland, and Germany were not idle. Names that today are familiar as types were then eager young men building and experimenting with airplanes; Alliot Verdun Roe (Avro) and Geoffrey de Havilland, Igor Sikorsky, Anthony Fokker.

Here in the United States, the Wright brothers did not hold a monopoly for long. Glenn H. Curtiss, a bicycle and motorcycle maker from Hammondsport, New York, full of ideas and encouraged by Alexander Graham Bell, formed a company to build airplanes. In his first product, the "June Bug," powered by an engine of his own design, he won the Scientific American Trophy in 1908 for the first officially observed flight (in America). With further improved models of the plane he gathered an impressive stack of records, including top honors at the First International Aviation Meet in Reims, France.

The lessons learned making fast, light motorcycle engines helped Curtiss develop an aviation power plant, the first American one manufactured, that gave a boost to U.S. air activity. Glenn Curtiss was also the first to devise a method of launching airplanes from water, by fitting a pontoon beneath one of his craft, retaining the wheel landing gear for take-off from land.

Thus the amphibian was born. Later, he built a special plane fitted with a boat hull—the ancestor of the flying boat. And a Curtiss landplane was the first to alight on and fly from the deck of a battleship.

During this period, designers were experimenting wildly with the airplane's shape. Every conceivable idea was tried, including the wholly circular wing. Gradually two standard types emerged, the monoplane and the biplane—and there were reasons for the latter's becoming predominant. Although the monoplane had cleaner design and hence greater speed, the biplane of those days presented an easier solution from the standpoint of structure as well as engineering. To attain a lift comparable to the biplane's, the mono had to have a longer wing. This large expanse of surface would require considerable structural strength, which meant much added weight with materials then available, and the external bracings also required by it created considerable drag and interfered with the air flow. On the other hand, the biplane, with one wing situated above another and tied in with struts and wires, was structurally more rigid, more stable, and more easily flown. The two wings gave it a larger over-all area, and thus it could carry greater loads than the monoplane.

The chief stability problems, by this time, had already been solved. The proper location of the center of gravity, ignorance of which had killed many an early pioneer, was known, as well as use of dihedral angle for lateral stability and *décalage* angle between wing and horizontal tail, where the tail is set at a negative, or forward-tilting, angle while the wing has a positive angle. (The negative angle of the tail causes a damping effect in the event of pitching motion.)

Improvement in engines also benefited lighter-than-air craft. Showing its first interest in the possibilities of flying, the U.S. Signal Corps purchased a dirigible built by Capt. Thomas Baldwin and equipped with a Curtiss engine. In 1910 an American newspaperman named Walter Wellman set out from Atlantic City in a big 228-foot "gas bag" to cross the Atlantic, but failed. (Three days and 550 miles out, Wellman, crew, and cat mascot were rescued by schooner from the storm-buffeted "America.") In Germany the following year, a huge rigid-type dirigible designed and built by Count Zeppelin was put into air passenger service, the world's first. On its maiden flight the "Schwaben" carried 32 people, and in the three years prior to World War I the Zeppelin Transportation Company flew 35,000 paid passengers to and from points on the Continent.

This period also saw air racing breeze into existence. In 1909 James Gordon Bennett, owner of the New York *Herald* and sponsor of balloon racing, underwrote the International Air Meet. The first one held at Reims was won by Glenn Curtiss—at a speed of 46 m.p.h. in his 26-foot-span "Golden Flyer" biplane. At the fourth annual meet the French entered a radical racing monoplane, the Deperdussin-Béchereau, the most streamlined machine of its time. It had a plywood shell fuselage, thin mid-mounted wings, streamlined landing-gear struts, and fully cowled 140-h.p. Gnome engine. Flown by Jules Vedrines, the airplane won the race at the amazing speed of 107 m.p.h. The next year, wearing a souped-up engine, it won with 125 m.p.h.

A feature of the Deperdussin was wheel control—from which comes the modern term "Dep control." And even then, thanks to recognition of the fact that race planes of the day suffered from drag and had poor take-off characteristics, designers were at least thinking in terms of retractable landing gears and variable-pitch propellers.

In 1913 another speed enthusiast, a wealthy Frenchman named Jacques Schneider, decided to sponsor international races for seaplanes, donating a $5,000 trophy and $5,000 in cash prizes. The opening meet was again won by France and a Deperdussin plane, a float version, at an average speed of 45.8 m.p.h.

But war was about to ring the bell on playtime for the airplane. Military were looking speculatively at this winged vehicle in terms of warfare. In England, Short and Vickers were experimenting with armed planes, as were Voisin and Farman in France. Great Britain's Royal Flying Corps, established in

1911, was a going concern; by 1912 the French Air Service was already the world's largest, having more than 200 planes. Around 1913 the U.S. Army Signal Corps formed a special aviation branch, equipped with biplane trainers turned out by the Wrights and Curtiss, and was soon ordering others from Glenn L. Martin, another early flying pioneer turned manufacturer. And Germany was bidding for the talents of the Dutch designer Fokker.

WRIGHT BROTHERS The Wright 1902 model glider was used by them to perfect the control system which they had invented. It marked a great step forward toward a practical airplane.

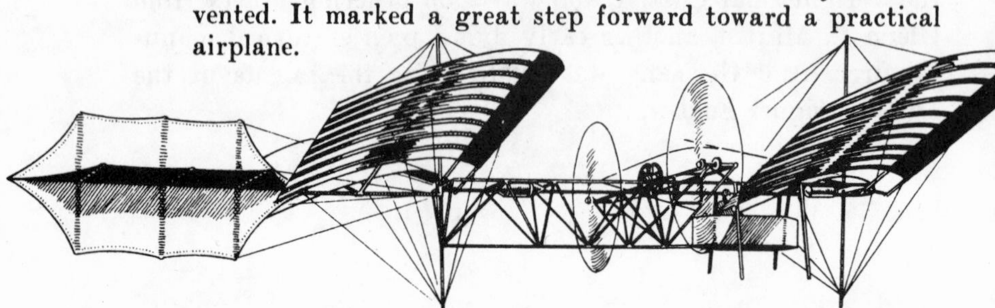

LANGLEY A full-scale development of Langley's earlier Model 5 was launched by catapult over the waters of the Potomac in October 1903. It fouled the take-off ramp and plunged into the river, but like the earlier Ader attempts remained for years a subject of bitter controversy on the subject of who actually flew first. Interesting to note is the fact that it was powered with the world's first radial gasoline engine. Many years later it was rebuilt and fitted with a Curtiss engine and actually flown by Glenn Curtiss in 1914.

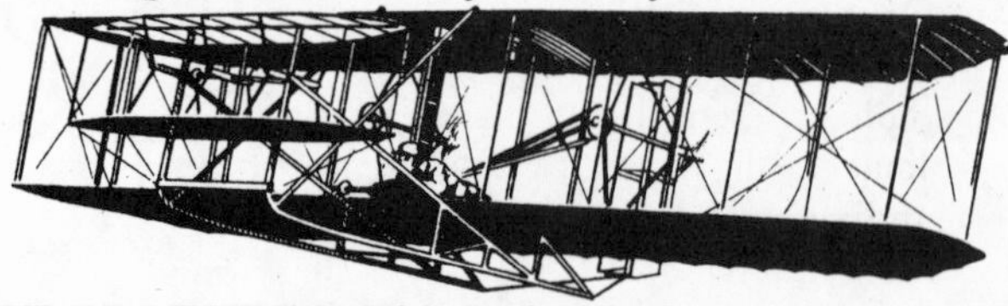

WRIGHT BROTHERS This is the airplane today recognized as the first to make a successful powered flight. It was powered with a 12-h.p. engine designed and built by the Wright Brothers. First flight of 120 feet was made by Orville Wright on December 17, 1903. Later in the same day Wilbur Wright flew the plane a distance of 852 feet.

SANTOS-DUMONT This Voisin-built biplane, powered with a 50-h.p. V-type Antoinette engine and piloted by Alberto Santos-Dumont, was the first airplane to fly in Europe (Bagatelle Field, Paris, France, Sept. 13, 1906).

BLÉRIOT Louis Blériot flew this prototype model of the famed 1909 cross-channel monoplane to complete the world's first officially recorded cross-country flight. The wing-tip ailerons are noteworthy.

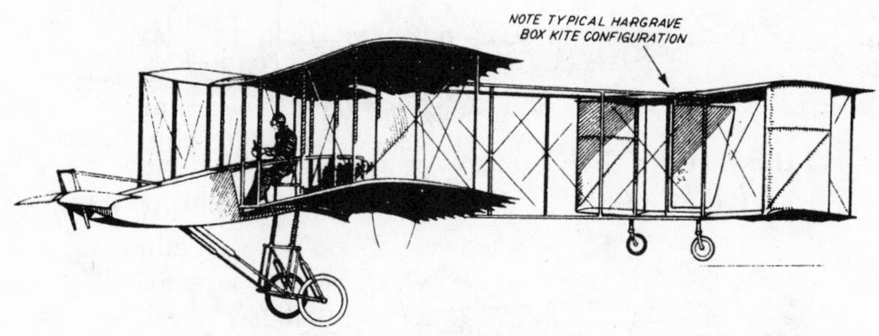

FARMAN This Voisin-built box-kite biplane with Henri Farman at the controls was the first airplane in Europe to complete a one-kilometer flight, returning to the point of departure before landing.

R.E.P. Robert Esnault-Peltrie introduced all-metal air frames, cantilever, internally braced wings, radial air-cooled engines, the stick control system, and the tandem-wheel landing gear.

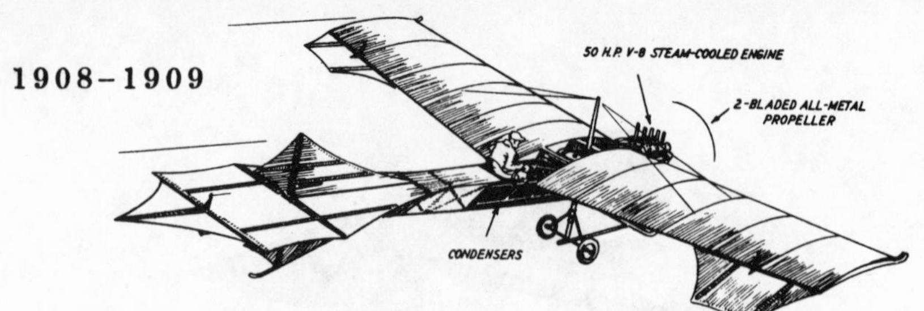

ANTOINETTE The graceful Antoinette monoplane designed by Levasseur and piloted by Hubert Latham was the first airplane in the world to attain an altitude of 500 feet and the first to fly in a wind of gale proportions. It was powered with a 50-h.p. Antoinette engine.

CURTISS "JUNE BUG" First genuine Curtiss design and winner of the first U.S.-sponsored airplane flight trophy.

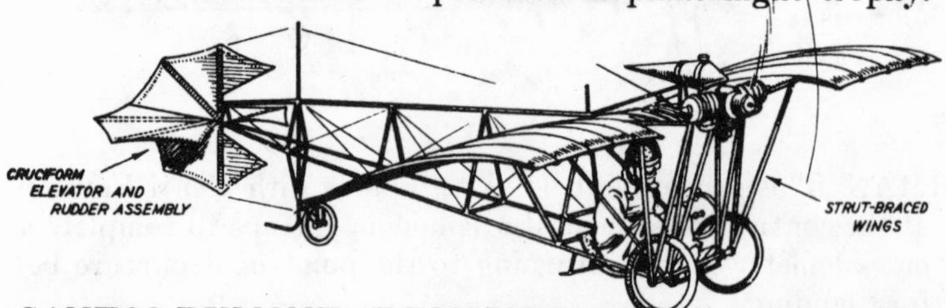

SANTOS-DUMONT "DEMOISELLE" The "Demoiselle" was the world's first ultra-light airplane. Powered with a 28-horsepower flat twin Darracq engine, it was largely constructed of bamboo. Although nicknamed the "Infuriated Grasshopper," it actually flew well with small pilots such as Roland Garros and Audemars and held the world's altitude record at one time.

CURTISS Powered with a 50-h.p. Curtiss engine and piloted by Glenn Curtiss, this biplane captured first place in the first Gordon Bennett speed races at Reims, France, in 1909. Average speed: 46 m.p.h.

WRIGHT BROTHERS This modified version of the earlier Model B was powered by a 30-h.p. Wright engine. Front elevators have disappeared.

DE HAVILLAND Geoffrey de Havilland's first successful airplane is a far cry from his present super-speedy jet-powered De Havilland's "Comet" air liners.

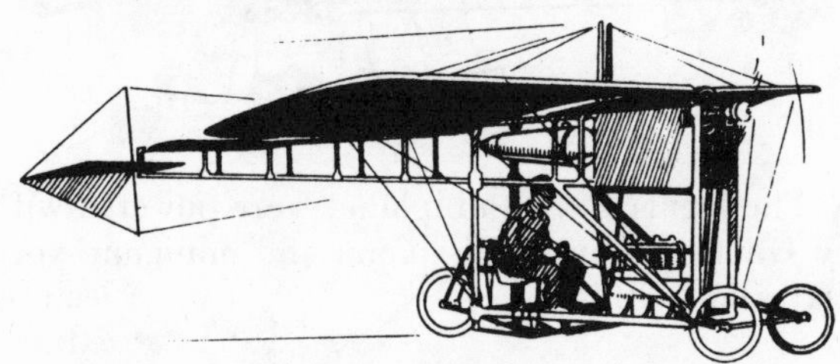

BLACKBURN Another early first by one of the still-leading aircraft firms.

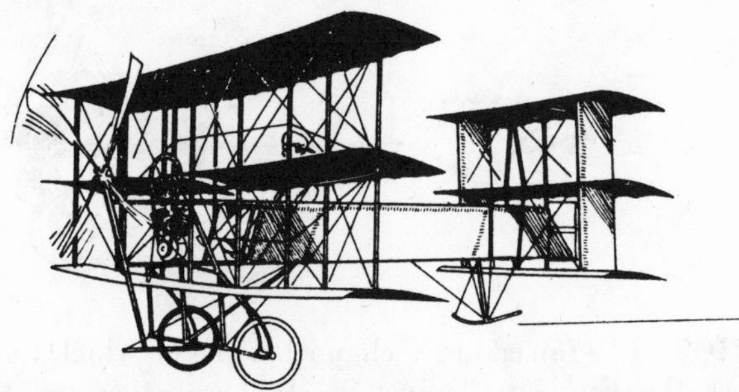

AVRO Yet another early design bearing a name still famous for its fine airplanes. A. V. Roe's little triplane was powered with a 9-h.p. J.A.P. motorcycle engine.

MARTIN And yet another first design from the stables of one of the world's leading aircraft firms. Engine was a 12-h.p. Ford.

FARMAN The Henri Farman biplanes were powered with 50-h.p. rotary Gnome engines. Maximum and minimum speeds coincided at about 38 m.p.h.

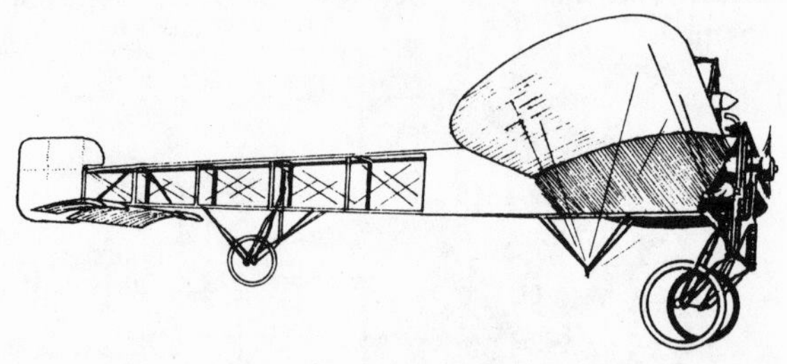

BLÉRIOT The famed cross-channel model on which Louis Blériot flew the English Channel in 1909 was powered with a 20-25-h.p. Anzani radial engine.

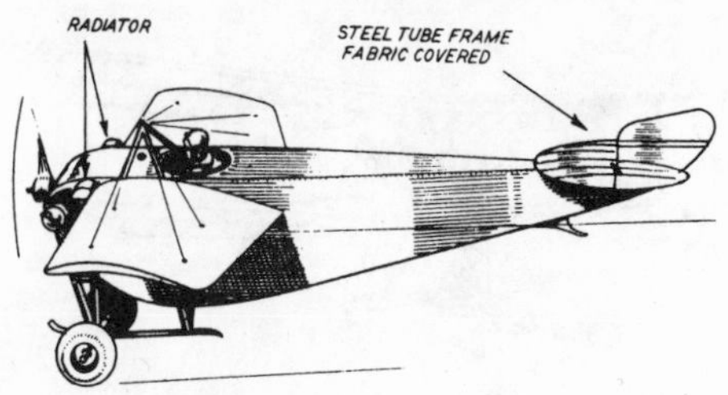

NIEUPORT Designed and built by Charles and Edouard Nieuport, this was one of the first airplanes in the world to approach streamline form and to use modern-type airfoil. With a 20-h.p. flat twin Nieuport engine it did about 80 m.p.h.

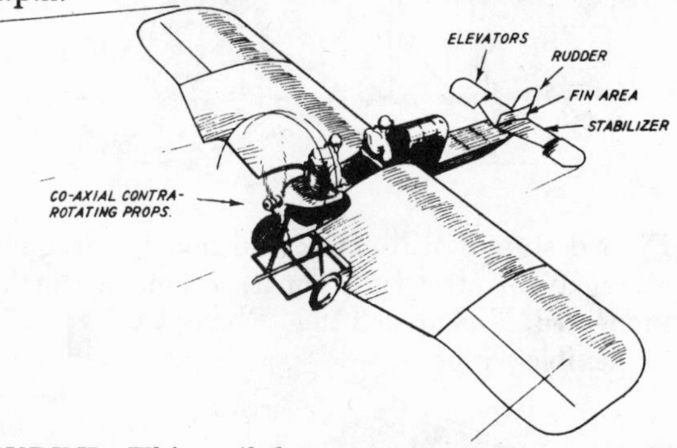

LEFEVBRE This tail-first monoplane was notable for having shaft-driven contrarotating coaxial propellers. Engine was mounted ahead of pilot's cockpit.

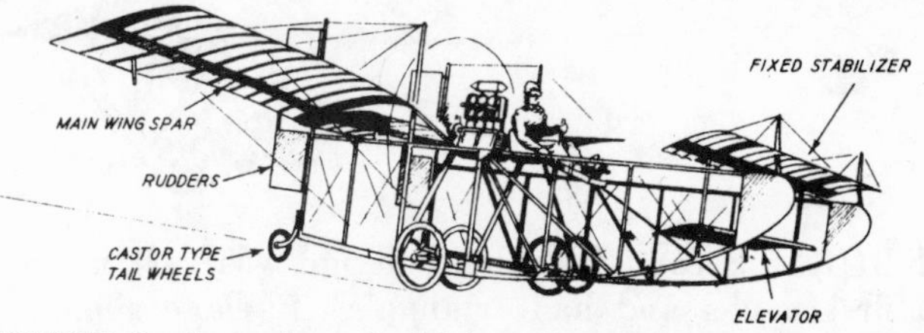

VALKYRIE 1 A curious British tail-first monoplane which had some success. Engine was a 35-h.p. Green.

WALDEN This first successful U.S. monoplane was far behind European designs of the period. It resembled a Curtiss biplane of the period minus the upper plane.

DUFAUX First successful Swiss airplane.

BREGUET First design of still-active and famous Breguet Company was largely of steel tube construction, in which Louis Breguet pioneered. Nicknamed the "Flying Coffeepot," it had single-spar flexible wings.

BLACKBURN Second Blackburn design was vast improvement on first model and had triangular fuselage similar to the Antoinette.

CURTISS Curtiss was first to introduce the single-float seaplane of the type shown here. They were used by the U.S. Navy.

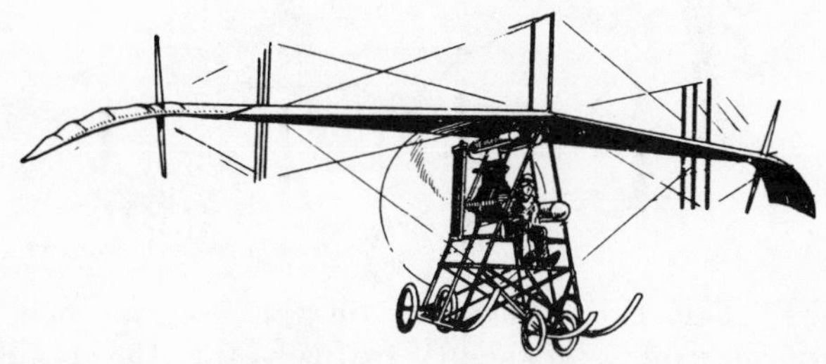

DUNNE D.6 This curious-looking plane was the predecessor of all swept-wing tailless airplanes. It was exceptionally stable.

EUGENE ELY Accomplished first ship-to-shore flight when he took off from a specially built ramp on the U.S.S. *Birmingham.*

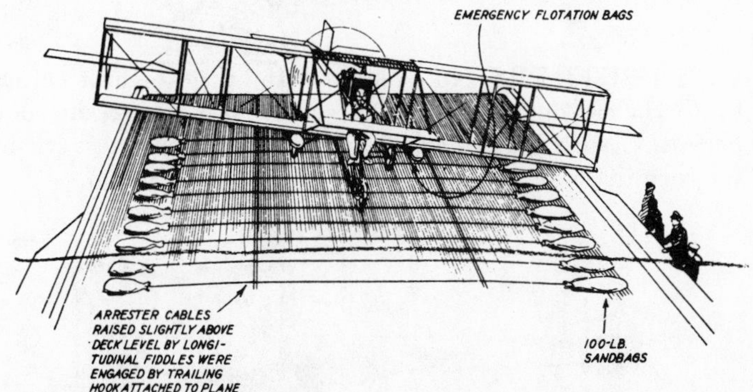

EUGENE ELY Made first round-trip ship-to-shore-to-ship flight when he landed on a specially equipped ramp on the U.S.S. *Pennsylvania.* A crude arrester device consisting of 100-pound sandbags attached to laterally spread cables was employed to slow down the airplane.

1911

BLÉRIOT This early adventure in the tail-first field reveals many incredibly advanced features for the period. The Blériot "Canard" ("Duck" to you) bristled with such things as streamlined struts, wing-tip rudders, and spring steel divided landing gear.

HANDLEY PAGE H.P.5 A name to be reckoned with even to-day, this was one of the most famous planes of its era. Nick-named the "Yellow Peril," it was one of the first British swept-back wing jobs and had a 50-h.p. Gnome engine.

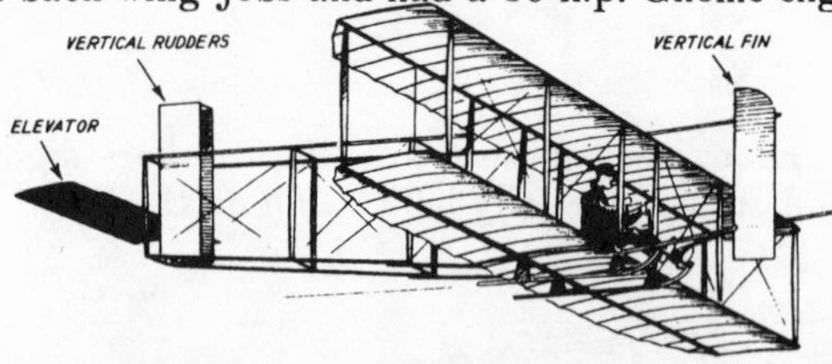

WRIGHT BROTHERS Not content with being the first actually to fly power-operated airplanes, the Wrights resumed ex-periments with gliders to pursue further their research into the then little understood problems of flight control.

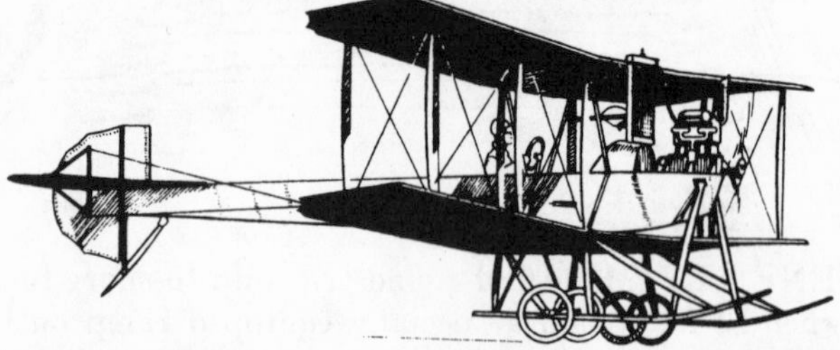

AVRO First Avro biplane was powered with a 35-h.p. Green 4-in-line engine. It was one of the world's first successful tractor biplanes.

CURTISS One of the first airplanes procured by the U.S. Army Signal Corps for the then infant air force. It was powered with a 50-h.p. Curtiss engine.

DEPERDUSSIN Designed by Béchereau, this was a training airplane. It was powered with a 50-h.p. 4-in-line Clerget engine. To Béchereau goes the credit for the invention of the present-day wheel control.

BRISTOL-PRIER Still a great name in aviation, the Bristol Company started out with box-kite biplanes. This was their first monoplane and was designed by Prier, a Frenchman. Power plant was the 50-h.p. rotary Gnome.

BREGUET Had all-metal air frame, oleo landing gear, metal-clad fuselage, horizontally mounted, liquid-cooled 100-h.p. engine with geared down drive to 4-bladed prop and single wheel control for all surfaces. It once carried 10 passengers and pilot.

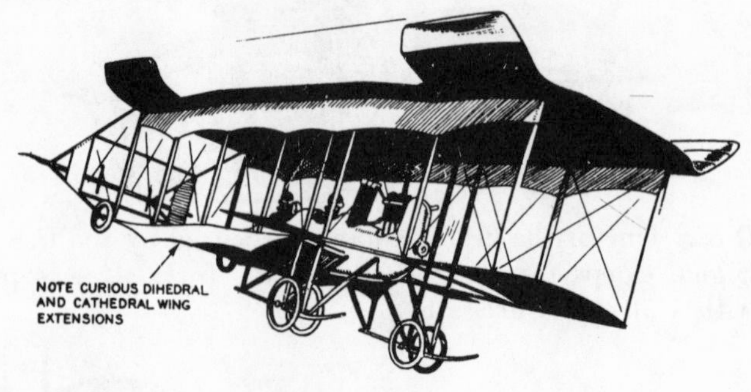

FLICK-REINIG The Flick-Reinig "Apteroid" was an experiment in ultra-low low aspect ratio.

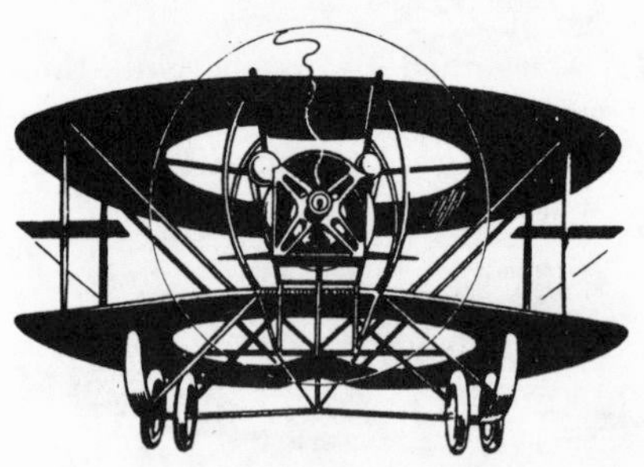

KITCHEN Early venture into the flying-saucer field, the Kitchen "Doughnut" was powered with a 50-h.p. Gnome rotary engine.

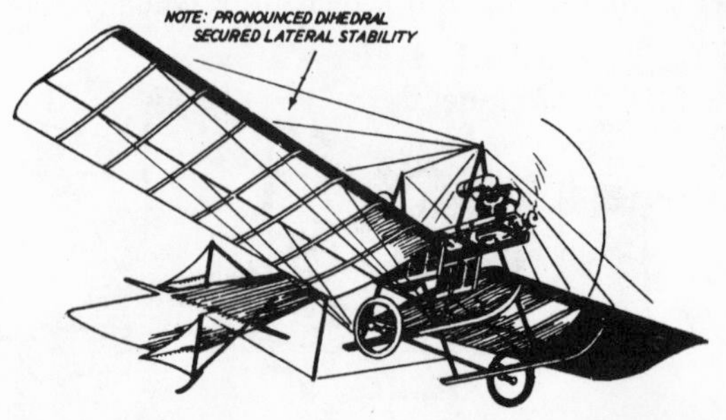

FOKKER The Fokker "Spider" was built by Anthony Fokker when he was 19 years old. No provision was made for lateral control, lateral stability being taken care of by the unusually large dihedral angle of the wings.

CURTISS Early Curtiss amphibian had single float, fixed landing wheels. Nose elevator seen on 1910 model eliminated.

DUNNE D.8 Developed from the earlier Dunne monoplane, this tailless design was so stable that it could be flown with the pilot standing outside the cockpit. There was also an American version—the Burgess-Dunne.

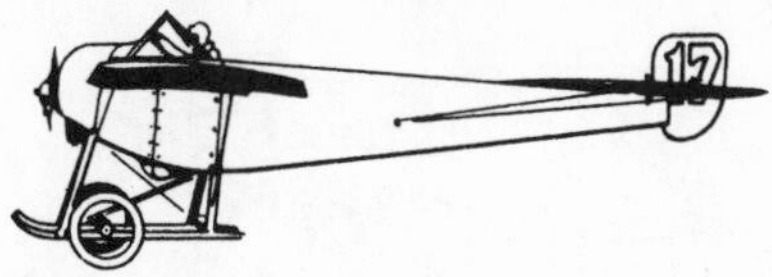

NIEUPORT-SABELLI Italian version of the Gnome-powered Nieuport monoplane, it was one of the fastest airplanes of its day.

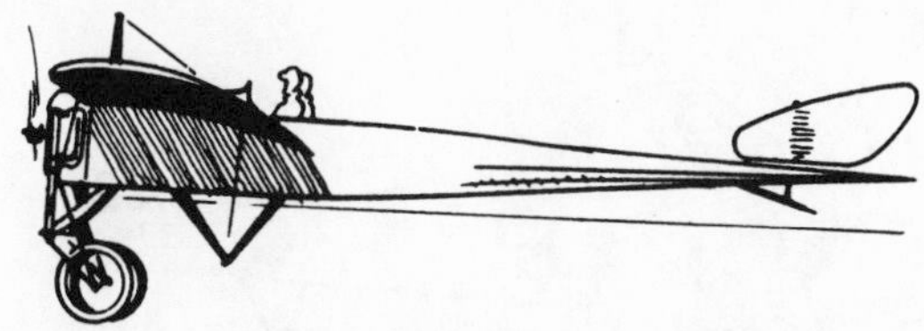

BLÉRIOT This fish-tailed side-by-side 2-seater was one of the least happy of the many Blériot designs. Inadequate fin area (note the balanced rudder) made it a sucker for spins.

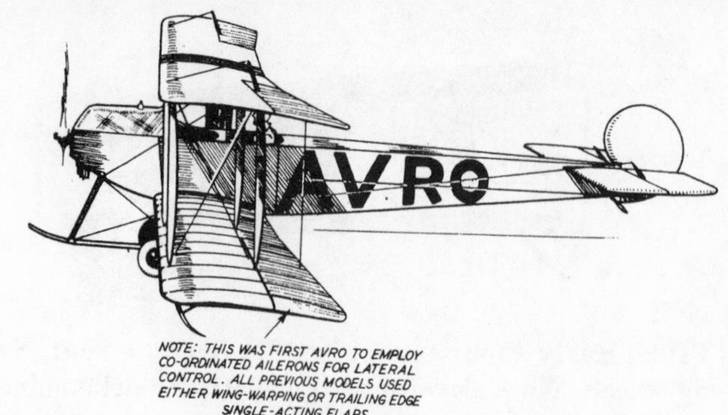

AVRO Prototype model of the famed Avro 504-K, which was standard R.A.F. trainer throughout World War I. It was powered with a 50-h.p. Gnome rotary radial engine and, in its day, was one of the best airplanes in the world.

AVRO Tandem 2-seat cabin biplane. First airplane in the world to recover from an involuntary spin (Lt. Wilfrid Parkes, R.N., solved the spin in 1912 by reversing the controls as a last resort).

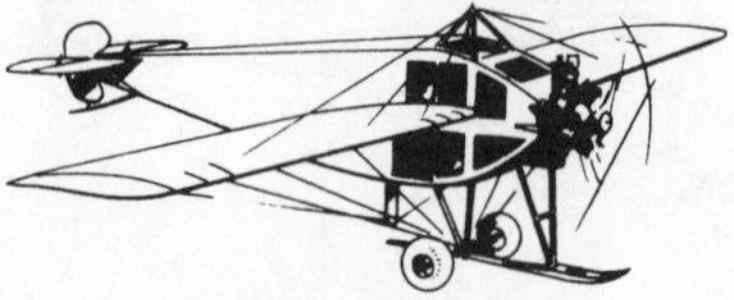

AVRO This experimental mid-wing cabin monoplane with radial engine gives some idea of the scope of some designer's imagination more than forty years ago.

HANDLEY PAGE H.P.6 This graceful monoplane had exceptionally clean lines for the period. Powered by an 80-h.p. Gnome rotary.

BLACKBURN One of these 1912 model monoplanes was recently reconditioned and flown with the original engine—a 50-h.p. Gnome rotary.

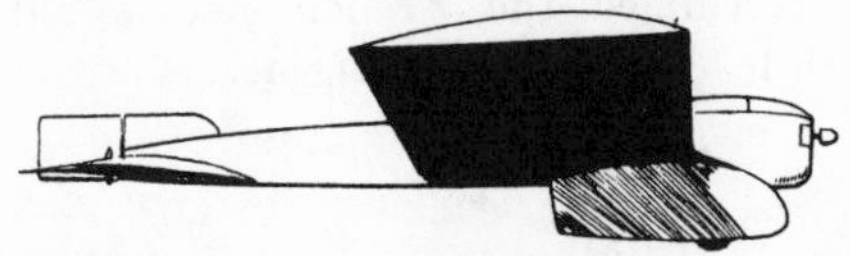

ANTOINETTE Levasseur's last design was remarkable in that at this early period it had full cantilever wings, was a true low-wing design, was a cabin monoplane, and had a fuel-injection steam-cooled engine.

CURTISS Built the world's first flying boat. This is one of the first models with stepless hull. It had a 50-h.p. V-8 Curtiss engine.

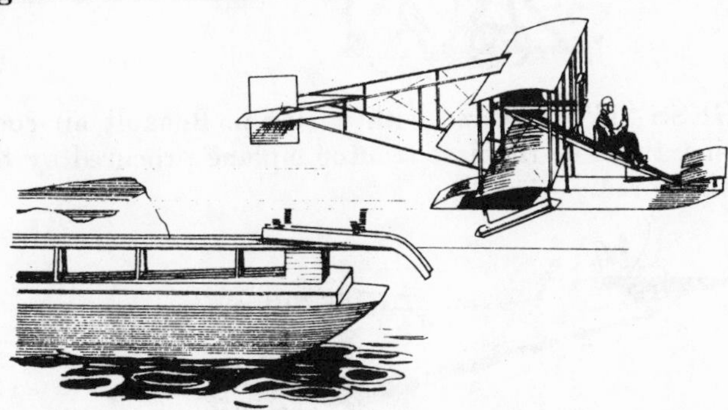

LT. T. G. ELLYSON, U.S.N. Made the first power catapult-launched flight from an anchored barge. The compressed-air catapault was developed under the guidance of Capt. Irvin Chambers, U.S.N.; early champion of shipboard flight.

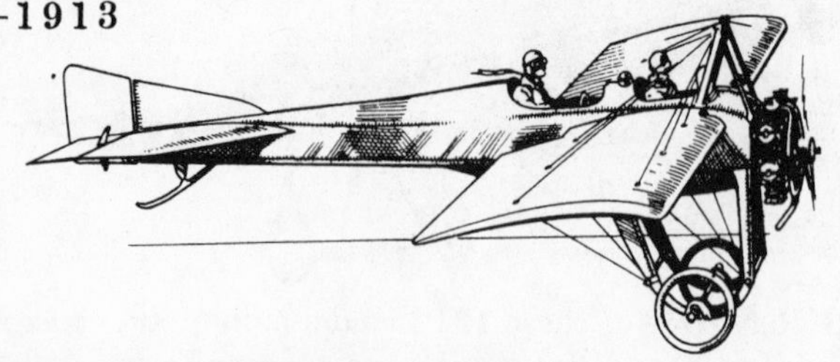

DEPERDUSSIN The British Deperdussin designed by Fritz Koolhoven resembled the French models but was powered with a 100-h.p. Anzani radial engine.

DEPERDUSSIN A Béchereau design, this 140-h.p. Gnome-powered monoplane won the Gordon Bennett races at Chicago in 1912 and was the first airplane in the world to exceed 100 m.p.h.

BURGESS "H" Powered with a 70-h.p. Renault air-cooled engine, this was the first tractor biplane procured by the U.S. Air Force.

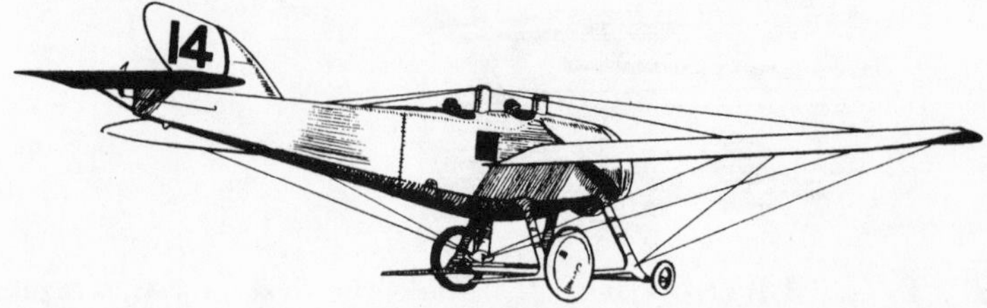

BRISTOL-COANDA Another example of advanced thinking is shown in this Gnome-powered military 2-seater produced and flown more than forty years ago.

SOPWITH Today known as the famed Hawker Company, producers of the Hawker "Hunter," this early biplane was their first tractor design and forerunner of numerous successful military designs. (See World War I.)

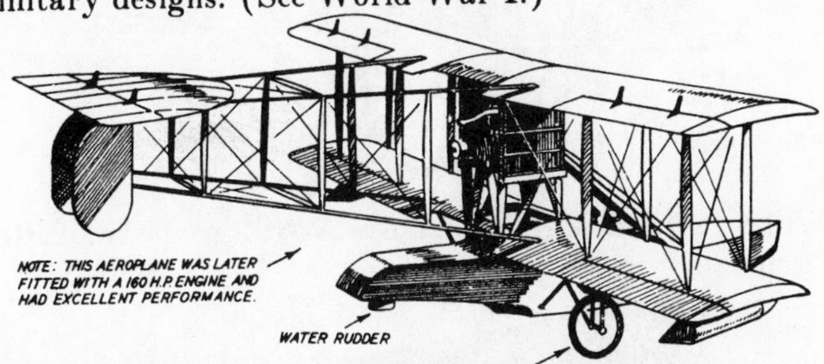

SOPWITH "BAT BOAT" The Sopwith "Bat Boat" was the world's first true amphibian. Powered with a 90-h.p. Austro-Daimler engine, it had a properly designed planing hull and retractable landing gear.

SHORT TYPE 38 First airplane in the world to be armed and to be radio equipped, it also has the distinction of being the airplane in which Sir Winston Churchill learned to fly.

BREGUET Was little changed from the earlier model but employed a direct-drive radial engine and/or a twin-row Gnome rotary.

CEDRIC LEE A development of Kitchen's "Doughnut," this was the first airplane in the world to employ elevons common to modern delta-wing designs today.

MARTIN Second Martin design was still crude but better engineered.

MARTIN First armored attack plane built in the U.S., this rotary-powered biplane marks a great improvement over previous designs but still clings to outmoded mid-wing ailerons.

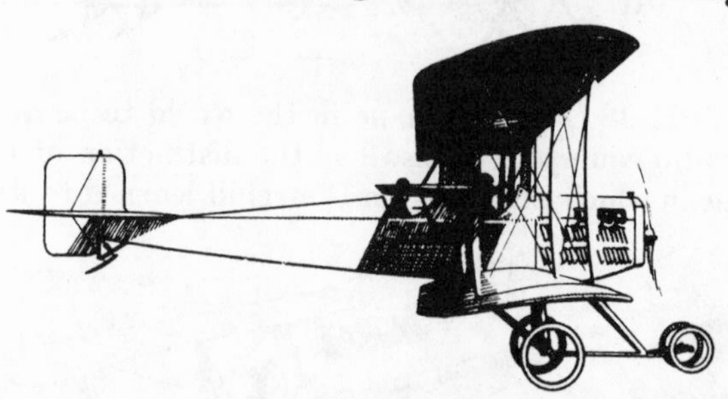

MARTIN The Model TT was a great improvement on previous Martin designs. One of the first Army planes to be procured in quantity, it was powered with a 90-h.p. Curtiss OX-2 engine.

MARTIN The "Great Lakes Tourer" 4-place float seaplane.

MORANE The little Morane-Saulnier monoplanes were among the best airplanes of this period. Fuselage and landing gear were steel tube, wings of fabric-covered wood. Absence of fixed tail surfaces was a Morane characteristic.

HANDLEY PAGE H.P.7 Swept-wing biplane, the H.P.7 had 100-h.p. Anzani radial engine, fine performance.

SOPWITH The Sopwith "Tabloid," powered with an 80-h.p. Gnome rotary engine, revolutionized all previous concepts of airplane performance and is generally regarded as the direct ancestor of all piston-engine single-seat fighters.

GRAHAM-WHITE "CHARABANCS" Powered with a 100-h.p. 6-in-line Green engine, this big pusher carried pilot and 10 passengers. It was used for joy riding at the Hendon airport.

B.E.3 Product of the Royal Aircraft Factory, the "Bloater" was noted for its bad spin characteristics and was withdrawn from service after a number of pilots had been killed.

CAUDRON These apparently frail little ships were in fact one of the safest designs ever built. Powered with the 35-h.p. Anzani radial, they were practically foolproof and easy to fly.

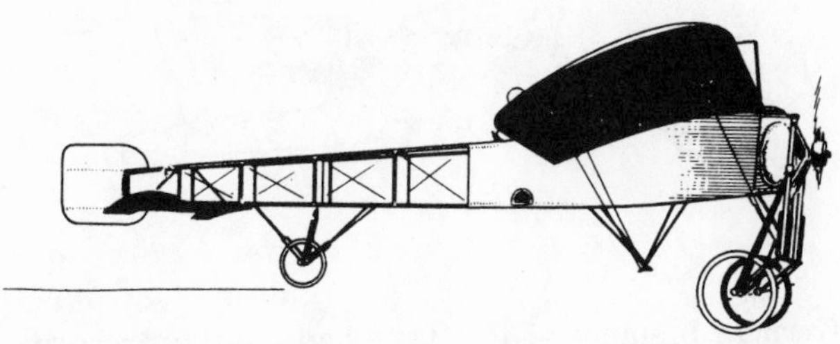

BLÉRIOT This tandem 2-seater was one of the most popular airplanes of its day. It was powered with 50- and 80-h.p. Gnome rotary engines and had warping wings.

BOREL This French float seaplane was the first airplane in the world specially designed as a torpedo plane.

VICKERS Still a top aviation firm, this is the prototype model of the famed Vickers "Gun Bus."

L.V.G. German biplanes of this type had hung up records of 24-hour nonstop flights at the end of 1913. The clean lines of this single-bay biplane are noteworthy.

FARMAN The Maurice Farman (brother of Henri Farman) "Longhorn" biplane was a slow but easy-to-fly airplane. It was powered with a 70-h.p. air-cooled V-8 Renault engine.

DEPERDUSSIN Last and most famous of the Deperdussin designs, it was powered with a 160-h.p. twin-row rotary radial engine and was the first airplane in the world to exceed two miles per minute (127 m.p.h.).

PART THREE

The First World War

1914-1918

WHEN THE WAR broke open in Europe in the summer of 1914, the military thought of the airplane mainly as an aerial scout. It began its martial career as a flying observation post from which terrain could be evaluated, enemy troop movements seen, and artillery fire corrected by means of dropped messages. In those early months pilots adhered to a code of chivalry that forbade trying to harm a fellow flyer, even if he was an enemy. Then one day some realistic-minded pilot took a shot at the opposition aloft . . . and the airplane became a weapon of destruction.

Pistols, rifles, and soon portable machine guns were carried aloft to battle enemy planes. A Frenchman, Roland Garros, mounted a fixed machine gun on his Morane-Saulnier to fire through the propeller arc, and fitted steel plates on the propeller shanks to deflect the bullets (about seven percent of the total fire) which hit it. Anthony Fokker, then working for the Kaiser in Germany, improved on this by inventing the interrupter gear that prevented the gun from firing when the propeller blades were passing the bullet path. And next a Rumanian-born engineer living in England, Constantinescu, topped Fokker's mechanism with the design of the hydraulically operated gun-synchronizing gear, which reversed the process by firing the gun at the moment when the propeller blades were not passing in front of the barrel.

Once pilots started shooting at each other, the question of plane performance leaped to No. 1 position. Rate of climb, diameter of a turn, straightaway or diving speed could spell death or survival. For a while Germany ruled the skies with her agile fighters built by Fokker. His famous triplane had good maneuverability by virtue of its small span and stacked-up wings, and a fast rate of climb. The French and British countered with Nieuports and Camels, biplanes that were speedier than the German triplane but not as maneuverable. In time, the weight of Allied production as well as the quality of Allied planes overwhelmed the *Luftwaffe*.

The race for greater performance and load-carrying capacity resulted in the development of high-output, reliable aircraft engines. Germany was quick to swing toward in-line water-cooled power plants like the 140-h.p. Argus and the 160-h.p. Mercedes. Allied engines, in the opening rounds, were predominantly of the 110-h.p. rotary type, built by Gnome-Rhone and Clerget in France and under French-granted licenses in England.

Although the rotary had the feature of being air-cooled—an advantage that in later postwar years was to give the real impetus to aerial transportation—the fact that the whole engine revolved around the crankshaft created terrible torque problems, making the plane very hard to control. Also, the rotary type often caught fire, had to operate either wide open or cut off, and the fumes or spray of the castor oil used as a lubricant made many a pilot ill in moments of more pressing peril.

Such drawbacks led to the design and production of famous water-cooled power plants like the Hispano-Suiza V-8 of France, the British Rolls-Royce, Beardmore, Napier, and the Italian Fiat—the latter being the only six-cylinder in-line of the Allied air forces. These worthy engines, ranging from 160 to 375 h.p., powered such worthy aircraft as the Spad, S.E.5, Bristol fighter, Ansaldo and various bombers, and others.

Added maneuverability coupled with more deadly fire power in airplanes brought on dogfighting. In order to get on an adversary's tail—or out of reach in case the other fellow managed that vantage point first—pilots voluntarily or through desperate accident entered into intricate evolutions which previously had been considered suicide. Loops, split-S turns, Immelmans (named after the German ace Max Immelmann and consisting of a half loop with a half roll on top, giving the plane a change of direction as well as a gain in altitude), and many others became integral parts of pursuit flying. In the period after the war these maneuvers were to be known as aerial stunting and acrobatics, the main attraction at air shows.

The specialized pursuit or fighter plane was born early in the conflict. The bomber had to wait a bit. Actually, aerial bombing preceded air-to-air fighting, the first bombs being hand grenades carried in the observer's lap and tossed overboard at low altitudes. Pot shots from ground troops then made low flying unsafe, and grenades exploded in mid-air when thrown from greater heights. The first "bombs" were just finned darts thrown overboard by the basketful. Then real aerial bombs came into being, first a 25-pounder, also hand tossed, and later a heavier missile requiring bomb racks, sights, and release mechanism. This in turn required a special bombing plane—one with more than a single engine, to manage the extra load.

At the start of the war neither the British, French, nor Germans had multi-engine airplanes. Only Russia could boast of one—the four-engined (German Argus, 100 h.p. each) "Russky Vitiaz" (Russian Knight) built in 1913 by Igor Sikorsky of subsequent helicopter fame. By early 1915 Russia had produced a number of improved Sikorsky bombers of the "Ilia Mourometz" type based on the "Grand," as the Knight was nicknamed, but with a span of over 100 feet, more powerful engines, and capable of carrying close to 1,000 pounds of bombs. These craft had machine-gun installation in the tail and a trolley arrangement between tail-gun post and the front crew quarters, not unlike that on such modern bombers as the B-50 and B-36.

Raids deep into enemy territory growing necessary, the other warring nations rose to the occasion with large multi-engine bombers—the German twin-engine Gotha, British twin-engine Handley Page, the Italian Caproni. By 1917 these craft were so far advanced that night raids became the rule and bomb sizes grew to 500-pound "blockbusters." (Heavy night bombing, of course, had been initiated by the Germans with their Zeppelin raids on London in 1915, but this method proved too costly: Allied fire contacting the hydrogen gas used in the huge bags caused too many devastating explosions.)

When the United States entered the war in 1917 its air force was pitifully small. The Aviation Section of the Signal Corps had 55 training planes, and the Navy counted 54. The great problem was suitable high-powered engines, which this country had not designed or produced. American cadets, though eventually receiving their primary training in native-built planes here, had to get their advanced instruction in French or English planes "over there," and with a single exception the craft in which they flew against the enemy were all British or European.

Soon realizing how short it had been caught, the U.S. mustered its aeronautical brains and resources. Before long it had in production one of the most powerful engines of its time, the 400-h.p. V-8 water-cooled Liberty. To expedite matters, licenses were acquired to produce existing European aircraft and engines in this country. A tidy nucleus of manufacturing concerns was already at hand—Curtiss, Boeing, Vought, L. W. F., Gallaudet, Burgess, the Dayton-Wright Company, to which Orville Wright had loaned his name and for which he acted as consulting engineer. In addition, auto plants were pressed into service to build planes and power plants.

The planes turned out in greatest number were the De Haviland DH-4, built under British license, a two-place observation craft powered by the Liberty, and the Curtiss JN-4 "Jenny" trainer, variously fitted with the Curtiss V-8 OX-5 90-h.p. engine or the 150-h.p. Wright-Hispano. American manufacturers discovered that it takes upward of two years to design, build, and "de-bug" a production airplane. Although many excellent planes of different types were under construction when the war ended, the only U.S.-made machine to see active service was the DH-4.

When the Armistice was signed the airplane was still not quite 15 years old, but the experience of war had jumped the boy into powerful manhood. The scattered sheds where a few men tinkered with wood and fabric had become sprawling factories representing an industry which during four years of war produced upward of 60,000 military airplanes. The plane itself had developed advanced features, many still to be fully utilized, such as the cantilever (unbraced) wing, all-metal body, superchargers that enable the engine to operate at much higher altitudes. Most significant was the growth of the engine, which made it possible for the plane to be big and carry heavy loads.

MARTIN Specially designed stunt plane for Lincoln Beachey, top U.S. pilot of the period. Gnome rotary powered. (Civil aircraft.)

SOPWITH Winner of the 1914 Schneider Trophy races. Powered with a 100-h.p. Gnome monosoupape rotary engine. (Civil aircraft.)

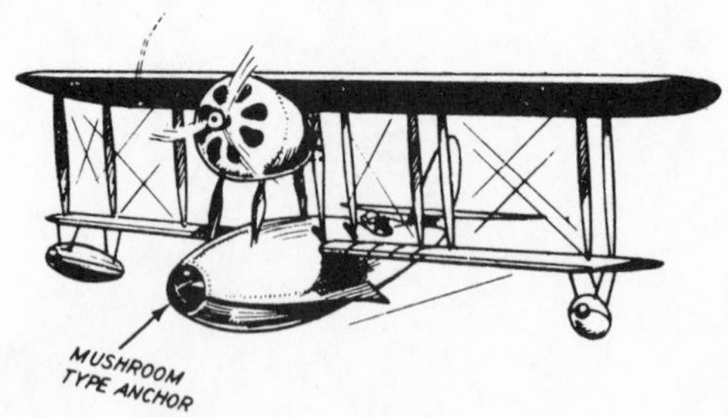

SUPERMARINE The extraordinary Pemberton-Billing Supermarine with completely encowled engine and streamline section hull was conceived forty years ago! (Civil aircraft.)

MAURICE FARMAN The Maurice Farman "Shorthorn," so named after the abbreviated landing skids, was powered with a 70-h.p. Renault engine and was used as an artillery spotter by the French during the very early days of the war. No armament.

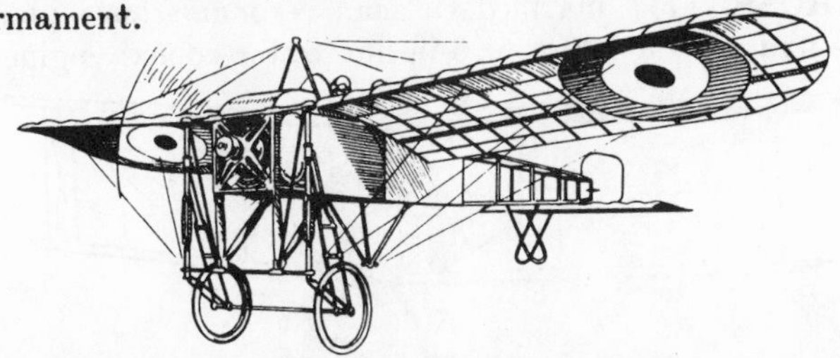

BLÉRIOT 80-h.p. Gnome engine. Used by French and British in early days of the war as reconnaissance airplane. No armament.

FARMAN Henri Farman reconnaissance plane. 80-h.p. Gnome engine. Used by French and British till 1915. No armament.

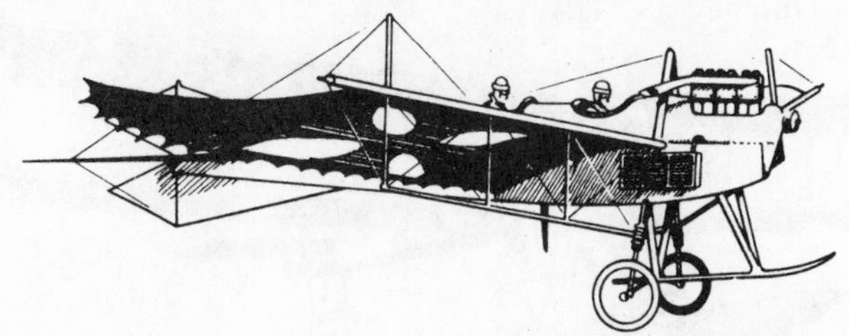

RUMPLER There were several "Taube"-type airplanes in service with the German Flying Corps at the outbreak of the war. This is a typical example. 100-h.p. Argus engine. Totally unarmed.

ALBATROSS This unarmed German reconnaissance plane was powered with a 100-h.p. 6-in-line water-cooled engine.

L.V.G. Another early unarmed German reconnaissance plane. Planes of this type took part in the first bombing attack on the city of London.

AVRO The Avro 504-K was used briefly by the British as a first-line military aircraft. From 1915 on it served as a primary trainer and was powered with a 100-h.p. monosoupape Gnome.

SHORT The Short Type 225 with 225-h.p. Sunbeam engine was used as a naval reconnaissance seaplane throughout the war.

CAUDRON With 35-h.p. and 50- and 80-h.p. engines, this model Caudron was widely employed as a primary trainer by the French air arm.

NIEUPORT The Nieuport "Scout," powered with 80-h.p. Gnome or Le Rhone rotary radial engines, was at first totally unarmed.

BRISTOL The Bristol "Scout," with 80-h.p. Le Rhone, was unarmed British equivalent of the little Nieuport.

MORANE The Morane *monoplan de chasse*, with 100-h.p. Le Rhone rotary, was the first airplane to be equipped with a fixed machine gun firing through the propeller arc. Steel deflector blades protected the propeller.

NIEUPORT The Nieuport "Scout" is shown here with one gun mounted to fire over the propeller arc and ten Prieur rockets, which were electrically fired.

FOKKER The Fokker E.IV, with 80-h.p. Oberursel rotary engine, was the first airplane in the world to employ a synchronized gun gear and caused such havoc among the either totally or poorly armed Allied aircraft that it was known as the "Fokker Scourge."

DE HAVILLAND The D.H.2 is generally credited with ending the Fokker Scourge. Powered with a 100-h.p. monosoupape Gnome, it was light and highly maneuverable.

MORANE The Morane-Saulnier "Parasol" was one of the first French reconnaissance planes to be armed. Gun was stowed in the observer's cockpit when not in use.

FARMAN The Farman F-40, known as the Horace Farman since it was the combined effort of Henri and Maurice Farman, was powered with a 130-h.p. engine and was lightly armed as shown.

B.E.2 This was long the standard British armed reconnaissance plane. It was powered with a 90-h.p. R.A.F. engine. Due to unfortunate position of the observer and his gun station, these planes proved to be veritable deathtraps as air fighting progressed.

VICKERS The Vickers "Gun Bus," with 100-h.p. Gnome monosoupape engine, was the first genuine 2-seat fighter to enter the war. One of these machines is credited with downing Immelmann, the great German fighter pilot of the period.

L.V.G. A typical example of armed German reconnaissance of the period. It was powered with a 120-h.p. Benz engine. Germans were the first to employ the rotating-ring gun mount, which completely changed defensive tactics at this time.

DE HAVILLAND The D.H.1 was a 2-seat fighter similar in appearance to the D.H.2 but powered with a V-8 air-cooled engine.

CURTISS The Curtiss JN-2 was predecessor to the famed JN-4 "Jenny." Most famous U.S. training plane of World War I.

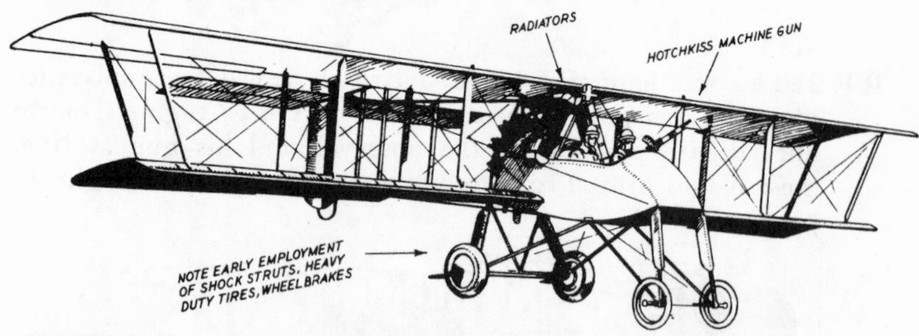

VOISIN French 2-seat fighter and day bomber was the first airplane to be armed with a shell-firing cannon in actual warfare. It was powered with a 200-h.p. Canton-Unne liquid-cooled radial engine; usually armed with one light machine gun.

JUNKERS The Junkers J.1 "Blechesel" (literally, "Tin Donkey") was the first all-metal airplane in the world. It was powered with a 120-h.p. Mercedes engine, did not go into production.

F.E.8 Royal Aircraft Factory's pusher fighter modeled after the De Havilland D.H.2. 100-h.p. monosoupape Gnome.

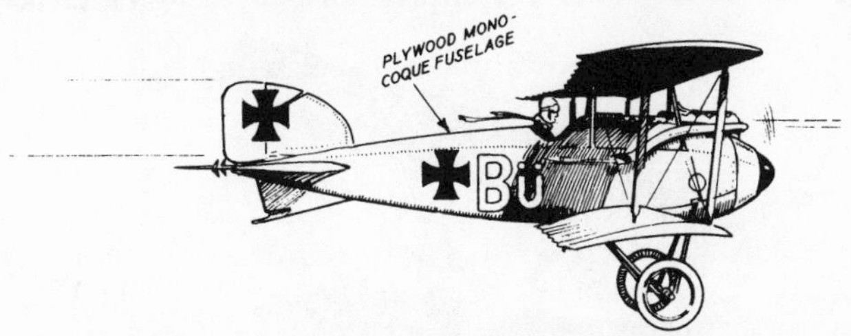

ALBATROSS The Albatross D.1's, powered with Benz or Mercedes engines, were heavy single-seat fighters with plywood monocoque fuselages and were excellent combat planes for the period.

ALBATROSS The Albatross D.111 was development of the earlier D.1 and was noted for its superior climbing qualities.

SOPWITH The Sopwith "Pup," with 110-h.p. Le Rhone rotary, mounted one fixed forward firing gun and outclassed the heavier Albatross D.1.

BOEING First Boeing-built airplane when the firm was known as Boeing and Westervelt. 200-h.p. Hall-Scott engine. A civil design.

B.B.2-E A modification of the earlier B.E. types but still poorly armed and a deathtrap under war conditions.

MORANE 110-h.p. Le Rhone engine. Briefly employed by the French and British air arms. Had poor defensive qualities.

BLACKBURN The Blackburn "Baby" was a small float seaplane scout used by the British Royal Naval Air Service.

SIKORSKY Over 70 of these huge bombers were built during World War I. Named the "Ilia Mourometz" (the giant), they were powered with four 100-h.p. Argus engines, mounted five flexible machine guns, including a tail gun station.

HANDLEY PAGE The H.P.0/400, with two 275-h.p. Rolls-Royce engines, was top Allied bomber of World War I. Over 400 were procured during the war.

DE HAVILLAND The D.H.3 was the first twin-engine bomber produced by this company.

ALBATROSS The Albatross C.3, with 225-h.p. Mercedes-Benz engine, is a typical example of later-model German reconnaissance planes.

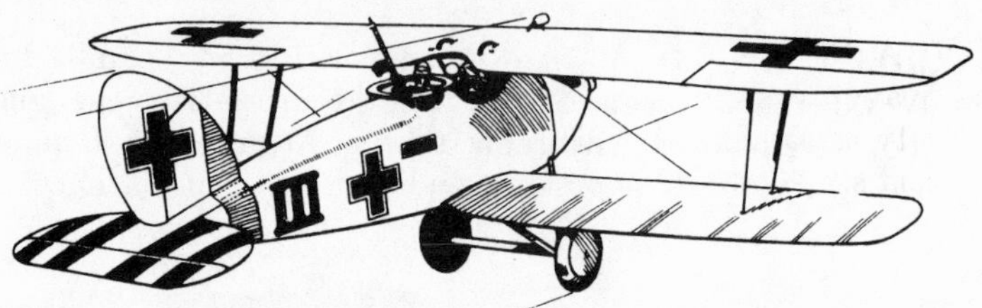

HALBERSTADT One of the top German 2-seat fighters of the period, it had monocoque wooden fuselage.

ROLAND The Roland "Walfisch" was another 2-seat German fighter. Washed-out wings were a feature of many German designs.

DE HAVILLAND The D.H.6, with 80-h.p. Renault engine, was a primary trainer designed for mass production.

GOTHA The Gotha Type 4, with two 260-h.p. engines, was the heavy bomber used in the more serious bombing raids on the city of London. It carried a crew of three, seven 112-pound and six 28-pound fragmentation bombs.

SUPERMARINE This curious quadraplane had swept wings, was partially cabinized, did not go into production.

CURTISS The Curtiss S-3, with 100-h.p. Curtiss OXX-2 engine, was one of the few U.S. pursuit-type planes built during the war. Only four were built and none saw combat service.

SOPWITH The Sopwith 1½-Strutter, with 130-h.p. Clerget rotary, was first British fighter with rear gun ring and fixed pilot's gun.

F.E.2 160-h.p. Beardmore engine. Standard short-range British night bomber after preliminary service as a 2-seat bomber-fighter. Note how gunner observer fought second gun against tail attack.

S.P.A.D. First appeared with a 200-h.p. Hispano-Suiza engine but was more heavily powered in later modifications. It was mostly used by the French and U.S. air arms. (Note: S.P.A.D. was revived Deperdussin. S.P.A.D.=*Société pour Production les Apparailles Deperdussin!)*

DE HAVILLAND The D.H.5, with 110-h.p. Le Rhone rotary, was a low-altitude fighter. Backward stagger gave unexcelled forward vision.

FOKKER The Fokker D.VII, with 185-h.p. B.M.W. belied its clumsy appearance; it was, in fact, one of the deadliest single-seat fighters of World War I. Cantilever thick section wings had no external bracing.

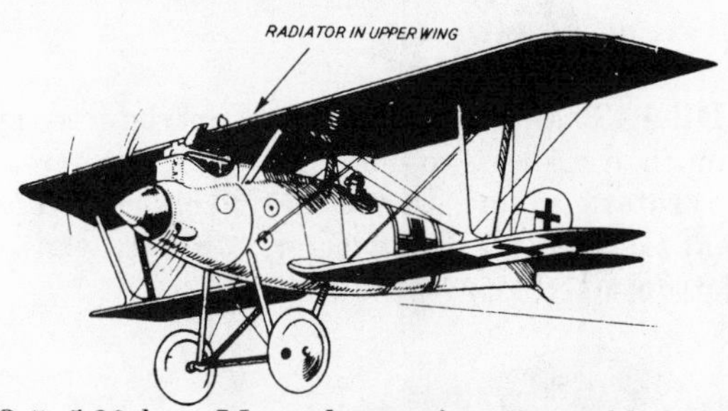

PFALZ D3.5 160-h.p. Mercedes engine. Resembled the Albatross D.3 and D.5 types but was considerably less rugged. Frequently broke up in the air during combat.

NIEUPORT 110-h.p. Le Rhone rotary. This odd-looking triplane fighter was a purely experimental design and was soon abandoned.

ALBATROSS D.V. 220 h.p. Mercedes-Benz engine. This was the last of the V-strut Albatross single-seat fighters and the deadliest.

FOKKER DR.1 Triplane fighters were introduced by the Germans and had a short vogue. The DR.1 was powered with a 110-h.p. rotary engine. It was in a machine of this type that the great German ace Rittmeister, Manfred von Richthofen, was shot down.

PFALZ 160-h.p. Siemens-Schuckert rotary engine. Another example of German triplane fighter design.

SOPWITH The Sopwith "Tripe" was powered with a 130-h.p. Clerget engine and was largely used by Royal Naval Air Service squadrons.

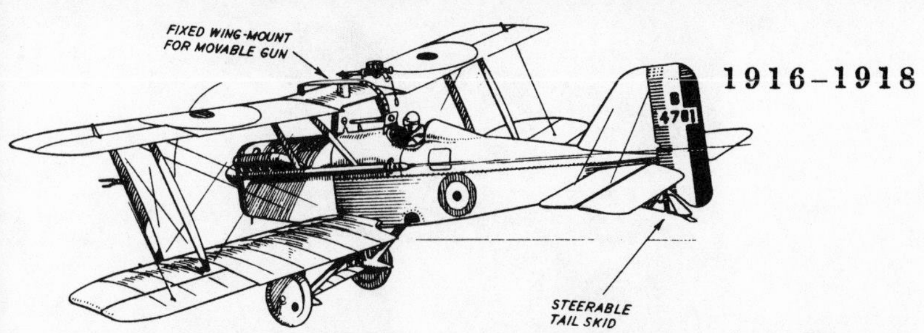

S.E.5 Produced by the Royal Aircraft Factory, the S.E.5 was powered with 150- and 200-h.p. Hispano-Suiza engines. It mounted two fixed guns firing through the propeller, one fixed overhead wing gun.

SOPWITH The Sopwith "Camel," variously powered with rotary engines ranging in power from the 110-h.p. Le Rhone to the 230-h.p. Bentley B.R.2, was noted for its remarkable maneuverability, its excellent climb, and its vicious habits in the hands of inexperienced or careless pilots.

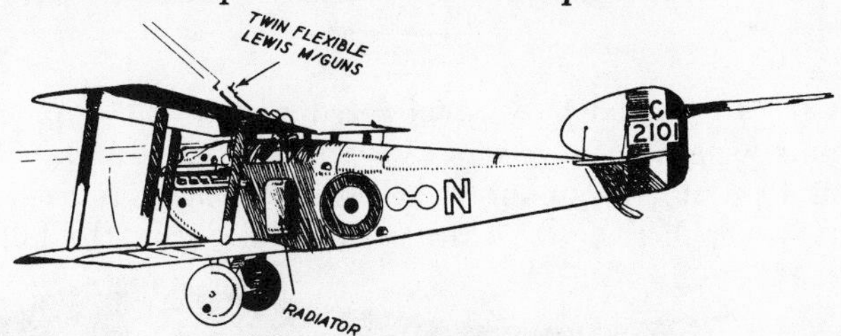

SOPWITH The Sopwith "Dolphin," with 220-h.p. Hispano-Suiza engine, was first armed with outboard wing guns as well as two fixed fuselage guns, but in its final form had two fixed guns and two semi-flexible guns in the center section as shown.

FIRST FIGHTER LAUNCHINGS AT SEA Shows "Camel" taking off from barge towed by destroyer. First introduced in 1917 for convoy protection.

ALBATROSS The D.XI, with 160-h.p. Siemens-Schuckert rotary, marked considerable departure from usual Albatross design.

ANSALDO The S.V.A. Ansaldo, with 220-h.p. liquid-cooled engine, was top Italian single-seat fighter during World War I.

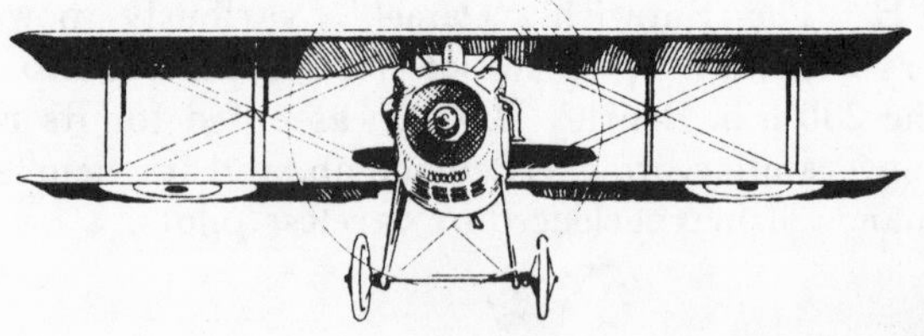

S.P.A.D. Last models were powered with a 235-h.p. Hispano-Suiza engine. There was also a Cannon-S.P.A.D., which was first pursuit to mount a shell-firing cannon. It fired through the propeller shaft, which was mounted on the hollow cam shaft.

SOPWITH The Sopwith "Snipe," with 230-h.p. Bentley rotary engine, was successor to the "Camel." A modified version, the "Salamander," had armored cockpit for low-level ground attack.

BLÉRIOT The clipped-wing Penguin was used by the French throughout the war to allow student pilots to get the feel of the controls while taxiing at high speed. 25-h.p. Anzani engine. It was not airborne.

CURTISS The famed JN-4D, with 90-h.p. Curtiss OX-5 engine, known as the "Jenny," was most widely used U.S. wartime trainer.

R.E.8 150-h.p. air-cooled R.A.F. (Royal Aircraft Factory) engine. Replaced the inadequately armed B.E. models as standard British observation model.

B.E.12 150-h.p. R.A.F. engine. Long-range fighter-photo-reconnaissance plane which saw limited service.

DE HAVILLAND D.H.9 230-h.p. Siddeley Puma engine. Used as a day bomber. Its more powerful sister, the D.H.4 resembled it outwardly but was powered with a 400-h.p. Liberty engine.

BRISTOL 275-h.p. Rolls-Royce engine. The Bristol fighter was one of the most formidable 2-seat fighters engaged in the war. It could outfly and outfight the best pursuits of the period and was armed with two flexible and one fixed gun.

BREGUET 14 Standard French long-range day bomber and photo-reconnaissance plane. One of the first airplanes in the world to have wing flaps.

DE HAVILLAND D.H.4 400-h.p. Liberty engine. Used by British and U.S. air arms as a long-range bomber-fighter.

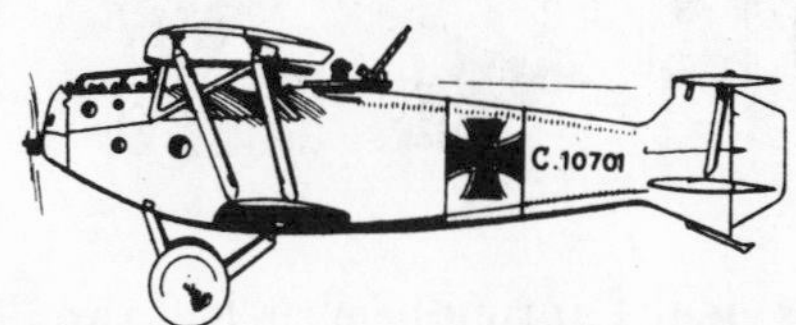

HANOVERANER 260-h.p. Mercedes-Benz engine. One of the most formidable of the German 2-seat fighters. The biplane tail is noteworthy.

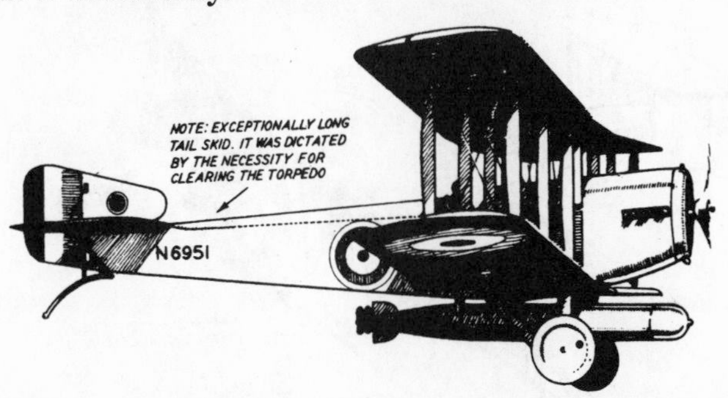

SOPWITH The Sopwith "Cuckoo," with 200-h.p. Hispano-Suiza engine, was only specially designed torpedo plane employed in this war.

JUNKERS J.4 First all-metal airplane employed in actual warfare. Used for ground attack, it was heavily armored, and no evidence exists that any of these machines were shot down by fighters.

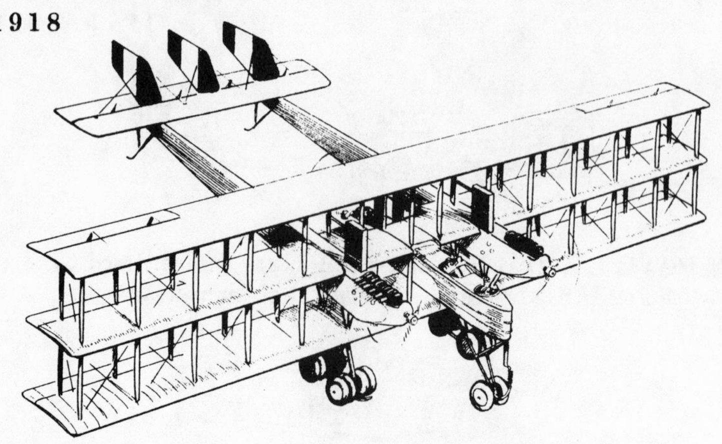

CAPRONI The giant Caproni bomber had two 300-h.p. engines, one 400-h.p. engine driving a pusher propeller.

HANDLEY PAGE V/1500 Four 275-h.p. Rolls-Royce engines. Designed for the intended bombing of Berlin, it was the B-29 of World War I; carried 3 tons of bombs and a crew of 4.

DE HAVILLAND D.H.10 Two 275-h.p. Rolls-Royce engines. In production at close of hostilities.

KONDOR D.VI 200-h.p. Goebel rotary engine. In production at close of hostilities. Upper wings were cut out at center section to improve pilot vision.

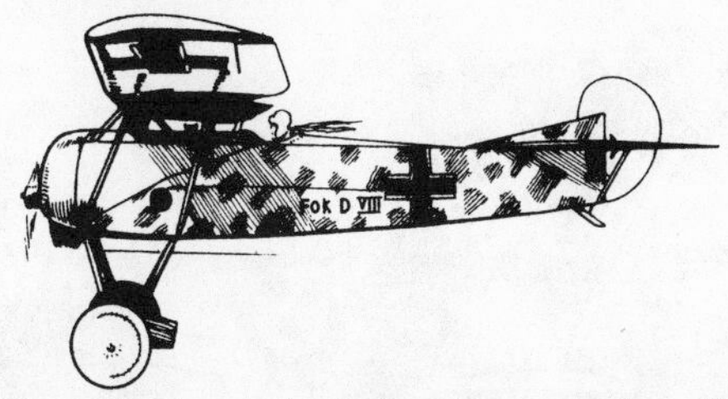

FOKKER D.VIII 200-h.p. Goebel rotary engine. Intended as a replacement for the Fokker D.VII, it was in test stage when war ended, but several had been engaged in actual combat. Cantilever internally braced wing is noteworthy.

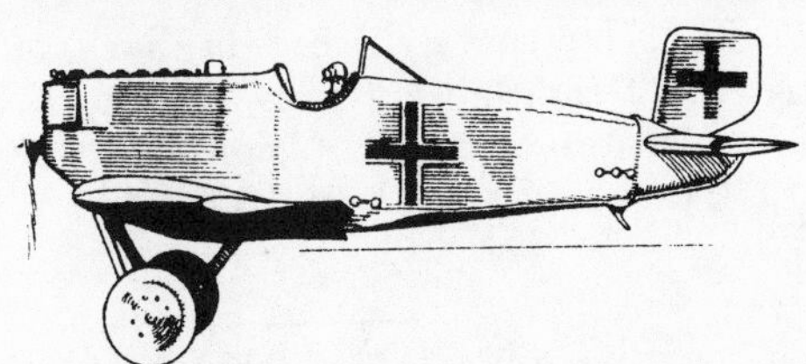

JUNKERS J.11 Arrived at the front too late to take much part in war but is noteworthy as first all-metal fighter in the world and is in striking contrast to planes employed at outbreak of World War I.

THOMAS-MORSE "SCOUT" Rotary powered. One of the few U.S. fighter designs. In production too late for service in war overseas.

JUNKERS J.10 All-metal low-wing attack plane on order for the German Air Force at close of war. Compare it with Allied aircraft of the period for some measure of German advanced thinking.

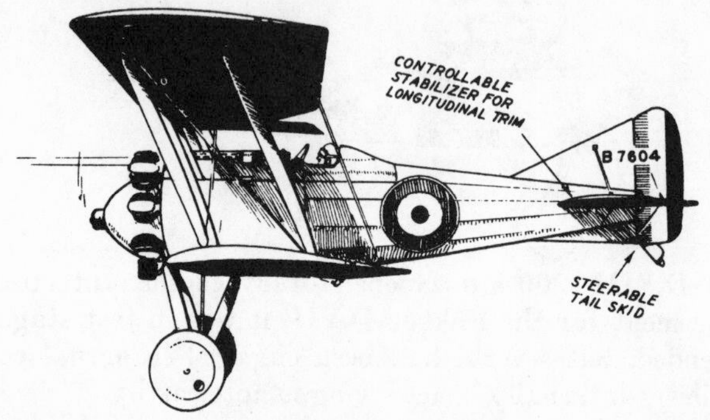

NIEUPORT Built by the British subsidiary of the Nieuport Company, the "Nighthawk," with 320-h.p. A.B.C. radial engine, was to be standard R.A.F. fighter if war had continued into 1919. Top speed was about 150 m.p.h.

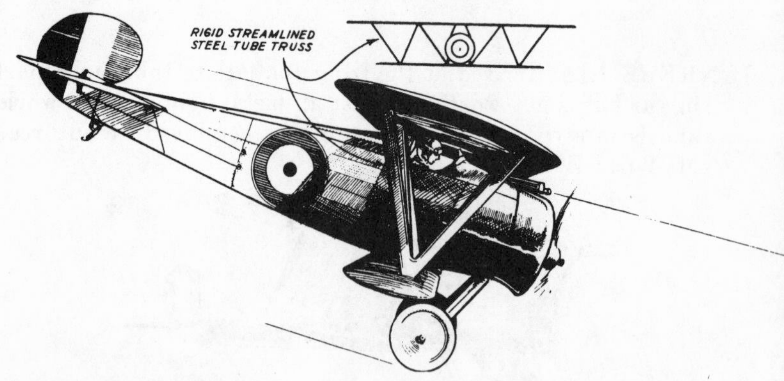

AVRO "SPIDER" 180-h.p. rotary radial. Rigid-truss single-seat biplane fighter.

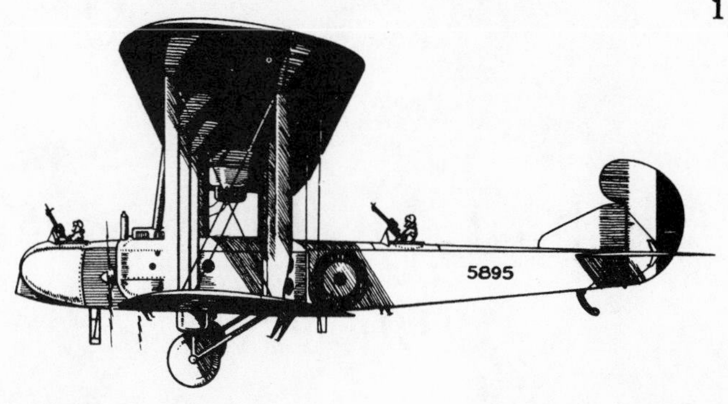

AVRO "PIKE" Two 230-h.p. engines. Another airplane which went into production too late to participate in the war. Night bomber.

MARTIN MB-1 Two 400-h.p. Liberty engines. Was to have been a U.S. contribution to the Allied aerial bombardment arm.

SOPWITH "SNAIL" 180-h.p. air-cooled radial. Plywood monocoque fuselage was complete departure from previous Sopwith construction.

PART FOUR

Birth of Air Transport

1919-1926

WITH THE AIRPLANE having proved it could carry large loads, travel faster than the best express train and fly comparatively long distances, the next step of transportation via the skyways was obvious. By the early 1920's Great Britain had four air lines organized to carry passengers, and in 1924 these merged to form the system that eventually became B.O.A.C. (British Overseas Airways Co., Ltd.). France had five such companies. But practically all the planes flown by these air lines were either converted bombers or observation craft, with enclosures built over open cockpits and seats installed. For one thing, airplane factories were not geared at war's end to produce transports, and surplus warplanes were cheap: why not let the public feel its way in them?

Germany's postwar role in this field amounted to a paradox. Forbidden by the Treaty of Versailles to build airplanes of more than 100 h.p., it was out of the transportation race. Teutonic flying interest turned to gliders, and in the all-embracing glider movement that followed many valuable new lessons in aerodynamic structure were learned that later served in designing their aircraft. At the same time the Germans cagily formed companies to work on transports in other European countries not affected by the treaty, including Russia. The paradox: when in 1925 Germany was finally allowed to conduct operations with this type, it was the only nation that possessed true, unconverted air transports.

Unlike its Allies, at peacetime the United States had no large surplus of bombers to convert for transportation, and anyway the leftover warplanes were not deemed reliable enough to cope with the greater distances to be covered in this country. However, in 1918 the U.S. Post Office Department inaugurated an air route between New York and Philadelphia to study the feasibility of carrying mail by air. The run was flown by Army pilots using Curtiss "Jennys." As the routes fanned out, more powerful converted DH-4's were pressed into service and civilian pilots hired. Then manufacturers began producing special mailplanes, better suited for the job.

Better flying qualities were a prime factor, inasmuch as mail carrying by air soon included night runs. Instrument aids were primitive and not yet suited for "blind flying." The art of controlling the aircraft was done by "seat-of-the-pants" feel, totally ineffective under "no visibility" conditions. One air-mail pilot, reminiscing about that kind of flying, recalled the night a storm tossed his plane about so mercilessly that he found it impossible to keep on even keel. At last, in desperation, he took his hands and feet off the controls and shouted: "Here, God, you take it—I've done all I can!" He ended his story: "And you know what? God cracked it up."

Though the airplane could fly high and fast, still greater altitude promised even higher speeds—and less dependence on weather—in the rarefied air of the upper strata. At these heights, however, the power plant lost power, gasping for combustion-sustaining oxygen. The problem was how to alleviate its breathing difficulties. The solution: installing of superchargers, centrifugal air pumps, which compressed the air and fed it to the engine in proper dosage. Two types came into use. One was the turbo-supercharger invented by the Frenchman Rateau and the American Sanford A. Moss of General Electric, which consisted of a turbine driven by the engine's exhaust gases that in its turn drove the centrifugal compressor feeding air under pressure to the engine. The other was the mechanical type whose compressor was driven by gears in the rear section of the power plant. It was in a Le Père-type observation plane powered by a turbo-supercharged Liberty engine that the

Army's Maj. R. W. Schroeder set a world's altitude record of 31,115 feet in 1920.

There remained still another goal to conquer—distance. In the postwar years, the challenge in the question: How far can an airplane really fly? brought on a succession of long-distance flight attempts.

On May 8, 1919, three huge U.S. Navy flying boats left Long Island to try to cross the Atlantic. Designed for that purpose, the series of NC (Navy-Curtiss) seaplanes had short hulls, outrigger-mounted tail surfaces, 126-foot wingspan, and four Liberty engines. Two of the flying boats were forced down at sea and their crews rescued by destroyers, but the other, the NC-4, commanded by Lt. Comdr. (now Admiral) Albert C. Read, reached its destination, the Azores. This was the first west to east crossing of the Atlantic by airplane.

The same May two Englishmen, Harry Hawker and McKenzie Grieve, failed in a try from Newfoundland in a single-engine Sopwith biplane, though rescue followed. A month later two other Englishmen, Capt. John Alcock and Lt. Arthur Whitten Brown, also took off from St. John's, in a Vickers "Vimy" bomber having two Rolls-Royce engines and jettisonable landing gear. After sixteen hours of battling wind, fog, and rain they reached Ireland.

The U.S. Army as well was making plans. In 1923 two of its pilots, Lts. John McCready and Oakley Kelly, flew nonstop from New York to San Diego, California, in an Army Fokker T-2 transport monoplane. A year later the Army tried a mass flight around the world with four large Liberty-driven Douglas DWC-1 biplanes. Two of them, piloted by Lt. Lowell Smith and Lt. Eric Nelson, made it—in 175 days.

Nor was the dirigible activity forgotten, though its ledger was red with tragedy. In the year following the war the British R.34 made a round trip between England and the U.S.—first crossing of the Atlantic by a lighter-than-air. The R.38, sold to America, broke in half during the trials in its homeland, killing 43 of its passengers. In 1922, the U.S. Navy ordered from Goodyear the "Shenandoah," built of the newly developed duralumin and the largest dirigible of its time. It perished in a violent storm over Ohio; 14 of the 29-man crew died. The "Los Angeles," later received by the U.S. Navy as war reparation from the Germans, lived to a ripe old age in test and training service.

In Spain a man by the name of Juan de la Cierva had an altogether different idea. Having suffered severe injuries as the result of "spinning in" with an airplane, he decided to make a flying machine without the airplane's disadvantages. He went back to the old dream of a rotary-wing aircraft—and produced the autogiro. But this was not a helicopter: its rotor blades were not connected to the engine. Mounted on a pylon rising above the conventional fuselage, they "windmilled"—rotated by the natural pressure of the air. The craft was powered by an engine in the front driving a conventional propeller, and had short stubby wings with ailerons to help share the lift work of the rotor blades and provide lateral control; at the rear of its fuselage were mounted the elevator and rudder for directional control.

Setting the blades into initial motion by means of rope-wind start that day in 1923, Cierva gunned his engine and rose above the Cuatro Vientes airport near Madrid. The machine made a complete circuit of over three miles at an altitude of 82 feet—the first officially observed flight of a successful roto-wing-type aircraft. In his subsequent models, Cierva connected the rotors to the engine by means of shaft and clutch that was disengaged immediately once the blades came up to take-off velocity, after which they windmilled freely as long as the "giro" was in motion.

Several months before the debut of the autogiro, a true helicopter with engine-driven rotors had made a flight in the U.S. —at the end of retaining ropes anchored to the ground. The big unwieldy craft, designed by the Russian-born mathematical wizard Dr. George de Bothezat and sponsored by the Army, eventually made a number of free flights, the longest lasting 2 minutes, 45 seconds, but performancewise it did not live up to the Army's expectations. Cierva's autogiro, on the other hand, was a flying machine in the true sense of the word, and the type became a common sight.

By 1926 the transport airplane had lost the look of a converted bomber. Manufacturers were designing planes better suited to air travel, with window curtains and meals for passengers' comfort and as many as four engines for safety. Fokker in Holland, Handley Page in England, and Junkers in Germany did most of the supplying. Fokker also established a plant to build transports here at Teterboro, New Jersey. Sensing a certain lack, Henry Ford bought William B. Stout's plant, moved it to Detroit and started production of the first U.S. all-metal transport designed by Stout. Soon its Liberty was replaced by three powerful air-cooled Wright or Pratt & Whitney engines. The famous tri-motor Ford, trade-marked by its corrugated-skin construction, was the greatest transport plane of the era. Besides being almost indestructible, it was easy to fly and could get in and out of small fields with heavy loads.

While both passenger and freight transports in the United States saw a rosy future ahead, private flying had to sing for its supper. In Europe aviation for the individual was subsidized by the government, which resulted in a plethora of flying clubs and specially designed light planes. Here, manufacturers were too busy trying to make a living out of contracts for the military and air-mail planes to consider John Q. Public.

But John Q., the countryman of Wilbur and Orville, was not content to sit on the ground. There were lots of war-surplus trainers to be had for approximately 300 dollars apiece, lots of ex-Army and Navy pilots, and soon a number of students who learned to fly by doing odd chores at the airports. From this combination emerged the barnstormers or "gypsies." These roaming daredevils, for a fee, put their creaky craft through all sorts of stunts, including wing walking and plane changing in mid-air. They took up passengers for ten dollars a head—or as low as a penny a pound per customer's weight. Some ranged as lone wolves, others organized flying circuses that followed the fairs around the land.

There is a story about a certain chute man caught in the middle of a little "misunderstanding" between an aerial circus and a lone wolf. One day in 1923 Clyde Pangborn, later a famed speed merchant and ocean hopper, but then a member of Gates Flying Circus, landed at a fair site in Montana where his outfit had an exclusive contract to do business. He found another barnstormer about to horn in, assisted by a tall, quiet young fellow acting as his chute man or parachute jumper. Pangborn had the pair ordered off the field. The chute man looked dejected. He had merely been hoping to earn another fee to help pay for flying lessons. The kid, whose name was Charles Lindbergh, wanted to be a pilot himself.

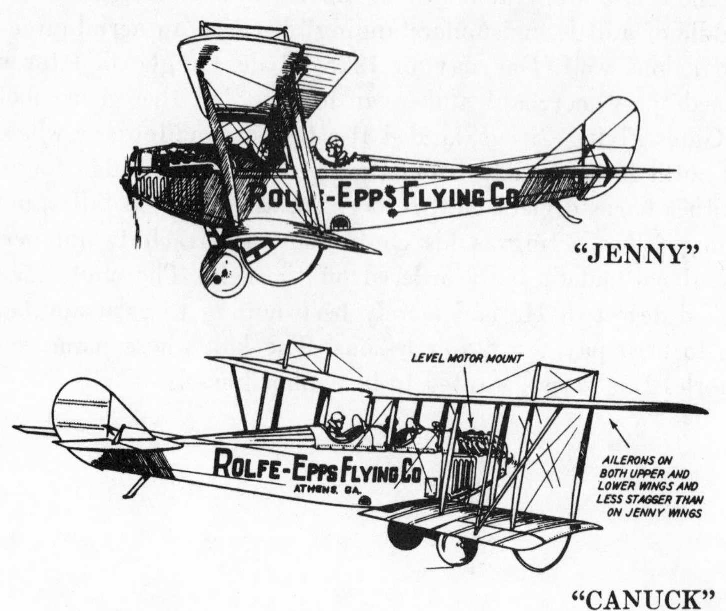

CURTISS JN-4D (Canadian version, the "Canuck." Differed from U.S. model, the "Jenny," in having ailerons top and bottom and level motor bed.) These war-surplus trainers were widely used throughout the U.S. after the war by barnstorming pilots.

JUNKERS J.13 Official designation D-1, 185-h.p. B.M.W. engine, was world's first all-metal transport airplane and first airplane specifically designed as a civil air liner. The original J.13 was still in service at the outbreak of World War II.

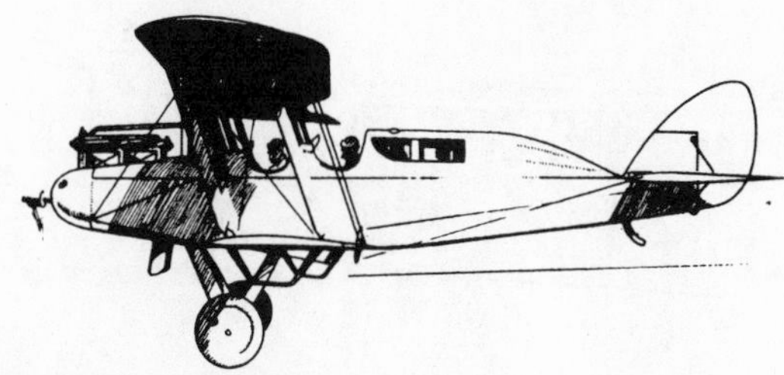

DE HAVILLAND Converted wartime D.H.9c was one of the first passenger planes employed on the newly established London–Paris run.

DE HAVILLAND D.H.4a Converted British bomber, similar to the D.H.9c, was also employed on embryo air lines.

CURTISS NC-4 Four 400-h.p. Liberty engines. The big NC boats had a wingspan of 126 feet, stood 22 feet high, were first to complete a South Atlantic crossing in 1919.

VICKERS "VIMY" Two 360-h.p. Rolls-Royce engines. This converted wartime bomber was the first airplane in the world to make a nonstop transatlantic flight (New Foundland to Ireland, June 14-15, 1919. Elapsed time of flight: 16 hours, 20 minutes).

VICKERS "VIMY" Two 360-h.p. Rolls-Royce engines. Similar to transatlantic "Vimy" but with modified 10-passenger cabin fuselage.

BOEING B-1 First commercial Boeing design. The original Boeing "Mail Boat" was powered with a 200-h.p. Hall-Scott engine, later fitted with a 420-h.p. Liberty. Plywood hull.

FARMAN "GOLIATH" Two 200-h.p. Salmson radial engines. Intended as a heavy bomber but converted at war's end into a 12-20-passenger air liner.

KOOLHOVEN FK.26 A postwar 5-passenger air liner by the same designer responsible for the 1912 British Deperdussin monoplane.

DE HAVILLAND D.H.4 420-h.p. Liberty engine. U.S.-built model which was used for some years on the air-mail routes here.

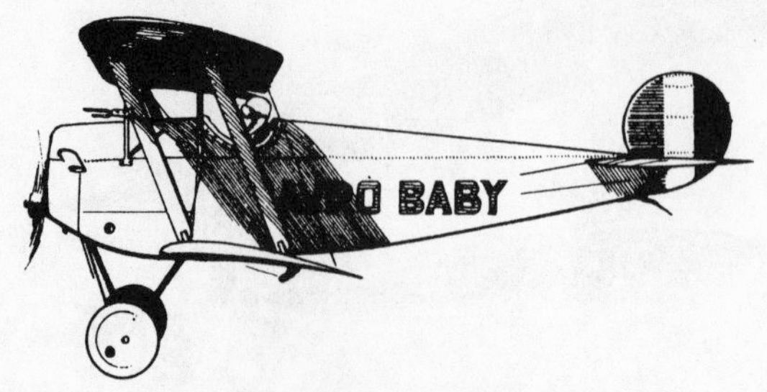

AVRO "BABY" This little single-seater sport plane was powered with the original 35-h.p. Green engine which was used on the 1911 Avro.

AVRO "BABY" This 2-place modification of the 1919 "Baby" was powered with a 60-h.p. Cirrus engine; had sensational performance.

SHORT "SILVER STREAK" First airplane in the world to employ stressed-skin all-metal monocoque fuselage structure.

FOKKER S.1 (U.S. Army designation: TW-4) Side-by-side 2-seat trainer powered with Curtiss OX-5 engine.

FOKKER D.11 Postwar modification of the Fokker D.VII; rotary powered.

HANDLEY PAGE H.P. Type W8b. Two 360-h.p. Rolls-Royce engines. Carried a crew of 2 and 14 passengers on regularly scheduled flights between London and Paris.

SAUNDERS "KITTYWAKE" Two 150-h.p. A.B.C. radial engines. This 9-place amphibian was built by the firm known today as the Saunders-Roe Company.

DOUGLAS First commercial design by the world-famed Douglas Company was the "Cloudster" shown here. 400-h.p. Liberty engine.

BARNHART "TWIN" Two 90-h.p. Curtiss OXX-5 engines; was early U.S. 4-passenger civil transport.

SAVOIA 470-h.p. Ansaldo engine. This neat little flying boat won the first postwar Schneider Cup races for Italy.

DE HAVILLAND The D.H.29 had a 450-h.p. Napier Lion 3-bank engine and carried 10 passengers. Note exceptionally clean lines.

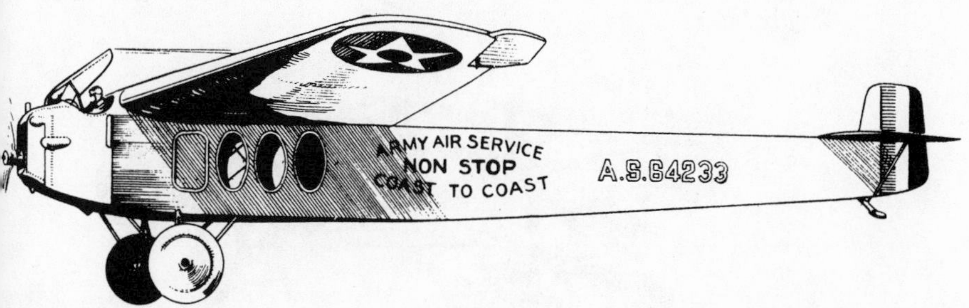

FOKKER F.1V (U.S. Army designation: T-2) 420-h.p. Liberty engine. Piloted by Lts. McReady and Kelly, this ship made the first nonstop transcontinental flight in February, 1923.

DOUGLAS DT-1 First military Douglas, this early torpedo bomber had folding wings.

MARTIN NBS-1 Two 420-h.p. Liberty engines; was development of the Martin MB series shown earlier. It was also used in modified form as a mail plane and as a 12-passenger cabin air liner.

FAIREY The Fairey "Flycatcher" shown here with H.M.S. *Eagle*, world's first genuine flattop, was one of the first specially designed shipboard aircraft.

THOMAS MORSE 400-h.p. Wright-Hispano engine. This Army Racer was a contestant in the 1921 Pulitzer races. Top speed was 162 m.p.h.

DE PISCHOFF Wingspan of the aerial scooter was only 12 feet. It was powered with a 20-h.p. flat twin. It ushered in a whole series of ultra-light, low-powered planes which appeared in the early twenties.

MARTIN MO-1 This shipboard observation plane was the first genuine all-metal airplane designed and built in the U.S.A.

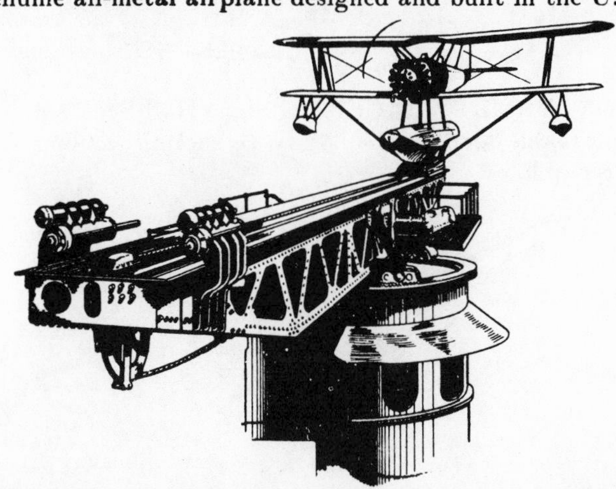

CATAPULTS First power-operated turntable catapults replaced fixed installations on battleships and cruisers about this time.

JUNKERS-LARSEN JL-2 First U.S. attack plane, it was armed with no fewer than 30 machine guns, all but two of which were remotely controlled for strafing ground troops. 42-h.p. Liberty.

AEROMARINE PG-1 Early U.S. fighter with cannon firing through propeller hub.

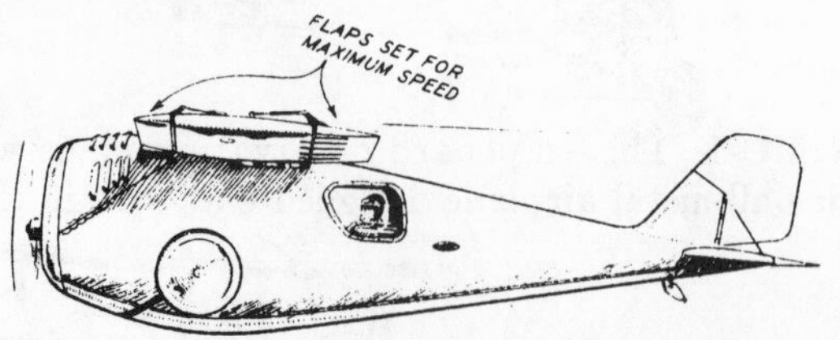

DAYTON-WRIGHT RACER 200-h.p. Hall-Scott engine. This remarkable airplane had fully retracting landing gear, hit 178 m.p.h.

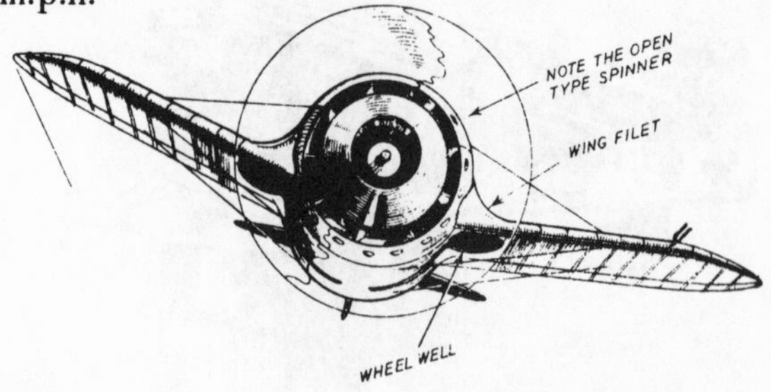

BRISTOL This remarkable experimental design anticipated the mid-wing monoplane fighter of World War II by nearly 20 years.

CURTISS R-6 ARMY RACER 460-h.p. Curtiss D-12 engine. The Curtiss racers were a milestone in the development of high-speed design. They placed first and second in the Pulitzer races of 1922, and although not strictly speaking a military type, played an important part in the development of all future piston-engine pursuit designs. Top speed 232 m.p.h.

CURTISS NAVY RACER R2C-1 General "Billy" Mitchell shattered all existing speed records in one of these planes—266 m.p.h.

FLATTOPS First U.S. flattop, a converted collier, was placed in service in 1922. Planes illustrated, Navy TS fighters.

ZOEGLING (Primary) GLIDER Due to the harsh terms of the Armistice and the restrictions placed on German aviation, there developed in the twenties a tremendous interest in gliding and soaring. This is a typical primary glider as developed in Germany.

LOENING "KITTEN" This neat little float seaplane was designed by Grover Loening. It was powered with a 35-h.p. Lawrence radial.

SUPERMARINE "SEA EAGLE" 365-h.p. Rolls-Royce engine. The seaworthy hull of this civil transport is noteworthy.

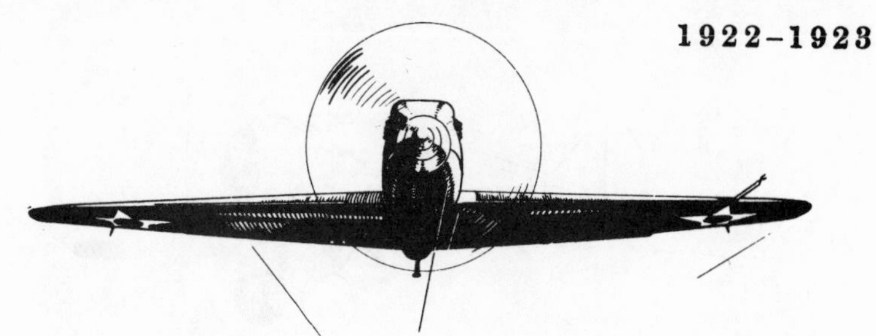

VERVILLE-SPERRY 400-h.p. Wright-Hispano engine. This U.S. Army Pulitzer racer had a top speed of 191 m.p.h.

FOKKER D.X This Dutch fighter was powered with a 335-h.p. Wright engine. U.S. Army designation was PW-5.

PENSUTI-CAPRONI The same company responsible for the giant Caproni bomber shown in the previous section produced this 13-foot triplane.

HANDLEY PAGE HP-21 This shipboard fighter was one of the first airplanes in the world to be equipped with full-length flaps, 7 slots.

CURTISS XPW-8 440-h.p. Curtiss D-12 engine. Developed from the R-6 racers and was prototype model of the famed "Hawk" fighters.

MARTIN MS-1 This diminutive float seaplane had folding wings, was designed for stowage aboard submarines.

VOUGHT UO-1 200-h.p. Wright radial engine. A catapult-launched shipboard spotter, it was ancestor of the famed Corsair series.

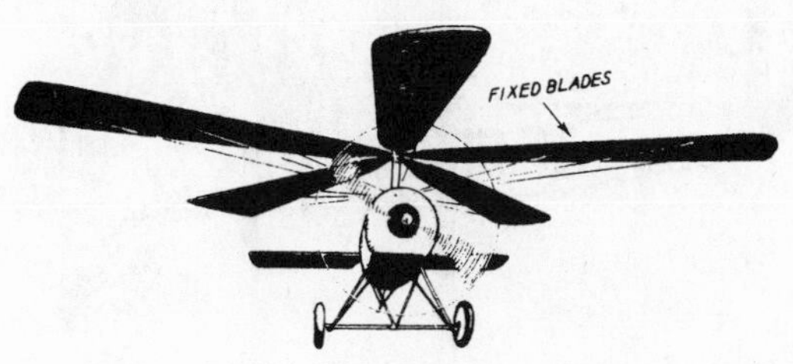

CIERVA Juan de la Cierva invented the autogiro, first practical application of rotary-wing flight. This early model had rigid rotor blades, tipped over on take-off.

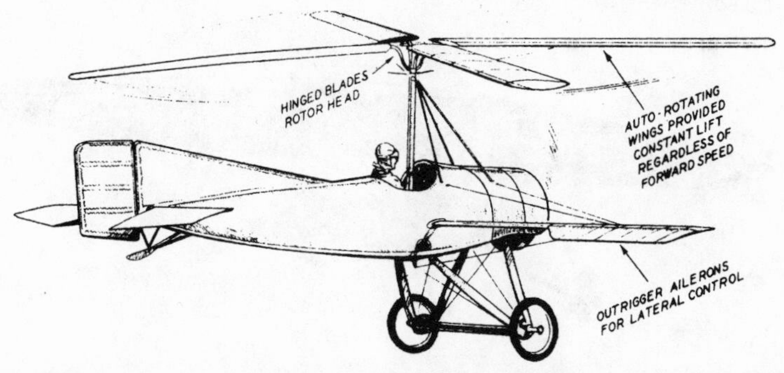

CIERVA First practical autogiro had articulated blades, normal airplane controls for lateral and longitudinal control.

BOEING PW-9 425-h.p. Curtiss D-12 engine. First of a long line of Boeing pursuits. Top speed was about 160 m.p.h.

CONSOLIDATED TW-3 First airplane built by what is now the famed Convair Company was this 150-h.p. Wright-Hisso-powered side-by-side trainer. Actually designed by former Dayton-Wright Co.

HAWKER "DUIKER" 400-h.p. Bristol Jupiter radial. One of the first products of the then newly formed Hawker Company (later Sopwith).

FOKKER FG.II World's first 2-place motorless plane. Anthony Fokker set many duration records with this in soaring flight.

DE HAVILLAND D.H.53 6-h.p. motorcycle engine. Flew well. With somewhat larger engine, it was used by R.A.F. as primary trainer.

PARNALL "PIXIE" Built by one of the top British aviation firms, this tiny airplane hit 100 m.p.h., won all the major speed events in the 1923 British Light Airplane Trials.

AVRO 506 Ultra-light monoplane which flew well with a 7-17-h.p. converted motorcycle engine.

AVRO NAPIER 1,000-h.p. four-bank Napier engine. Largest single-engine plane of the period, it makes a striking contrast with the little motor glider produced during the same year and shown immediately below.

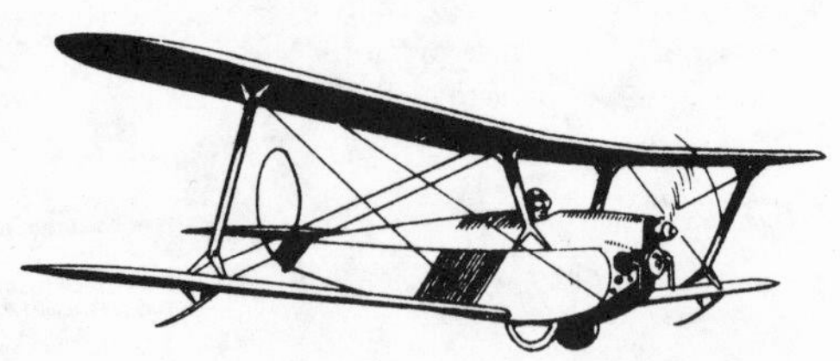

AVRO MOTOR GLIDER 3½-h.p. converted motorcycle engine. Another ultra-light Avro which flew consistently well.

BEARDMORE "WEE-BEE 1" 32-h.p. Bristol Cherub engine. One of the most successful ultra-light planes yet produced.

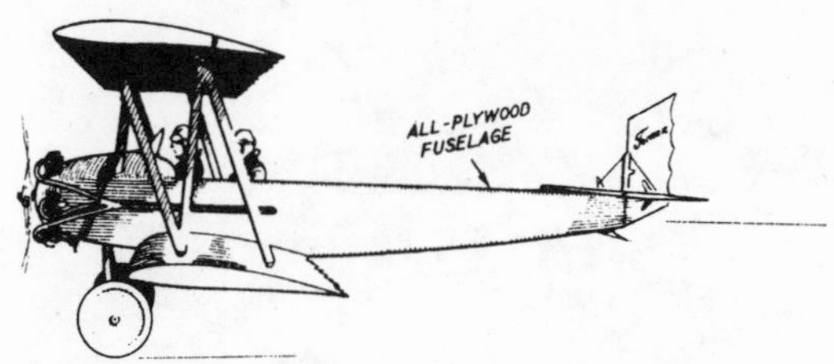

FARMAN "SPORT" 60-70-h.p. Anzani radial engine. Another 1924 design.

FARMAN "MOSQUITO" 35-h.p. Anzani fan-type radial engine. A French ultra-light airplane.

AVIA B.H.16 A 1924 Czech venture into the ultra-light plane field.

HAWKER "CYGNET" 32-h.p. Bristol Cherub engine. Ultra-light plane.

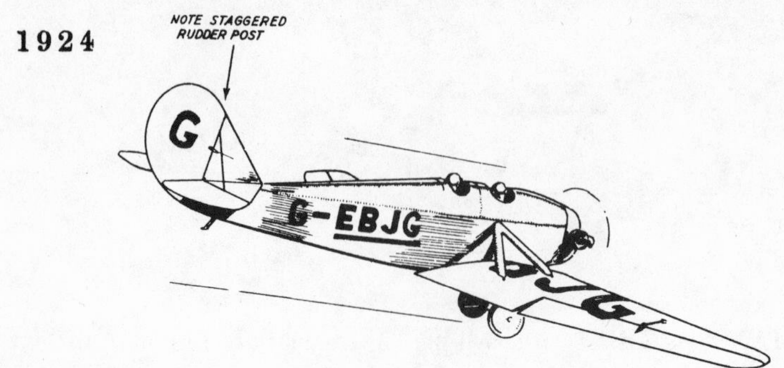

PARNALL "PIXIE III" 32-h.p. Bristol Cherub engine. The 2-place "Pixie" had folding wings for easy storage.

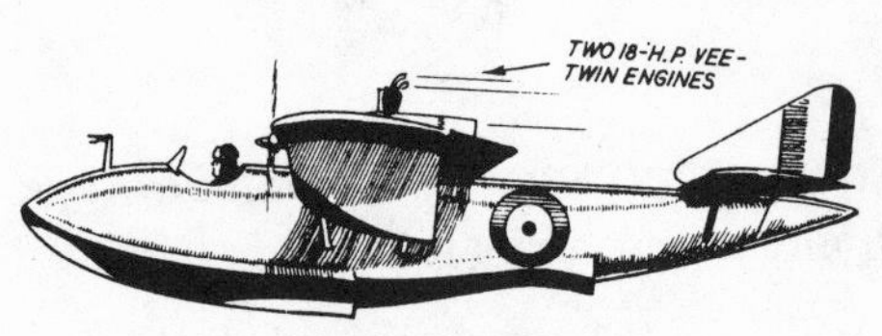

SHORT "COCKLE" Two 7-h.p. (suped-up to 18 h.p. each) Blackburn motorcycle engines. Ultra-light all-metal flying boat.

SHORT "SATELLITE" 32-h.p. Bristol Cherub engine. All-metal ultra-light 2-seater.

IRWIN "METEORPLANE" 20-h.p. Irwin X-type radial engine. Was an ultra-small U.S. light airplane.

BRISTOL "BROWNIE" 32-h.p. Bristol Cherub engine. Produced by world renowned Bristol Aeroplane Company.

R.A.E. "HURRICANE" A 1924 amateur-built design which flew well.

DORMOY "BATHTUB" 20-h.p. Henderson motorcycle engine. Ultra-light home-built U.S. design which flew well.

FORD "FLIVVER" 20-h.p. flat twin engine. Henry Ford's entry in light-plane field.

ALBATROSS SPORTFLUGZEUG 32-h.p. Bristol Cherub engine. Ultra-light airplane by the famed World War I pursuit manufacturers.

MYERS "MIDGET" One of the most original light planes entered in the 1924 U.S. Light-Plane Contest was this rigid-truss 16-foot biplane.

SCHULZ The Germans were first to perfect soaring motorless flight. The Schulz *Segelflugzeug* is one of the earlier types.

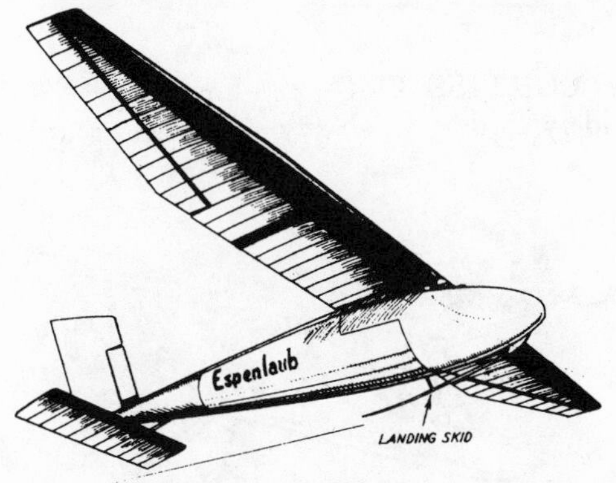

ESPENLAUB Another 1924-model German high-performance *Segelflugzeug* or sailplane.

CURTISS CR-3 500-h.p. Curtiss D-12a engine. Float version of the 1923 Navy Racer, it set new speed record of 227 m.p.h.

U.S. NAVY CURTISS F4-C 220-h.p. Lawrence radial engine. Was widely used by the Navy as land- or seaplane.

CONSOLIDATED PT-1 180-h.p. Wright-Hisso engine. The Consolidated "Trusty" was long the standard trainer of the U.S. Army Air Corps.

TSCHERANOVSKY This parabolic-wing 2-seater was a 1924 Russian design.

BLACKBURN "DART" 450-h.p. Napier Lion engine. First specially designed torpedo bomber by this still-famous British company.

MARTIN SC-2 Was a U.S. torpedo bomber of the 1924 period.

BRISTOL 100-h.p. Bristol Lucifer radial engine. Civil or military 2-seat trainer.

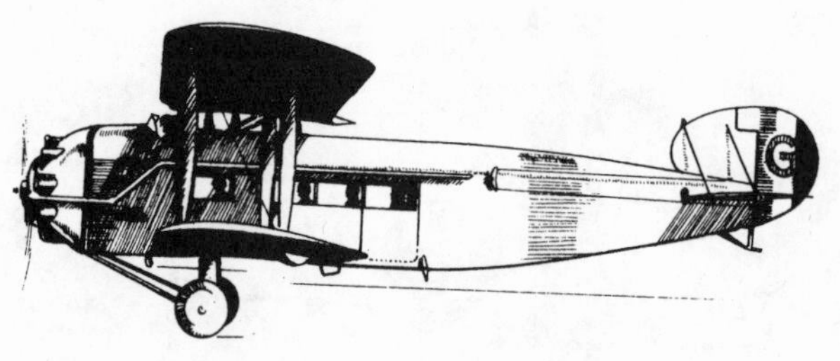

BRISTOL "BRANDON" Single-engine 10-passenger transport.

LOENING AMPHIBIAN 400-h.p. inverted Liberty engine.

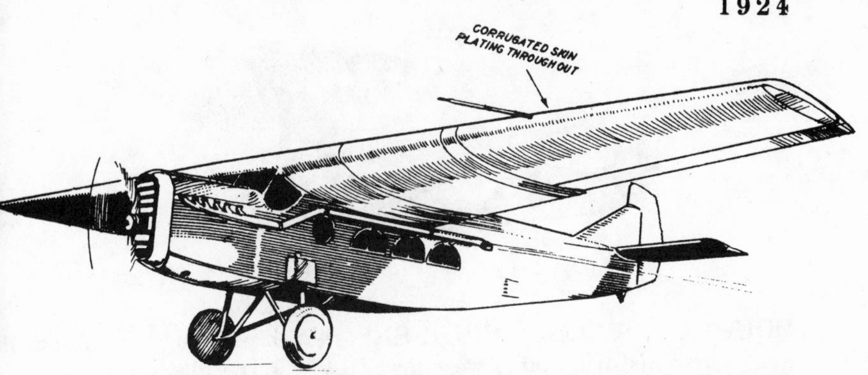

FORD-STOUT "PULLMAN" 420-h.p. Liberty engine. First U.S. all-metal air liner; carried 6 passengers and crew. Speed: 110 m.p.h.

FARMAN "JABIRU" Four 180-h.p. Hispano-Suiza engines. 10-passenger air liner produced by the pioneer Farman Company in 1924.

REMINGTON-BURNELLI RB-2 Burnelli was pioneer proponent of lifting airfoil-type fuselages. Note the completely buried engines.

DOUGLAS "WORLD CRUISER" 420-h.p. Liberty engine. These historic planes were first to girdle the globe.

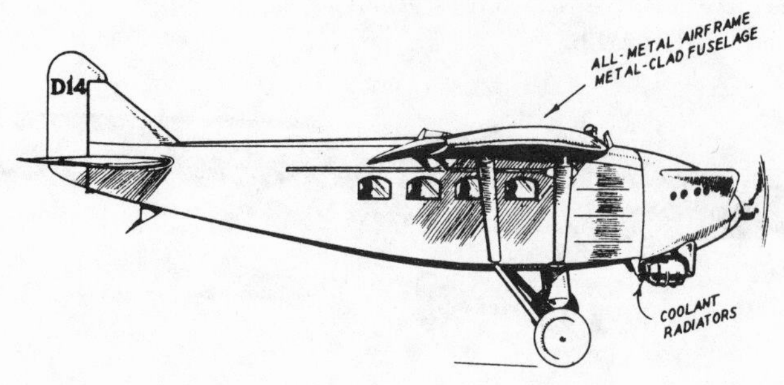

DEWOITINE D-14 450-h.p. Lorraine-Dietrich engine. Dewoitine was early exponent of all-metal aircraft. 8- to 10-passenger air liner.

DE HAVILLAND D.H.54 650-h.p. Rolls-Royce Condor engine. 14 passengers and crew. Top speed: 120 m.p.h.

ROHRBACH Two 375-h.p. Rolls-Royce engines. This large German flying boat carried a crew of 2 and 12 passengers.

FOKKER B.11 Powered with a Rolls-Royce Eagle engine. Had all-metal hull and wing-tip floats.

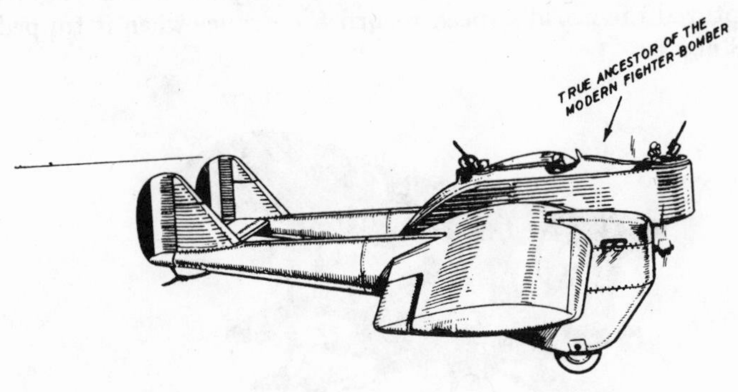

SCHNEIDER Two 500-h.p. Lorraine engines. This all-metal French attack bomber had a top speed of 136 m.p.h.

AERO BH16 300-h.p. Walter engine. This little Czech racer averaged 164 m.p.h. over a pylon course.

BERNARD-FERBOIS 450-h.p. 3-bank Hispano-Suiza engine. Captured the world's speed record for France when it topped 278 m.p.h.

GLOSTER "GREBE" Builders of today's Gloster "Meteor" jet fighters supplied this single-seat fighter to the R.A.F. in 1924.

HUFF DALAND 190-h.p. Wright V-8 engine. This plane was built when the present president of the McDonnell Company was engineer and test pilot for Huff Daland.

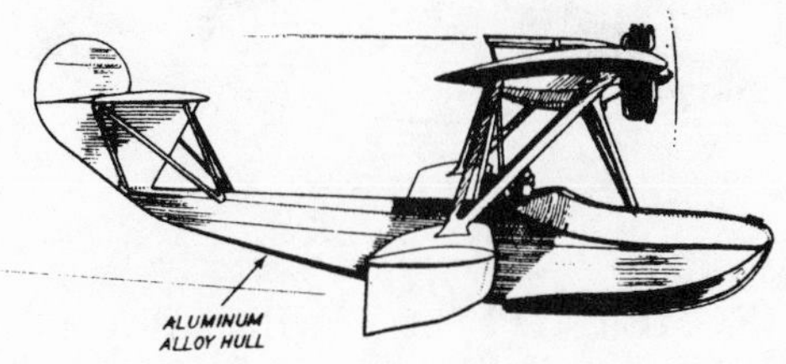

AEROMARINE E.O. 70/80-h.p. Anzani radial engine. A trim U.S. 3-place seaplane with all-metal hull.

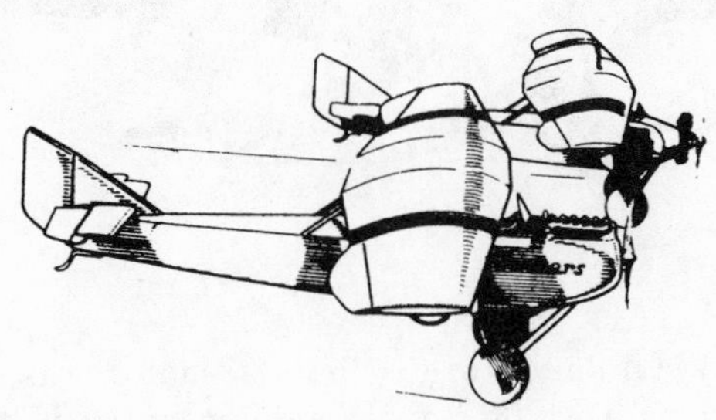

JUNKERS TYPE T 60-h.p. Junkers 6-in-line or Siemens-Halske 50-h.p. radial. These rugged little all-metal trainers were advanced designs.

KOOLHOVEN F.K.33 Recall the old British Deperdussin? Well here is Fritz's idea of what a 12-passenger air liner should look like.

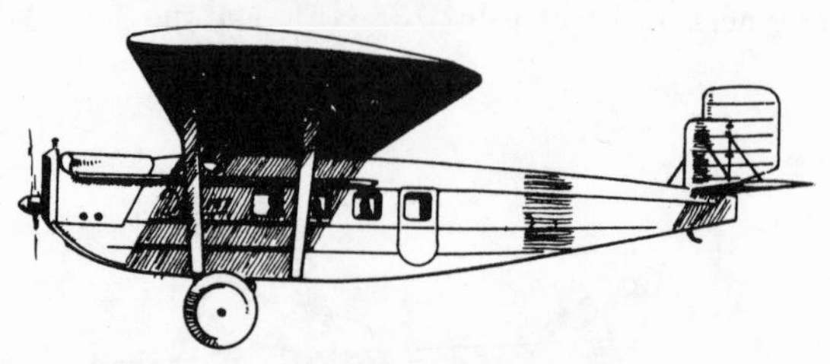

DORNIER "KOMET III" 360-h.p. Rolls-Royce engine. 6- to 8-passenger air liner by the pioneer German designer of transport planes.

FOKKER F.VIIB-3m World's first tri-motor was actually the old F.VII with a 200-h.p. Wright mounted in the nose and two more of the same engines slung from the wings. Many notable long-distance and transoceanic flights were made with this type.

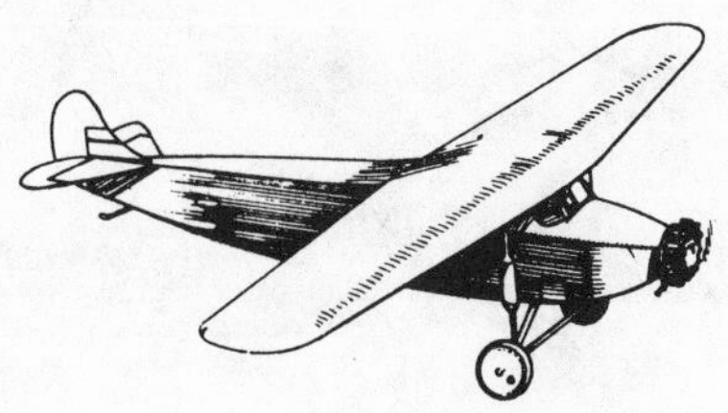

FOKKER F.VII Variously powered. At this time Fokker air liners were predominant all over the world and used engines native to the country in which they happened to be employed.

AVRO 563 650-h.p. Rolls-Royce Condor engine. And here is another old-timer's conception of the 12-passenger air liner in 1925.

RYAN-STANDARD First Ryan production was this Hisso-powered converted Standard JR-1, a wartime trainer. Originally a 2-seat open-cockpit biplane, it came out of the Ryan shops a 5-place cabin biplane.

DOUGLAS O-2 435-h.p. Liberty engine. Replaced the De Havilland 4 as standard observation plane in the Army Air Corps.

EPPS 17-h.p. Indian Chief motorcycle engine. One of the many amateur U.S. light planes developed during this era.

POWELL 32-h.p. Bristol Cherub engine. The Powell Racer was miniature perfection for the period. Fuselage was all-plywood construction.

BOEING MAILPLANE First of a long series of Boeing mail and passenger transports.

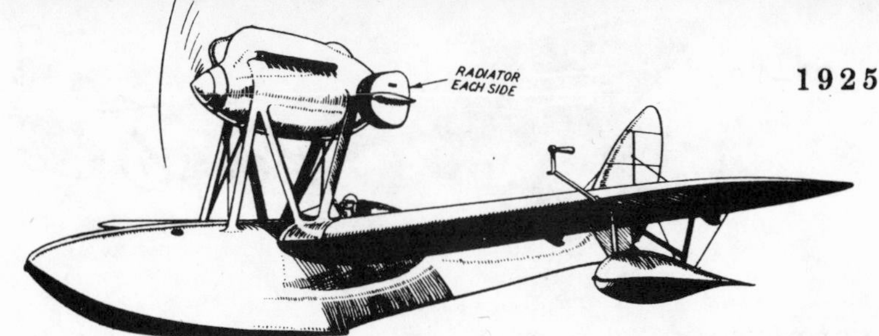

MACCHI 33 450-h.p. Curtiss D-2 engine. From the first the Italians had a flair for clean-looking, fast flying boats. This one was a Schneider Cup racer, had a top speed of about 250 m.p.h.

DE HAVILLAND D.H.60 27-h.p. Cirrus engine. First of the famed "Moth" series and first practical personal plane, the "Moth" was a simple, foolproof airplane with excellent performance.

FOKKER D.XIV This semi-cantilever fighter gives some idea of the range covered by Fokker designs during this period.

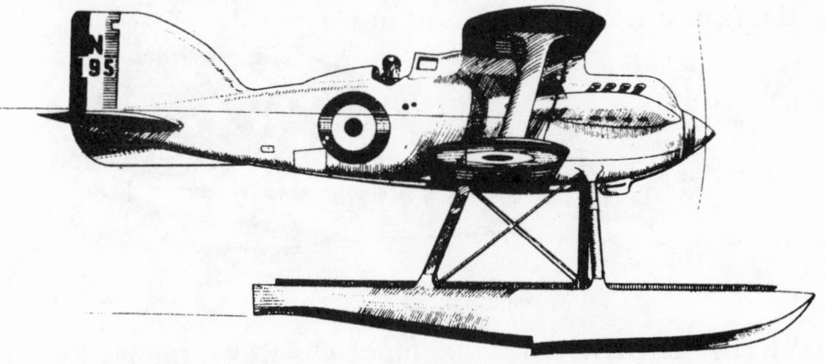

GLOSTER III 1,275-h.p. 3-bank Napier engine. Placed second in the 1925 Schneider Cup races. Maximum speed: 234 m.p.h.

FORD-STOUT Three 200-h.p. Wright Whirlwind radials. Bill Stout took up Fokker's tri-motor idea and used it on this 12-passenger all-metal design which was the backbone of U.S. air lines for years.

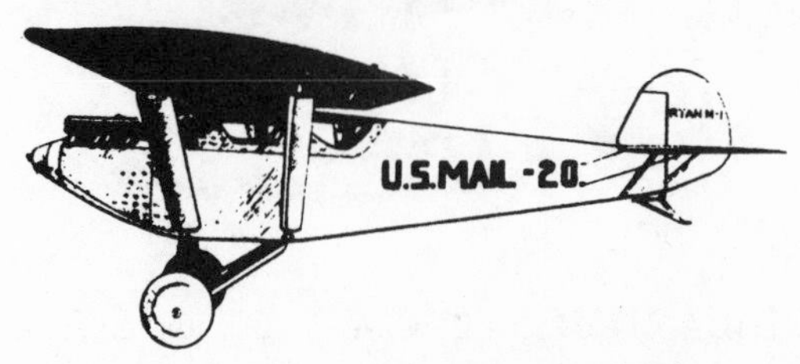

RYAN M-1 First authentic Ryan design. Hispano-Suiza engine.

AVRO "AVENGER" 525-h.p. 3-bank Napier engine. In its day the fastest single-seat fighter in the world.

HAWKER "HORNBILL" 700-h.p. Rolls-Royce engine. First of the high-speed Hawker biplane fighters which culminated in the "Furies," which in turn preceded the "Hurricanes." Top speed of the "Hornbill" was 196 m.p.h.

BREGUET XIX Prototype model of the plane which made first nonstop Paris-New York flight some years later.

BRISTOL "BLOODHOUND" First new Bristol 2-seat fighter-reconnaissance plane since the famed Bristol fighter of World War I.

STINSON First type produced under the Stinson name, this 200-h.p. cabin biplane introduced wheel brakes in the U.S.A.

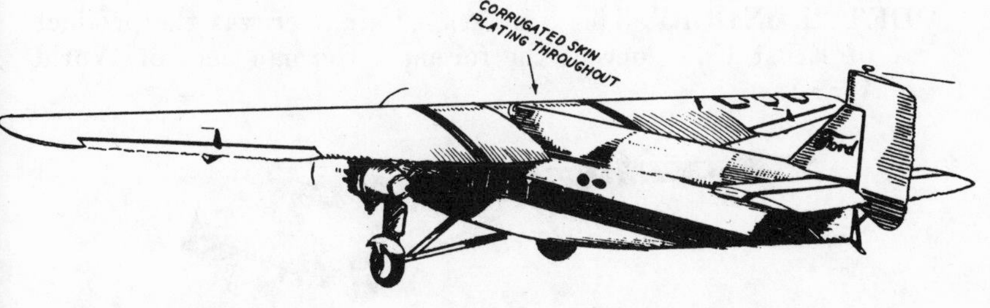

FORD 4-AT A modification of the first U.S. tri-motor air liner, it had enclosed cockpit instead of the open affair shown on the preceding plane. This is the famed "Tin Goose," of historic interest.

DOUGLAS M-2 400-h.p. Liberty engine. This mailplane had a useful load capacity of 2,000 pounds.

CURTISS "CARRIER PIGEON" This was 1926 Curtiss bid for mailplane contracts.

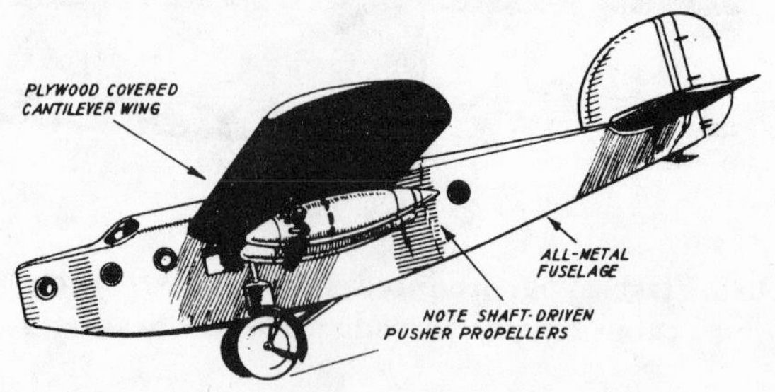

UDET "KONDOR" This 8-passenger air liner was the product of Ernst Udet, one of the foremost German aces of World War I.

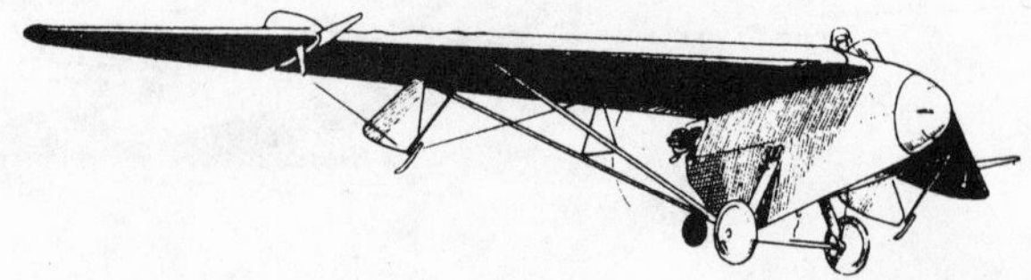

HILL TAILLESS 32-h.p. Bristol Cherub engine. Prototype model of the later Westland-Hill "Pterodactyls" and ancestor of the present-day jet-powered tailless fighters.

FOKKER F.VIII A twin-engined modification of the F.VII-3m type, it was a 15-passenger air liner used on the Dutch airways.

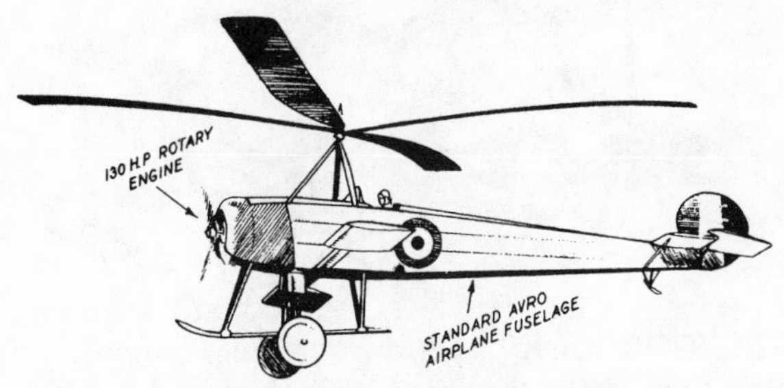

CIERVA AUTOGIRO 130-h.p. rotary radial. British development of original Cierva design. Autogiros of this period were handicapped by lack of any mechanical means of setting rotor blades in motion—a necessary prelude to the take-off.

PENHOET Five 450-h.p. Bristol Jupiter radials. Illustrates the French aircraft industry's interest in large flying boats.

BLACKBURN "BLACKBURN" This curious-looking fleet-spotter, naval observation plane is notable for the fact that in profile it anticipated the present trend in similar naval air-craft.

GLOSTER "GORCOCK" 525-h.p. Napier engine. The name Gloster has been associated with fast fighter aircraft for nearly 30 years.

JUNKERS K-47 This all-metal attack plane was built in Sweden at the time when all military aircraft were forbidden to the defeated Germans of World War I.

BOEING XF2B-1 First Boeing radial-powered shipboard fighter.

CURTISS P1-A "HAWK" 435-h.p. Curtiss D-12 engine. In variant forms, the famed "Hawk" was for years the standard U.S.A.A.C. fighter and derived from the earlier Curtiss Racers.

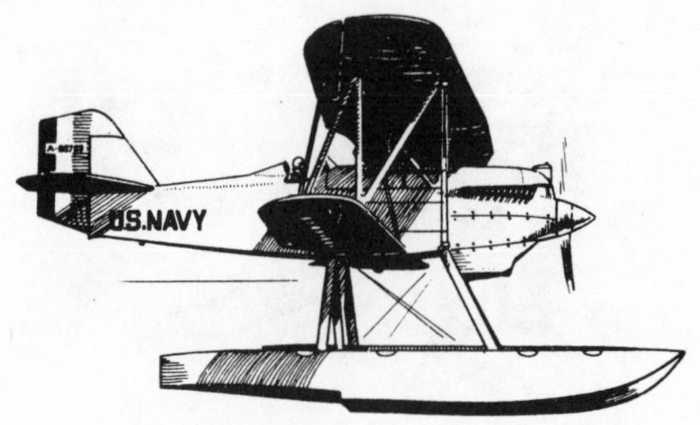

CURTISS F6-C "HAWK" U.S. Naval version of the "Hawk" pursuit.

BLACKBURN "IRIS" Three engines, total horsepower, 2,100. Long-range patrol bomber and civil air liner.

BOEING FB-3 600-h.p. Packard engine. Easily convertible to land-based fighter. Later versions were radial powered.

CONSOLIDATED "HUSKY" Similar to the famed "Trusty" trainer but powered with a 225-h.p. Wright J-5 radial engine.

RYAN M-2 "BLUEBIRD" First of the Ryan cabin monoplanes and precursor of the famed "Spirit of St. Louis." Hisso engine.

PART FIVE

The Golden Age of Aviation

1927-1932

BARNSTORMERS HELPED. In the years immediately following World War I the visiting pilots who hopped passengers from cow pastures and the daredevils who thrilled the crowd at county fairs made the American public air-conscious. By 1927 the matter of flying was no longer regarded as a form of insanity or a special brand of talent.

In that year Lindbergh's feat of spanning the Atlantic solo in a nonstop flight from Roosevelt Field, Long Island, to Le Bourget in Paris, followed by Chamberlin and Byrd, gave the spark to this accumulated interest—a spark that burst into the Golden Age of Aviation. For five eventful years, till the depression began to weed out the merely experimental or induce economic pause in even the boldest, the airplane leaped ahead from one major development to another. The general activity might be gauged by the fact that in the United States alone, at one time during this period, there were upward of 150 aircraft manufacturers producing every type of flying machine from the 26-h.p. "grasshopper" to the multi-engined "air yacht."

The development in engines was outstanding. Already the airplane had undergone structural change, with the spruce of the barnstormer's "Jennys" and "Standards" giving way to the metal tubing welded fuselage frames in open cockpit of three-seaters like the "Travelair," "Waco," "Eaglerock," "Swallow," and other biplanes. Such improved craft were faster and more stable than the vintage warriors. Though still powered by surplus 90-h.p. Curtiss OX-5's or 150-h.p. Wright-Hispanos, they became available—for the more affluent—with the powerful Wright J-5 "Whirlwind" 220-h.p. radial air-cooled engine mounted in the same air frame. They could take it.

The "Whirlwind" and its more muscular sister, the 400-h.p. "Wasp," changed the whole aeronautical picture. Without these two nine-cylinder air-cooled radials, the former manufactured by the Wright Aeronautical Corporation and the latter by Pratt & Whitney, the rapid progress in air transportation that occurred during the Golden Age would have been impossible. Lighter in weight than the previously liquid-cooled plants due to the elimination of cylinder water jackets, radiator and cooling liquid with its attendant plumbing and pumps, these perfected radials made it feasible to build airplanes with larger payloads and greater range.

The weight saving on the "Whirlwind," for instance, meant an increase in fuel capacity on an ordinary plane that enabled it to extend its range by at least 200 miles.

Simple in construction, economical, and most pleasantly reliable, these engines laid the foundation for the expansion of both commercial and military aviation. Though built under license and copied by many other countries, including Russia, they did not radically alter the preference of the Europeans for the liquid-cooled "V" type as exemplified by Britain's magnificent Rolls-Royce or France's Hispano-Suiza or Lorraine. Here in America the trend grew definitely in their favor for civilian use. Even the military was being partially won over. While the Air Corps leaned toward the liquid-cooled V-12's such as the Curtiss D-12 and the 600-h.p. Conqueror, the Navy chose radials produced by Wright and Pratt & Whitney.

The quest for better streamlining was responsible for the development of bonded wood structures, wherein plywood was used as outer fuselage and wing covering, giving an exceptionally smooth outer surface which greatly reduced drag and increased the efficiency of the wing. This construction was pioneered by Fokker with his wooden cantilever wing and by Lockheed with their "Vega," "Executive," and "Air Express" high-wing monoplanes.

The shape of the airplane was being altered during this period. Slowly the biplane moved aside first for the high-wing monoplane and later for the low-wing. Though the biplane retained certain advantages from the standpoint of maneuverability and lower stalling speed, its awkward mounting of one wing above the other with bracing struts and wires caused high drag and considerable interference of airflow between the two wings. The biplane continued as the favorite in the military service and in the smaller, open-cockpit craft flown by civilians, but all the larger airplanes, at least in the United States, became the more efficient monoplane type.

It was the demand for still higher speeds, especially in the field of aerial transportation, that decided the manufacturers to go into low-wing design. Heretofore this had been an exclusive characteristic of racing planes. The low-wing shape permitted a better all-round streamlining and provided space for the wheels of the retractable landing gear. At the same time it achieved a wide undercarriage tread, the extra distance between wheels giving the airplane better ground stability in take-offs and landings.

Since the radial engine, sitting out in the breeze on the front of the airplane, created considerable drag, it was first enclosed in a narrow ring, known as the Townend ring. Later NACA developed the deep chord cowl as presently used, which not only streamlined the engine but also improved its cooling through use of baffles which guided the air around the cylinders.

During these years the development of cockpit instruments and navigation devices began to overcome the bugaboo of blind flying. Aviation leaders, realizing that air transportation could never reach the status of big business unless airplanes could keep to schedules no matter what the weather or kind of visibility, took definite steps to crack the problem. Fortunately there was at their disposal the genius of Elmer Sperry, who adapted the gyroscope to flight instruments. The gimbal-mounted spinning disk with the uncanny ability to maintain a fixed orientation in space became the basis of all instruments that guided the pilot through darkness, rain, snow, and sleet.

With the help of financier Harry Guggenheim and the Bureau of Standards, the Sperry, Pioneer, and Kollsman instrument companies introduced in 1927 such devices as the Artificial Horizon, which told the pilot the altitude of his plane; the Gyro Direction Indicator, graduated in compass degrees, that could instantly show any change in direction and did not have the "hunting" qualities of a magnetic compass; and the Earth Inductor Compass, which was not affected by large masses of iron ever-present in an airplane, or by vibration and the effects of the earth's field. This last-named device played an important role in the success of Lindbergh's flight.

These instruments, along with the sensitive altimeter capable of measuring heights as low as 20 feet, the turn and bank indicator showing the rate of an airplane's turn, and also radio beams acting as highways of the sky all served to guide the pilot through the murky atmosphere when his senses were unable to do so. But instruments alone could not keep a plane on an even keel or on course, for man is so constructed that his senses fool him when he cannot see, and such is his nature that he will depend on them no matter what. It was necessary, therefore, to teach pilots to trust the dials rather than their sense of balance. This task fell on a young Army lieutenant, James H. Doolittle, who in 1927 demonstrated the infallibility of the blind-flying system by taking off and landing in a completely enclosed cockpit of a Vought airplane at Mitchell Field on Long Island. Then Howard Stark and Charles A. Lindbergh further proved that man could fly without visual reference to landscape horizon.

The invention of the automatic pilot by Sperry in 1932 was another victory for the plane in its contest with the medium of air. And the variable-pitch propeller—the gear shift of the airplane—did much to extend the useful life of the engine, to reduce take-off run and increase operational efficiency.

Air races during this era spurred the development of the high-speed airplane. They acted as the proving ground for engine endurance, aerodynamics, and air-frame strength under the most grueling conditions. It was at the 1929 National Air Races in Cleveland that Jimmy Doolittle, flying a stubby Gee Bee racer, established a world speed record of 294 m.p.h. Even greater speeds were attained at the Schneider Cup meets, during one of which in 1931 in England a Supermarine S6B racing seaplane hit 407.5 m.p.h. The Schneider Cup Trophy races were greatly responsible for the evolvement of the "Spitfire," heroine of the Battle of Britain, in World War II; R. E. Mitchell, the "Spitfire's" designer, also drew up the S6B.

During the Golden Age Germany was the world's strongest booster for the lighter-than-air travel craft. It was the first to build a dirigible passenger liner, the "Graf Zeppelin," which in October of 1928 made its inaugural voyage with 23 paying passengers from Lake Constance to Lakehurst, New Jersey. As though trying to make up for time lost because of the Versailles Treaty restrictions, this country also produced some remarkable large transports. The most interesting example was the Dornier DO-X, a twelve-engine monster, which on its trial flight lifted 169 passengers; it visited the U.S. in 1931.

Prior to 1927 Germany had been forced to concentrate mainly on motorless flight for its aeronautical exercises. The soaring plane was an extremely useful research instrument, and the highly developed program centered around it started paying off dividends. It was the early experiments of Dr. Alexander Lippisch of Darmstadt with tailless gliders that eventually handed the *Luftwaffe* the Me.163 rocket fighter, and to the world, later on, the arrowhead-shaped flying wing and delta airplane.

This era saw autogiros emerging from the experimental stage. They were being built in quantity by both the United States and Great Britain.

In this period the trick of air-to-air refueling was performed in a big way for the first time. The magicians were the Air Corps' Major Carl Spaatz (General "Toohey" Spaatz of World War II fame), Captain (now General) Ira Eaker, and Lieutenant "Pete" (now General) Quesada. They remained aloft for 150 hours and 40 minutes in an Army tri-motor Fokker transport that obtained fuel from an aerial tanker.

The blueprint for the future was on the drawing table.

RYAN SPECIAL 220-h.p. Wright J-5 radial engine. The famed "Spirit of St. Louis" with which Charles Lindbergh completed world's first nonstop New York–Paris flight.

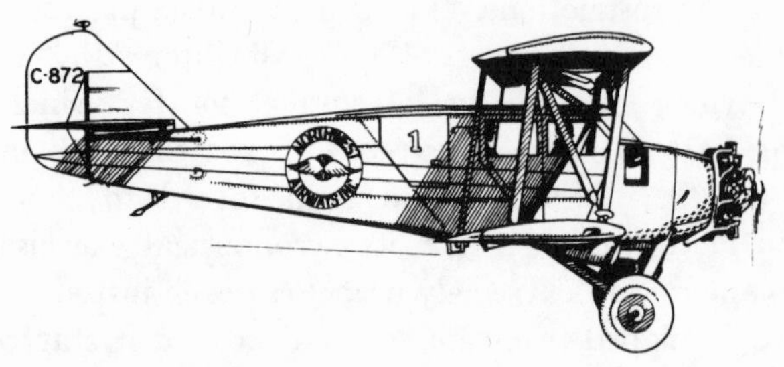

STINSON "DETROITER" 220-h.p. Wright J5-Ca radial. 4-place passenger mailplane. It was first real equipment of today's great Northwest Airlines, lasted for years as a feeder-line passenger and mailplane.

STINSON SM-1 220-Wright engine. Noted chiefly for its 12,995-mile flight to Japan with Bill Brock at the controls.

MARTIN T4M-1 U.S. Navy's first large carrier-based torpedo-bomber.

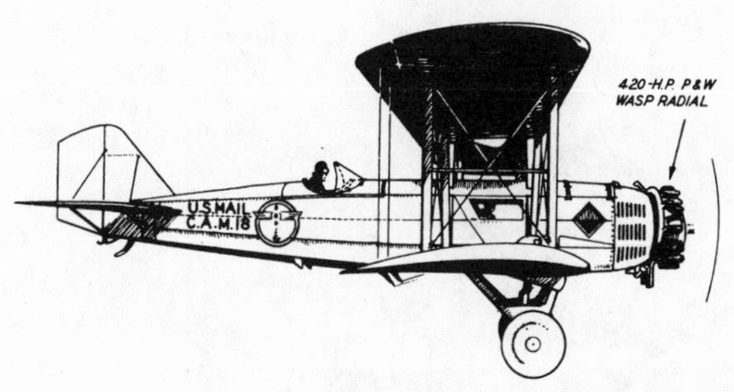

BOEING 40 420-h.p. Pratt & Whitney Wasp radial. Pioneer passenger mailplane and used on first night coast-to-coast routes.

RYAN B-1 BROUGHAM First volume-produced cabin monoplane in U.S. Production model had 200-h.p. radial instead of 150-h.p. Hispano-Suiza on prototype.

CURTISS HAWK P-1B 450-h.p. Curtiss engine.

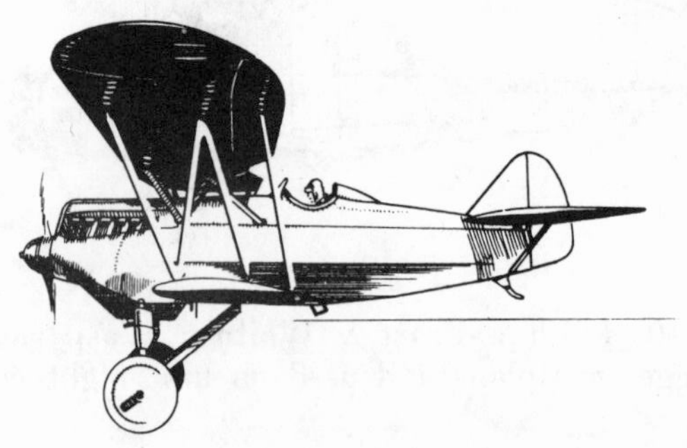

HEINKEL H.D.43 500/700-h.p. B.M.W. engine. This German pursuit closely resembled the Curtiss Hawks of the period.

HEINKEL H.20 Two 320-h.p. Wright radials. Supposedly a commercial airplane, it was in fact a thinly disguised military plane built in defiance of the Armistice terms.

DE HAVILLAND D.H.66 Three 450-h.p. Bristol Jupiter radials. 14-passenger air liner. Top speed: 130 m.p.h.

LOCKHEED "VEGA" 200-h.p. Wright radial. First of the Lockheed "Star" series. All-plywood fuselage. One of the fastest 6-place planes of the period.

PITCAIRN "MAILWING" 220-h.p. Wright radial. A typical example of the small short-haul mailplanes of the period.

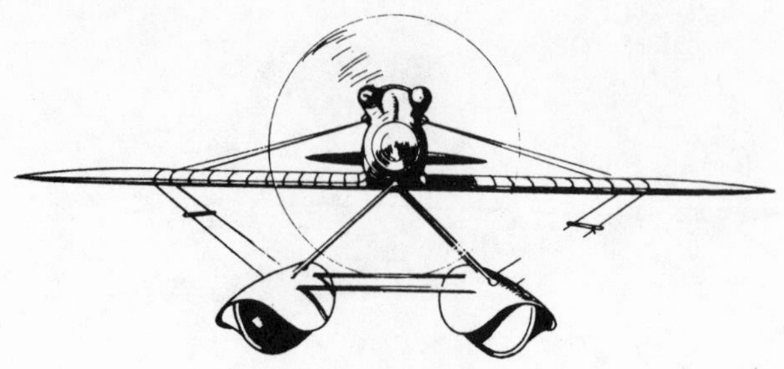

MACCHI M.39 800-h.p. Fiat engine. Italian winner of the Schneider Cup races in 1926.

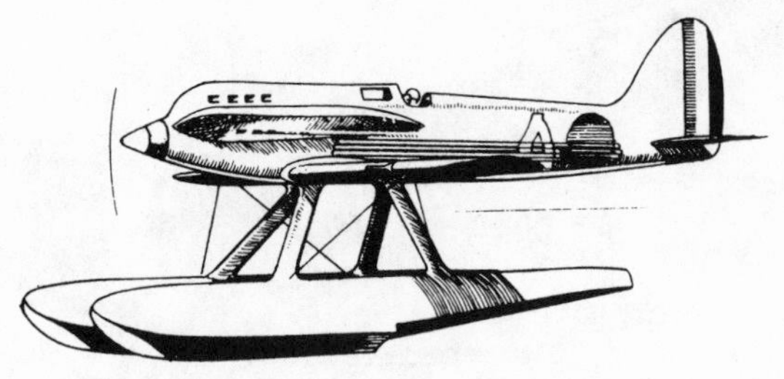

SUPERMARINE S.5 900/1,050-h.p. Napier 3-bank engine. Regained the Schneider Cup for Britain in 1927 at 281 m.p.h.

KIRKHAM RACER 1,250-h.p. 24-cylinder Packard X-type engine. Built for Al Williams, it established an unofficial record of 322 m.p.h.

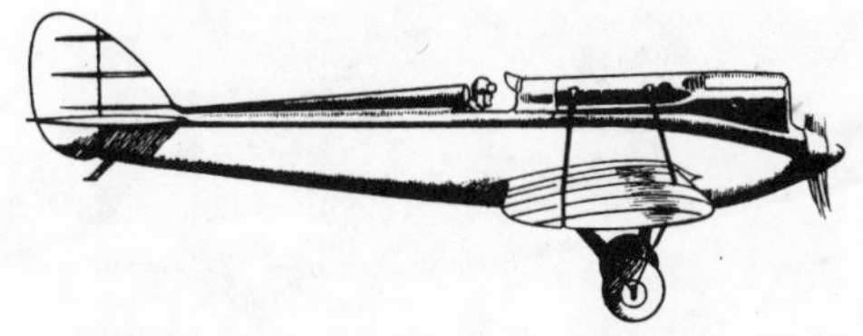

DE HAVILLAND "TIGER MOTH" 115-h.p. De Havilland engine. This specially designed little racing plane had a top speed of 187 m.p.h.

MOHAWK "PINTO I" 60-h.p. radial engine. One of the first low-wing personal planes to appear in the U.S.A.

ROHRBACH "ROLAND" Twin-engine German air liner produced in 1928.

BOEING 80A Three 525-h.p. P. & W. Hornet engines. The tri-motor Boeing carried 15 passengers and crew, cruised at about 110 m.p.h.

FOKKER The Fokker Super-Universal single-engine air liner was first ship turned out by the newly created American branch of the firm. It was a cleaned-up version of the basic F.VII design.

SHORT "CALCUTTA" A typical example of the large multi-motor flying-boat air liners favored by the British on their overseas airways.

CURTISS B-2 "CONDOR" Two 600-h.p. Curtiss Conqueror engines. Maximum speed: 133 m.p.h. One of the standard heavy bombers of the U.S. Army Air Corps for several years.

LOCKHEED "AIR EXPRESS" This high-wing passenger-air-mail monoplane established two coast-to-coast records. East-West: 19 hrs.; West-East: 18 hrs., 49 min.

MARTIN XT5M-1 Prototype model dive bomber. First Navy bomber to carry a 1,000-pound bomb in a terminal velocity dive.

BLACKBURN "LINCOCK" 215-h.p. radial engine. One of the few single-seat fighters produced during the long history of this pioneer firm.

STINSON JUNIOR SM-2 110-h.p. Warner Scarab engine. Stinson pioneered in the 4-place personal cabin plane.

VELIE MONOCOUPE 40/60-h.p. Velie radial engine. Side-by-side 2-place personal plane popular in the U.S. for many years.

AERONCA C-2 28-h.p. Aeronca flat twin-engine. Prototype model of a series of interesting little 1- and 2-seat personal planes.

HAMILTON METALPLANE 420-h.p. Wasp radial. First Hamilton all-metal air liner when McDonnell, producer of the famed "Banshee" and "Cougar" jet fighters, was chief engineer at Hamilton's.

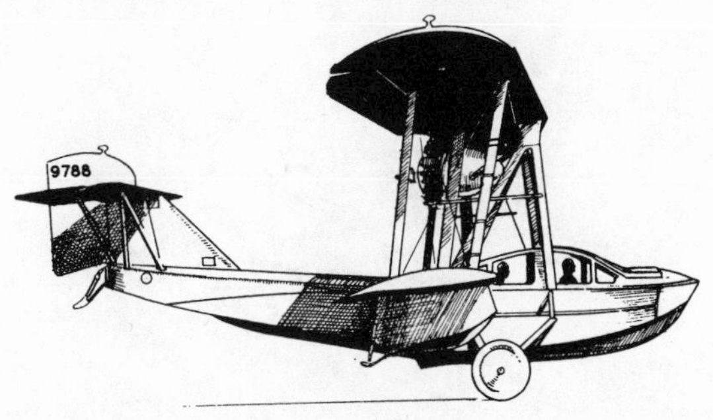

IRELAND "NEPTUNE" 420-h.p. Wasp radial. 5-place executive amphibian.

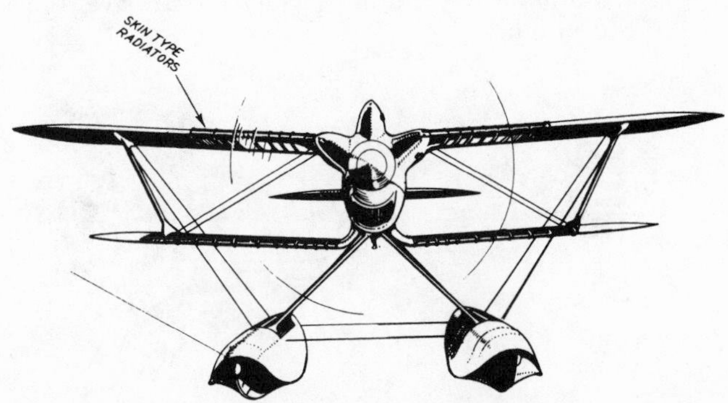

GLOSTER IV 1,275-h.p. Napier engine. Runner-up in the 1927 Schneider Cup races; attained a speed of 294 m.p.h. in preliminaries.

HANDLEY PAGE H.P.21 ("Harrow") The "Harrow" was one of the few departures from large military designs made by the firm over the years. Like most H.P. designs, it had full-length slots and flaps.

HEATH "BABY BULLET" 32-h.p. Bristol Cherub engine. Ed Heath, a small-size man himself, whipped this diminutive mid-wing monoplane round the pylons at an average speed of over 140 m.p.h.

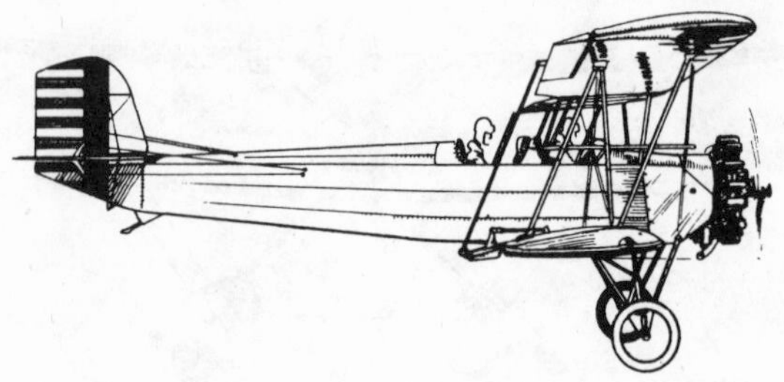

CONSOLIDATED The "Husky" and "Trusty" trainers as they appeared in 1928.

DE HAVILLAND D.H.60 Improved "Moth" with 110-h.p. Gipsy engine; had wing slots.

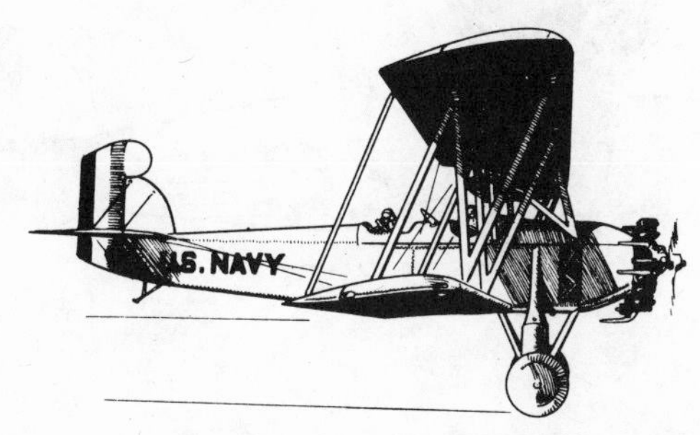

CURTISS N2C-1 220-h.p. Wright radial engine. The "Fledgling" was an unbeautiful but practical U.S. Navy trainer.

MOHAWK "PINTO II" 70-h.p. Velie radial. Tandem seats replace the staggered side-by-side seats of the original "Pinto."

BRISTOL "BULLDOG" 515-h.p. radial engine. For many years standard R.A.F. single-seat fighter, it had a combat speed of about 175 m.p.h.

HAWKER "HORNET" 450-h.p. Rolls-Royce engine. Prototype of the "Fury." Although it had 350 h.p. less than the "Hornbill," it was 20 m.p.h faster (214 m.p.h.).

FAIREY "FIREFLY III" 535-h.p. Rolls-Royce Kestrel engine. Was one of the fastest British fighters of the period.

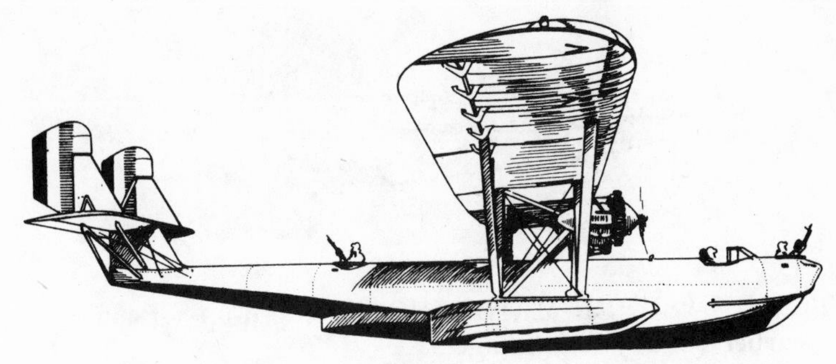

CONSOLIDATED XPY-1 First Consolidated (Convair today) Navy patrol boat. A civil version with cabinized cockpit was known as the "Commodore."

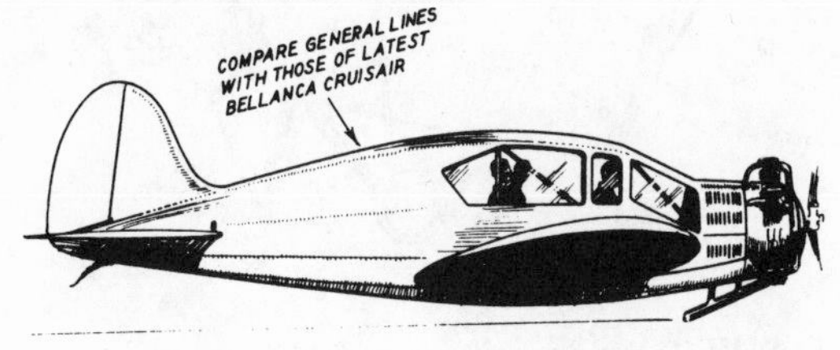

ALEXANDER EAGLEROCK "BULLET" 160-h.p. Wright or 125-h.p. Kinner engine. With four people and their baggage this advanced design cruised at 127 m.p.h., had a top speed of 150 m.p.h. This, plus the retractable landing gear, brings it close to modern designs.

GLENNY & HENDERSON 40-h.p. A.B.C. Scorpion flat twin engine. An interesting British single-seat personal plane with cantilever wing.

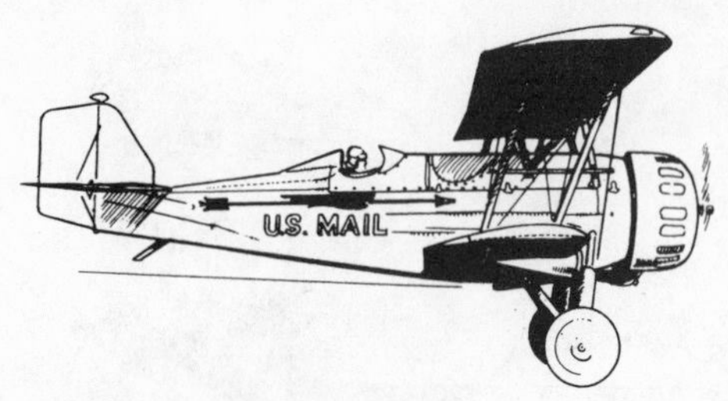

PITCAIRN "SUPER-MAILWING" A suped-up version of the earlier (1927) "Mailwing."

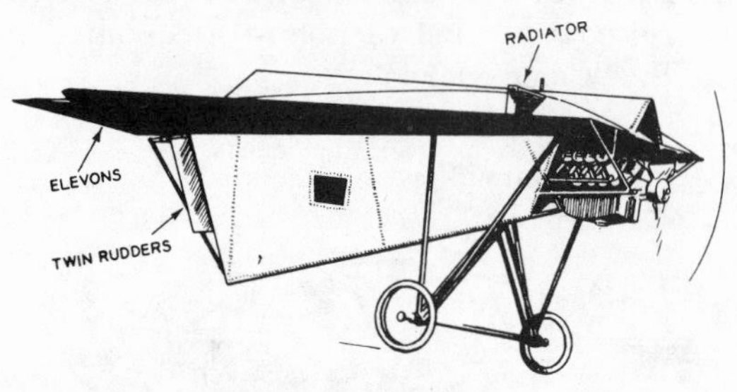

SCROGGS "DART" 90-h.p. Curtiss OXX-5 engine. A freak design at the time but interesting for its approach to the modern delta-wing design. No record of actual flight.

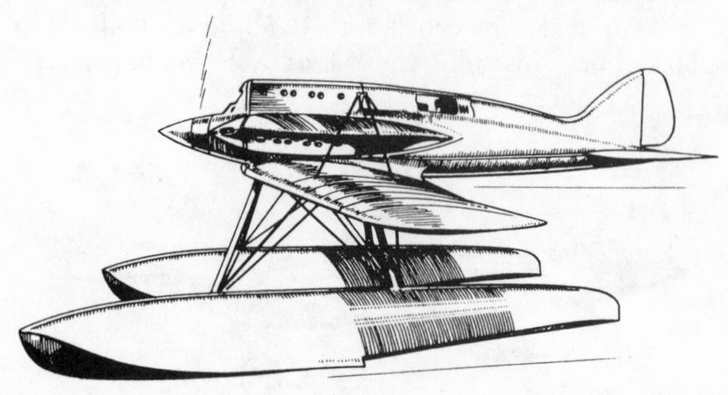

NIEUPORT-DELAGE 1,200-h.p. 18-cylinder Hispano-Suiza engine. Last effort of this pioneer firm to crack the Schneider Cup races. It was completed too late but attained an estimated speed of 400 m.p.h.

DORNIER Do.X Originally 12 550-h.p. Siemens radials (*this model shown*). Twelve 615-h.p. Curtiss Conqueror engines. Gross weight, 55 tons: span, 157 feet, 5 inches. Maximum speed about 130 m.p.h.

HAMILTON The improved Hamilton Metalplane was powered with a 525-h.p. P. & W. engine. It was used extensively as a short-haul civil transport.

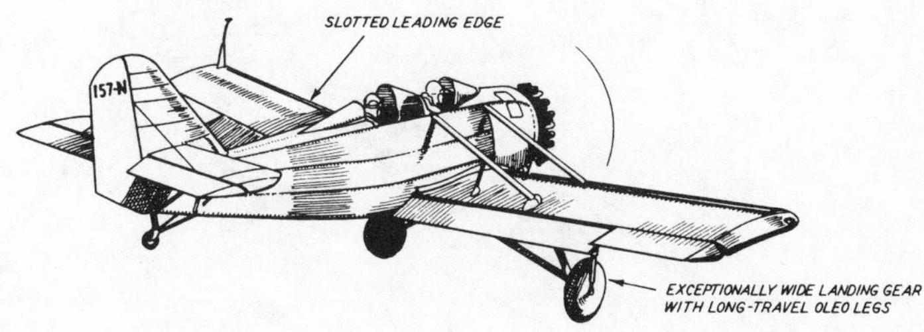

McDONNELL "DOODLEBUG" First airplane to appear under the McDonnell label, it had full slots and flaps and could operate at what in normal designs would be regarded as critical speeds. 110-h.p. Warner.

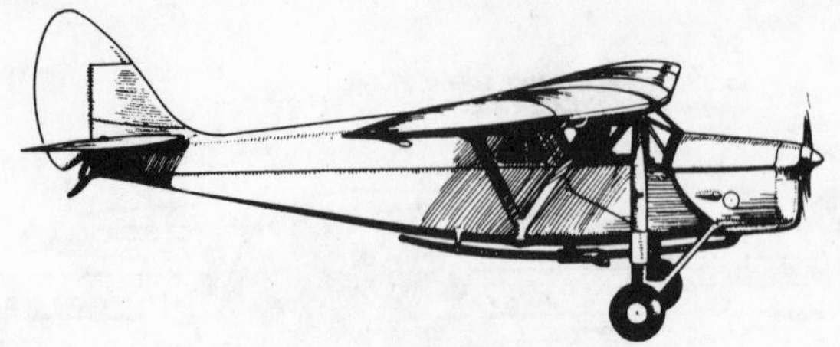

DE HAVILLAND D.H.80 "PUSS MOTH" 100/20-h.p. inverted D.H. Gipsy engine. Folding wings. This 2- to 3-seat job cruised at 105 m.p.h., had a top speed of 125 m.p.h. Prototype model of "Puss Moth" series.

RAAB-KATZENSTEIN "RAKETE" Experimental tail-first test bed intended for rocket power. Flight tests were made with conventional engine.

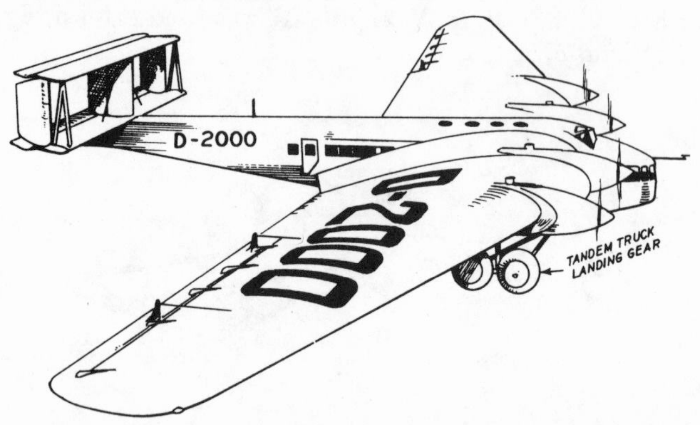

JUNKERS G-38 Total h.p. 2,400. This huge (20 tons) airplane, produced by the pioneer builders of all-metal aircraft, introduced buried engines, tandem-truck heavy-duty landing gear.

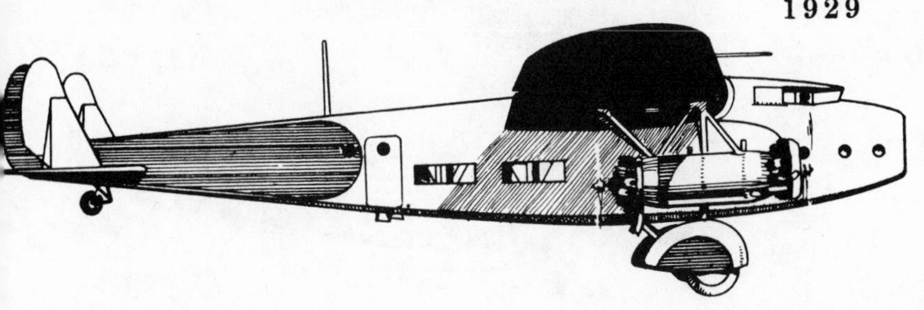

FOKKER F-32 Four 525-h.p. P. & W. Hornet engines. Produced by the U.S. subsidiary of the Fokker Company, it carried 32 passengers at about 120 m.p.h.

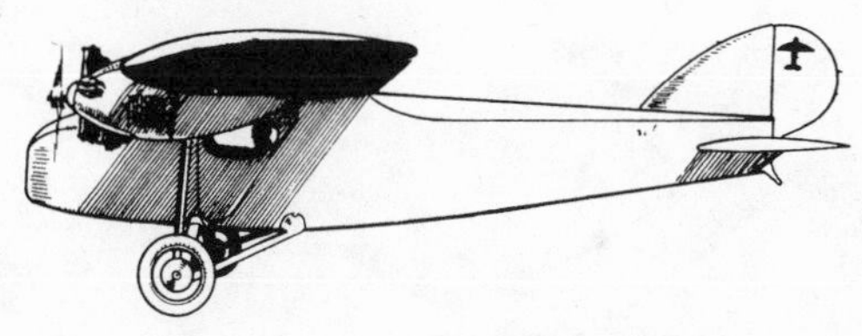

ALBERT A-20 Two 60-h.p. Walter radial engines. A French conception of the feeder-line mailplane.

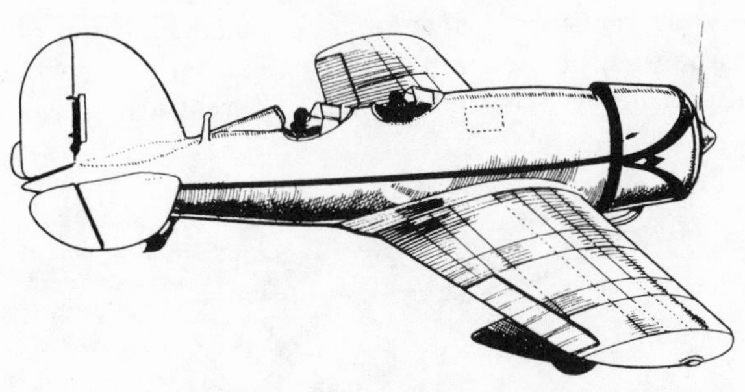

LOCKHEED "SIRIUS" Specially designed for Col. Lindbergh, this was first low-wing Lockheed. It lowered the West-East nonstop transcontinental record to 14 hours, 45 minutes.

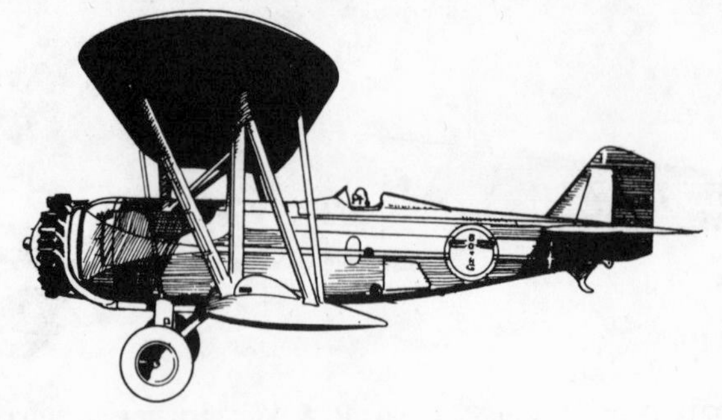

BOEING 95 525-h.p. P. & W. radial engine. Long-range fast mailplane.

SCHWABE *SEGELFLUGZEUG* Although at first glance merely an enlarged Zoegling or primary-type glider, the Schwabe was, in fact, a highly efficient sailplane which raised the duration record to 14 hours, 43 minutes.

SAVOIA-MARCHETTI S.65 Two 1,000-h.p. engines mounted in tandem. Italy's bid for the 1929 Schneider Cup, won for the second time in a row by the British entrant.

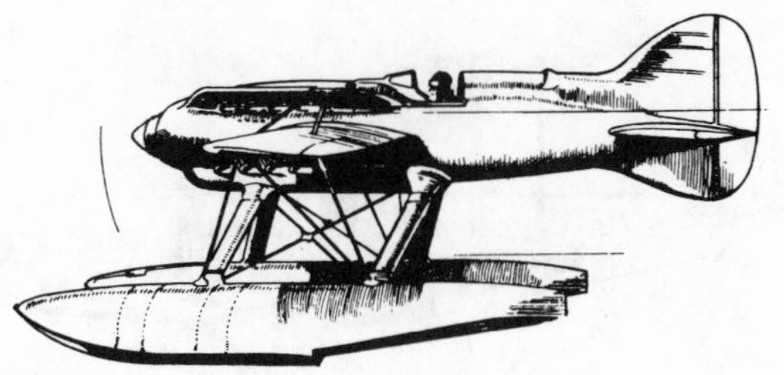

MERCURY "SPECIAL" 1,250-h.p. Packard X-type engine. Last and unsuccessful racer used by Al Williams in attempt to regain the Schneider speed trophy for the U.S.A.

VOUGHT "CORSAIR" 425-h.p. P. & W. engine. First to bear the name "Corsair," this was a rugged ship-based spotter specially designed for catapult launching and rough sea landings.

DEWOITINE D-27 Shown here with 300-h.p. Titan radial but usually fitted with 500-h.p. Hisso V-8 engine. All-metal French pursuit.

LIORÉ ET OLIVIER Le.O.21 Two 500-h.p. V-12 Renaults. 18-passenger French air liner of the period.

A.N.T. TYPE 5 A typical Soviet transport which followed universal trend toward tri-motor design. Engines were 370-h.p. Gnome-Rhones.

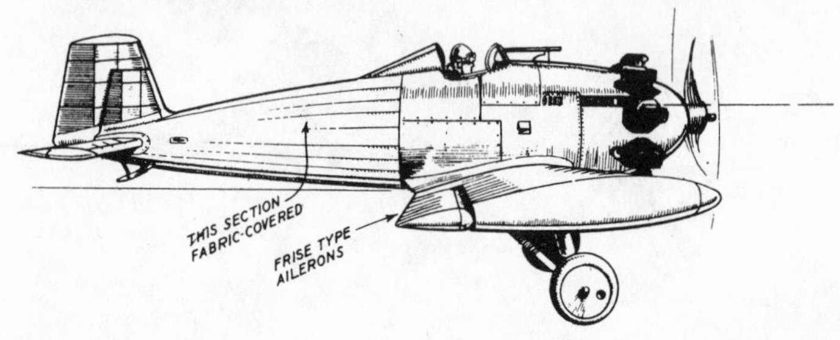

VICKERS 151 Another metal, but not quite all metal, fighter of this period, this is one of Vickers' least conventional designs.

FORD 5-AT Three 450-h.p. Wasp radials. Improved 12-passenger version of earlier Ford tri-motors.

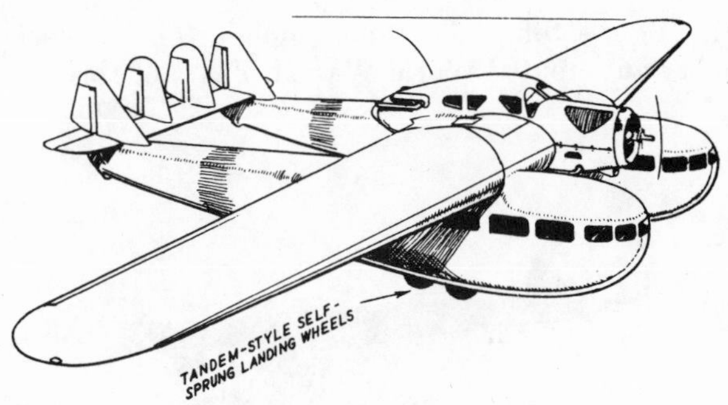

BLÉRIOT 125 Two 500-h.p. Hispano-Suiza in tandem. A curious 12-passenger twin-cabin French air liner.

CURTISS XF6C-F "HAWK" 600-h.p. Curtiss Conqueror engine. Crashed, killing its pilot, after averaging 207 m.p.h. for several laps in the 1930 Thompson Trophy races.

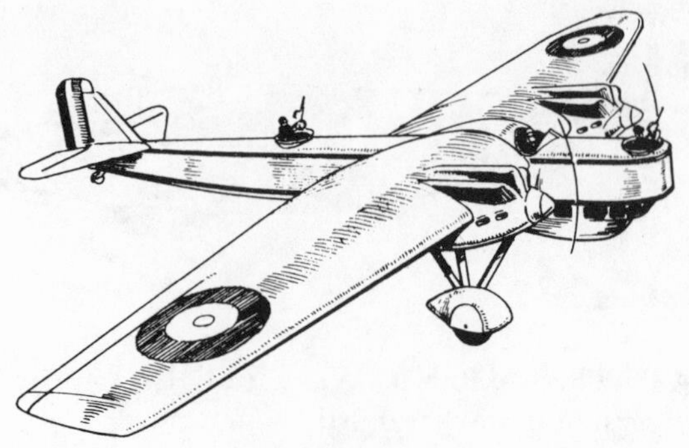

S.E.C.M. Two 450-h.p. Lorraine engines. This French fighter-bomber anticipated World War II planes of this type.

LIPPISCH "STORCH" 7/9-h.p. D.K.W. engine. No landing wheels were provided on this German tailless design. Catapult-launched.

WESTLAND-HILL "Pterodactyl" 70-h.p. Armstrong-Siddeley Genet radial. Development of the 1926 Hill tailless monoplane. Note wing-tip elevons.

BUHL This experimental autogiro was the only pusher-type rotary-wing aircraft ever built.

STINSON R 220-h.p. Lycoming radial engine. Predecessor of the Reliant series of personal aircraft.

STINSON TRI-MOTOR Three 240-h.p. Lycoming radial engines. First Stinson venture in the multi-motor field, it carried 10 passengers.

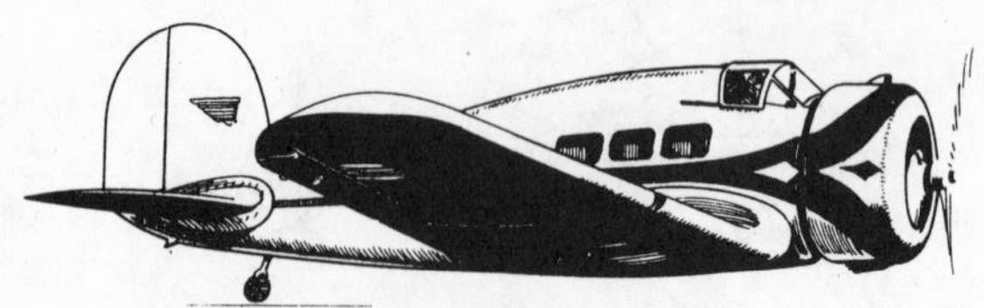

LOCKHEED "ORION" First Lockheed to employ a fully retractable landing gear. Set new West-East transcontinental record—just over 13 hours.

DOUGLAS O-31 600-h.p. Curtiss Conqueror engine. Army observation plane.

DOUGLAS O-35 Two 600-h.p. Curtiss Conqueror engines. Another Douglas U.S. Army observation type. Both appeared about 1930-31.

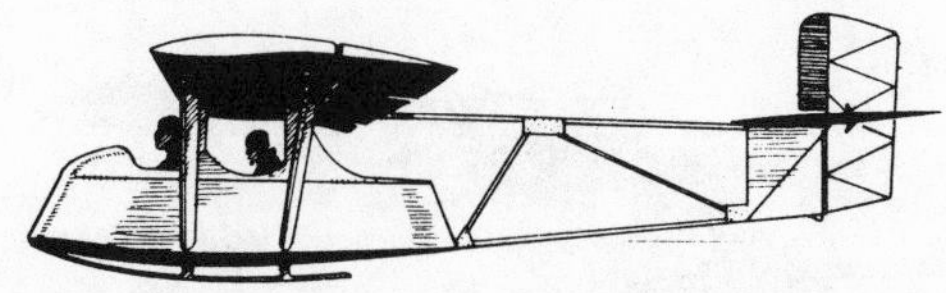

KEGEL "PRUEFLING" (secondary) **TRAINING GLIDER** Typical 2-seat German glider of the period was development of Zoegling-type glider.

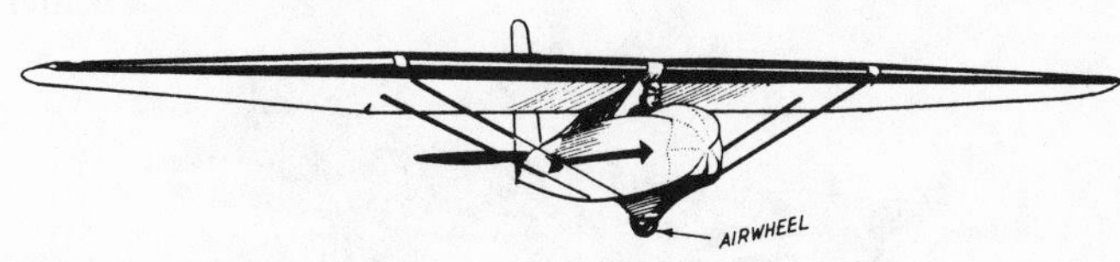

BAKER-McMILLAN "CADET II" Fully aerobatic U.S. secondary sailplane.

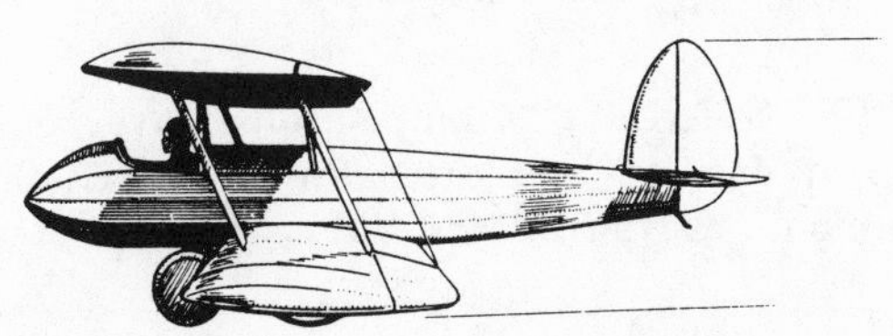

HEATH "SUPER-SOARER" This was, in fact, a glider rather than a sailplane. It was the first motorless aircraft in the world to be looped (Ed Heath).

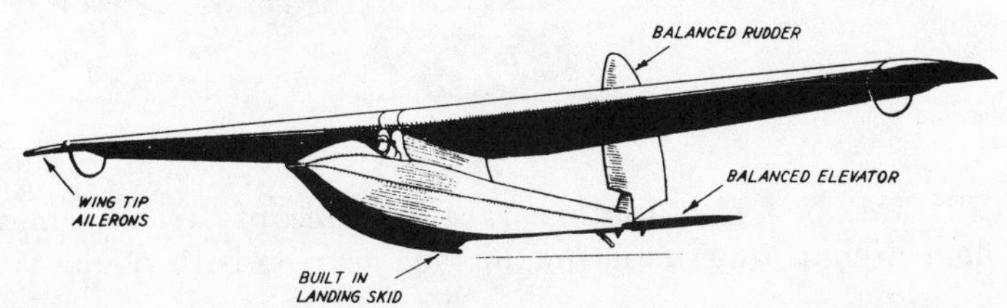

BOWLUS "ALBATROSS" First high-performance U.S. sailplane, it closely followed accepted practice of the Germans—originators of the art of soaring flight.

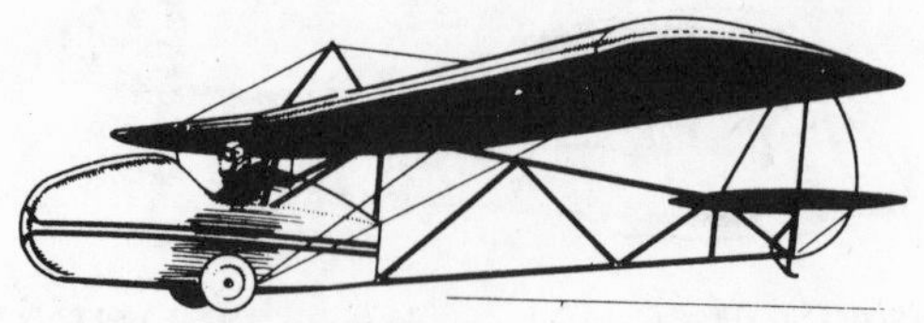

BRALEY "SKYPORT" A U.S. modification of the simple Zoegling, or primary glider, originated in Germany.

SHORT "GURNARD" 680-h.p. Rolls-Royce engine. Central-float seaplanes are not often found in British designs. The amphibious "Gurnard" and "Mussel" are noteworthy exceptions.

SHORT "MUSSEL" Another rare example of British single-float design. The simple amphibious gear on both planes is of interest.

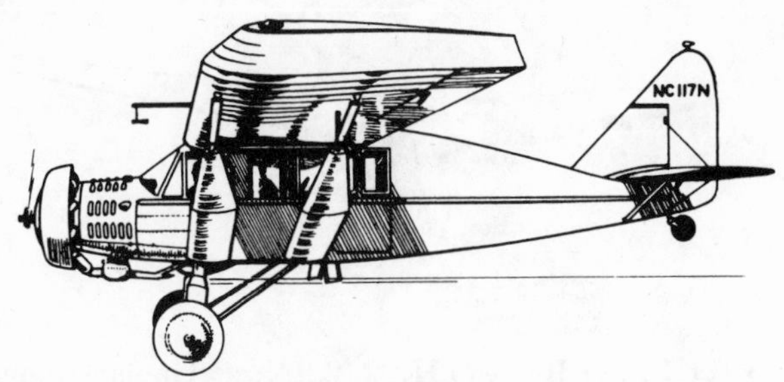

BELLANCA "SKYROCKET" One of the most efficient airplanes of the period. Earlier model, the "Pacemaker," made many outstanding long-distance flights.

BREGUET Developed from the earlier Breguet Type 19, this plane made first nonstop westbound transatlantic flight (Paris–New York, September 1930, Coste and Bellonte).

FAIRCHILD 71 Widely used land and seaplane employed here and in Canada for mail and passenger service.

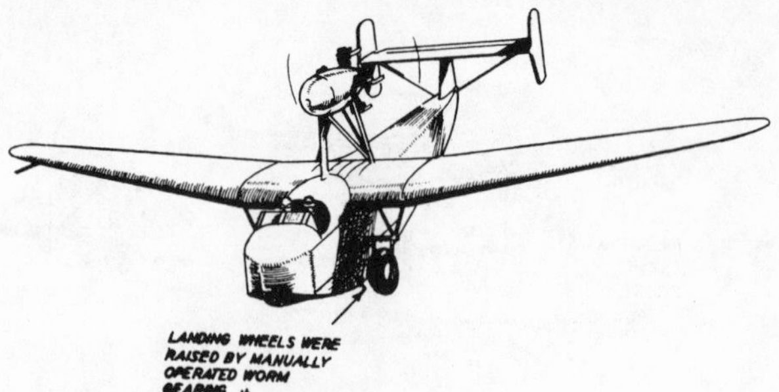

LIORÉ ET OLIVIER Le.O.H.22 230-h.p. Gnome-Rhone Titan radial engine. A French approach to the small 2-place amphibian.

SAUNDERS-ROE "CUTTY SARK" Two 130-h.p. Cirrus engines. This 4-place amphibian was one of the first types produced after A. V. Roe left the famed Avro company and joined forces with Saunders', noted British boat builders.

FIZIR A.F.2 85-h.p. Walter radial engine. A rare Yugoslavian amphibian with many advanced features for the period.

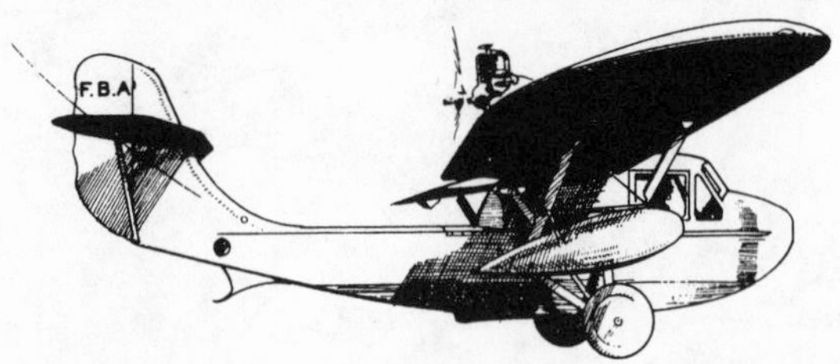

SCHRECK F.B.A.310 120-h.p. Lorraine radial engine. Designer of the Republic "Sea Bee" must have had this one on his mind when he got to work some 15 years later! Oleo-hydraulic wheel retracting gear.

BUEHL "PUP" 40-h.p. 1-place sport plane with metal fuselage.

BRISTOL "BULL-PUP" 520-h.p. Bristol Mercury engine. High-altitude single-seat interceptor-fighter.

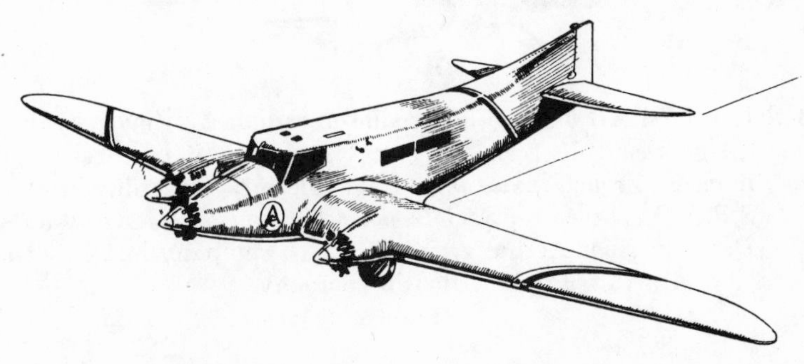

COUZINET 100 Three 40-h.p. Salmson radial engines. An extremely interesting, small (3-place) French tri-motor produced in 1930.

VICKERS "VIASTRA" British air liners of this period were not noted for their beauty. This 12-passenger transport is an example.

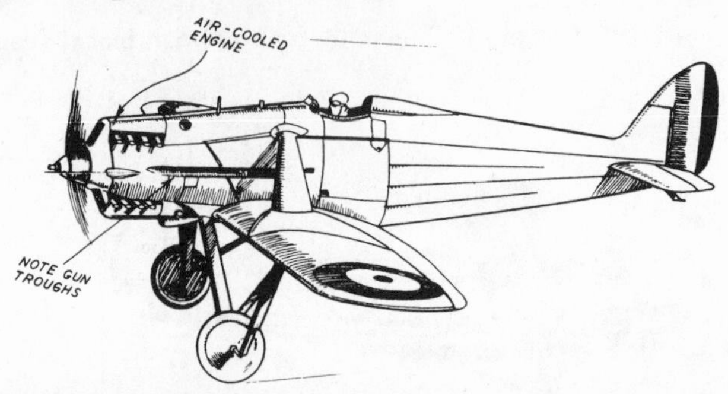

DE HAVILLAND D.H.77 300-h.p. D.H. Gipsy H-type engine. The amazing versatility of De Havilland design is exemplified in this high-altitude interceptor-fighter.

BLÉRIOT-SPAD 540 95-h.p. Salmson radial. A primary-trainer design resulting from the merging bit by bit of three great pioneer French aviation firms: Blériot, Deperdussin, and S.P.A.D. (literally, *Société pour Production les Apparailles Deperdussin*). Actually, the S.P.A.D. company lost its identity with the old Deperdussin company.

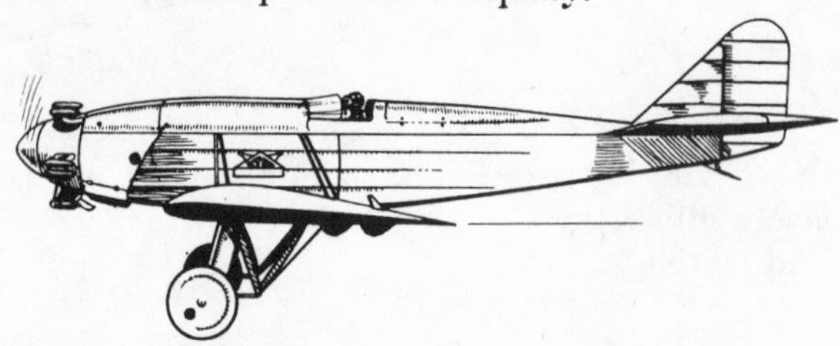

AVRO "AVIAN" A trim sport and racing plane produced by a historic firm.

AVRO 621 "TUTOR" 215-h.p. Siddeley Lynx radial engine. Was first Avro military trainer to appear after World War I. Up till this time the old 504-K model (in various modifications) was still the standard R.A.F. primary trainer. Surely a record of some sort!

CONSOLIDATED "FLEETSTER 17" This clean-looking 6-passenger liner resembled the Lockheed "Vegas" outwardly.

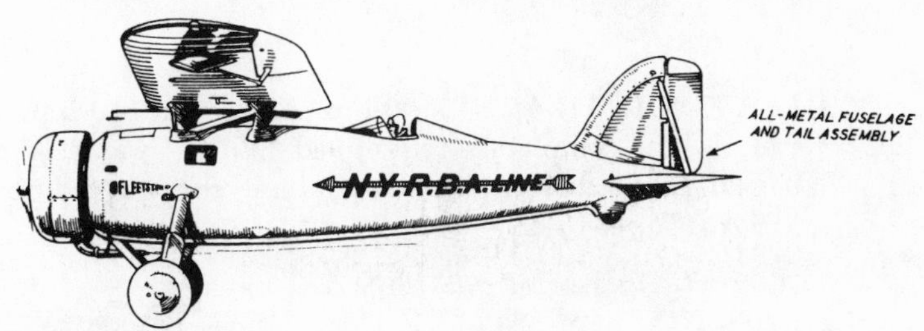

CONSOLIDATED "FLEETSTER 20" High-wing express mail-plane version of the Model 17. All-metal fuselage, plywood-skin wings.

LINCOLN PT-K 100-h.p. Kinner radial engine. One of the last products of the pioneer airplane company responsible for the Lincoln-Standard training biplane which shared honors with the famed "Jenny" during World War I and in postwar commercial aviation.

BOULTON PAUL "SIDESTRAND" Two 460-h.p. radial engines. The "Sidestrand," a medium-range fighter-bomber, was extremely maneuverable.

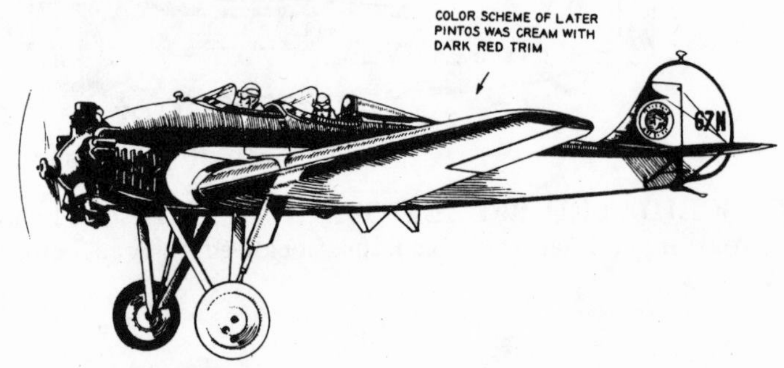

MOHAWK "PINTO M-1C" 90-h.p. Kinner or 110-h.p. Warner radial. The completely redesigned "Pinto" was a larger and considerably better airplane than the preceding model "Pintos."

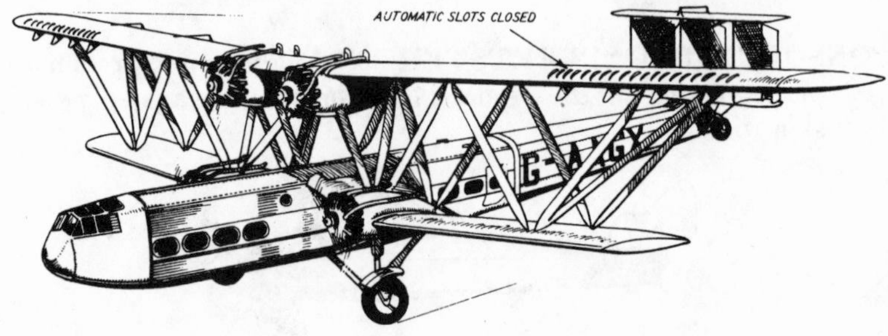

HANDLEY PAGE H.P.42 "HANNIBAL" Four 490-h.p. radial engines. Slow but efficient 38-passenger air liner used on Far East routes.

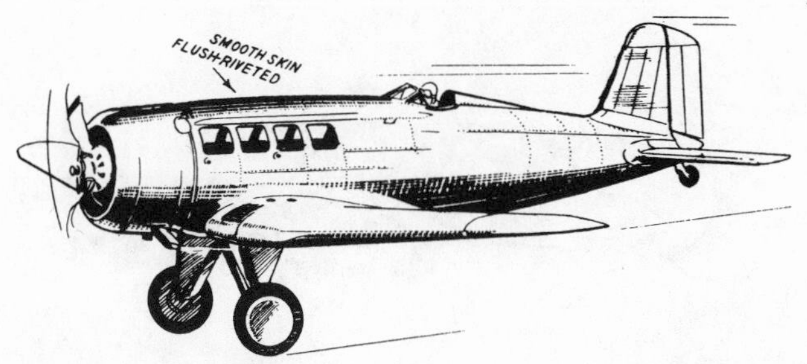

NORTHROP "ALPHA" This 6-passenger 150-m.p.h. transport was first U.S. plane to have all-metal, stressed-skin monocoque fuselage.

BLERIOT 110 This very large, externally braced cabin monoplane was one of the last Blériot designs. Long-distance record breaker.

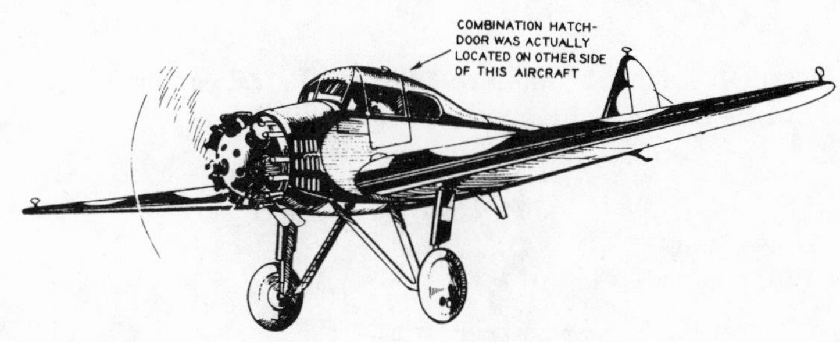

MOHAWK "SPUR WING" Warner radial powered. This tandem-seat cabin personal plane was last Mohawk production model.

GEE BEE "SPORTSTER D" First approach by Granville Brothers to the famed Gee Bee racers. Variously powered with 95-h.p. and 125-h.p. Menasco or 110-h.p. Cirrus engines, the Model D had a top speed of 159 m.p.h. with the 125-h.p. engine.

NIEUPORT 62-C.1 500-h.p. Lorraine Petrel engine. Single-seat *avion de chasse* by pioneers of pursuit design.

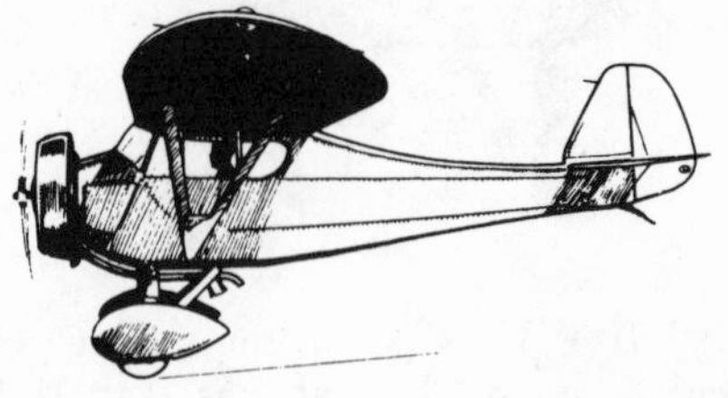

WARNER MONOCOUPE 110-h.p. Warner radial engine. Refined version of the earlier Velie Monocoupe and one of the best personal planes ever produced in the U.S.A.

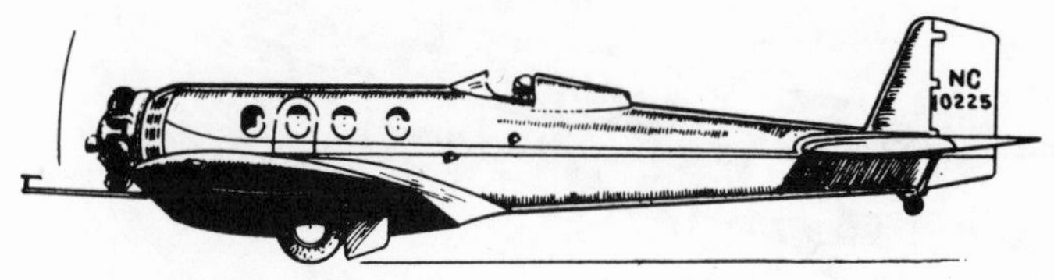

BOEING "MONOMAIL 200" The Boeing "Monomail" design
BOEING "MONOMAIL 221" marked a new era in high-speed mail and passenger transport. These all-metal aircraft were powered with the 575-h.p. P. & W. Hornet radial.

SAVOIA-MARCHETTI S-55 Two 500-h.p. Fiat engines. A flight of these curious twin-hulled boats, 23 in all, flew the Atlantic in 1933.

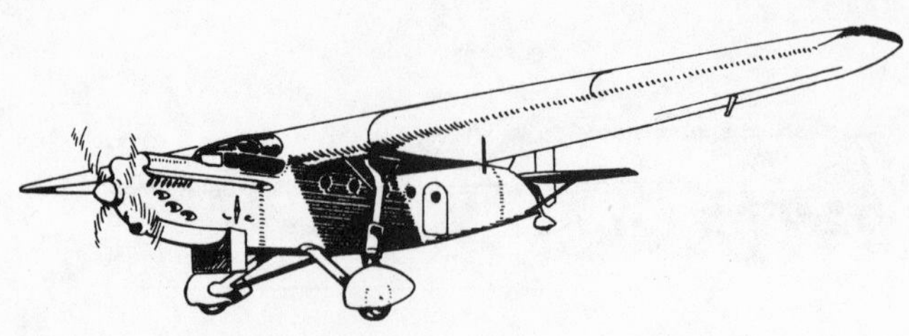

FORD FREIGHTER 650-h.p. Hispano-Suiza engine. A little-known Ford single-engine transport. Only one was built.

MARTIN XP2M-1 Three 575-h.p. Wright Cyclone radials. Commercial version of this U.S. Navy patrol boat carried 33 passengers.

BOOTH This interesting little pusher boat had a conventional 32-h.p. outboard boat motor mounted in the hull with shaft and gear drive to the propeller.

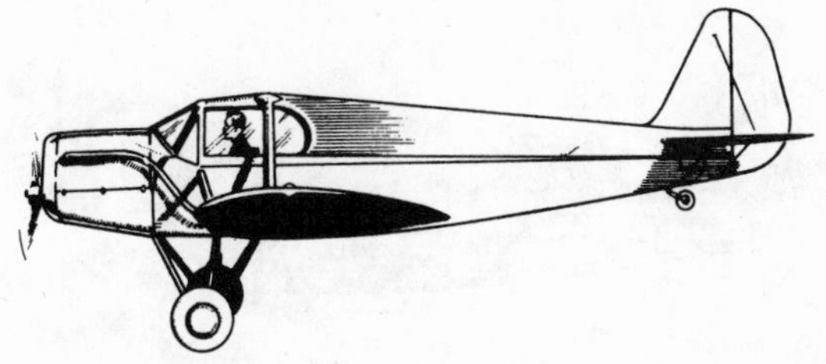

CURTISS-WRIGHT COUPE 90-h.p. Wright Gipsy engine. 2-place side-by-side-seating cabin monoplane. Personal plane.

FOCKE-WULF "ENTE" (Duck) Two 110-h.p. Siemens radial engines. Front stabilizer was set to stall before main wing reached stalling point, making it virtually stall-proof.

GEE BEE SPORTSTER MODEL YL Powered with a 300-h.p. Wasp radial engine, it placed fourth in the 1931 Thompson Trophy races.

HANRIOT H-131 230-h.p. Lorraine radial engine. Product of a pioneer French aviation firm and winner of the 1931 Coupe Michelin.

WESTLAND-HILL "PTERODACTYL Mk. 4" 120-h.p. inverted D.H. Gipsy engine. A further modification of the previous designs. 3-place cabin and wing-tip rudders are innovations.

CURTISS F9C-1 "SPARROWHAWK" 400-h.p. Wright radial. World's first airship-based fighter. Carried on U.S. dirigibles.

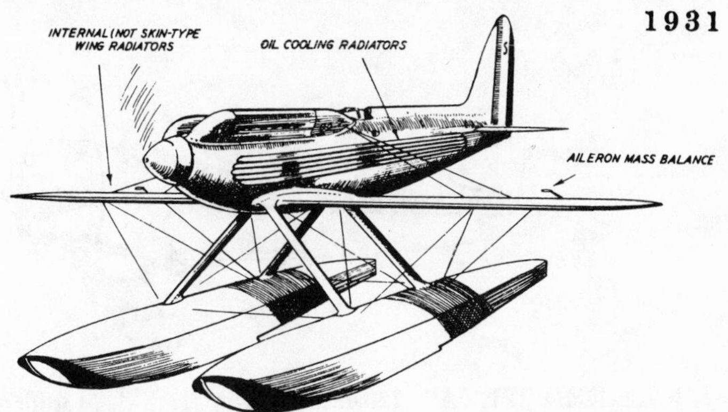

SUPERMARINE S.6B 2,300-h.p. Rolls-Royce engine. Won the Schneider Cup outright for Britain in 1931. It averaged 407 m.p.h. and later set an unofficial straightaway record of nearly 500 m.p.h. Direct ancestor of the "Spitfire."

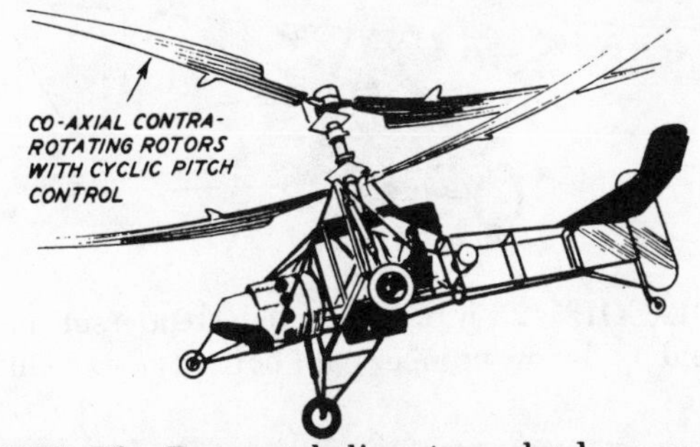

BREGUET The Breguet helicopter solved many of the problems of rotary-powered flight years before the first Sikorsky flew, but it was not developed beyond the experimental stage.

CURTISS-WRIGHT JUNIOR 40-h.p. Szekeley engine. Curtiss revived the pusher configuration for light 2-seat sport-trainer.

LOCKHEED "VEGA" 420-h.p. P. & W. radial. Modified version of original "Vega." First airplane to circle the globe in less than 8 days (Wiley Post, 1933).

HEATH "PARASOL" 23-h.p. converted Henderson motorcycle engine. Sold in large numbers in both flyaway and knock-down form.

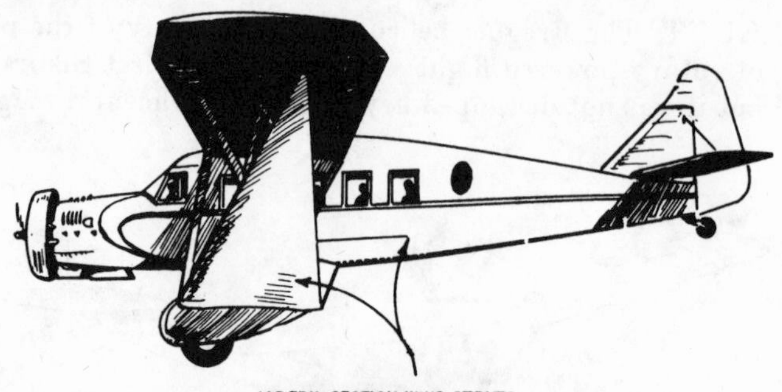

BELLANCA "AIRCRUISER" 575-h.p. Wright Cyclone radial. Like all Bellanca designs, this 10-passenger transport was highly efficient. Airfoil section wing struts and fuselage were designed to reduce drag, increase lift.

DOUGLAS "DOLPHIN" Two 350-h.p. Wright radial engines. Military, naval, and civil 8-place amphibian. Stem profiles varied on some of the earlier models.

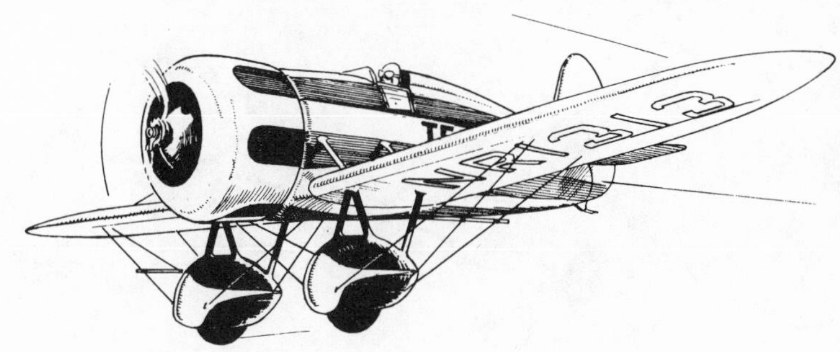

TRAVEL-AIR S MYSTERY 300-h.p. Wright radial. Sponsored by Texaco and flown by the famed Frank Hawks, it set up several notable transcontinental flight records.

BOEING P-12E (Navy designation: F4B) Substantially the Boeing F4B-1 with more powerful engine and drag ring cowling.

GRUMMAN FF-1 This all-metal shipboard reconnaissance fighter was first of a long line of famous aircraft by this company.

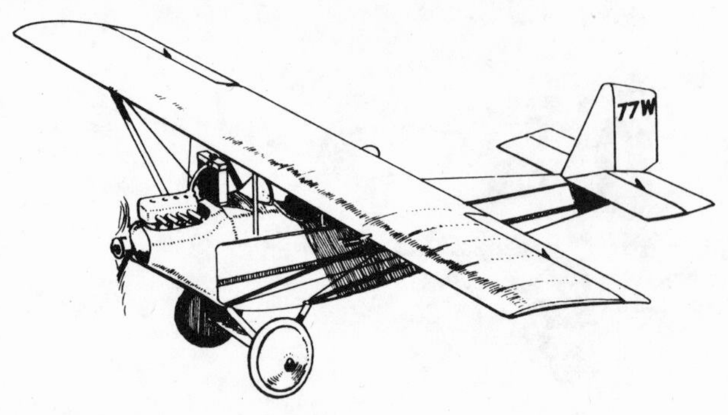

PIETENPOL "AIRCAMPER" 40-h.p. converted Ford Model A engine. One of the better amateur-produced small aircraft made during the thirties.

SIKORSKY S-39 400-h.p. P. & W. radial. 5-place amphibian.

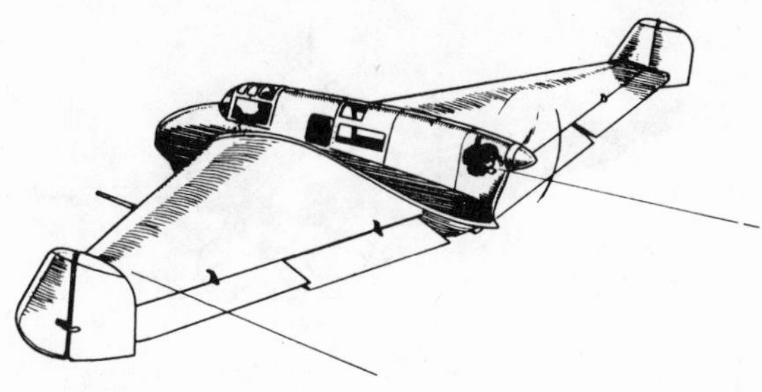

LIPPISH 32-h.p. Bristol Cherub engine. Experimental all-wing design from Germany. Ailerons, flaps, and wing-tip rudders effected control.

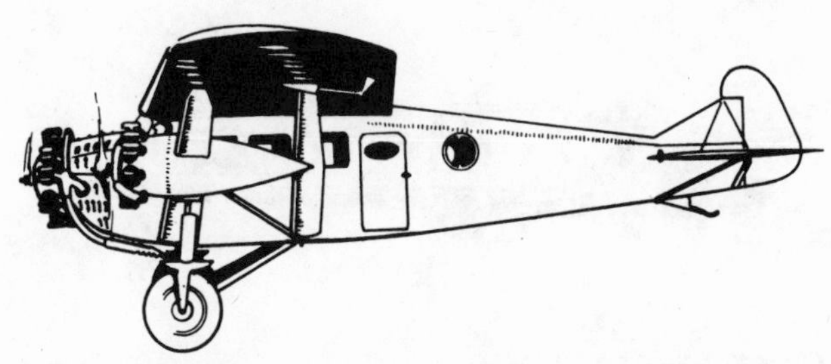

BACH "AIR YACHT" One Wasp and two 225-h.p. Wright engines. A little-known 10-passenger U.S. air liner of the period.

DEWOITINE 500-h.p. Hispano-Suiza liquid-cooled engine. Variant of the radial-powered fighter illustrated earlier.

BOEING P-26 550-h.p. P. & W. radial. With a top speed of 215 m.p.h. this was one of the fastest single-seat fighters of the period and long the standard U.S. pursuit plane.

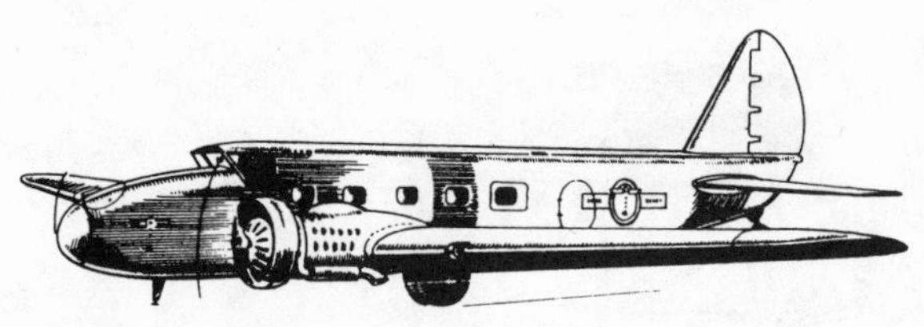

BOEING 247 Two 570-h.p. P. & W. radials. First really modern air liner, it cruised at 165 m.p.h. (later, 180 m.p.h.). 10 passengers.

BOEING B-9 Two 575-h.p. P. & W. Hornet radials. First U.S. all-metal twin-engine heavy bomber. Top speed was about 186 m.p.h.

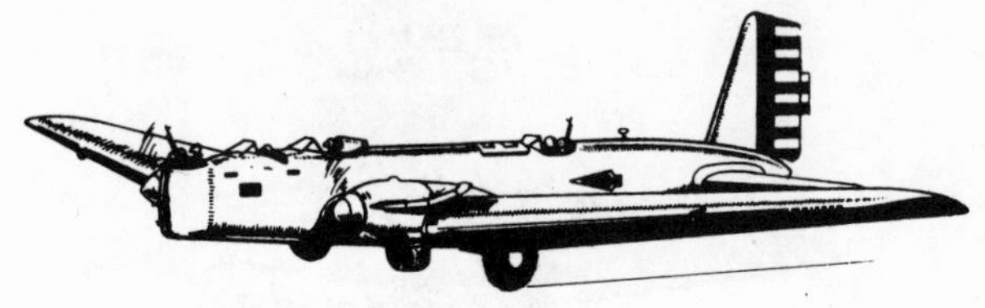

BOEING Y1B-9 Two 600-h.p. Curtiss Conqueror engines. Modified version of B-9.

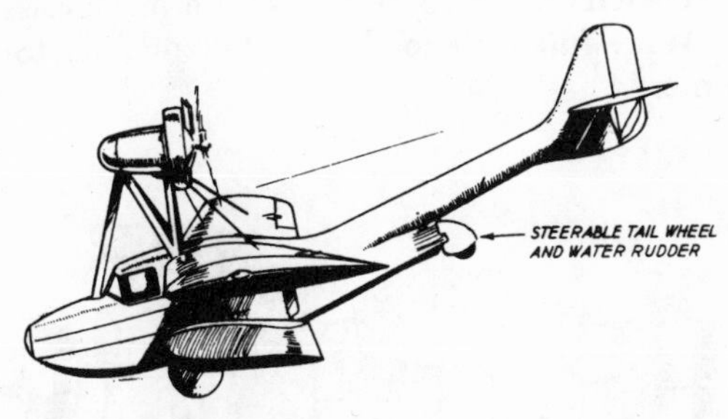

PRIVATEER P-III 165-h.p. Continental radial engine. Neat little personal cabin 2-place amphibian built by Amphibians, Inc.

GERE "SPORT" 40-h.p. converted Chevrolet auto engine. This workmanlike little single-seater was amateur-built by a teenager and properly powered would have compared with the best factory jobs.

CURTISS "CARRIER PIGEON" 600-h.p. Curtiss Conqueror engine. With full mail load of 3,300 pounds top speed was 150 m.p.h.

BRISTOL 120 General-purpose military plane. Enclosed gun ring marks final step before introduction of power-operated turrets.

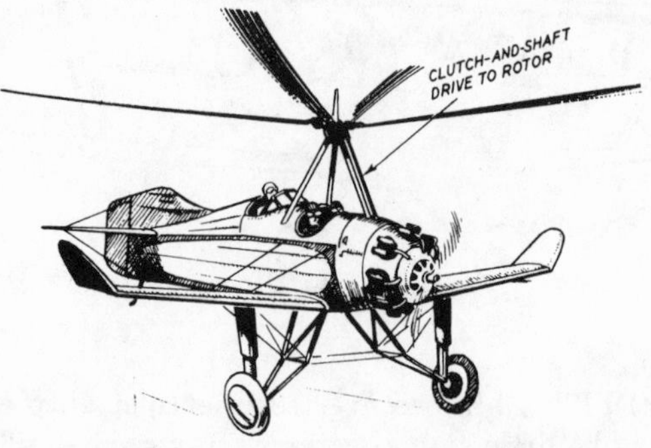

PITCAIRN PCA-2 AUTOGIRO Retained fixed wing of early giros but had engine drive to rotor head to start blades revolving.

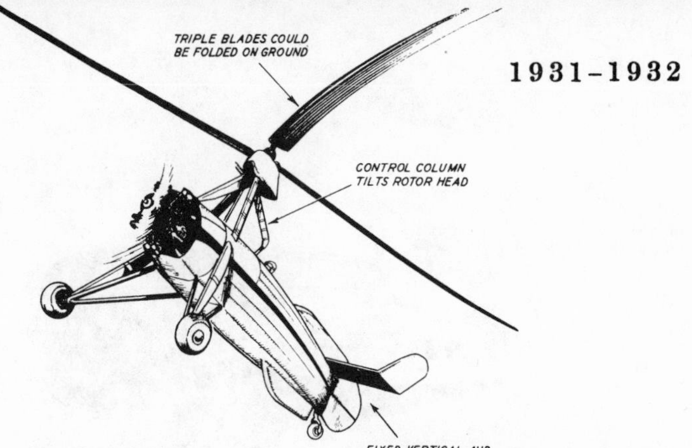

CIERVA AUTOGIRO Dispensed with fixed wing and airplane-type controls. All control effected through tilting rotor head. This, Cierva's invention, paved way for the present-day helicopter.

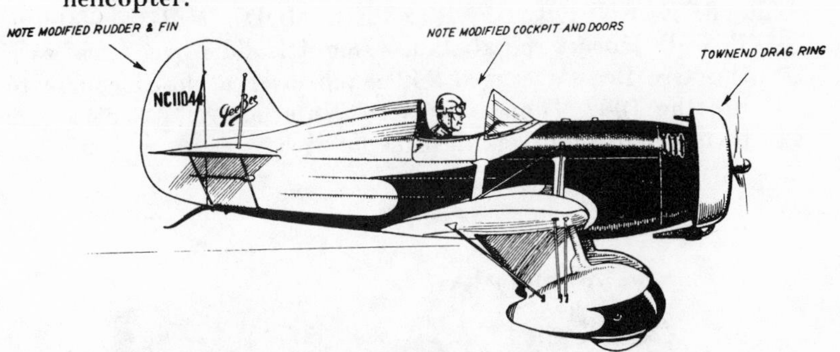

GEE BEE SPORTSTER MODEL E 110-h.p. Warner radial with Townend drag ring. High-speed (148 m.p.h.) 1-place sport plane.

GEE BEE SUPER SPORTSTER MODEL Z First of the stubby Thompson Trophy racers. Powered with a 535-h.p. P. & W. Wasp Jr. engine, it won the 1931 races at an average speed of 236 m.p.h. In a later attempt to break the existing world's speed record it hit 281.9 m.p.h. but broke up in the air, killing the noted racing pilot Lowell Bayles. Note canopy.

GEE BEE SUPER SPORTSTER MODEL R-1 800-h.p. P. & W. Hornet radial. James Doolittle did a great deal with this Gee Bee—averaged 252 m.p.h. over a closed course to win the 1932 Thompson races. Note how pilot's office has been shoved way back into the fin area!

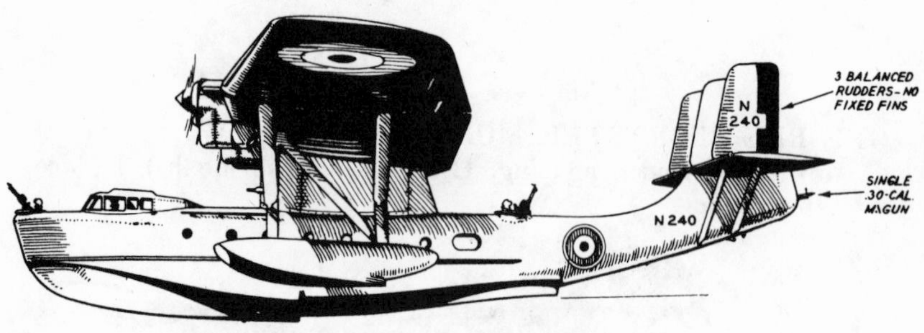

BLACKBURN "SYDNEY" Three 535-h.p. Rolls-Royce engines. This large British naval patrol boat suggests configuration of the much later Consolidated PBY patrol boats of World War II.

PART SIX

Air Power

1933-1938

STREAMLINING and "cleaning up" the airplane to attain greater speed was rapidly becoming a science. The faster the plane flew, the more drag was created by even the smallest protuberance, and the more power was required to overcome this speed-killing resistance. Rivets, which held the metal skin to the basic frame, were the greatest offender. (Thousands were needed in a small fighter, for example.) Their round heads protruding into the rushing air stream reduced the plane's speed considerably. To overcome this particular drag, countersunk, or "flush," rivets were introduced about 1932. Fitting into conical depressions in the skin, the rivet heads conformed to the smooth outer contour of the skin structure.

Revved-up speed to get the passenger there faster meant more powerful engines, heavier wing loadings, and these in turn presented new problems. For example, how to keep down the stalling and therefore the landing speed of the airplane? This was solved by the use of flaps, additional hinged surfaces in the wing's trailing edge that were deflected downward on landing. Flaps were part of the low-wing twin-engine Model 247 that Boeing introduced in 1934—the first modern air liner. It carried ten passengers and cruised at 180 m.p.h. Douglas Aircraft then soon came out with the 14-passenger DC-2, father of the almost legendary DC-3. Lockheed entered the picture with its Model 10, and later produced the larger "Lodestar," a high-speed transport noted for its exceptionally large flaps, which also extended rearward on tracks.

Instruments had by no means lifted the threat of weather. Turbulence and thunderstorms could still toss big liners about like corks, and passengers felt keenly on the matter. It was decided to minimize this by flying high above the weather, in regions of usual calm. But although the plane itself could easily function in the "troposphere," the passengers could not—at least without individual oxygen masks, a measure deemed undesirable. The answer was the pressurized cabin, which kept the air inside at low-altitude pressure, equal to that at about 8,000 feet, while the plane cruised at 20,000 feet. Using Army experimentation in 1937 as a basis, the Boeing firm designed and built the world's first pressurized passenger plane—the four-engine "Stratoliner." This was contracted for by TWA and Pan American Airways.

The latter, the only U.S. air line with service to foreign countries, also had need of a large flying boat to overcome the limited fuel capacity of landplanes in order to negotiate long overwater flights with safety. The need was supplied by Igor Sikorsky, the brilliant Russian designer who had fled the Communist revolution to settle in the United States. His big S-40 four-engine amphibian was an unusual-looking craft with a short hull and tail surfaces fixed on outriggers. This versatile pioneer in the flying-boat field later, in 1935, built the S-42, a large conventional four-engine craft of its kind that could carry 44 passengers. Along with the Boeing and later the Martin Clippers, it was destined to cover Pan American's transocean routes.

In a few short years developments like the foregoing made America the leader in air transportation. Soon European and other countries were buying U.S.-built passenger craft.

The thirties also witnessed a new, grim milestone in aviation history—the emergence of "air power." For the first time it was a realized fact that the airplane could be a major weapon of aggression, a deciding factor in warfare. Germany's whole air industry, ever since the dropping of treaty restrictions, had been a thinly disguised military machine going full blast. In Italy Mussolini too had concentrated on his air force, and the mere threat to use his bombers caused the British fleet in the Mediterranean to stand by and offer no block when he moved to conquer Ethiopia. Japan dispatched planes to help grab Manchukuo. The Spanish Civil War was seized as an excuse by Hitler and Stalin to try out their respective warplanes.

At the time Communist Russia was just beginning to expand its aviation industry, but Nazi Germany already had the world's most formidable military air arm. A significant example of its planes to receive "blooding" in Spain was the Messerschmitt Me.109 (then known as the Bf.109), an advanced fighter armed with cannon and capable of speeds in excess of 350 m.p.h. Its entire engine, a 1,100-h.p. Daimler, could be taken out and replaced in 40 minutes; the same chore in a U.S. fighter, for instance, required a whole day. There was no longer doubt that Hitler meant to use air power for a grand program of destruction and conquest.

By 1938 the Nazis had several thousand first-rate modern combat planes. The British, despite expansion programs, had only a handful that were comparable in quality: Hawker "Hurricane" and Supermarine "Spitfire" fighters. France could not point to a single modern warplane. Its aircraft industry had been nationalized, and most development work had ceased due to intra-governmental strife. The only modern combat planes the United States could wheel out of the hangar were Curtiss P-36 and Seversky P-35 fighters, in small total. Our air force was geared for defense, and planes like the Martin and Douglas bombers were rapidly becoming obsolete.

The P-35 with retractable landing gear was the first up-to-date U.S. fighter, an outgrowth of Seversky's famous amphibian designed and built by him in 1934. The latter, a powerful low-wing monoplane mounted on ingenious floats that could change angles for water landings and with retractable wheels, established a world speed record of 230.5 m.p.h. for its type. The P-35 in civilian version, called the EP-1, set a number of impressive speed marks and was flown by such luminaries as Jimmy Doolittle, Frank Fuller, Jacqueline Cochran, and the designer himself.

Alexander de Seversky, a Russian émigré from the Communist paradise, also developed here the gyroscopic bombsight, which took the by-guess-and-by-gosh aiming out of aerial bombing. This was the forerunner of the U.S. "super-secret" Norden bombsight already being perfected in 1938.

The highly limited production in warplanes in this country on the eve of Hitler's march into Poland did not mean the American military had been either idle or insensible to danger. The vaunted Nazi dive-bombing technique, for example, had already been developed by us with the Martin BM-1 dive bomber. Even by the mid-thirties the Navy could roster three large aircraft carriers with five smaller ones on order. By 1938 the world's largest bomber, the Douglas B-19, was almost ready to fly. This 200-foot-span giant was the ancestor of our super-bombers.

The reason for our lag in production lay in public apathy toward the threat across the water, and the consequent small appropriations for military aviation. Nevertheless the Army and the Navy, besides constantly improving methods and accessories, had been selecting types and placing orders with professional foresight. The result was that by the time the war started in Europe the U.S. at least had in some stage of design or construction or testing the various aircraft it would need to meet the challenge forced upon it—the "Lightning," the "Airacobra," the "Tomahawk," the "Mitchell," the "Flying Fortress," and others.

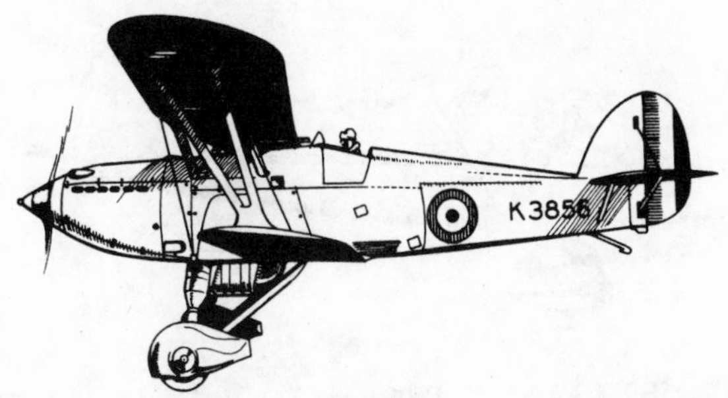

HAWKER "SUPER FURY" 480-h.p. Rolls-Royce engine. The Hawker "Furies" were last biplane fighters produced by this famous firm, which was the old Sopwith Company under a new name.

BOLTON PAUL MAILPLANE Two 565-h.p. radial engines. Carried a useful load of 4,375 pounds. A typically British design of the era, the P-64 has the blunt lines of the earlier military Sidestrand fighter-bomber.

KNIGHT "TWISTER" 40-h.p. converted Ford Model A auto engine. One of the speediest amateur-built racers of the period.

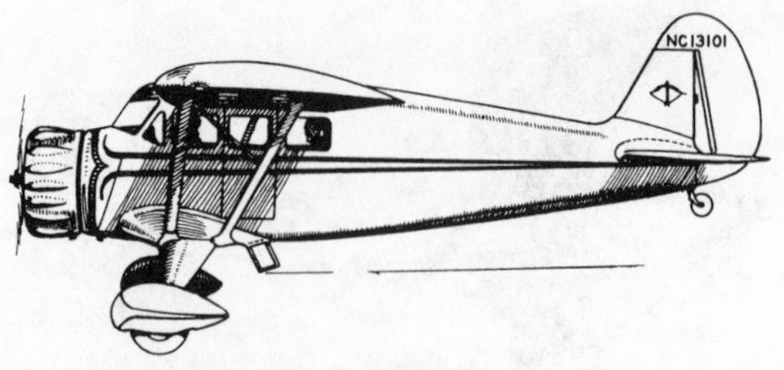

STINSON "RELIANT" 225-h.p. Lycoming radial. First of a series of excellent 4-place personal planes by this firm.

LOCKHEED "ALTAIR" Was a modified version of the Lockheed "Sirius" and had retracting landing gear. It was first to make a nonstop East-West transpacific flight (November, 1934).

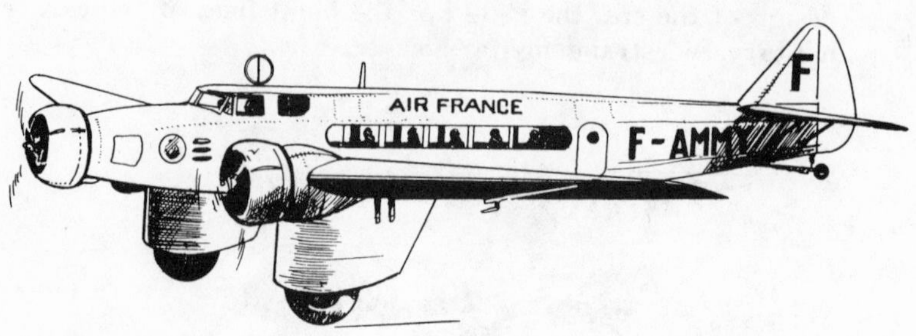

DEWOITINE D.332 Three 600-h.p. Hispano-Suiza engines. This French air liner carried 14 passengers at 155 m.p.h.

FOKKER F.XX Fokker's conception of the 12-passenger air liner powered with three 640-h.p. Wright Cyclone radials.

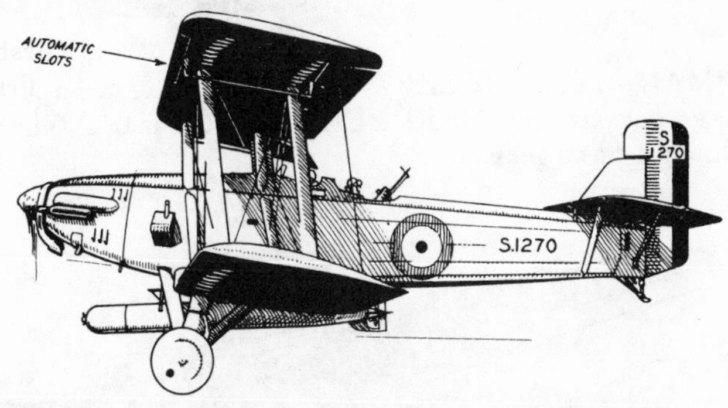

BLACKBURN "RIPON" Variously powered with either liquid-cooled or radial engines, this was standard British torpedo-bomber for years. Blackburn specialized in naval aircraft then as it does today.

BLACKBURN "SEAGRAVE" Two 120-h.p. D.H. Gipsy engines. This 4-place executive airplane marked one of the occasional departures from military aircraft by Blackburn.

NORTHROP "GAMMA" All-metal mailplane produced in the U.S.A. in 1933.

GRUMMAN J2F-1 "DUCK" Was the result of a happy marriage between the Model FF-1 and Grumman's famed amphibious float gear.

CONSOLIDATED XBY-1 A little-remembered U.S. Navy dive bomber. All-metal.

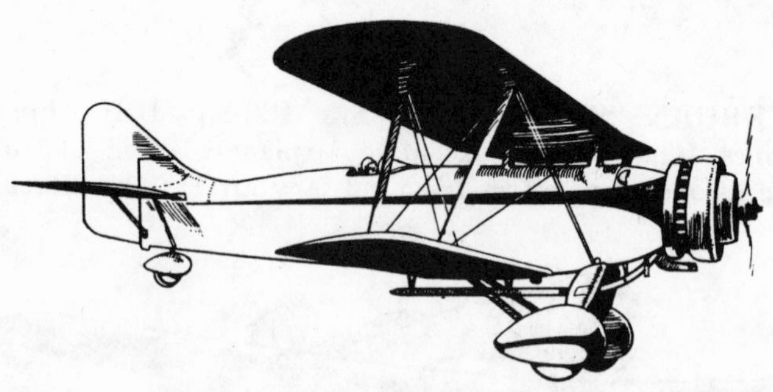

AVRO MAILPLANE Followed the trend for single-engine express mailplanes during this period. Cruising speed was 176 m.p.h.

AVRO 626 Standard R.A.F. trainer for many years. Appeared in 1933.

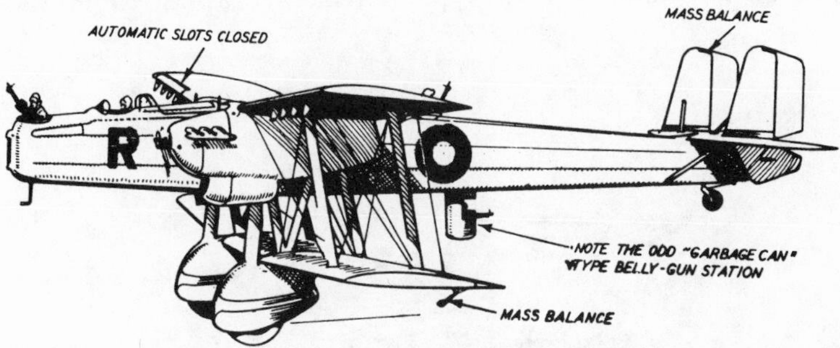

HANDLEY PAGE H.P.50 "HEYFORD" Two 525-h.p. Rolls-Royce engines. Heavy long-range British bomber of the period.

MARTIN P3M-1 Large U.S. Navy patrol bomber. It was produced fitted with amphibious gear.

DE HAVILLAND D.H.86 This is the 1934 modification of the De Havilland Rapide types which first appeared in 1933.

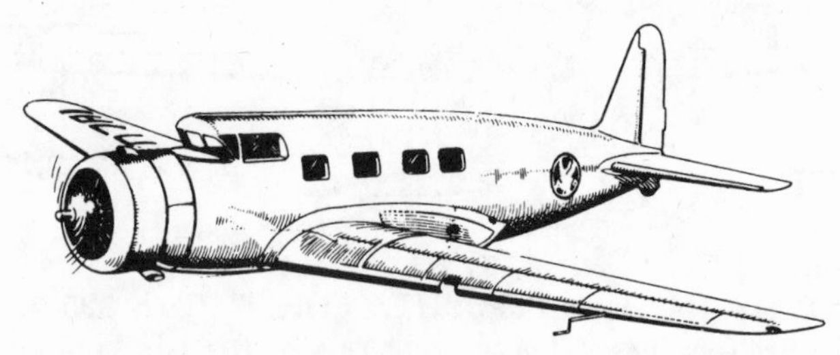

VULTEE V-1 735-h.p. Wright radial. 8-passenger air liner. First Vultee.

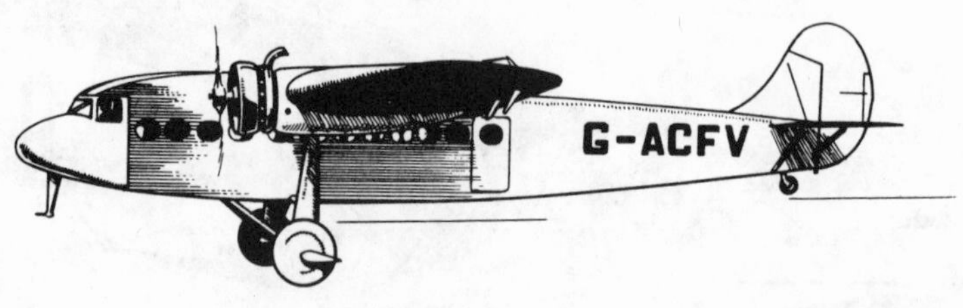

AVRO 642 This 16-passenger shoulder-wing air liner appeared in 1934.

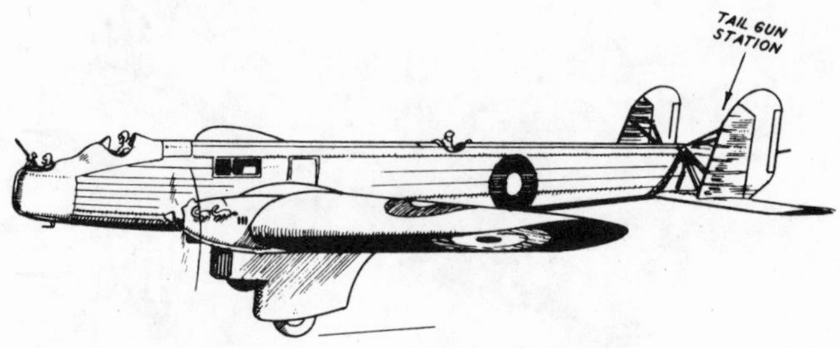

FAIREY "HENDON" Two 480-h.p. Rolls-Royce engines. First large low-wing heavy long-range bomber.

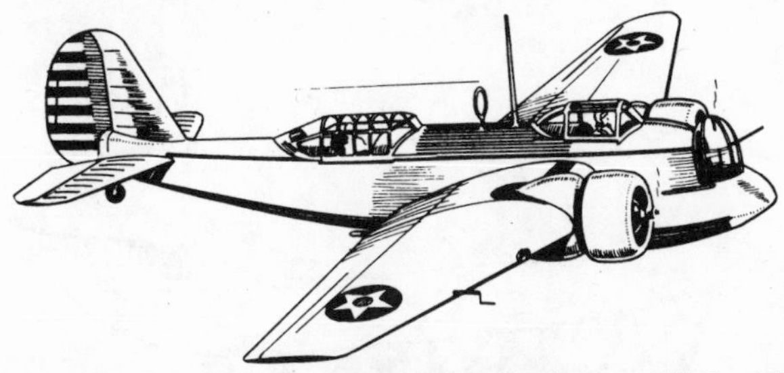

MARTIN B-10 Two 750-h.p. Wright Cyclone radials. This was one of the all-time highs in this pioneer company's many succesful designs. All-metal mid-wing. Speed was 215 m.p.h.

LOCKHEED "ELECTRA" Two 420-h.p. P. & W. engines. First of the fast all-metal multi-engine air liners for which this company is famed. Carried 10 passengers at 203 m.p.h.

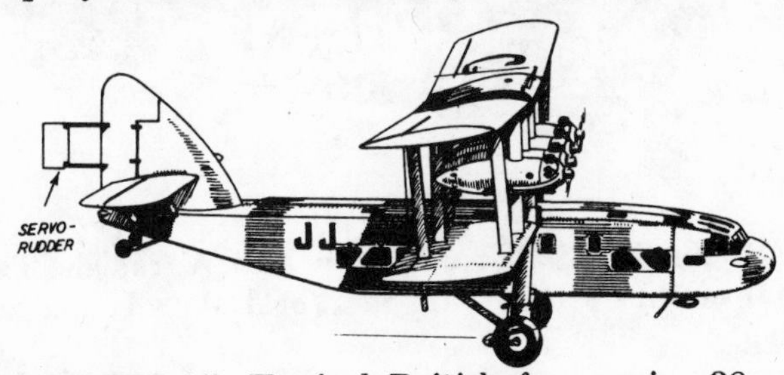

SHORT "SCYLLA" Typical British four-engine 38-passenger air liner of the period.

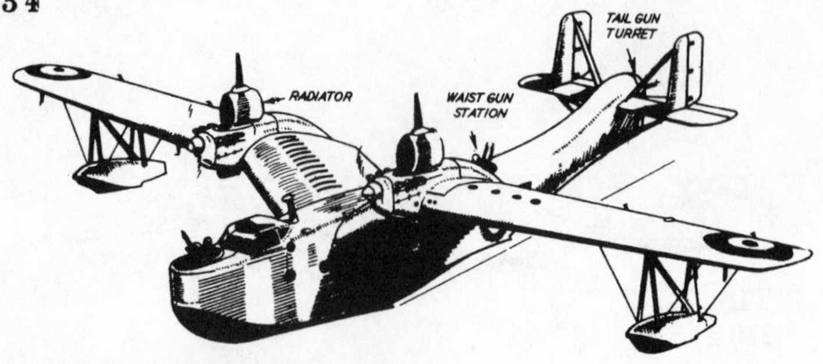

SHORT R.24/31 This large all-metal gull-wing flying boat preceded the Empire flying boats, which appeared in 1936.

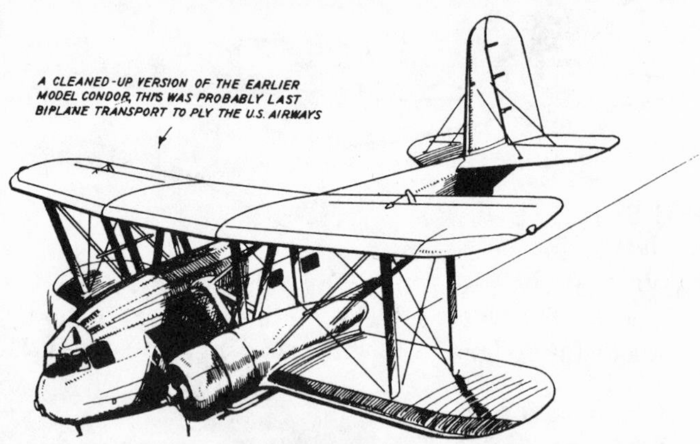

CURTISS "CONDOR" Two 700-h.p. Wright Cyclone radials. Was last U.S. biplane air liner; first sleeper plane in the world.

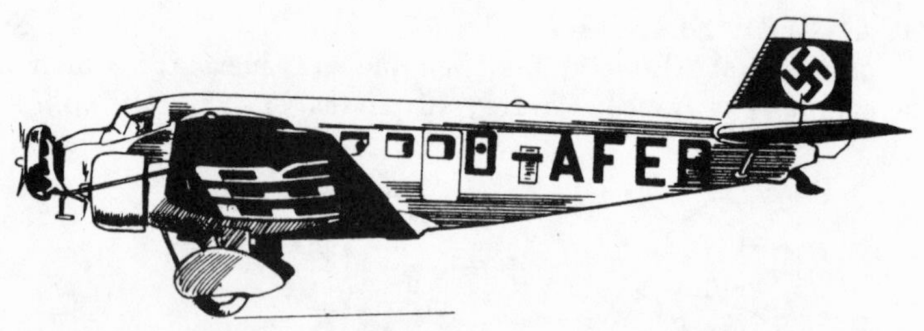

JUNKERS Ju.52/3M Three 575-h.p. B.M.W. radials. These all-metal air liners took part in World War II and are still flying.

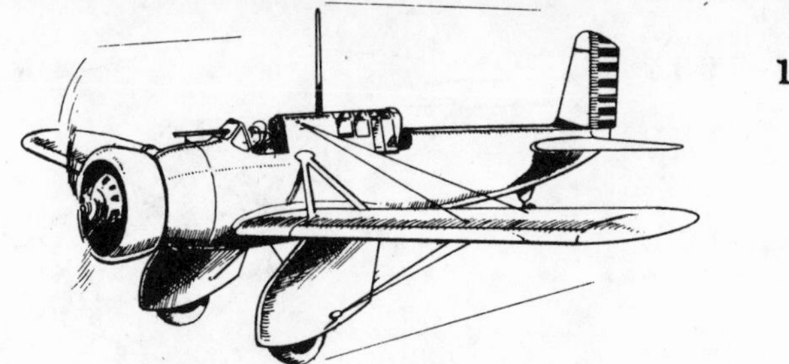

CURTISS A-12 "SHRIKE" 750-h.p. Wright Cyclone radial. 210 m.p.h. U.S. attack plane.

GEE BEE R-6 700-h.p. P. & W. radial. The "Q.E.D." was the last of the famed Gee Bee racers and was specially built for Jacqueline Cochran to compete in the England-Australia MacRobertson Race.

BLACKBURN "SHARK" 700-h.p. radial engine. Last biplane torpedo-bomber by this firm. Obsolescent in 1939, it was nevertheless used as a front-line plane during early days of World War II.

SEVERSKY AMPHIBIAN This early ancestor of the World War II Republic fighter held world's amphibious speed record at one time.

WESTLAND-HILL Rolls-Royce Goshawk engine. Final form of the Hill "Pterodactyl" designs. This was intended as a 2-seat fighter. Note the enclosed observer's gun station.

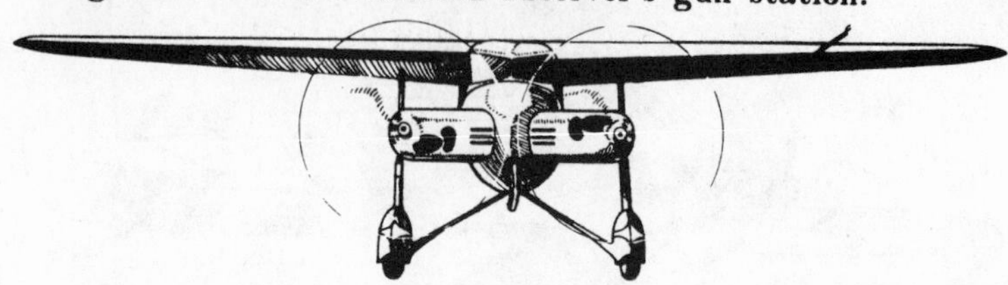

LOUGHEAD ALCOR DUO-6 Two 6-in-line air-cooled supercharged Menasco engines. Strictly speaking not a Lockheed production but designed by one of the Loughead brothers. This was an unusual and most interesting compact twin-engine design.

DE HAVILLAND "COMET" (D.H.88) Not to be confused with the "Comet" shown on page 305, this small, fast medium-powered twin-engine cabin racer won the Robertson England–Australia race in 1934 pitted against the world's best pilots and aircraft.

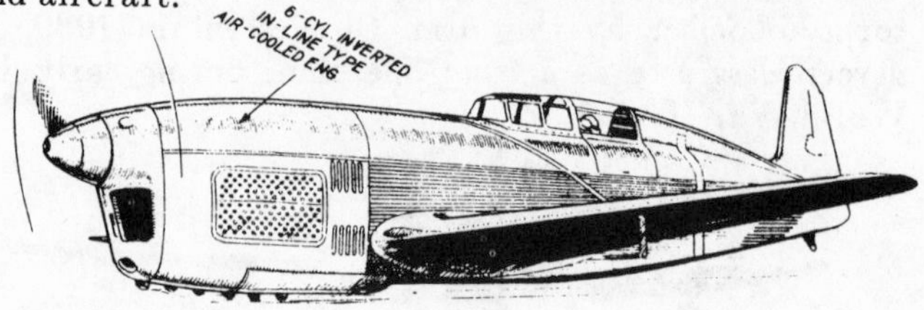

CAUDRON C-46 RACER 340-h.p. Renault air-cooled in-line engine. Set a new world's record for landplanes at 314 m.p.h., and although it had about half the power of the other competing aircraft, it won the 1936 Thompson Trophy races at 264 m.p.h.

FLYING SAUCER This unusual-looking airplane was built by Miami University.

HUGHES RACER 700-h.p. Twin Wasp Jr. radial. Set new world's speed record of 352.46 m.p.h. in 1935 for U.S.A. (Howard Hughes, pilot).

LOENING AMPHIBIAN Specifically designed for private owners, this 4-place amphibian had a cruising speed of 110 m.p.h.

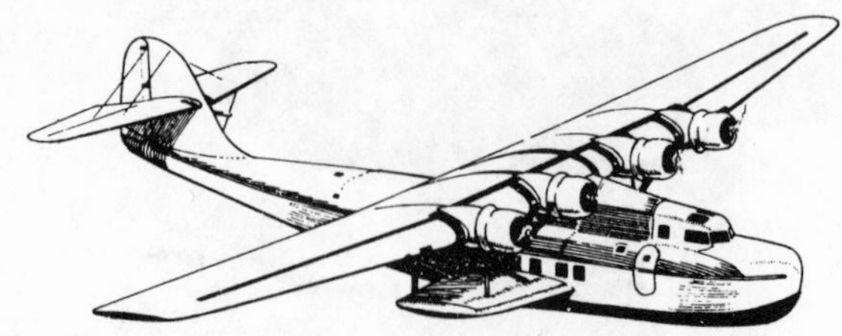

MARTIN M-130 The famed "China Clipper" had a total horsepower of 3,300 and carried 46 passengers plus a crew of 6.

PITCAIRN PA-36 Took the autogiro evolution another step forward with vertical-jump take-off. This was attained by speeding up the rotors at zero incidence, then increasing pitch.

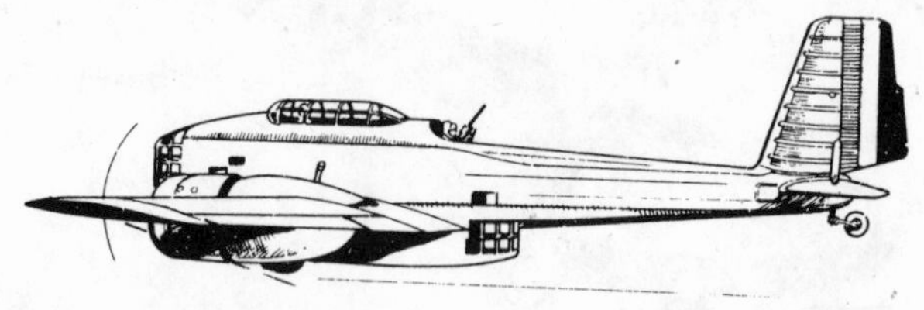

BREGUET 460 Two 820-h.p. Gnome-Rhone radials. Heavy all-metal French bomber with top speed of 235 m.p.h.

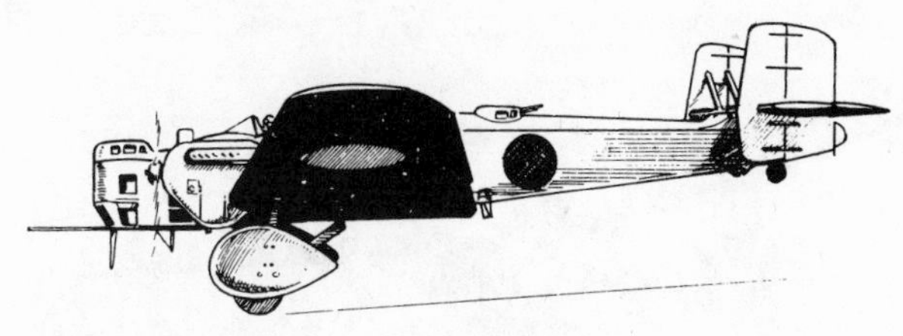

MITSUBISHI 93 Two 700-h.p. radial engines. Japanese fighter-bomber with maximum speed of 137 m.p.h.

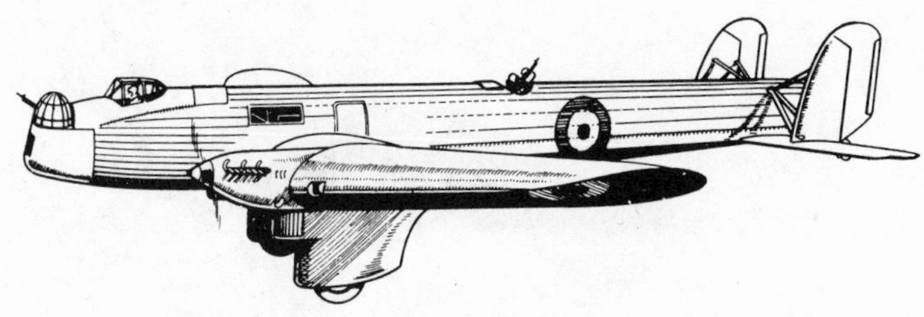

FAIREY "HENDON" Modified Hendon bomber had more powerful engines, enclosed pilot's cockpit and forward gun station.

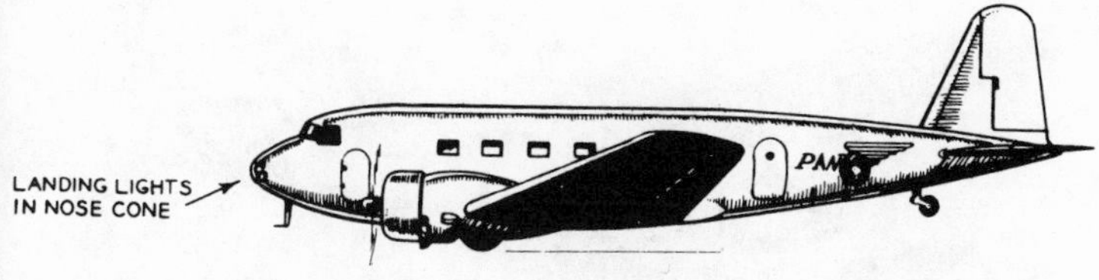

DOUGLAS DC-2 Forerunner of the existing DC series, it was powered with two 700-h.p. Wright radials, carried 14 at 185 m.p.h.

BURNELLI U.B.-14 Two 675-h.p. P. & W. Hornet radials. A development of the original Burnelli airfoil fuselage configuration.

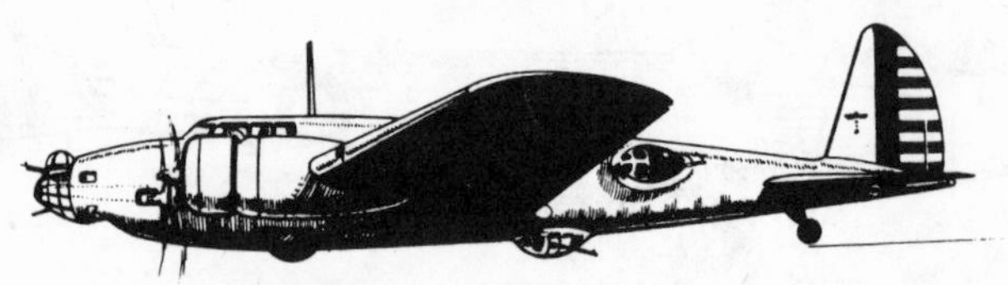

BOEING 299 Four 750-h.p. P. & W. Hornet radials. First 4-engine Boeing bomber and direct ancestor of the "Flying Fortress" of World War II fame.

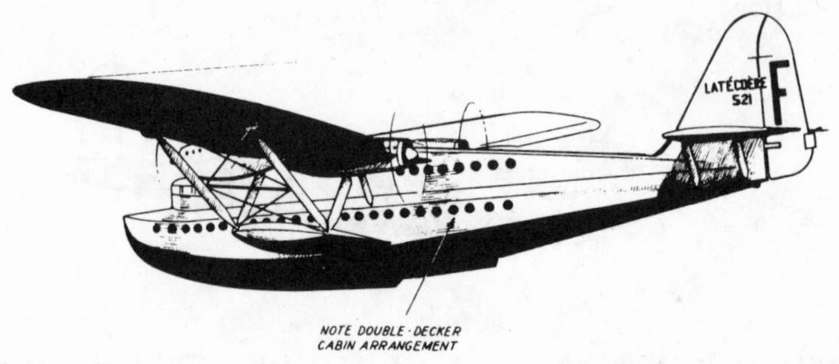

LATÉCOÈRE 521 35-ton double-decker flying boat. This huge French boat could accommodate up to 70 passengers.

BLACKBURN 600-h.p. single-seat day and night fighter. A comparatively unknown type by this famous firm.

CONSOLIDATED PB-2a Supercharged 675-h.p. Curtiss Conqueror engine. Also produced in modified form as a single-seat fighter.

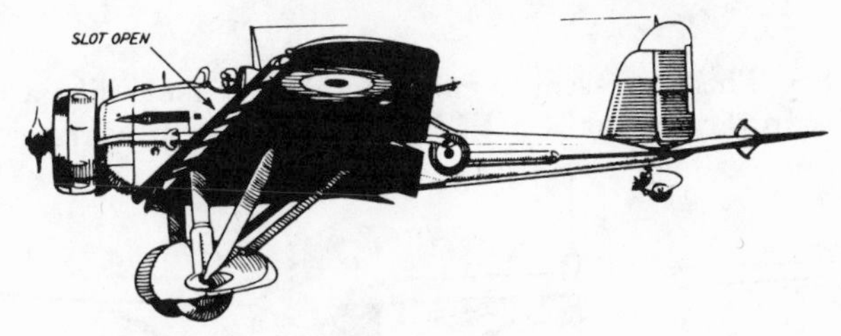

HANDLEY PAGE H.P.47 680-h.p. Bristol radial engine. All-metal general-purpose Army 2-seater.

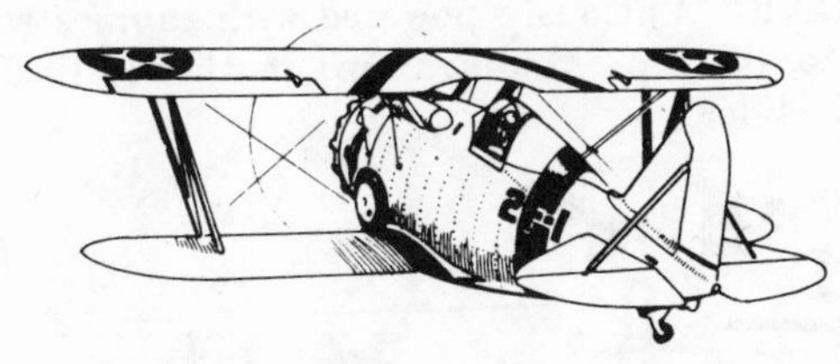

GRUMMAN F2F-1 650-h.p. U.S. Navy shipboard fighter. Pratt & Whitney engine.

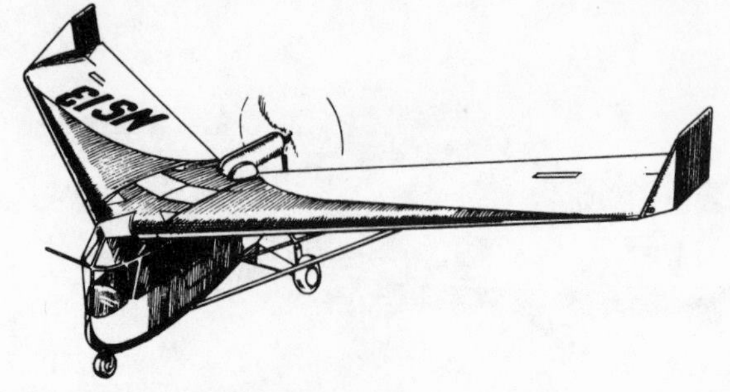

WATERMAN ARROWPLANE 95-h.p. inverted Menasco engine. One of the first serious U.S. designs in the tailless field.

CURTISS This 5-passenger cabin amphibian looks like a throwback to the original Curtiss boats so far as appearance goes.

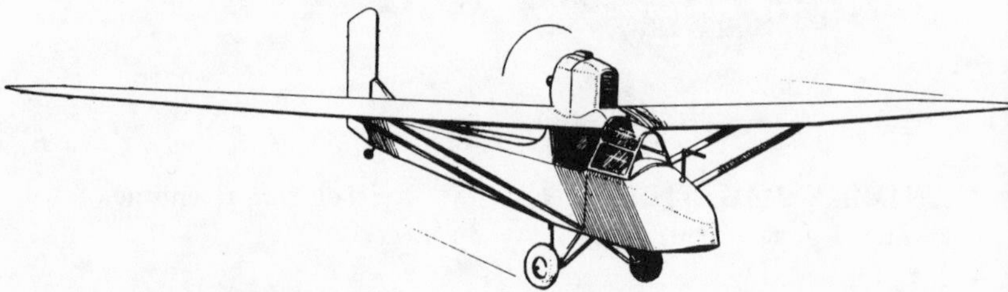

B.A.C. "DRONE" Variously powered with engines ranging from 6 h.p. to 35 h.p. Modification of the 1932 Lowe-Wylde powered glider.

LUTON "BUZZARD" Another small British light plane, 25/35 h.p.

MIGNET POU DE CIEL ("Flying Flea") Variously powered with 17- to 35-h.p. engines. Front wing could be tilted for lateral control, incidence changed for longitudinal control. Supposedly a foolproof airplane, its certificate of airworthiness was withdrawn after a long series of fatal crashes.

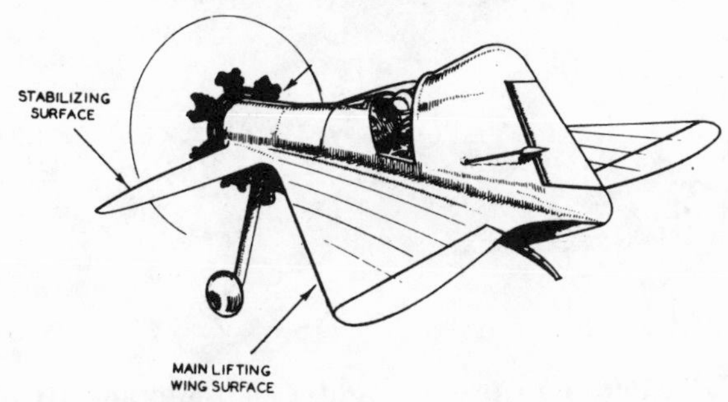

PAYEN "FLECHAIR" 400-h.p. radial engine. A very interesting French design which proved unsuccessful on account of excessive torque, but which would have made an admirable jet-power airplane.

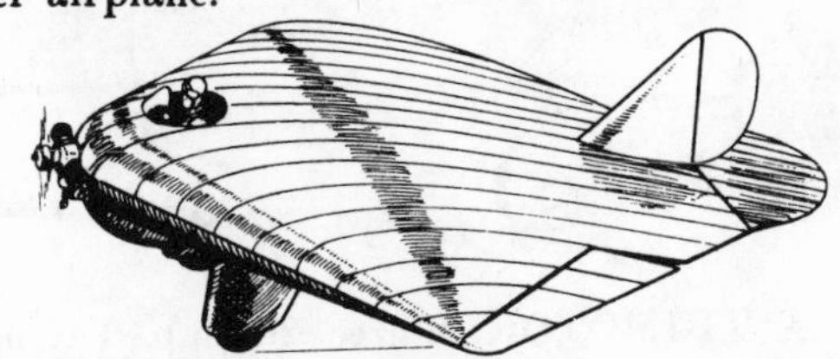

CANOVA ALL-WING An experimental design with normal control surfaces.

SEVERSKY P-35 900-h.p. P. & W. radial; top speed: 285 m.p.h. This was the last model procured by the U.S.A.A.F. before renaming as Republic Aviation. Predecessor of famed World War II "Thunderbolt."

BUECKER JUNGMANN Bu. 139 70-h.p. inverted Hirth engine. Built and used in defiance of the Armistice terms to train future *Luftwaffe* pilots.

HEINKEL He.50 Top prewar fighter of the crack Richthofen *Geschwader* and last biplane fighter used by the *Luftwaffe.*

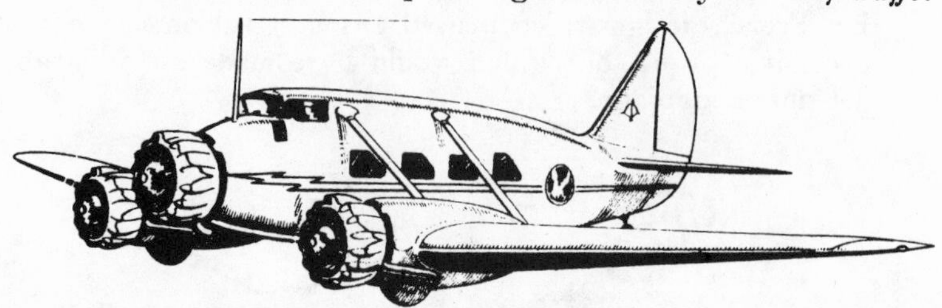

STINSON A TRIMOTOR Three 260-h.p. Lycoming radials. Cruised at 163 m.p.h. with eight passengers and crew.

BRISTOL 142 Prototype model of the famed Blenheims. First British approach to the fast twin-engine fighter-bombers of World War II.

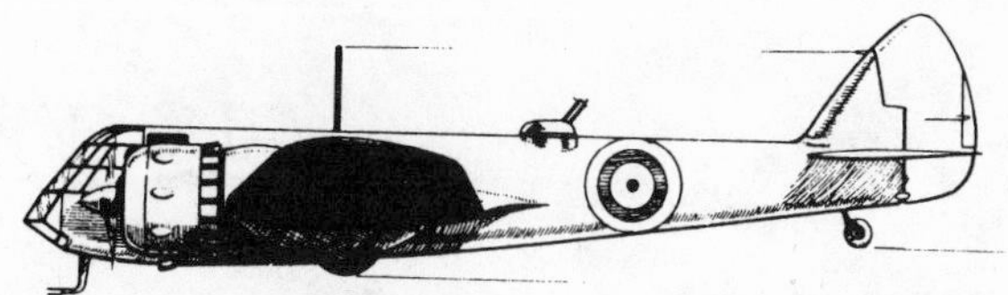

BRISTOL 142-M Immediate predecessor of the Bristol Blenheim.

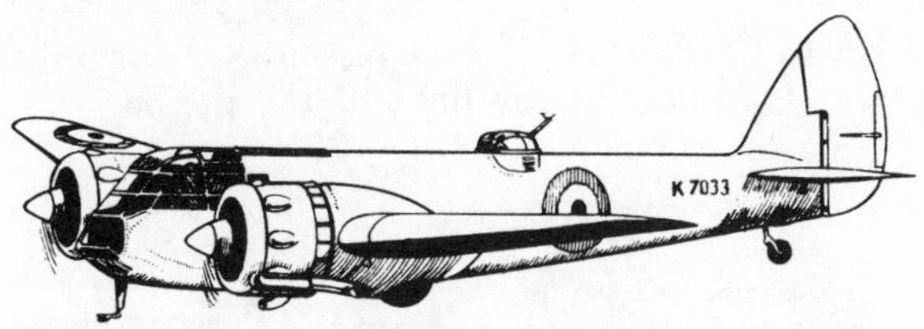

BRISTOL BLENHEIM Mk.1 Two 935-h.p. radial engines. Cruised at 240 m.p.h. with range of 1,000 miles. Saw service in World War II.

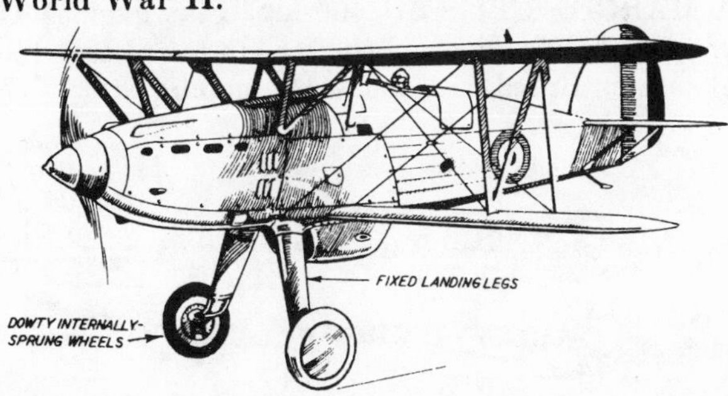

HAWKER "SPANISH FURY" 745-h.p. Rolls-Royce engine. Last and fastest of the "Furies," it had a top speed of 252 m.p.h. The simple landing gear with fixed legs and internally sprung wheels is notable.

HAWKER F36/34 PROTOTYPE "HURRICANE" 1,030-h.p. Rolls-Royce Merlin engine. Prototype model was test-flown in late 1935. First production model of the famed World War II fighter had cantilevered tailplane.

BOEING B-314 CLIPPER This huge boat was largest and most luxurious transoceanic air liner of the period.

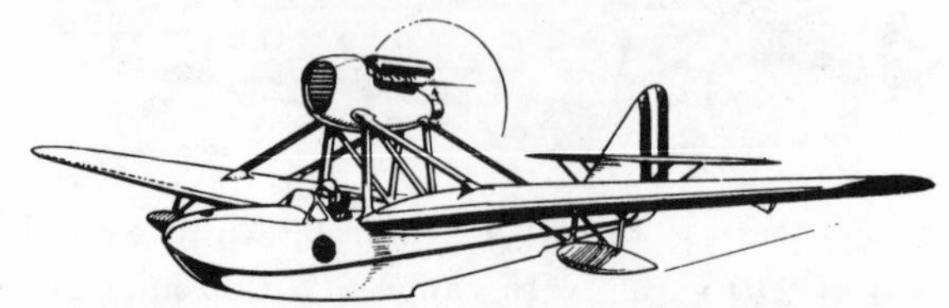

SAVOIA-MARCHETTI, S-67 400-h.p. Fiat engine. This little single-seat fighter displays the Italian talent for clean flying-boat design. Speed was about 140 m.p.h.

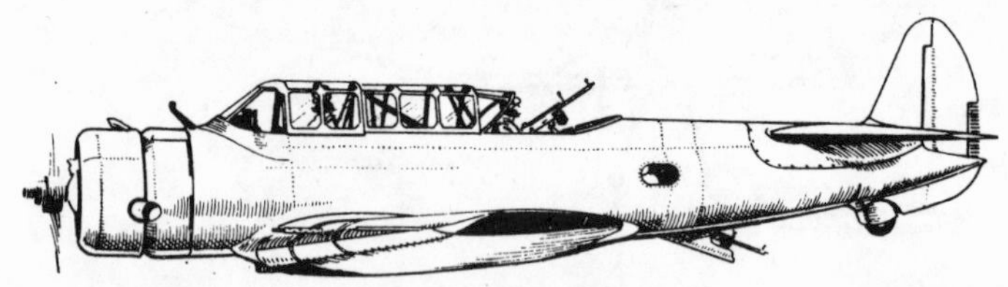

CONSOLIDATED-VULTEE V-11-GB 3-place attack plane. Modification of first military Vultee, the Model V-11, produced in 1936.

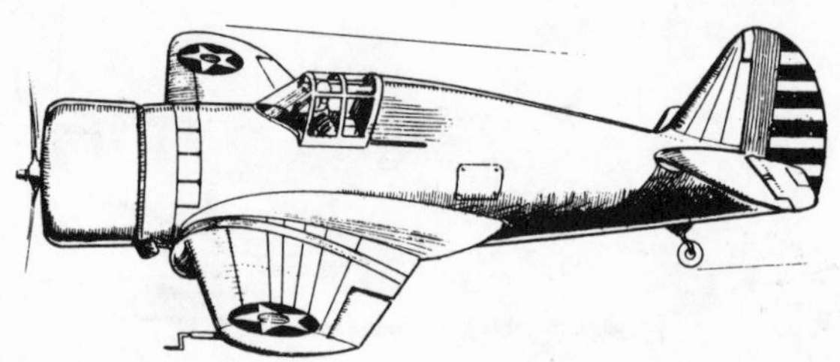

CURTISS P-36 1,150-h.p. P. & W. radial. First all-metal low-wing Curtiss fighter and prototype model of Hawk 75-A (350 m.p.h.).

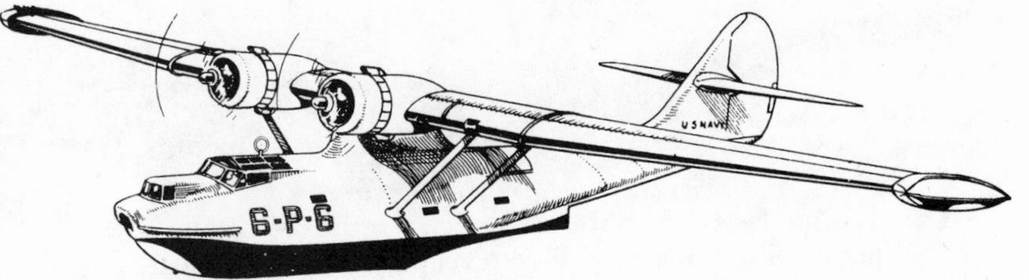

CONSOLIDATED PBY-1 First of the fabulous Catalinas which were the most widely used U.S. Navy long-range patrol boats of World War II.

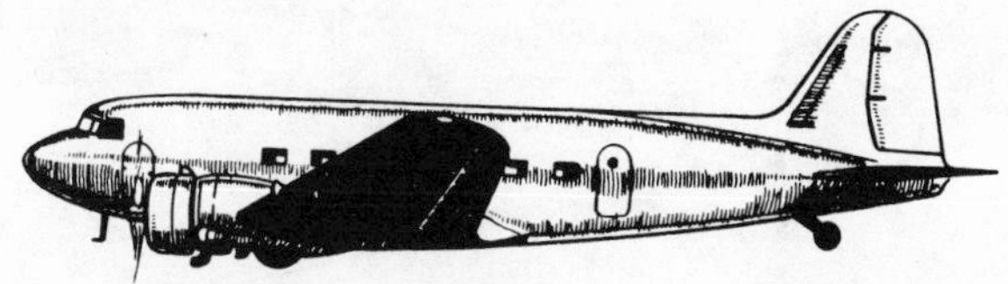

DOUGLAS DC-3 One of the most remarkable airplanes in the world. During World War II alone more than 10,000 military versions of the DC-3 were built, and it is still in service as an air liner in many countries.

BOEING XB-15 Four P. & W. 1,000-h.p. radials. Forerunner of the Super Forts. Only one of these giant ships was built.

DOUGLAS B-18A Military version of the DC-2 air liner. 214 m.p.h. Similar to the B-18 except for modified nose.

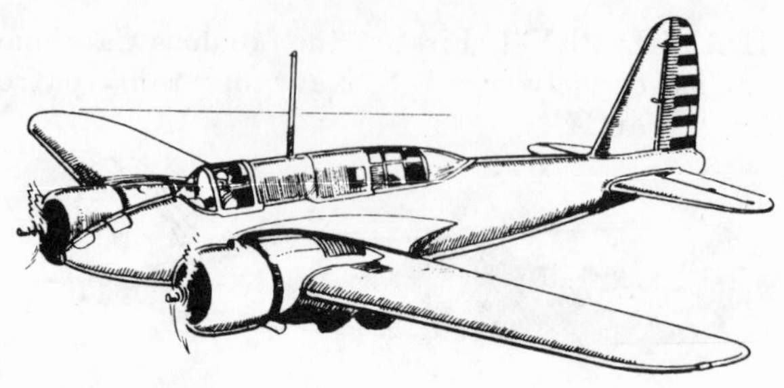

CURTISS Y1A-18 First U.S. twin-engine attack plane.

FOCKE-WULF "AGHELIS" Regarded by many as world's first successful helicopter, it certainly demonstrated free helicopter flight but was not developed.

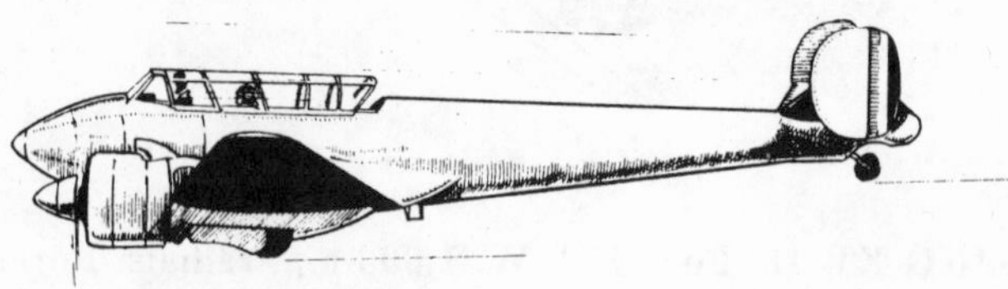

POTEZ 63 This twin-engine French attack plane suggests the future Me.110 of World War II.

GRUMMAN SF-1 Typical U.S. Navy prewar carrier-based scout-bomber.

AVRO "ANSON" Served throughout World War II as an R.A.F. coastal command reconnaissance plane.

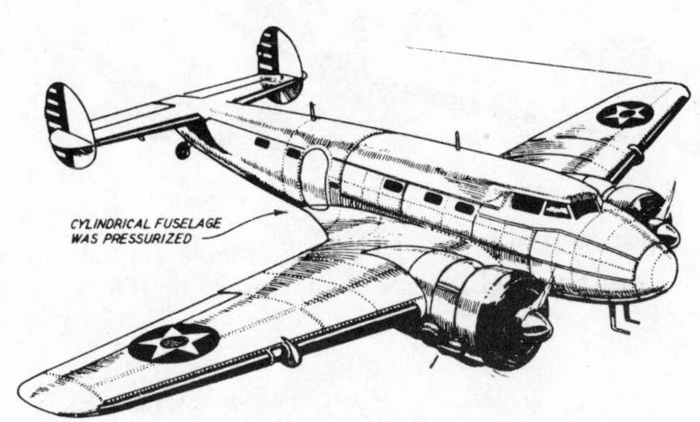

LOCKHEED XC-35 U.S. Air Force stratospheric experimental plane. Initial tests produced 350 m.p.h. at 21,000 feet altitude.

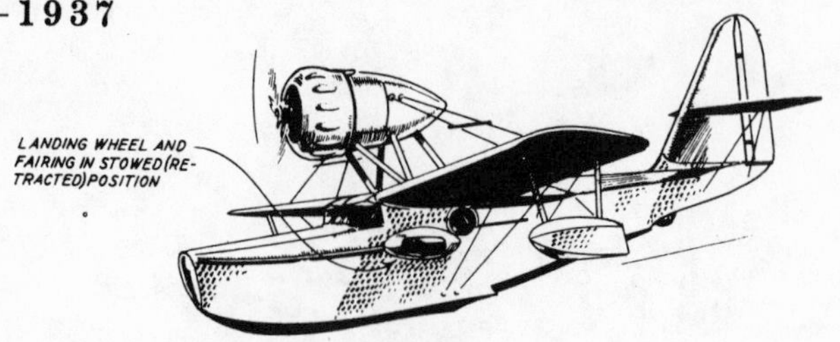

FLEETWING "SEA BIRD" 285-h.p. Jacobs radial engine. 4-place amphibian with stainless-steel hull. Speed: 135 to 150 m.p.h.

AVIONS "TIPSY" 40-h.p. flat twin Train engine. Belgian light plane with a top speed of 124 m.p.h. Still actively flying.

BELTRAME "COLIBRI" 18-h.p. Beltrame engine. This interesting tail-first light plane is of Italian origin.

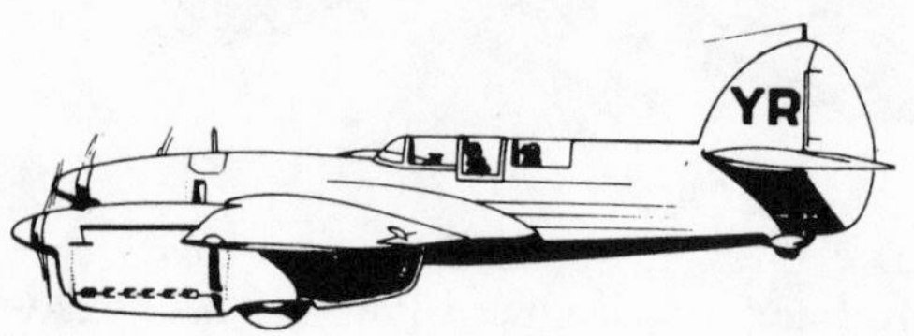

BELLANCA Special twin-engine long-distance New York—Bucharest model.

CONSOLIDATED XPB2Y-1 Prototype model of the Coronado-class U.S. Navy patrol bombers.

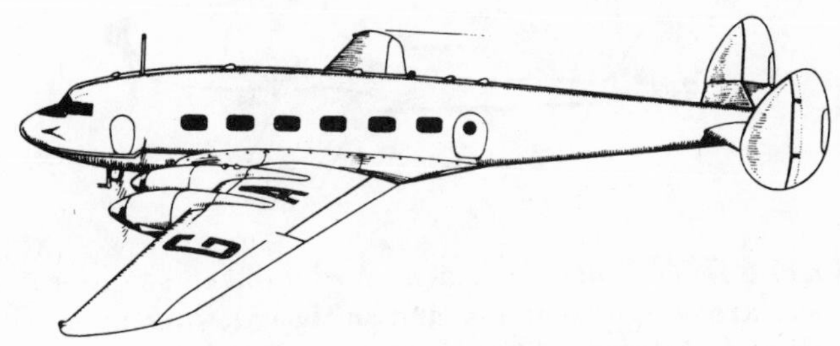

DE HAVILLAND D.H.91 "ALBATROSS" This was a promising four-engine air liner with bonded plywood fuselage. War interrupted development.

SHORT 14/38 "STRATOLINER" An experimental high-altitude air liner which was abandoned due to the outbreak of war.

FOKKER D-21 Last single-engine fighter by Fokker before the war. It was behind U.S., British, and German fighters in design.

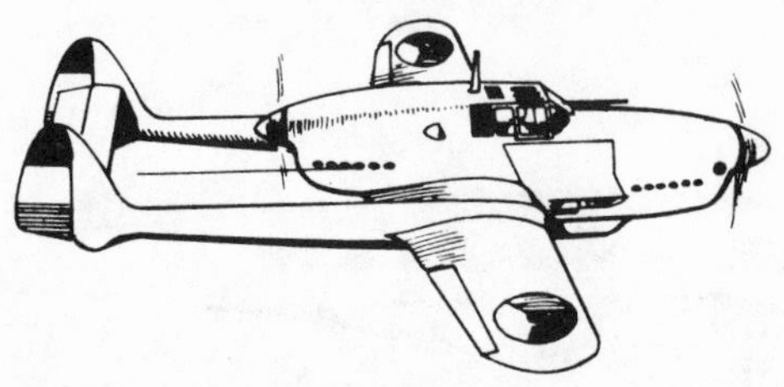

FOKKER D.23 This tandem-engined Fokker single-seat fighter was armed with cannon and outboard wing guns. Overrunning of Holland by the Nazis terminated development of this advanced design.

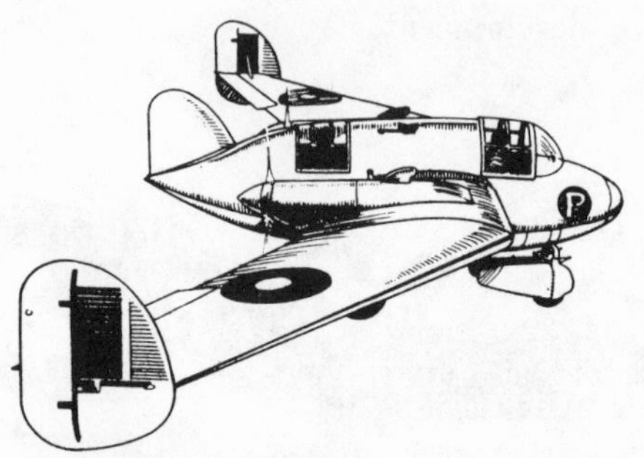

HANDLEY PAGE H.P.75 "MANX" This twin-engine experimental tailless design was dropped during the war but experiments were renewed after the cessation of hostilities.

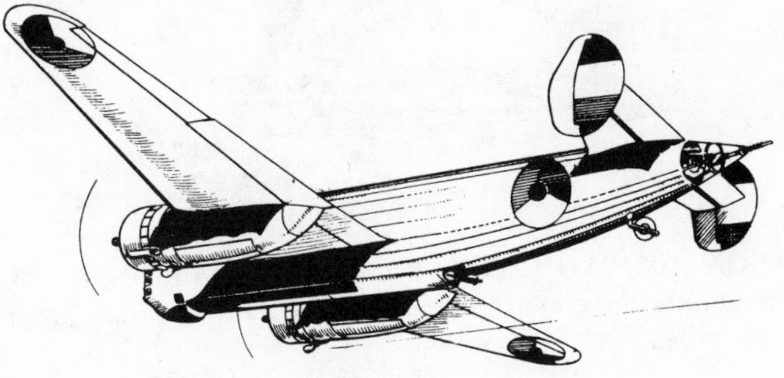

FOKKER T.5 Another interesting prewar Fokker design. This time a twin-engine heavy bomber built for the Dutch Air Force.

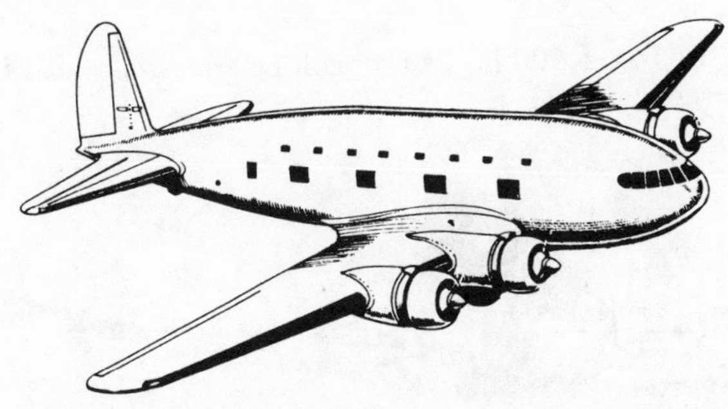

BOEING 307 "STRATOLINER" Prototype model of world's first high-altitude air liner with fully pressurized cabin. Production model was modified to include a large dorsal fin.

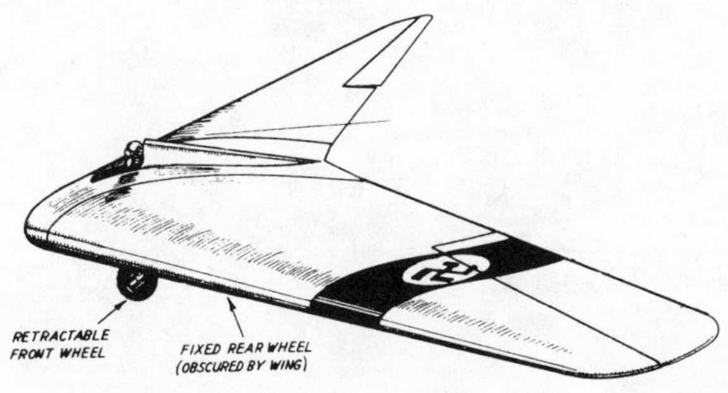

HORTEN "SOARING WING" A very advanced prewar German all-wing sailplane.

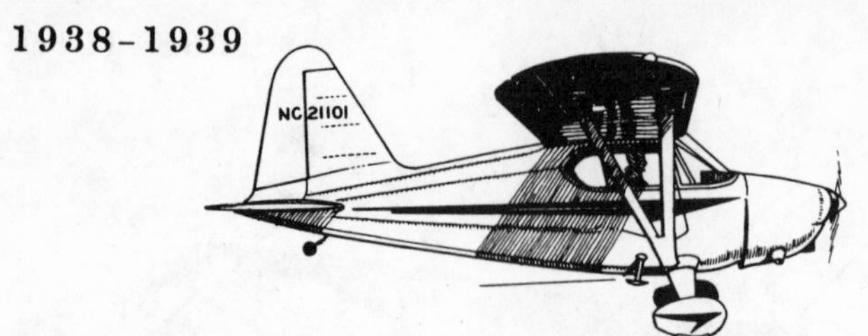

STINSON 105 "VOYAGER" 90-h.p. Franklin engine. 3-place personal plane with cruising speed of 105 m.p.h.; range: 395 miles.

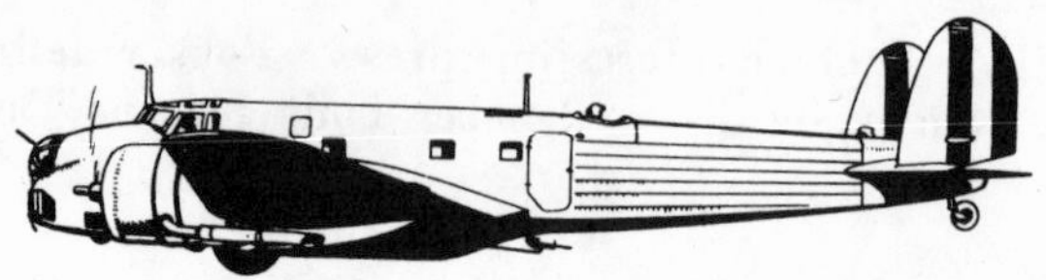

FIAT B.R.20 Two 1,000-h.p. Fiat radial engines. Typical Italian prewar heavy bomber.

HANDLEY PAGE H.P.52 "HAMPDEN" Two 1,025-h.p. Bristol radial engines. Obsolescent at outbreak of war but used in early days as bomber.

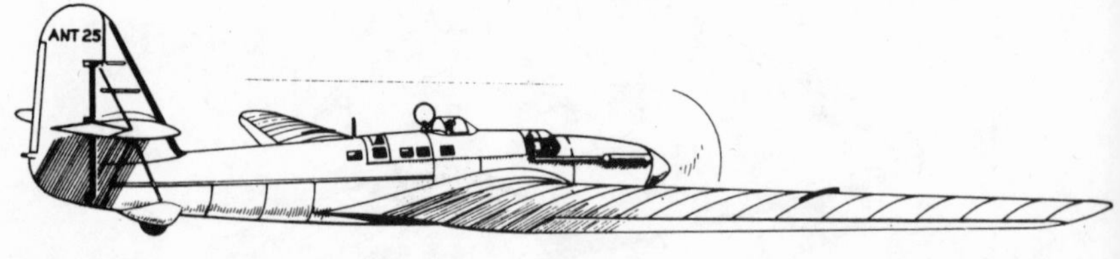

A.N.T. 25 All-metal single-engine Soviet long-distance record breaker.

DEWOITINE D.510 One of the many obsolete types with which France entered war and which were no match for the *Luftwaffe* fighters.

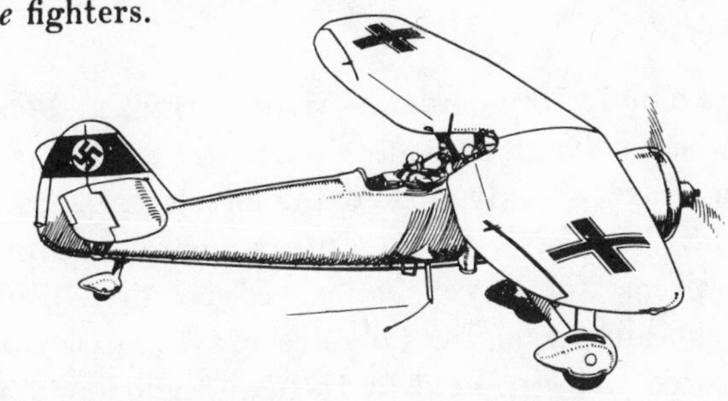

HENSCHEL He.126 High-wing *Luftwaffe* observation and general-purpose army co-operation plane. Employed in early days of World War II.

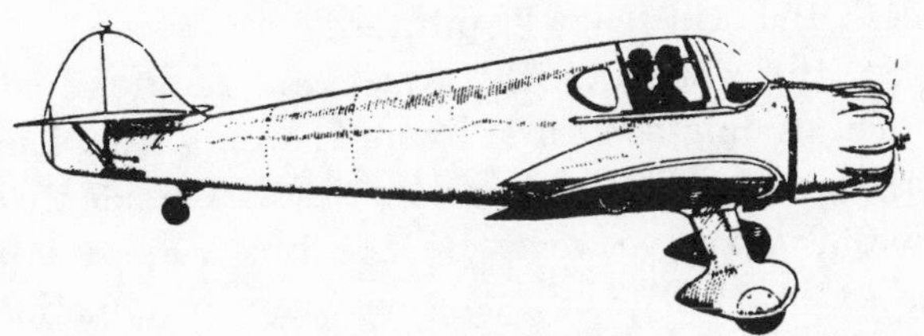

RYAN S-C 145-h.p. radial engine. This neat little all-metal 2-seat personal plane cruised at 135 m.p.h., which would be considered good by present-day standards.

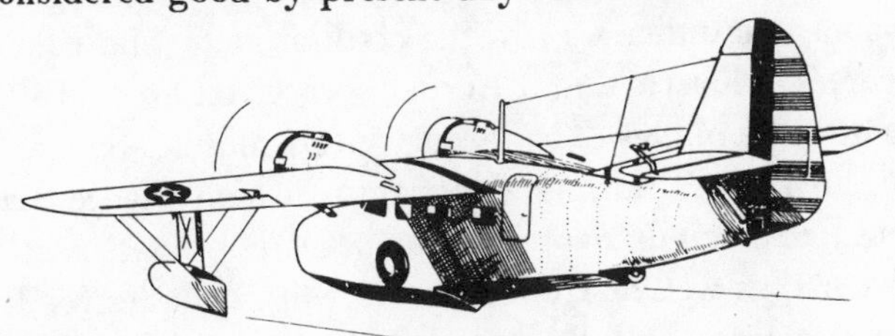

GRUMMAN "GOOSE" (Navy designation: JRF-1; Commercial designation: G-21A) First Grumman departure from float-fuselage-type seaplanes.

PART SEVEN

World War II

1939-1945

On September 1, 1939, Adolph Hitler attacked Poland, and three days later England and France declared war on Germany. The Nazis quickly proved the effectiveness of total air power. Their Junkers Ju.87 Stukas, many equipped with shrieking sirens for psychological effect, dive-bombed and strafed everything in sight. Poland's brave but wholly inadequate air force was wiped out by them on the ground and aloft by Me.109's. Then France, already hamstrung by internal strife, fell before the onslaught, and England retired to her island fortress to fight the valiant Battle of Britain with her "Hurricanes" and still fewer "Spitfires."

Sluggishly the wheels of the American aviation industry began to turn, stimulated at first by small orders from England and France and later by the dramatic call of President Roosevelt for 50,000 planes a year. By the time Japan attacked Pearl Harbor in 1941, U.S. military plane production was around 19,500 annually, and in 1944 soared to a peak of 96,315 that year.

Though the turnout of military planes was lagging here in '39, a boom was under way in the civilian field. Manufacturers like Piper, Taylorcraft, and Aeronca were rolling forth a good number of light planes. The incentive to produce stemmed from the Civilian Pilot Training Program in which the government contracted with civilian operators to train pilots, mostly college students, as well as from orders for light planes for liaison, artillery spotting, and limited ambulance work in the armed services.

The story of the airplane in this greatest of wars, especially at the outset, is filled with instances of hasty "make-do" and feats beyond the call of original purpose. "Frail" Lockheed P-38 "Lightning" fighters in Europe were often loaded with as much as 4,000 pounds of bombs. When our daylight bombing raids deep in Germany proved too much for the range of our early escort fighters, big B-17 "Flying Fortresses" were rushed into service equipped with 20 machine guns to play protector. Commercial transports too went to war, and modified DC-3's (C-47's) and DC-4's (C-54's) made flights and carried loads far in excess of designed capacity.

And most spectacular was the raid on Tokyo by sixteen B-25 "Mitchells" commanded by the then Col. "Jimmy" Doolittle. They took off fully loaded in April 1942 from the deck of the aircraft carrier *Hornet* to fly overwater to a target 820 miles distant—a job for which this medium bomber had certainly never been intended.

In the space of three years after entering the war, with only a small quantity of advanced fighters, the U.S. had, through production and effective use, achieved air power that ruled the heavens. It was an accomplishment bought at a dear price. Most bitter of the early lessons learned was that the Japanese had a large and excellent air force, with fighters like the "Zeke," "Oscar," and "Tony" easily able to outclimb and outmaneuver our P-40's and P-39's.

But once the lesson was learned we were quick to correct our mistakes. The Navy's magnificent Grumman F4F "Wildcat" and later the F6F "Hellcat," the Vought F4U "Corsair," and the Army's "Lightning," "Thunderbolt," and the "King of the Skies," the P-51 "Mustang," ended the supremacy of the Jap fighter. The enemy's shipping got short shrift from extra heavily armed "Mitchells," while B-24 "Liberators" bombed the Nip out of his island installations. And Navy TBM torpedo-bombers and SB2C dive-bombers annihilated the Emperor's navy.

In Europe, where U.S. lend-lease planes by the thousands had been augmenting the air forces of our Allies, American mass daylight and British night bombing raids were gradually crippling the Nazi war industry. The British "Spitfire," having undergone a number of improvements, had become the scourge of the Me.109's and Focke-Wulf 190's. The English "Mosquito," a very fast twin-engine plane of unusual wooden "sandwich" construction, served in triple-threat duty as fighter, bomber, and pathfinder for the big night-raiding bombers.

Toward the final year, U.S. P-47 "Thunderbolts" and P-51 "Mustangs," equipped with jettisonable fuel tanks, had the range to escort American day bombers all the way to Berlin. The "Mustang," a sleek design, had originally been ordered by the British. It featured the radical "laminar flow" wing profile developed by the National Advisory Committee for Aeronautics which produced about one-half the drag of the conventional airfoil, thus enabling the airplane to fly faster on the same power that it would if fitted with standard airfoiled wing. Characteristics of the "laminar flow" were a sharper leading edge and generally symmetrical shape, with the thickest portion carried back to the halfway point of the chord instead of one-third, as in the standard airfoil, whence it "dished in" toward the trailing edge. The "Mustang," in its early stages, bore a superficial resemblance to the Me.109, and many an R.A.F. pilot, following an aerial battle with Messerschmitts, briefly joined the homeward-flying enemy formation by mistake. In the war's last months the "Mustang" developed into probably the fastest propeller-driven fighter, capable of speeds around 475 m.p.h.

Just as the Allies gained virtual control of the air, Germany sprang an alarming surprise by introducing jets. The opener was a little batwing plane without propeller that whizzed through a formation of "Flying Fortresses" one summer day in 1944. The startled crewmen, had they been able to examine the apparition, would have described it as the Me.163, a monoplane with low, swept-back wings that was powered by a liquid-fuel rocket engine and capable of a speed of 560 m.p.h. It was armed with four 30-mm. cannon, could climb 5,550 feet per minute, and had a range of eight minutes. A most dangerous antagonist, it died in production because of bickering among Nazi manufacturers.

Hard on the heels of the 163 there appeared the Me.262 jet fighter. Powered by two jet engines (the "true" kind, which took air in at the front, mixed it with fuel, and ejected it at the rear in a searing blast), this one did considerable damage among our bombers by virtue of its four cannon and 500-m.p.h. speed. It could have done more had not Hitler's lack of foresight relegated it to the lowly duty of ground attack craft against the onrushing tanks of General Patton. Damage also was done by another utilization of jet power by the enemy—the "buzz bomb" aimed at English cities, a winged pilotless missile that was essentially an aircraft.

Germany's lead in this whole field of "reaction propulsion" was due to the fact she had been busy experimenting long before the war. The world's first jet-powered plane, the air frame and engine of which were built by the Heinkel firm, made its initial flight on August 27, 1939. Following their Axis partner, the Italians delved into the subject, and the Caproni-Campini Company flew its first jet airplane in 1941. So secret had the Nazi experiments been that Italy mistakenly received credit for first appearance. The Caproni-Campini job, however, left much to be desired, and the project was dropped.

Despite Germany's lead, the Allies were really not far behind in jet development. In England the then Squadron Leader Frank Whittle of the R.A.F. started work on a gas turbine jet engine back in 1929. As a consequence, the Gloster E28/39 jet plane took to the air in May 1941. It was a purely experimental craft, its Whittle engine developing a mere 655 pounds of thrust—still faster than the "Spitfire." The Gloster Company's second attempt was the "Meteor," built specifically as a fighter powered by two Whittle jets, these later being replaced by Rolls-Royce Derwent jet engines. The Gloster "Meteor" was the only service jet plane of the Allies, but it never saw combat in World War II.

Investigating British jet progress while in England, the U.S. Army Air Force head, Gen. "Hap" Arnold, made immediate

TEXAS STATE TECHNICAL INSTITUTE
ROLLING PLAINS CAMPUS – LIBRARY
SWEETWATER, TEXAS 79556

arrangements to have a Whittle engine sent to this country. A B-17 under top-secret orders helped speed delivery to the General Electric Company. At the same time, Bell Aircraft in Buffalo was asked to construct an air frame to be powered by two G.E. turbo-jets based on the Whittle design. The airplane was rushed to completion in 1944 and taken to the then hush-hush Muroc test base in California. On the last stage of the frantic race it had to be towed five miles from Muroc's assembly shops to the flying field—with a dummy propeller fixed on its nose for camouflage. The Bell XP-59A "Airacomet" zoomed into the sky in September 1944 flown by company test pilot Robert M. Stanley and Col. (now Gen.) Lawrence Craigie of the Air Force.

In its subsequent flights over the Muroc desert the "Airacomet" created quite a stir among the flyers training at a near-by bomber base. The pilots would return to their field with eyes still popping to report encounter with a peculiar mid-wing plane streaking past without benefit of a propeller and, so help them, its pilot wearing a bowler hat. At first the medical officer wearily murmured something about training fatigue and ordered a rest. Later the boys were to learn among other things that the gent in the nonregulation hat was Stanley. The "Airacomet" was not a fast airplane as jets go, its top speed being 409 m.p.h. Only 14 were ordered, for pilot training. Lockheed already was building the P-80 (later designated F-80) "Shooting Star," which was the U.S.A.A.F.'s first service-type jet fighter.

Jet power arrived at a time when the possibilities of the piston engine were fairly well exploited, thanks to the latter's ever-increasing complexity and size in order to gain additional h.p. Engine firms like Pratt & Whitney, Allison, Wright, and others quickly tooled up jet-wise. For definitely the age of super-speed was here, with the coveted speed of sound not far distant, and even the multiple of it.

That was a new dream. An old one, in which a helicopter kept appearing, was now quietly being made to come alive by Igor Sikorsky. Though helicopters had been built and flown with moderate success by Brequet in France and Focke in Germany, this designer and manufacturer in Connecticut had developed a truly practical rotary-wing craft. His R-4 with enclosed cabin, fathered by his earlier bird-cage-like VS-300, was ordered in number toward the end of the war by the Army. Sikorsky ingeniously solved the problem of torque imposed by the whirling blades of the overhead rotor by counteracting it with a small vertical propeller located at the tail, facing left. The pitch of these tail rotor blades could be altered, thus increasing or decreasing the torque for directional control.

Though the war with Germany terminated in May 1945, the Japanese still hung on. Our newest bombers, the mammoth B-29 "Superforts," hammered their heartland incessantly from bases in the Marianas, a 2,500-mile round trip to Tokyo and back. These sleek planes, powered by four 2,500-h.p. Wright engines, were the last word in aircraft design, structure, and equipment of electronic nature. A special airfoil shape developed by Boeing gave them a top speed of over 300 m.p.h., and their wing loading (weight carried by each square foot of wing) of 74 pounds per was the heaviest up to that time.

It was a B-29 nicknamed "Enola Gay" that dropped an atom bomb on Hiroshima August 6, 1945. A second such bomb on Nagasaki a few days later ended World War II.

BÜCKER Bu. 133 "JUNGMEISTER" Prewar single-seater employed by the *Luftwaffe* for advanced and aerobatic training.

FAIREY "SWORDFISH" Standard British carrier-based torpedo-bomber at outset of World War II.

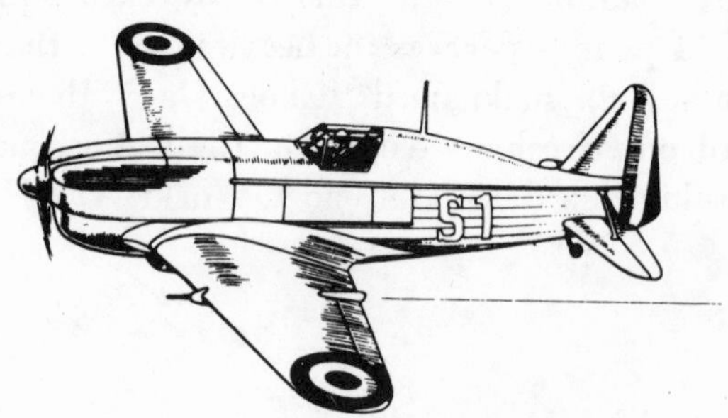

MORANE-SAULNIER 406 A prewar design but one of the better French fighters in service at outbreak of the war. It was powered with a 860-h.p. engine.

HEINKEL HE-178 World's first turbojet powered aircraft, flew August 1939; single-seat research craft had monocoque aluminum fuselage, all-wood wing. Speed 435 m.p.h.

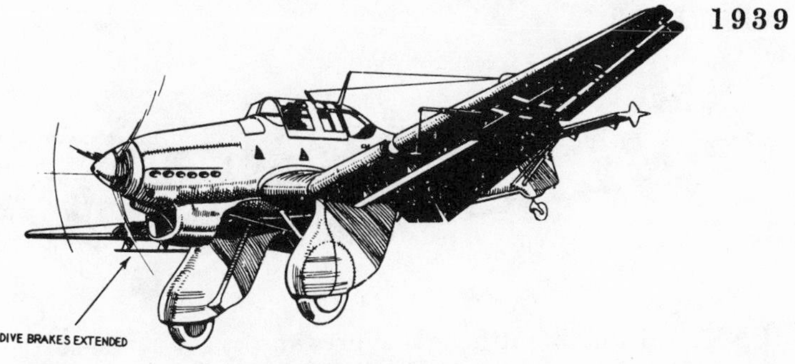

JUNKERS Ju.87 1,000-h.p. Junkers Jumo engine. Symbol of Nazi ruthlessness, the Stuka played an important if ignoble role in the defeat of Poland and France.

HEINKEL He.111-K Variously powered and in many variant forms, the He.111, a prewar design, was one of the most widely used heavy bombers in early days of the war. Poorly armed, it was vulnerable to determined enemy fighter attack.

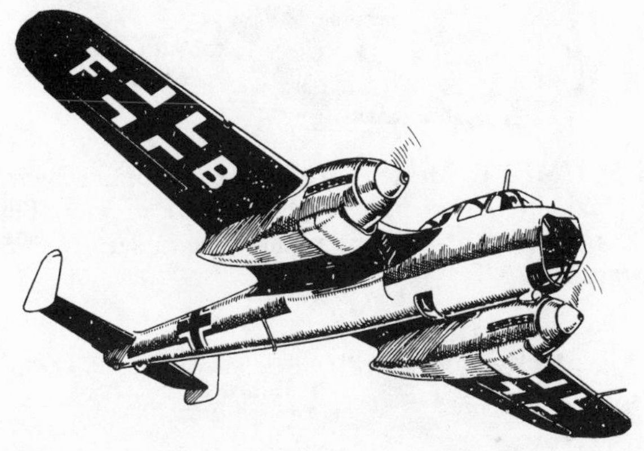

DORNIER Do.215 Two 1,150-h.p. engines. Top Nazi medium-range bomber at outbreak of war. Radial-powered versions existed too.

JUNKERS Ju.52 Although a prewar design, it served as the *Luftwaffe*'s workhorse throughout the war. Heavy bomber, troop carrier, glider tug, and cargo plane, it was powered with three 700-h.p. radials.

GLOSTER "GLADIATOR" 830-h.p. Bristol radial engine. An obsolescent prewar design, it was the only biplane fighter in the war and saw limited use—chiefly in Norway and at Malta.

MESSERSCHMITT Me.109 1,050-h.p. Daimler-Benz engine. Top Nazi single-seat fighter at outbreak of war. Top speed: 375 m.p.h. Variants of this plane were in service throughout the war.

MESSERSCHMITT Me.110 Two 1,395-h.p. engines. Top Nazi 2-seat fighter and fighter-bomber at outbreak of war.

LOCKHEED "HUDSON" **Military version of Lockheed 14 air liner, it was an export medium bomber used by the R.A.F. Coastal Command.**

BRISTOL BLENHEIM Mk. IV **Had modified nose, more powerful engines. Top speed of the fighter-bomber: 295 m.p.h.**

VICKERS SUPERMARINE "SPITFIRE" 1,030-h.p. Rolls-Royce Merlin engine. Armed with 8 wing guns, the Spit was highly maneuverable. Prototype appeared 1935.

HAWKER "HURRICANE" 1,030-h.p. Rolls-Royce Merlin engine. Battle of Britain model had anti-spin ventral fin; otherwise resembled first production model of "Hurricane." Companion fighter to "Spitfire" in Battle of Britain, "Hurricane" cut the heart out of the *Luftwaffe* in the Battle of Britain.

ARMSTRONG-WHITWORTH WHITLEY Two 918-h.p. radials. A prewar R.A.F. heavy bomber which saw limited service during early war days.

VULTEE BT-13A (PROTOTYPE MODEL) 450-h.p. P. & W. Wasp radial. More than 11,000 "Valiants" were procured for the U.S.A.A.F. during the war.

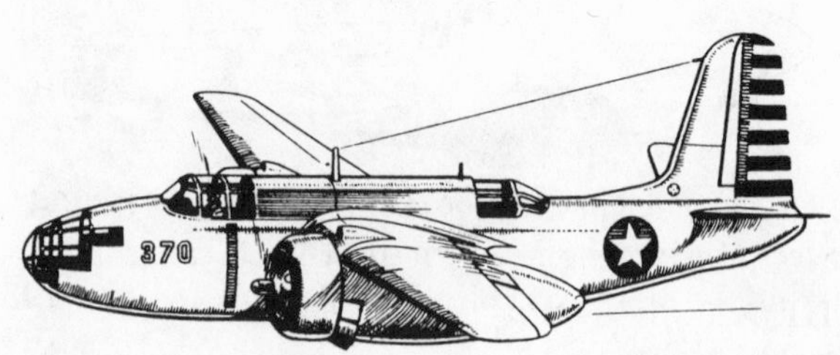

DOUGLAS DB-7 Two 2,000-h.p. P. & W. radials. R.A.F. designation: "Boston." Became U.S.A.A.F. A-20 light attack-bomber.

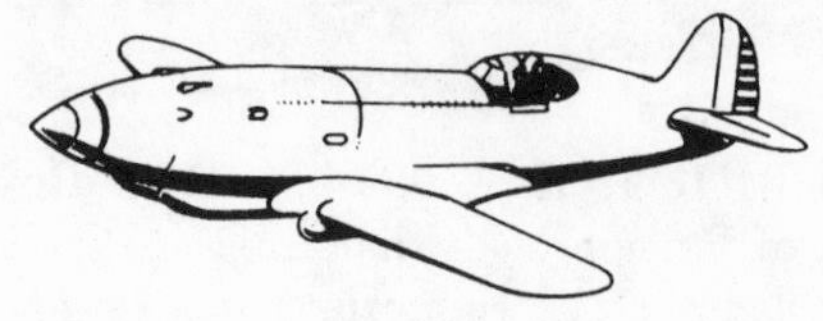

CURTISS P-37 Forerunner of famed P-40 Hawk.

VICKERS "WELLINGTON" Two 1,100-h.p. radial engines. Most formidable R.A.F. heavy long-range bomber at outbreak of war. Twin gun power turrets at nose and tail provided it with excellent protective armament. The "Wimpy" was still in service at close of hostilities.

MACCHI C.202 1,200-h.p. Daimler-Benz engine. Italy's standard World War II fighter. Four .50-caliber machine guns in nose.

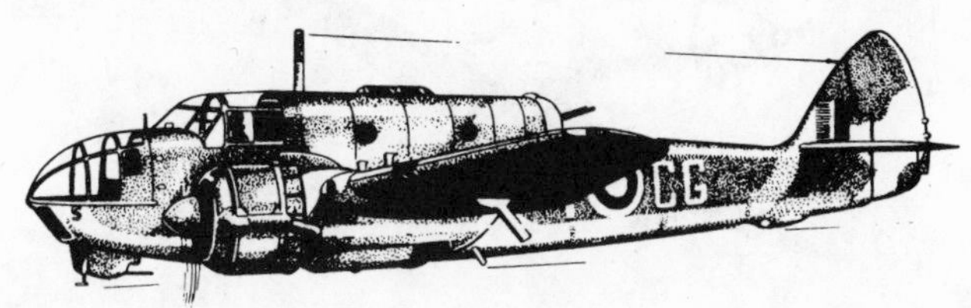

BRISTOL "BEAUFORT" R.A.F. Coastal Command torpedo-bomber. Also employed as coastal patrol reconnaissance plane.

DORNIER Do.217 Formidable *Luftwaffe* dive-bomber in service throughout World War II.

JUNKERS Ju.88 With many modifications, standard *Luftwaffe* medium bomber throughout World War II.

LOCKHEED XP-38 Prototype of famed P-38 Lightning. Two 1,150-h.p. Allison engines. On its maiden cross-country flight, it hung up new transcontinental record (7 hours, 45 minutes).

BELL P-39 "AIRCOBRA" 1,100-h.p. Allison engine behind pilot with cannon firing through propeller hub. Prototype of fighter in limited service with U.S.A.A.F. but popular with Russians as a tank buster.

SHORT "SUNDERLAND" These large R.A.F. Coastal Command patrol boats were development of the Empire class boats of 1936. Under fighter attack, technique of defense was to fly just above the waves, discouraging dive attack by fighters.

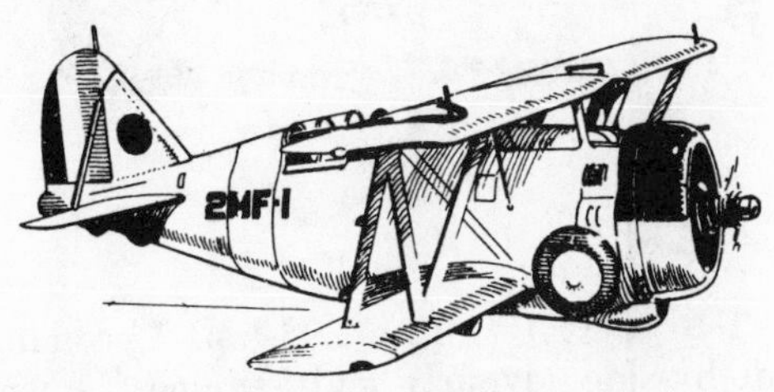

GRUMMAN F3F-3 1,000-h.p. Wright radial. A prewar U.S. Marines fighter in use at outbreak of war.

CURTISS SNC-1 450-h.p. P. & W. radial. In limited use by the U.S. Navy for advanced training at this time.

AVRO "TUTOR" 215-h.p. Armstrong-Siddeley radial.

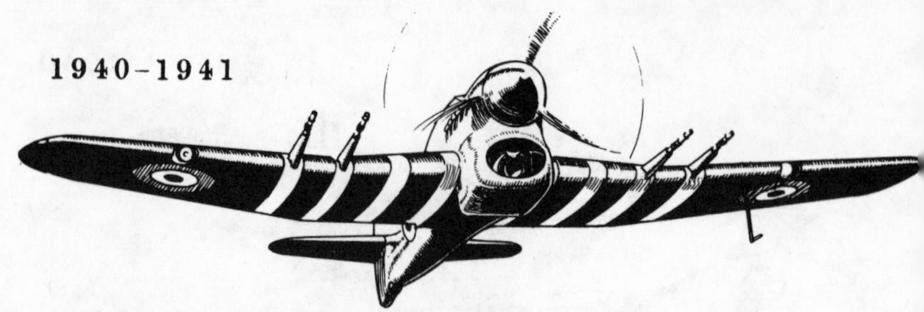

HAWKER "TYPHOON" 2,240-h.p. H-type Napier engine. Armed with four 20-mm. cannon and with a top speed of 416 m.p.h., it was one of the most formidable Allied fighters in the war.

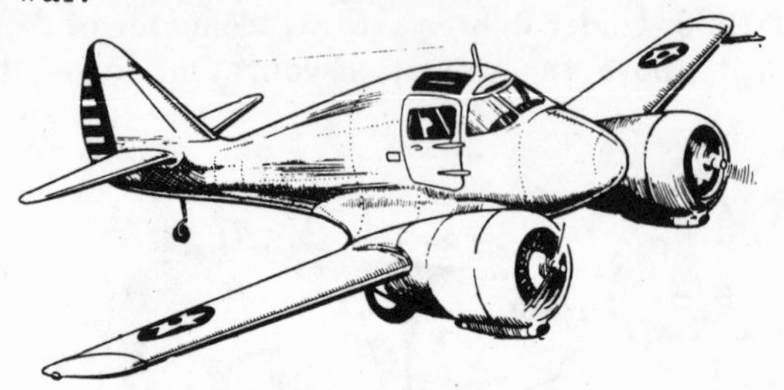

CURTISS AT-9 "JEEP" Two 295-h.p. Lycoming radials. 2-place side-by-side advanced multi-engine trainer.

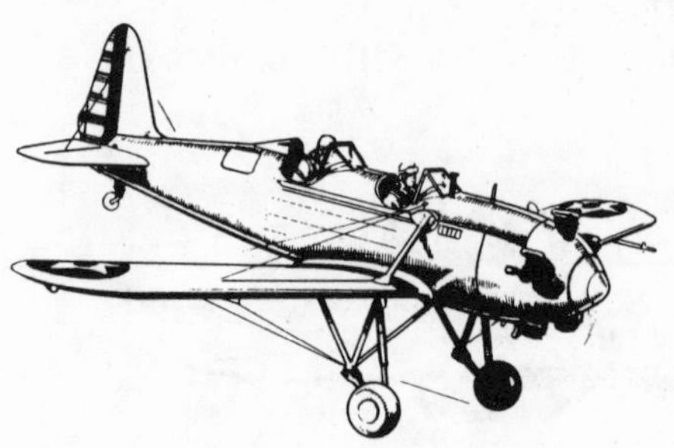

RYAN PT-20 160-h.p. Kinner radial engine. All-metal primary trainer.

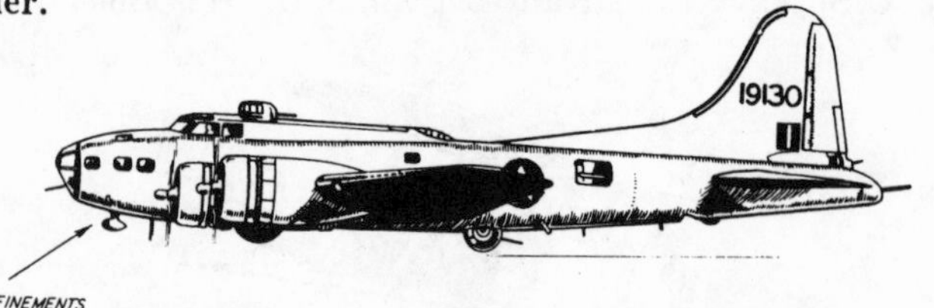

BOEING B-17F "FLYING FORTRESS" Most famous U.S. heavy long-range bomber of the war. Four 1,250-h.p. Wright radials. Essentially a development of the prewar Boeing 299.

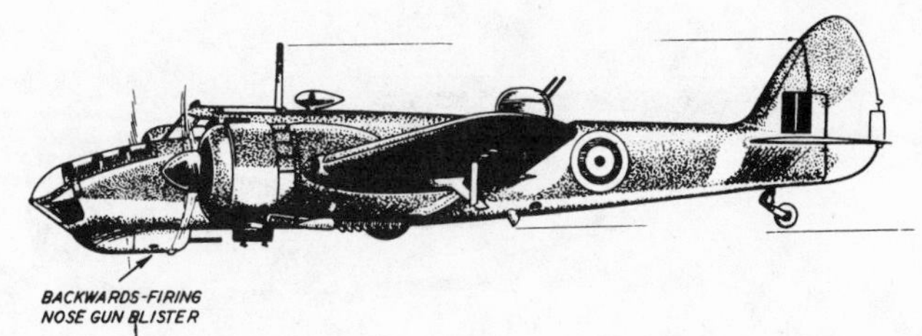

BRISTOL BLENHEIM V-D Two 1,065-h.p. Bristol radials. Long-range day bomber. Chin turret gun covered rear lower hemisphere.

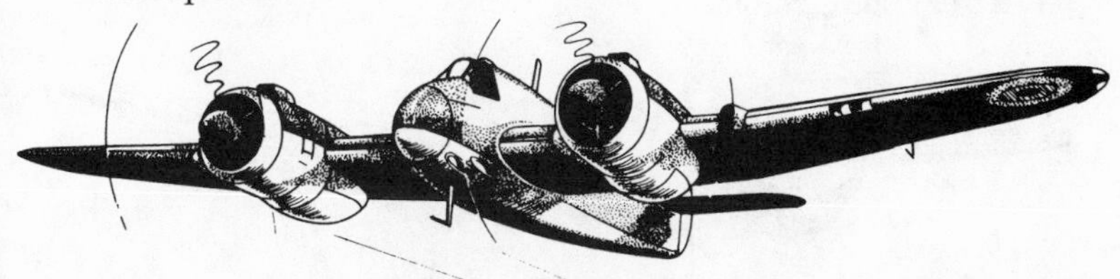

BRISTOL "BEAUFIGHTER" **Was formidable long-range 1- or 2-seat day and night fighter used by the R.A.F. Two 1,065-h.p. engines.**

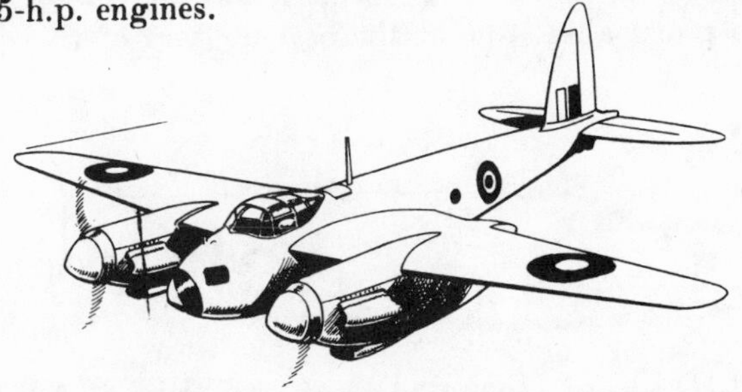

DE HAVILLAND D.H.98 "MOSQUITO" The all-wood "Mosquito" was one of the fastest and most versatile military aircraft of World War II. Armed reconnaissance, fighter-bomber, unarmed bomber escort fighter, and unarmed photo-reconnaissance variants of the design appeared. This is first.

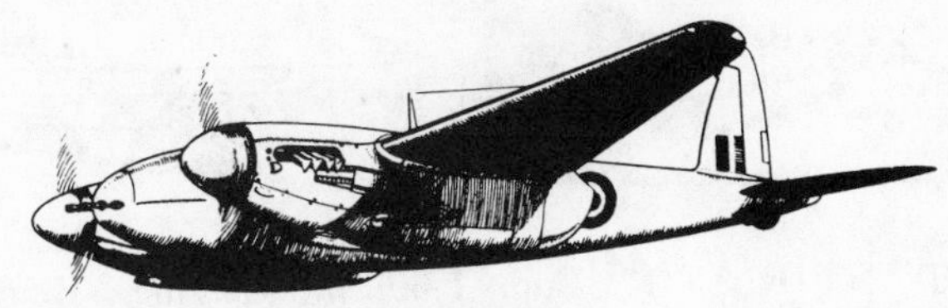

DE HAVILLAND D.H.98 "MOSQUITO" **Fighter-bomber version with fighter nose.**

CONSOLIDATED PBY-5A Two 1,200-h.p. P. & W. radials. U.S. Navy patrol amphibian. Used by the British also, who named it the "Catalina." Famed U.S. Navy workhorse, it had a very long range.

LOCKHEED P-38 Two 1,150-h.p. Allison engines (later increased to two 1,475-h.p. engines). Known to the German pilots as the "Fork-Tail Devil," it was feared by German and Jap pilots alike. One of the best fighters of the war.

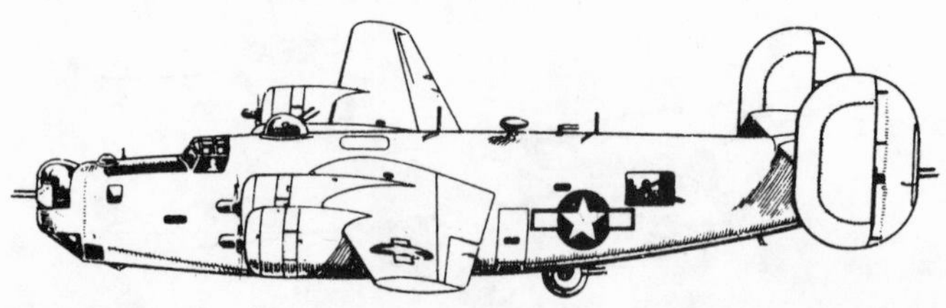

CONSOLIDATED (CONVAIR) B-24J "LIBERATOR" Four 1,200-h.p. P. & W. radials. Probably the most widely used U.S. heavy bomber of the war. More than 18,000 were built before close of the war.

SHORT "STIRLING" Four 1,600-h.p. engines. Britain's first really large long-range bomber. Carried a 8- to 10-ton bomb load at 280 m.p.h.

REPUBLIC P-47 "THUNDERBOLT" 2,100-h.p. P. & W. radial. One of the toughest single-seat fighters of the entire war. This is later model with bubble canopy.

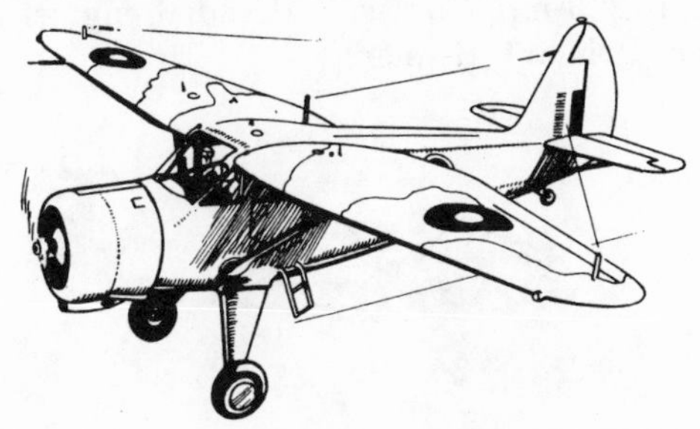

STINSON AT-10 Military version of the Stinson Reliant. Lend-leased to Britain and Russia as navigational trainer.

STEARMAN N2S-5 (Air Force designation: PT-17) 220-h.p. Continental radial engine. Widely used primary trainer of World War II.

RYAN S-TM 125-h.p. inverted Menasco engine. Primary trainer.

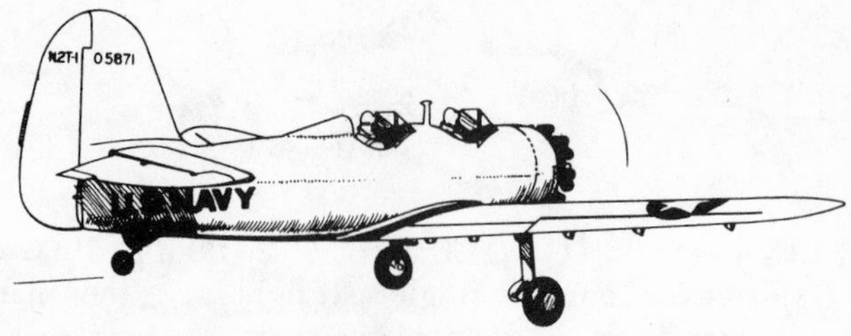

TIMM N2T-1 220-h.p. Continental radial engine. All-wood construction. Primary trainer.

FAIRCHILD PT-23 220-h.p. Lycoming radial. A variant of the lower-powered PT-19 primary trainer.

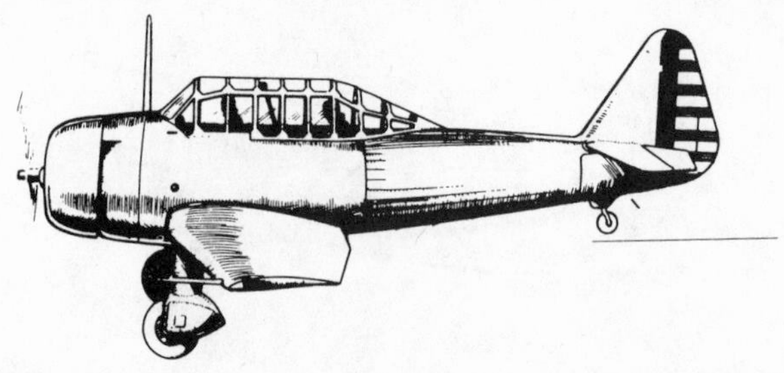

FLEETWINGS BT-12 450-h.p. P. & W. radial. Basic trainer in limited use.

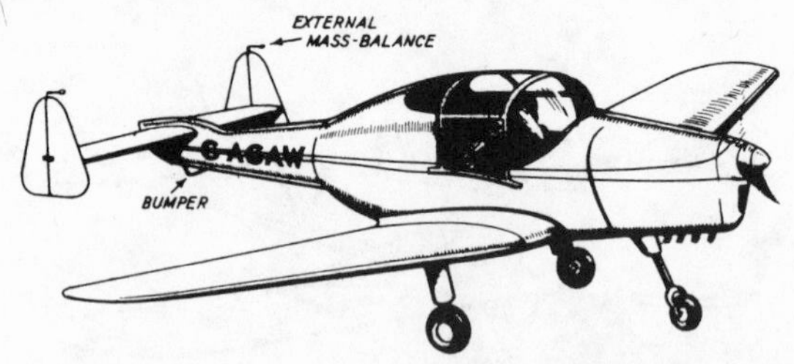

GENERAL AIRCRAFT "CYGNET" 150-h.p. inverted Cirrus engine. A civil type resembling U.S. Ercoupe used as military trainer.

MARTIN B-26 "MARAUDER" Two 2,000-h.p. P. & W. radials. Medium bomber that could carry large bomb loads, or formidable ground attack bomber.

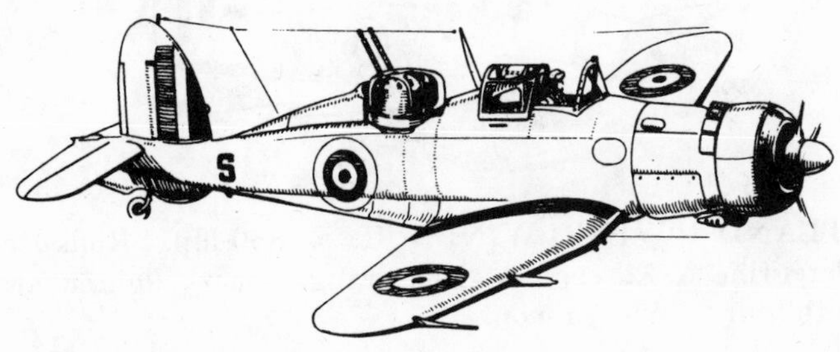

BLACKBURN ROC 905-h.p. radial engine. British Navy two-seat fighter, a poor design not much used in the war. Its cousin, the Blackburn Skua, was similar except for power turret.

NORTH AMERICAN B-25 "MITCHELL" There were many variants of this design. Earlier model with plexi-nose was first to bomb Tokyo; 75-mm. cannon armed version was used in Pacific against Jap destroyers.

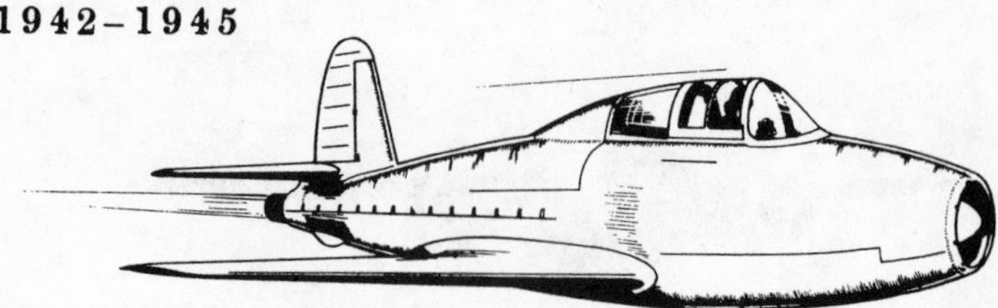

GLOSTER E.28/39 First Allied plane to be jet-powered. This was not a service fighter but a flying test bed for the new Whittle jet engine.

WESTLAND "WHIRLWIND" Two 850-h.p. Rolls-Royce Peregrine V-12 engines. Long-range escort fighter armed with four 20-mm. cannon.

VOUGHT F4U "CORSAIR" 2,000-h.p. P. & W. Double Wasp. One of the most formidable carrier-based fighters and fighter-bombers used by the U.S. Navy in World War II. This crank-wing fighter was reactivated for service in the Korean war.

GRUMMAN F4F-4 "WILDCAT" 1,200-h.p. Wright or P. & W. engine. This carrier-based fighter was stand-by during early Pacific war.

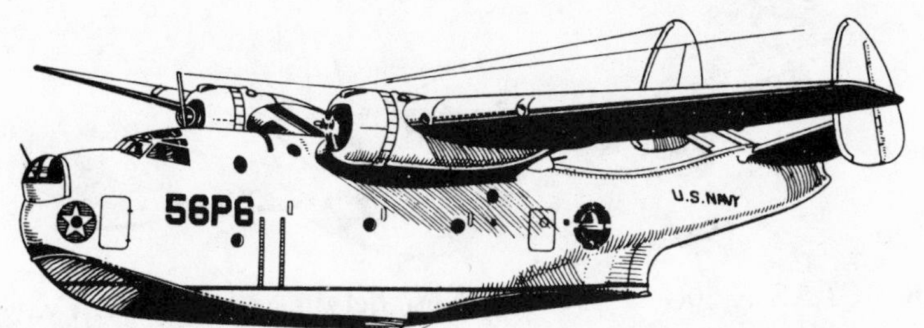

MARTIN PBM-3 "MARINER" Four 1,600-h.p. Wright Cyclones. Like the "Catalina," this large Navy patrol boat was a pre-1941 design.

HAWKER "TEMPEST V" 2,400-h.p. Napier Sabre H-type engine. One of the fastest and most formidable World War II fighters. Used with great success against the buzz bombs in Britain.

DOUGLAS SBD-4 "DAUNTLESS" Carrier-based dive-bomber. At beginning of Pacific war it was mainstay of U.S. Naval aviation. 1,200-h.p. radial.

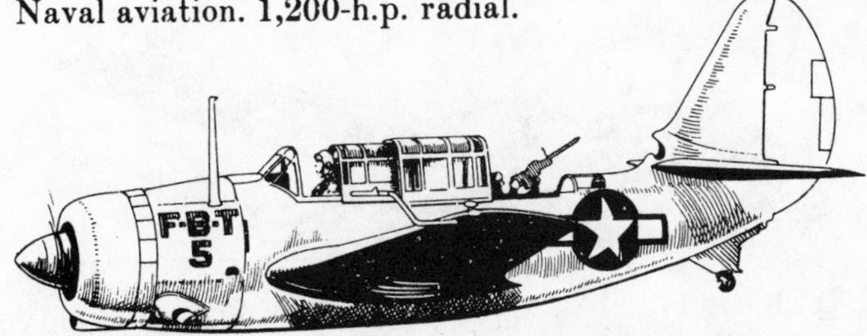

CURTISS SB2C "HELLDIVER" 1,600-h.p. Wright radial. Carrier-based dive-bomber. Saw extensive service with U.S. Navy throughout Pacific war.

DOUGLAS A-20G "HAVOC" Nose details and armament varied on this ground attack bomber used by U.S.A.A.F., R.A.F., and the Russian air arm in World War II.

DOUGLAS A-26 "INVADER" Two 2,000-h.p. P. & W. radials. One of the fastest and most heavily armed attack-bombers produced in World War II. Redesignated after the war as B-26—all-purpose medium bomber.

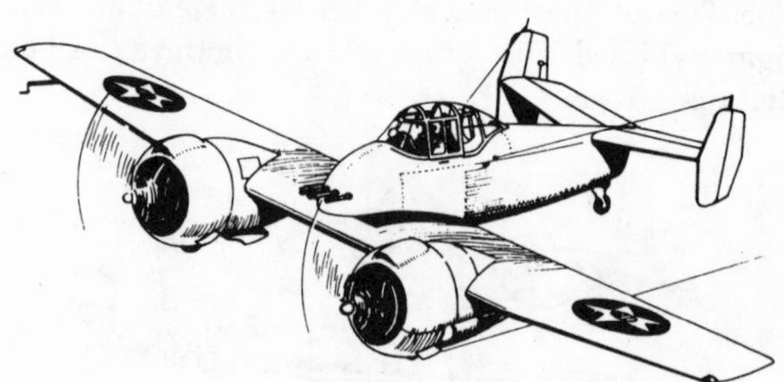

GRUMMAN F5F "SKYROCKET" Was an experimental twin-engine Navy fighter and ancestor of the Grumman F7F "Tigercat."

DORNIER Do.17z Two 1,000-h.p. Bramo 323 radial air-cooled engines. This plane was predecessor of the famous 217 series extensively used by the *Luftwaffe*.

AVRO "LANCASTER 1" Four 1,280-h.p. Rolls-Royce engines. Largest R.A.F. bomber of World War II. Could carry large bomb load, including famed 10-tonner "blockbuster." With crew of 7 and full load, it hit 300 m.p.h.

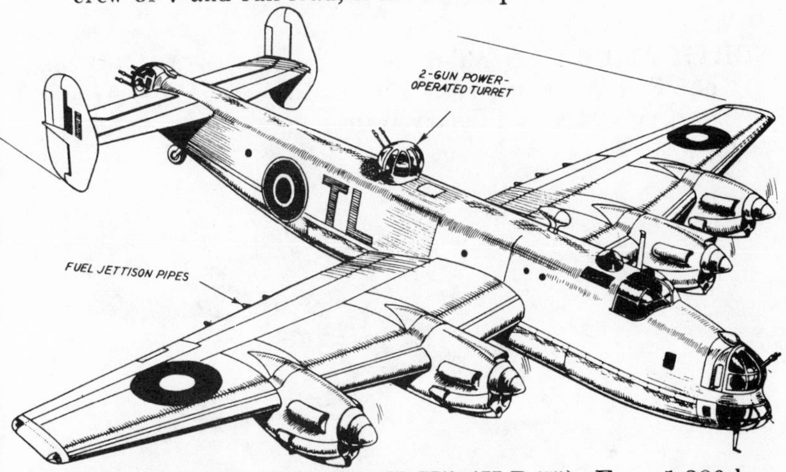

HANDLEY PAGE "HALIFAX II" (H.P.57) Four 1,280-h.p. Rolls-Royce engines. One of the best long-range heavy bombers used by the R.A.F. in World War II. Heavy defensive armament was feature of all British bombers.

AVRO "LINCOLN" Four 1,760-h.p. Rolls-Royce Merlins. Intended to replace the Lancaster bomber, it carried up to 11 tons of bombs. In production during closing days of World War II.

NORTH AMERICAN AT-6 (Navy designation: SNJ-4) 600-h.p. P. & W. radial. Widely used advanced trainer. After the war, classed as a primary trainer.

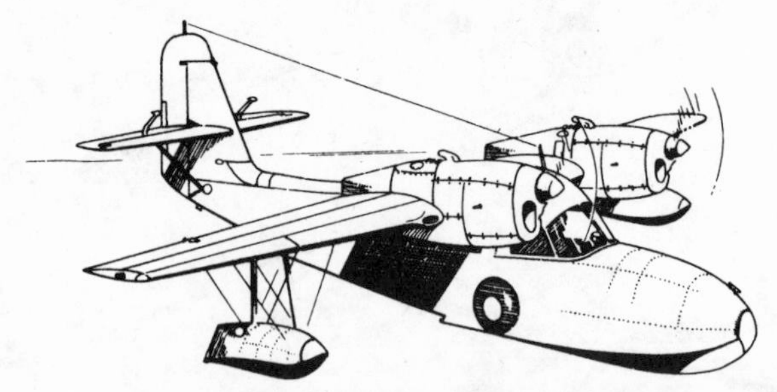

GRUMMAN J4F-1 "WIDGEON" Two 200-h.p. Ranger engines. (The civil version, G-44, appeared in 1939.) Used as rescue plane by U.S. Navy.

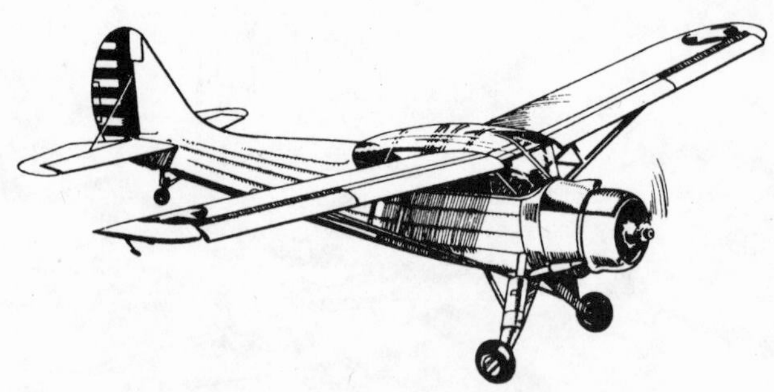

STINSON L-1 "VIGILANT" 280-h.p. Lycoming engine. One of the many light aircraft used by the U.S.A.A.F. for liaison and observation purposes in World War II.

FOCKE-WULF Fw.190 1,800-h.p. B.M.W. radial engine. Top Nazi single-seat piston-engine fighter of World War II. First to employ a cockpit canopy that may be jettisoned.

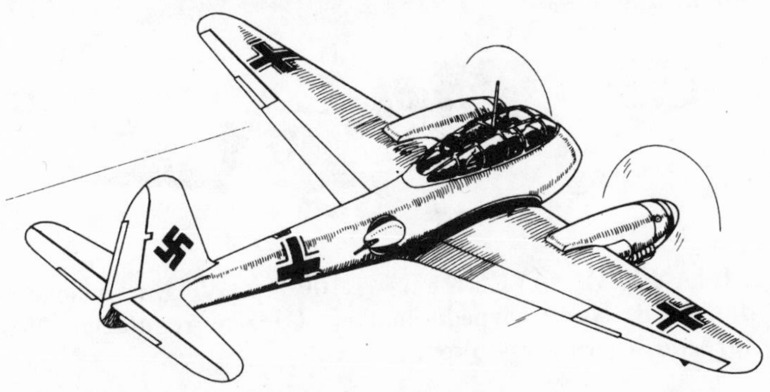

MESSERSCHMITT Me.410 Final evolution of the Me.110, this fighter-bomber had a top speed of 380 m.p.h.

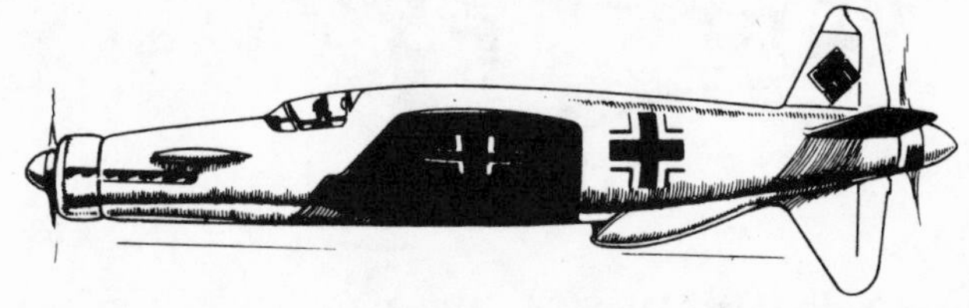

DORNIER Do.335A Radical tandem-engine day and night fighter. With a top speed of 475 m.p.h., it was fastest piston-engine fighter produced during the war. Night-fighter version seated two.

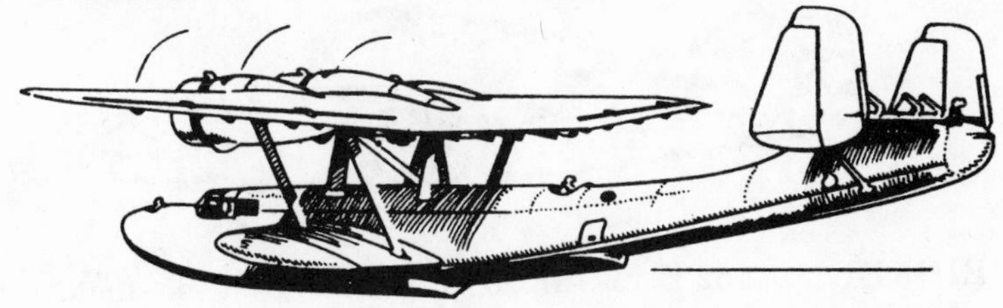

DORNIER Do.24 Three 880-h.p. B.M.W. engines. This and the four-engine Do.26 were final developments of the Do.WAL.

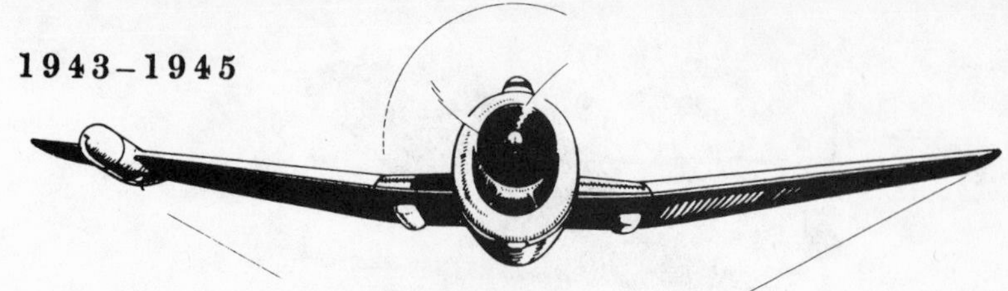

GRUMMAN F6F-5N "HELLCAT" 2,000-h.p. P. & W. double Wasp radial. Carrier-based Navy night fighter. First low-wing Grumman single-engine fighter and scourge of the Jap air arm in 1944-45.

GRUMMAN TBF "AVENGER" 1,700-h.p. Wright Cyclone radial. U.S. Navy torpedo-bomber. Carried regulation Navy torpedo internally stowed.

AMERICAN P-51D "MUSTANG" 1,490-h.p. Packard Merlin engine. Top U.S. single-seat fighter in World War II, it had a top speed of about 435 m.p.h. and was operational as late as the Korean war.

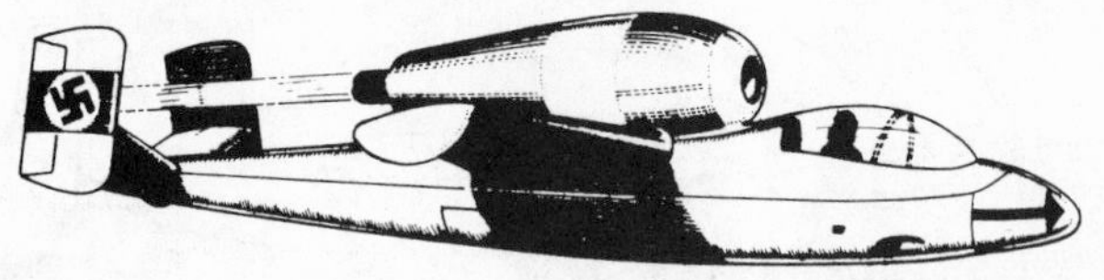

HEINKEL He.162A "VOLKSJAEGER" Last of the *Luftwaffe*'s jet fighters, it had a maximum speed of about 490 m.p.h.

GLOSTER "METEOR" Twin-jet fighter. Only Allied jet in World War II, it saw limited service in Britain and Belgium and was chiefly directed against enemy buzz bombs.

MESSERSCHMITT Me.163 Rocket-propelled interceptor-fighter. Duration: 8 minutes; speed: about 580 m.p.h, Catapult-launched, it landed on central skid. Armed with four cannon.

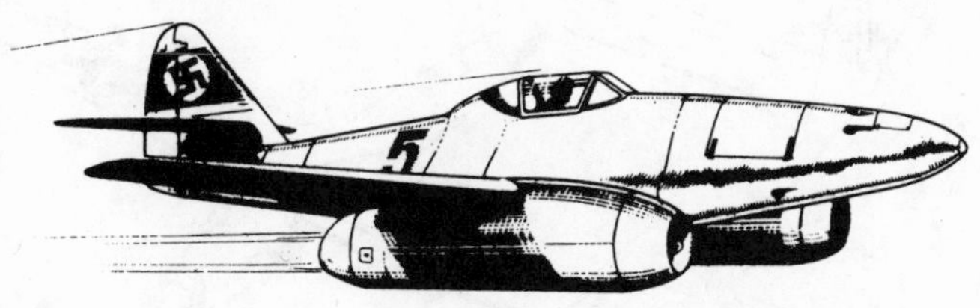

MESSERSCHMITT Me.262 Two Junkers Jumo jet engines. First operational jet fighter in the world. Maximum speed 500 m.p.h. plus.

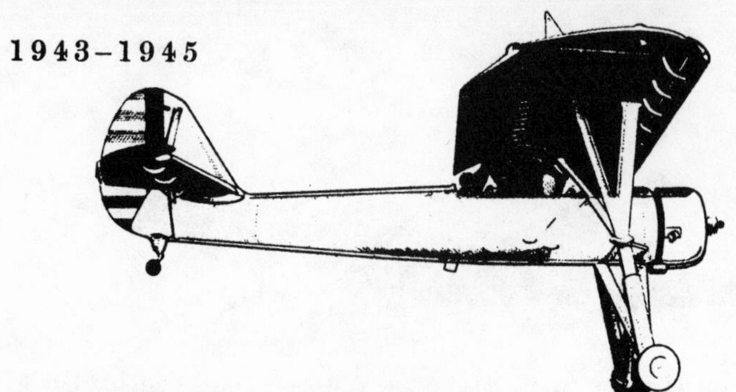

RYAN YO-51 "DRAGONFLY" 450-h.p. P. & W. Wasp. U.S. equivalent of the Fiesler "Storch." With full-span flaps and slots it could fly at very low speeds.

CAPRONI-CAMPINI First jet plane in the world to make a cross-country flight. Powered with a conventional gasoline engine driving a 2-stage compressor. Top speed: about 176 m.p.h.

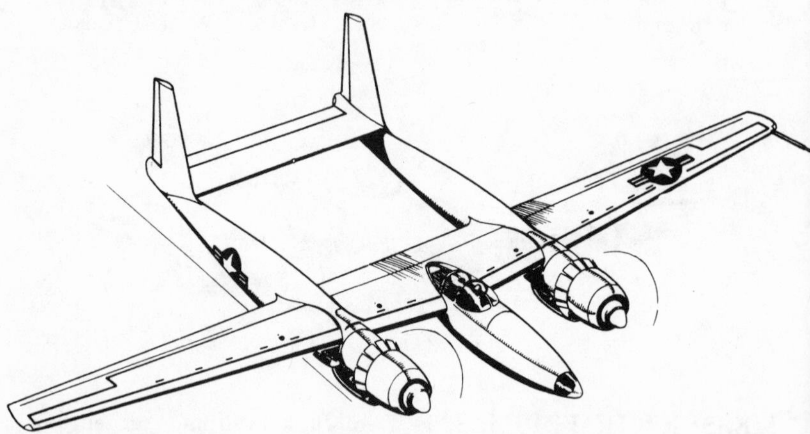

HUGHES XF-11 Two 3,000-h.p. P. & W. radials driving contrarotating propellers. This experimental photo-reconnaissance plane mounted 8 cameras.

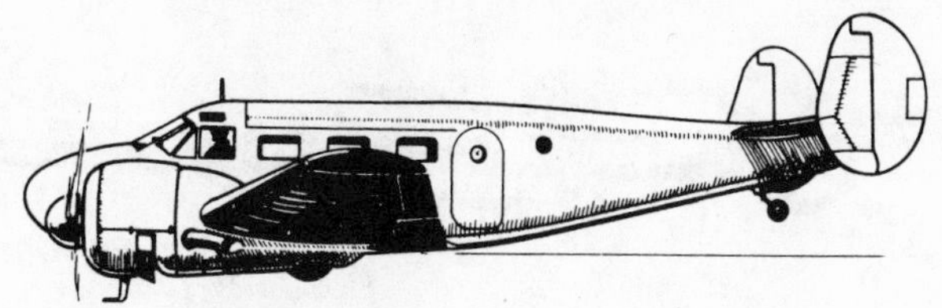

BEECH 18S Two 450-h.p. P. & W. radials. As the C-45 it was used in various forms throughout the war as a medium transport (prewar design).

CURTISS C-46 "COMMANDO" Twin-engine U.S. military transport widely used during the war, particularly in flying the "Hump" in China. As a war-surplus transport, it was still in use as late as 1953.

MESSERSCHMITT Me.323 One of the largest troop transports employed by the *Luftwaffe*—notably in ferrying troops to North Africa. It was more of a 6-engine converted glider than a normal airplane. Span: 181 feet. Carried 130 men.

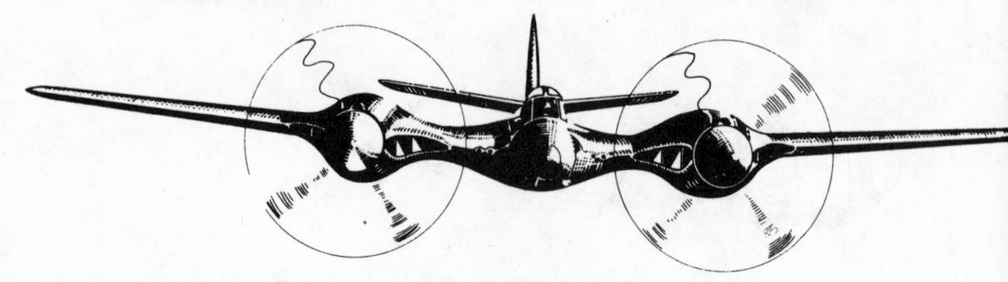

McDONNELL XP-67 Two 1,250-h.p. Continental engines. Experimental twin-engine high-altitude fighter with pressurized cockpit.

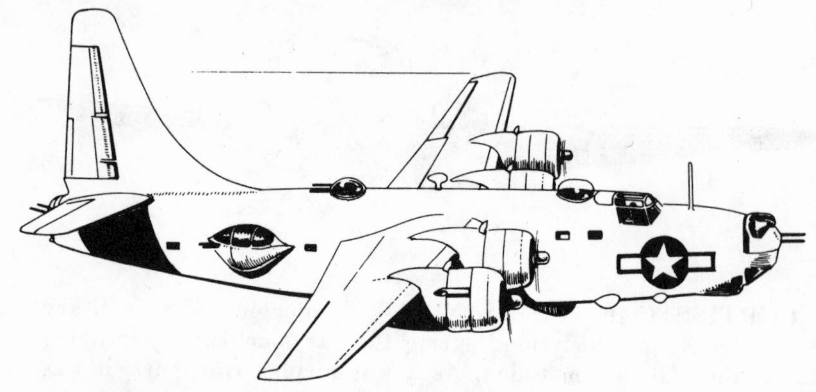

CONSOLIDATED PB4Y-2 "PRIVATEER" Four 1,200-h.p. P. & W. radials. U.S. Navy land-based patrol bomber.

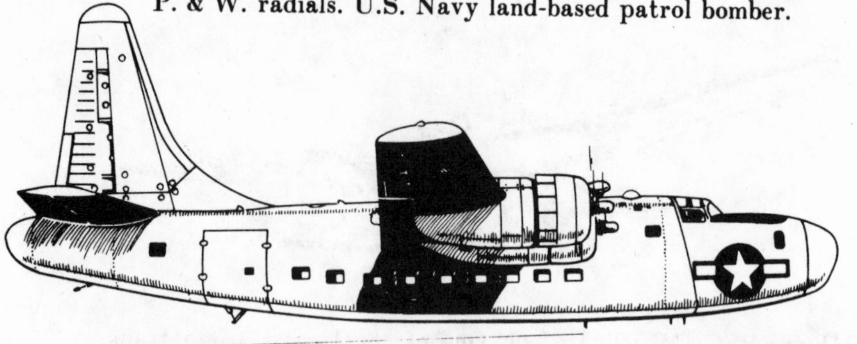

CONSOLIDATED RY3 Navy transport version of the "Privateer" patrol bomber was unarmed. It could carry up to 10,000 pounds of cargo or personnel.

GRUMMAN F7F-3N "TIGERCAT" Twin-engine Marine fighter. The 2-seat night-fighter version used by the Marines is shown here.

GRUMMAN F8F "BEARCAT" 2,500-h.p. P. & W. radial. Most powerful and fastest of the "Cat" series. In production at close of the war.

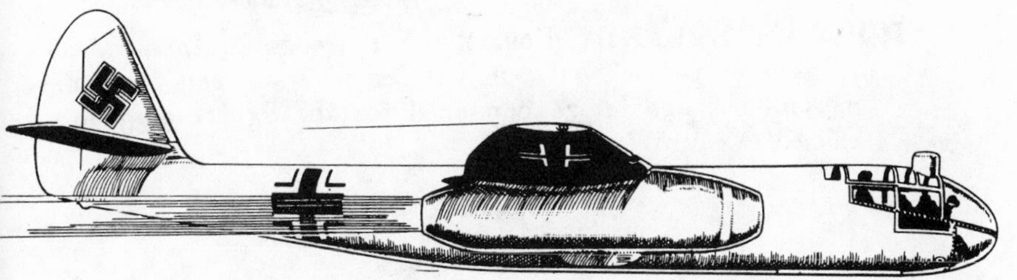

ARADO Ar.234 Four-jet reconnaissance and tactical bomber. In production at end of the war, it had a top speed of 475-540 m.p.h.

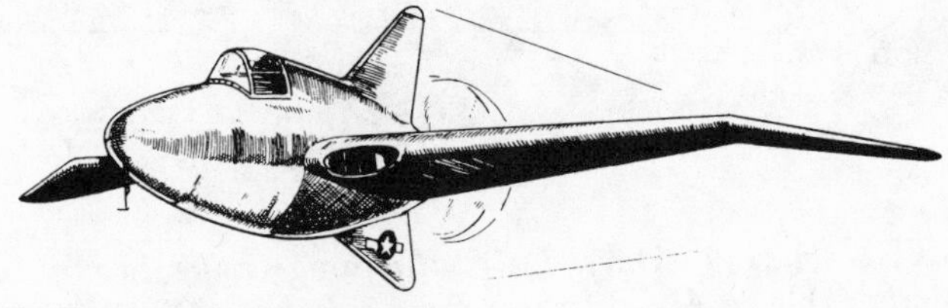

NORTHROP XP-56 2,000-h.p. P. & W. radial-driving pusher prop. Experimental tailless fighter based on previous flying-wing experiments by this firm.

CURTISS SC-1 "SEA HAWK" Shipboard scout reconnaissance; catapult-launched from cruisers and battleships. Replaced Chance Vought types.

SHORT "SHETLAND" Four 2,425-h.p. engines. Intended as long-range patrol boat but modified at war's end for commercial use and later abandoned for the lighter and more efficient "Solent."

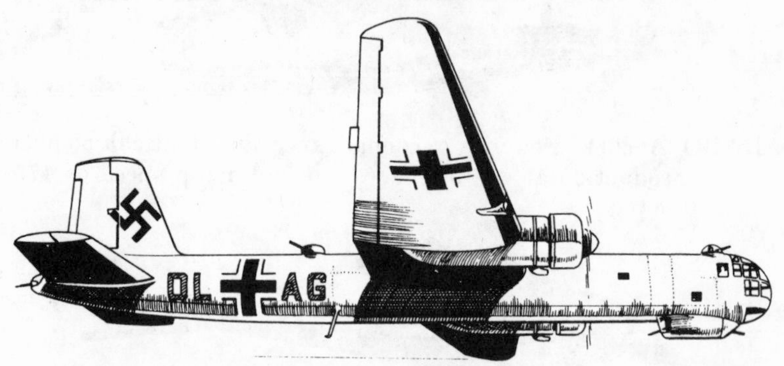

HEINKEL He.177 Only *Luftwaffe* long-range heavy bomber comparable to Allied types. Twin side-by-side engines in each nacelle-driving single propeller.

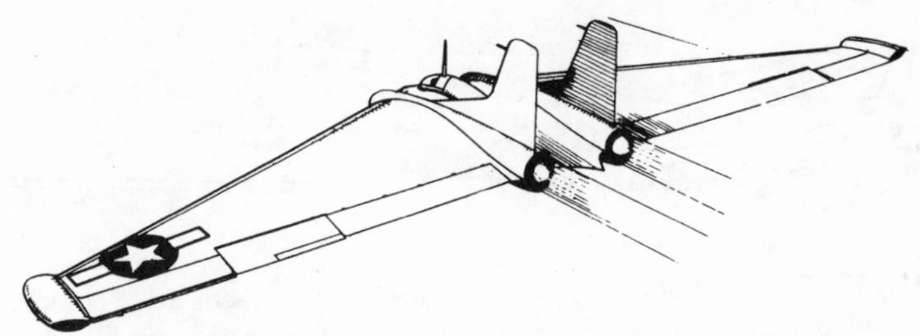

NORTHROP XP-79B Two Westinghouse 19b jet engines. Experimental tailless fighter featured prone pilot position, was towed into flight.

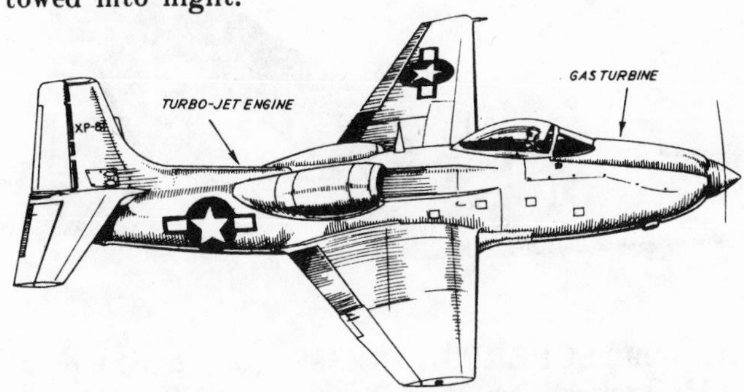

CONVAIR (VULTEE) XP-81 General Electric J-33 jet engine. World's first turbo-prop plus jet-powered fighter. This 4,000-h.p. fighter was not operational in actual war.

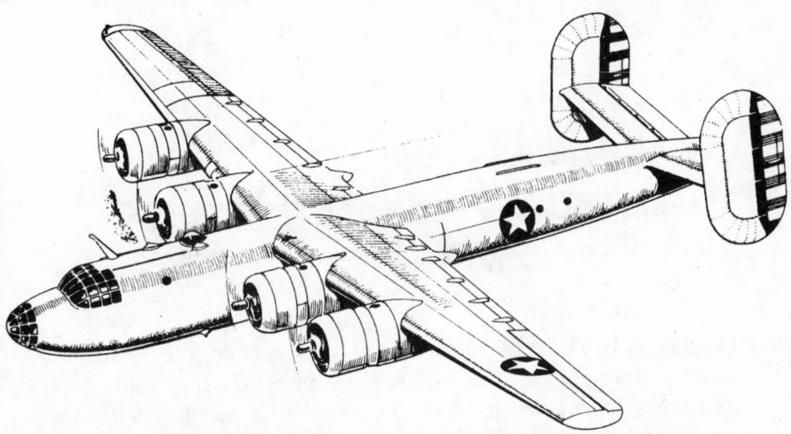

CONVAIR XB-32 Prototype of B-32 "Dominator." Pressurized fuselage and twin-rudder configuration were eliminated on production model.

JUNKERS Ju.290 Very large *Luftwaffe* 4-engine transport; also employed as a long-range spotter against Allied convoys. (Goering's personal plane.)

BOEING B-29 "SUPERFORTRESS" Four 2,200-h.p. Wright radials. Largest bomber of World War II, it carried the war into the heart of Japan and did much to reduce that nation into submission. First aircraft in the world to employ remote-control power-operated gun turrets.

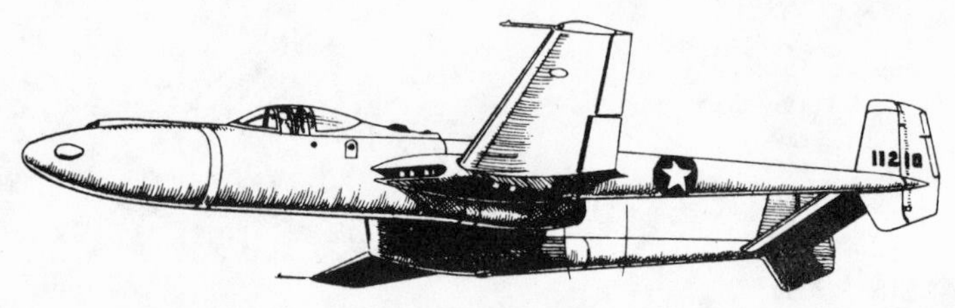

CONVAIR XP-54 2,300-h.p. flat Lycoming engine; contrarotating propellers. Still in the experimental stage, this was a Vultee project when that company was merged with Consolidated Aircraft Company.

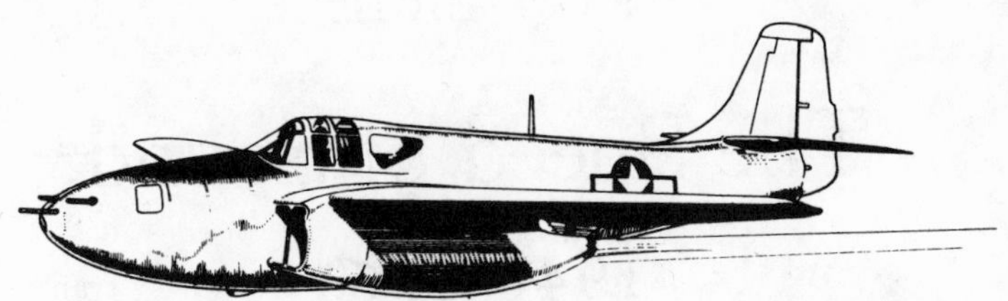

BELL P-59A "AIRACOMET" First U.S. jet fighter (but not operational). It was powered with two General Electric 1-16 engines developed from a British Whittle turbo-jet flown over from England.

CHASE CG-14A All-wood troop-carrying glider accommodated 16 armed men.

STINSON L-5 "SENTINEL" 185-h.p. Lycoming opposed engine. Had phenomenal take-off qualities. The original "Flying Jeep" and first U.S. airplane to land on Iwo Jima.

PART EIGHT

The Speed of Sound

1946-1951

THE MAN couldn't believe it. Yesterday, in the excitement of V-J Day, he hadn't been able to contact Eula Brooks. Phone service in Santa Monica seemed all tied up, including that at the big aircraft plant where she worked. But he'd been dating the girl practically every day for two years! And now the landlady had just told him: "Eula? Why, she's packed up and gone back to Iowa."

With that same kind of suddenness, plane production in the U.S. came to a halt with the end of hostilities. In 1946 only 1,669 military aircraft were produced. The disarmament process wrecked our air power for several years to come.

However, public demand for air transportation skyrocketed. The return to the air lines of their war-loaned planes failed to meet the need, which called for larger and faster craft. So there appeared the passenger version of the DC-4, the Lockheed "Constellation," the big DC-6, and the Boeing "Stratocruiser" that had begun life as the C-97 able to carry a hundred fully equipped soldiers. This quartet of four-engine transports marked a new era in air travel. They seated from 50 to 70 passengers, had fully pressurized cabins complete with lounges, and all cruised at around 300 m.p.h. With the new Instrument Landing System and Ground-Controlled Approach radar developed in the war, they could fly in weather that would have canceled flight in pre-Pearl Harbor days.

In addition to these luxurious big transports, vastly improved two-engine air liners made by Convair and Martin began to report for duty on the expanding networks.

As after the First World War, private flying increased—though not in the "plane for every family" way so rosily predicted. Surplus craft of all kinds were bought. Bucking this market, a number of manufacturers went in for the personal plane—if only to keep their key workers. North American introduced the "Navion," a four-passenger personal with retractable landing gear that obviously was related to the company's "Mustang"; Republic floated out the four-place Sea Bee amphibian.

Despite its commitment to a program of minor orders for military planes, the government realized it could not afford to lag far behind in jet propulsion and asked various companies to institute research in sonic speed possibilities. The first U.S. research high-speed aircraft—meaning 500 or more miles an hour—was the Bell XS-1 (Experimental Sonic). It had an extremely thin straight wing, was powered by four rocket engines. With the duration of fuel only two to five minutes, it was built to be carried aloft tucked underneath a B-29 and then released at high altitude, whereupon its pilot would fire his rockets. The initial flight, however, was without the use of power, the XS-1 being merely glided to learn flying and landing characteristics.

After this war, Germany had been temporarily prohibited from flying even model airplanes, much less gliders. France, still reeling from the effects of Nazi occupation, had to resort to glider building to prevent the demise of its aircraft industry. But Russia was investigating the data on jets "liberated" from the Nazis, and England's progress in this field led the world. She had two jet fighters in service, the twin-boom De Havilland "Vampire" and the Gloster "Meteor." The latter was the first plane to touch 600 m.p.h., which it did on several occasions.

And then it happened. At Muroc in 1947 the Bell XS-1, later known as the X-1, cracked the speed of sound with the Air Force's then Capt. Charles Yeager in the cockpit. (The speed of sound is 1,100 feet per second at sea level at 59° F., or approximately 762 m.p.h.) At the same time Douglas was in the midst of building a supersonic jet job, the D-588-1 "Skystreak," and Northrop had the tailless X-4 research plane on the board. Now the experiments were shifting into high gear—and trouble.

As airplanes neared the point of sonic speed, they began to yaw and roll and cut other weird didos. The culprit was the "shock wave," which so disturbed the air flowing over the wings and tail that it became extremely turbulent, upsetting the lift as well as the control characteristics of the aircraft. Use of exceptionally thin wings helped some, and the "swept-back" or arrowhead-shape wing helped even more. But much work lay ahead to achieve the necessary stability at such high speeds. The Northrop Company, even before war's end, had been experimenting successfully with the "flying wing" type of airplane, which did away with tail and fuselage and concentrated everything in the wing. Now, they modified their huge XB-35 bomber in this category to take eight jet engines, but the resulting YB-49 proved too unstable.

It was Russia's clearly inimical attitude toward the democratic world and the U.S. in particular that caused America to start building up its air power again in 1948. Even if Russia weren't known to have jet aircraft, which it did, plans and training procedure called for immediate conversion of our air arm along the new high-speed lines. The plants began to hum.

Since we might find ourselves without overseas bases in case of war with our potential enemy, a major need was felt to be a fast, long-range bomber. Consolidated Vultee solved the range with the mammoth B-36, which first came out with six piston engines and later acquired four turbo-jets in addition. Then the world's largest bomber, it was capable of flying as much as 5,000 miles with a 10,000-pound bomb load and returning. This plane on its appearance met with criticism about its vulnerability: with a top speed of only 435 m.p.h., and lacking the protection of jet fighters because of the latter's limited range, the B-36 would be a sitting duck for the faster enemy fighters, or so it was claimed.

Consolidated Vultee also designed and built the world's first "delta-wing" fighter, whose radical triangle-shape wing was expected to prove effective in the supersonic realm. And Boeing answered the call for air power with the B-47 "Stratojet," world's fastest bomber. Its sharply swept wing, unusually clean form, and six jet engines put it in the "over 600 m.p.h." class —a speed equal to that of the advanced fighter. Like the B-36 and the B-45 four-jet light bomber, the "Stratojet" could carry the atom bomb. Before long the Air Force was in a position to list eight or nine jet fighters, including the F-86 and F-84, and the Navy had four.

The high-speed airplane was rapidly becoming a Frankenstein monster. Day by day it grew in complexity. Man was flying faster than he could think, faster than his reflexes could function. More and more artificial means had to be installed to think for him, or to take over.

At the new speeds a pilot did not have time to spot the enemy, aim, and shoot, so radar found the other plane and the automatic gunsight did the aiming and told him when to fire. (The electrical wiring alone in today's bomber would stretch for 40 miles.) Since the air pressure on the plane's control surfaces was so great that at 600 m.p.h. it would require the strength of a hundred men to move them, hydraulic power had to be applied through stick, wheel, and rudder pedals. For a pilot to bail out in the rushing gale at jet speed was either impossible or suicide; this necessitated a special ejection seat, with a 37-mm. cartridge underneath that literally fired him into the air, seat and all.

There also rose the problems of physical effect on the pilot. Flying at altitudes of 40,000 feet required the military plane's cabin to be fully pressurized. Suffering from the heat was no small item. At 650 m.p.h. the heat created by the friction of the plane's outer surfaces cutting through the air could raise the temperature inside to 125° F. Every bomber and fighter therefore had to be equipped with a refrigeration system. (It was not uncommon, when the system wouldn't keep pace with the sudden changes in altitude and pressure, for snow flurries to pass through the "office.")

The already crowded living conditions in the cockpit got more and more so. The home of the fighter pilot was being furnished with still more dials, levers, buttons, winking lights, and a variety of "magic boxes." And his bulky costume made for even less room. . . . "If it gets much worse," commented a fighter pilot in Korea, "they'll have to breed a special race of midgets to fly these here things." A squadron mate retorted, "No, the trouble is, aeronautical engineers just don't like people. Pretty soon these here things will take off, fly, fight, and come back with *nobody* at the stick." As a matter of fact, an experimental job has been built which will do exactly that.

But attendant problems did not slow down jet experimentation. The stakes were too large, the goal too enticingly limitless. The promising delta wing was being readied for its debut in military planes. The U.S. had one such craft under construction, though in modified form—the Vought F7U "Cutlass." England put a couple of experimental deltas into the air, built by Avro and Fairey. As part of her program of refurbishing its transport fleet, which now included the Bristol "Brabazon" air liner, roughly the size of the B-36, England also was trying jet propulsion on for size in commercial planes and was the world's pioneer in this respect. France was producing its first jet, and Italy was taking up where it had left off. Rumors seeping out of Russia indicated the USSR was well on its way to catching up with England and America in reaction propulsion.

The Korean war beginning in the summer of 1950 meant the heavy involvement of the airplane in conflict for the third time since its birth less than half a century before. Unlike the other two, this war contributed little in the way of major progress as far as the plane itself was concerned. It did, however, answer many questions on the merits of the jet and the helicopter in battle. Both had as yet been untried, and both covered themselves with glory.

Long before the start of the "Police Action," the U.S. had planes on the board and in the assembly line far in advance of anything it would need to use in Korea. The famous F-86 "Sabre" jet was already in limited production in 1950. It was then the most magnificent fighter in existence. Though at first maligned because it was a trifle slower in speed and rate of climb than the Russian MiG-15, its combat ability cannot be disputed in the face of its superior record of 14-to-1 ratio of kills over the MiG. And along with the decisive performance of such fighter-bombers as the Republic F-84 "Thunderjet," the Lockheed F-80 "Shooting Star," and the Navy's "Skyknight" and "Banshee," it helped show in practical application that piston-engine planes were indeed outmoded.

The helicopter proved itself in truly heroic fashion. On hundreds of mercy missions these unarmed and most vulnerable craft landed behind the lines to evacuate wounded GI's or crashed pilots pinned down by enemy fire, or snatched Navy pilots from death in the icy waters of the Sea of Japan. The helicopter's service as an "aerial truck" was highlighted by its feat in kidnaping a MiG. Settling beside one of these downed enemy planes, a Sikorsky H-19 transport and cargo 'copter disgorged a salvage crew that dismantled the MiG, partly with the aid of hand grenades. Despite Red flak, the lumbering H-19 reached its rendezvous at an island off the coast, and the Communist plane was shipped to the U.S. for evaluation.

As the war progressed it was evident that speed could mean survival more than ever, and back in America the quest for it and for better planes continued without letup. At Muroc, now renamed Edwards Air Force Base, various advance-type jets and turbo-prop aircraft were undergoing tests. (The turbo-prop—wherein the jet engine drives a propeller—had advantages in better take-off characteristics and fuel economy in the lower speed ranges.) Douglas had at Muroc the XF4D-1 "Skyray," a bobtailed fighter with deltalike wings. Martin sent its **XB-51** ground attack bomber with two jets mounted beneath the fuselage and a third one in the tail; this plane had a wing whose angle of incidence could be varied.

Another Douglas plane being given tryouts was its **D-558-II** "Skyrocket." On one of its flights, with test pilot Bill Bridgeman at the controls, this jet attained the incredible speed of 1,238 miles an hour at the altitude of 79,494 feet. Two years later, Marine Colonel Marion Carle exceeded Bridgeman's altitude record by reaching the height of over 85,000 feet in the same plane.

GLOSTER "METEOR IV" First standard R.A.F. jet fighter. Established world's speed record of 606 m.p.h. in 1946. Two Rolls-Royce Derwent jet engines.

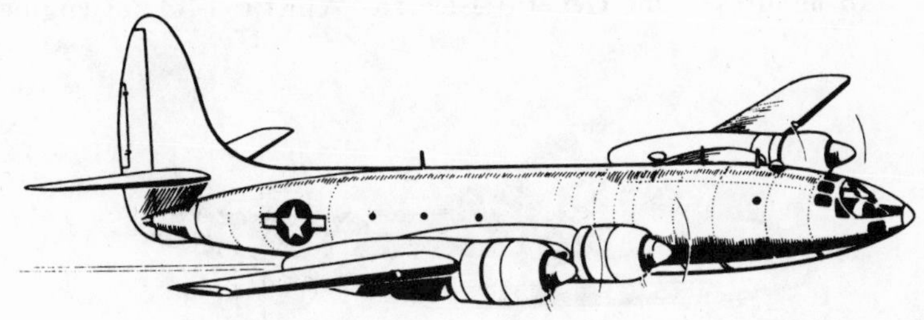

REPUBLIC XF-12 "RAINBOW" Long-range photo-reconnaissance plane under construction at close of the war. Only two built (both crashed). Unusual in that the four 3,000-h.p. P. & W. engines had turbo-boost thrust.

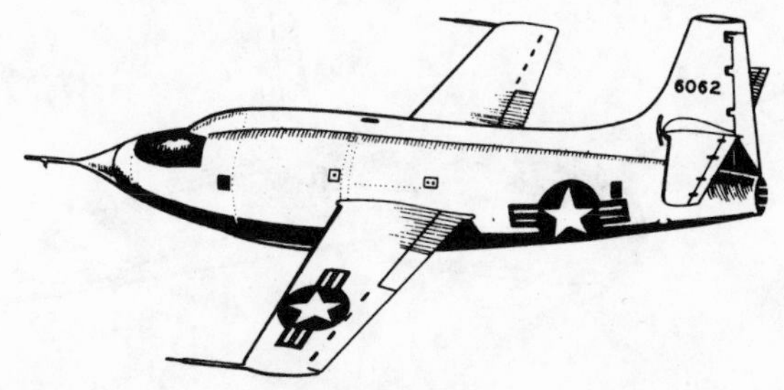

BELL X-1 "SKYROCKET" First airplane to reach the speed of sound. 4-nozzle 6,000-pound-thrust rocket engine.

LOCKHEED P.80 "SHOOTING STAR" First U.S. operational fighter. Set new West-East coast-to-coast record (4 hours, 13 minutes). One General Electric–Whittle J-33 jet engine.

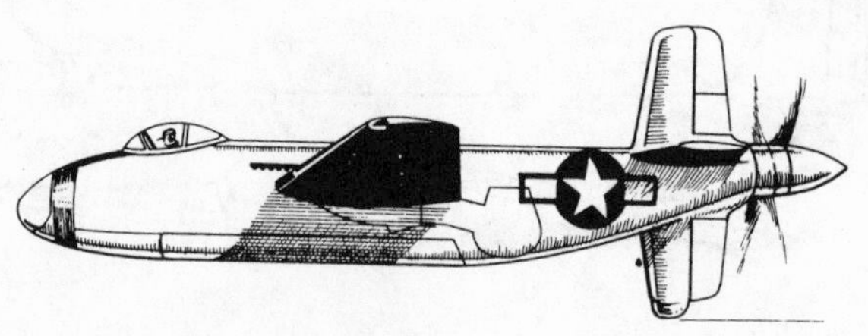

DOUGLAS XB-42 "MIXMASTER" Experimental pusher-type medium bomber. Two 1,800-h.p. Allison engines; contrarotating propellers.

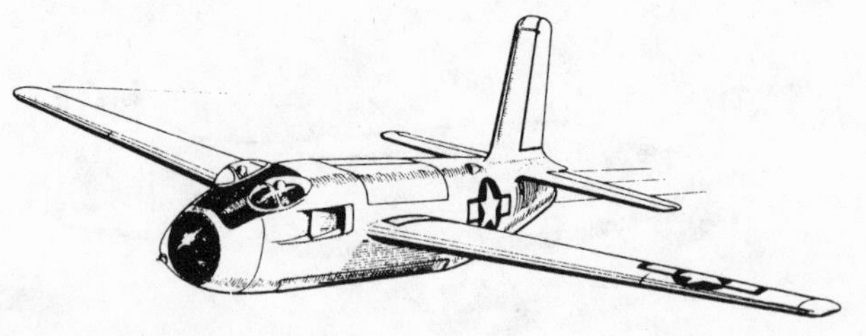

DOUGLAS XB-43 First U.S. jet bomber. Same air frame as XB-42. Two General Electric TG.180 jet engines.

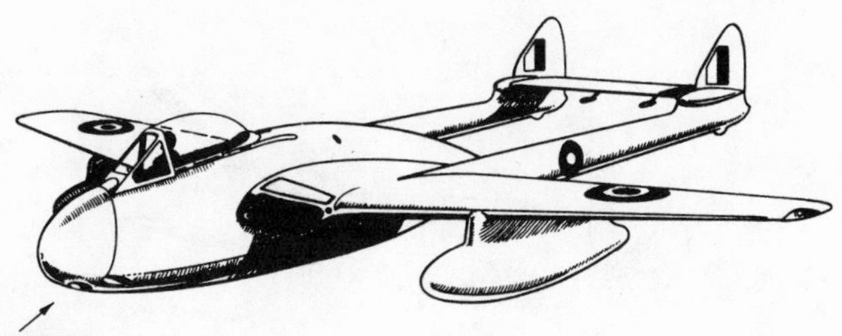

DE HAVILLAND D.H. 100 "VAMPIRE" Second R.A.F. operational jet fighter. First jet aircraft to operate from a carrier at sea and first to make an Atlantic crossing (1948).

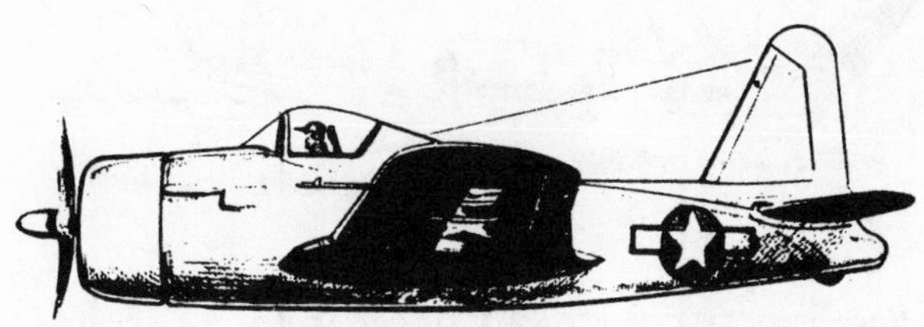

RYAN FR-1 "FIREBALL" Composite piston-engine jet shipboard fighter. 1,350-h.p. Wright radial-driving propeller; General Electric I-16 jet in tail.

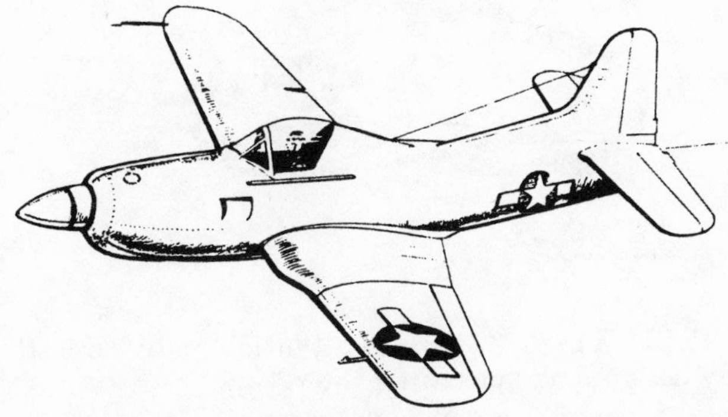

RYAN XF2R "Dark Shark" Turboprop engine in the nose and jet engine in rear of fuselage. Advanced development of "Fireball."

McDONNELL RTV-2 "GARGOYLE" Experimental ground-to-air guided missile with 1,000-pound war head and proximity fuse.

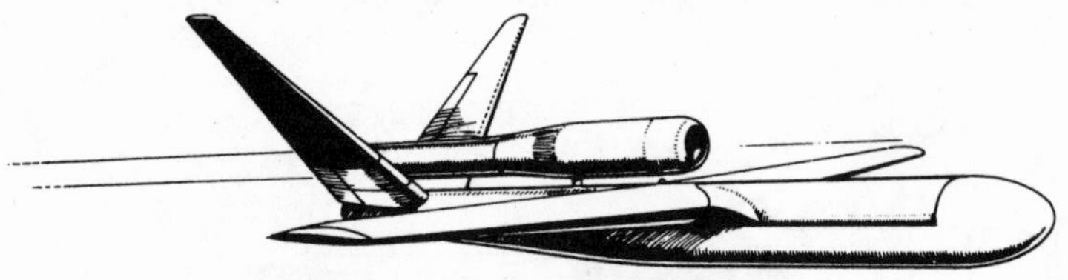

McDONNELL KDH-1 "KATYDID" Radio-controlled target drone with dorsally mounted reso-jet engine. For air-to-air target practice.

McDONNELL XF-85 "GOBLIN" World's only aircraft specially designed as "parasite fighter."

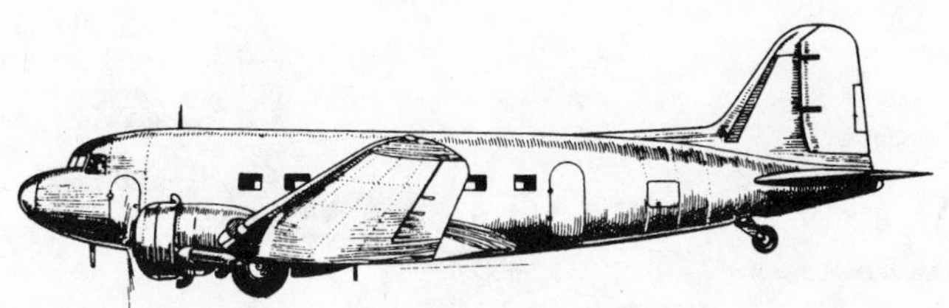

DOUGLAS DC-3 One of the world's truly great airplanes. It appeared in 1936 and immediately became the world's top air liner. As the C-47 it served throughout the war as a military transport and after the war formed the backbone of civil aviation both here and abroad. It is still—more than thirty years after its debut—in service all over the world.

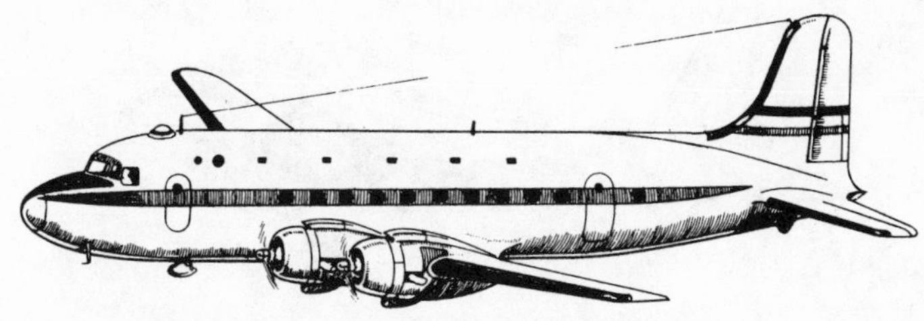

DOUGLAS DC-4 First Douglas 4-engine air liner, it appeared in 1939 and has a record paralleling that of the DC-3. Still active.

DOUGLAS DC-6 A postwar design. In effect, a larger, more powerful version of the DC-4.

LOCKHEED "CONSTELLATION" First 4-engine Lockheed air liner. Served as a military transport during the war. One of the world's best air liners and used by all major air lines here and abroad.

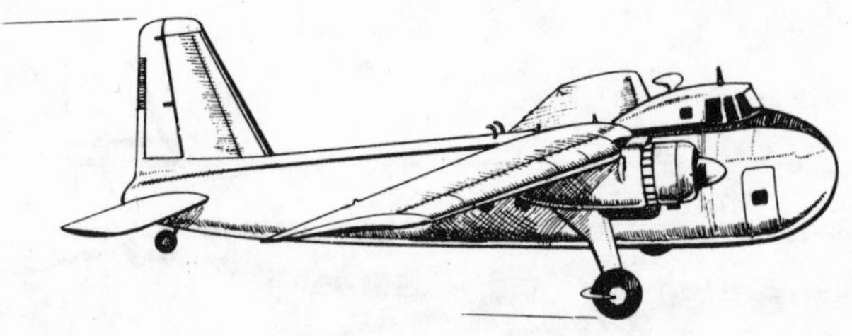

BRISTOL "FREIGHTER" A successful postwar cargo plane by one of the pioneer aircraft companies. Used chiefly as a car ferry between England and the Continent.

SHORT "SOLENT" Last of the big Empire boats. Four 1,700-h.p. radials. Double-deck arrangement accommodated 30 passengers.

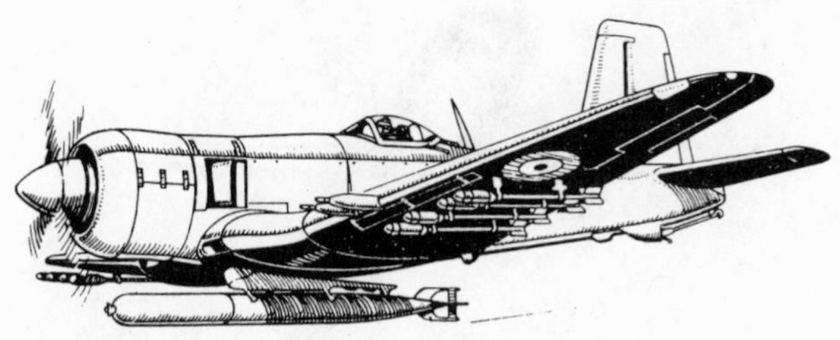

BLACKBURN "FIREBRAND V" Postwar British Navy strike fighter. 2,500-h.p. engine. Heavily armed with cannon, rockets, and either torpedo or bombs.

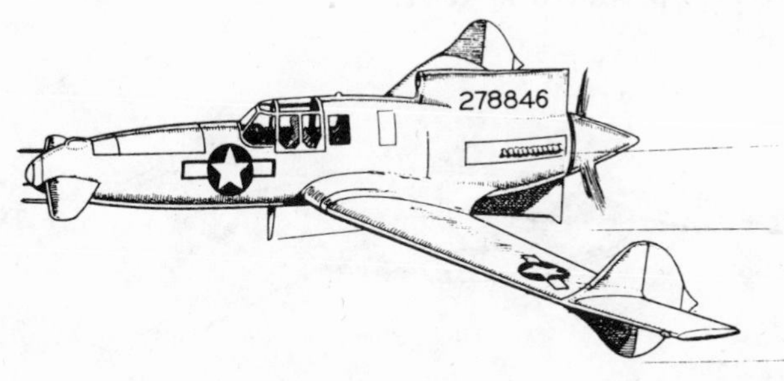

CURTISS XP-55 "ASCENDER" Experimental Canard (tail-first) fighter. Powered with 1,275-h.p. Allison engine.

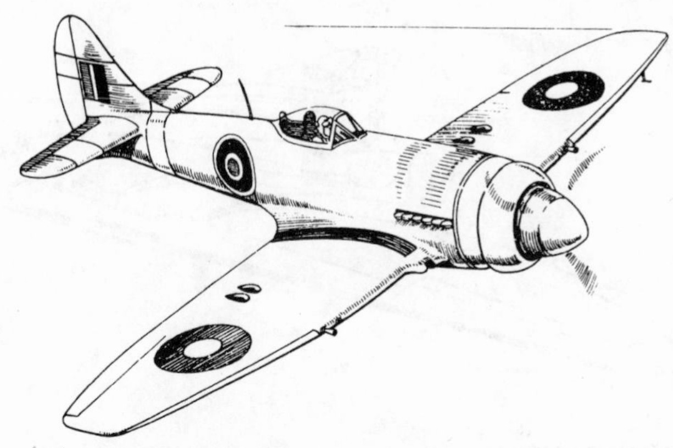

HAWKER "TEMPEST VI" 24-cylinder 2,300-h.p. Sabre engine with annular radiator. "Tempest" can be traced back in direct line to the famed Sopwith fighters of World War I.

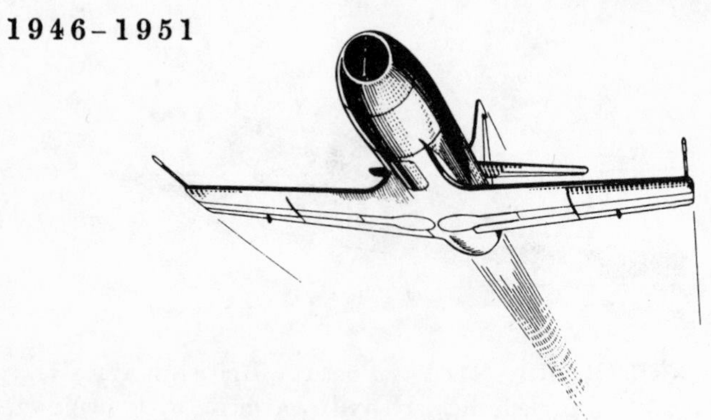

DOUGLAS D-558-1 "SKYSTREAK" A high-speed research jet aircraft produced in 1947.

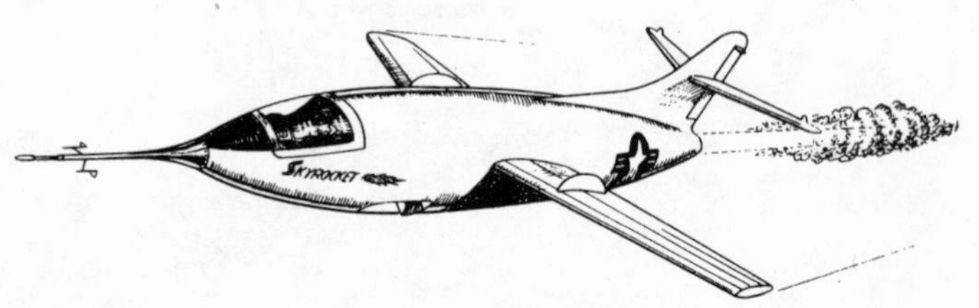

DOUGLAS D-558-2 "SKYROCKET" First version of the airplane which flew twice the speed of sound.

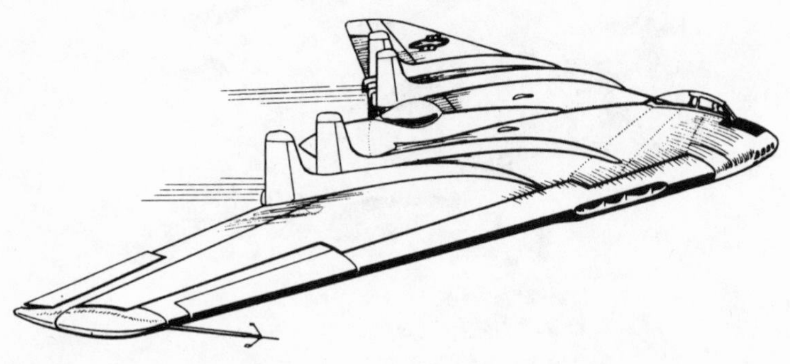

NORTHROP YB-49 Final development of the experimental Northrop flying wings. This large bomber was powered with eight 4,000-pound-thrust Allison J-35 jet engines.

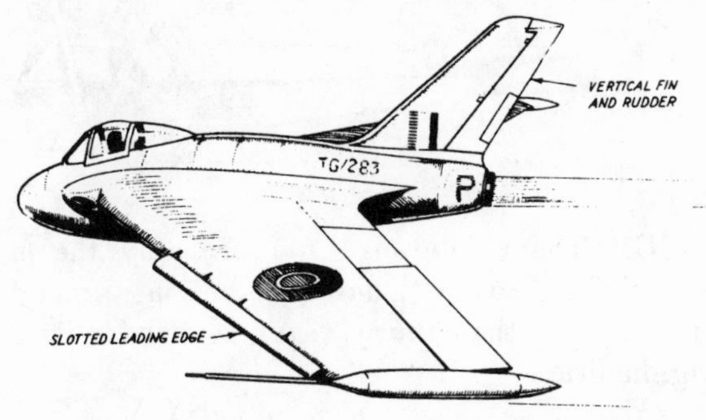

DE HAVILLAND D.H.108 One of the first experimental jet-powered tailless monoplanes built by this pioneer firm for high-speed research.

SAUNDERS-ROE SR/A1 World's first jet-powered flying-boat fighter. Powered with two Metrovick axial-flow jet engines.

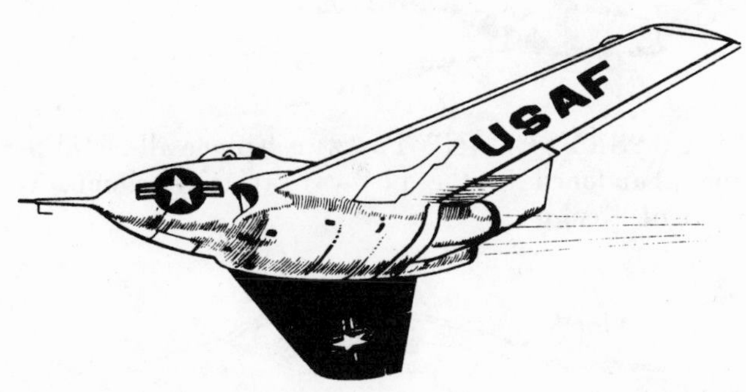

NORTHROP X-4 "BANTAM" U.S. experimental high-speed tailless aircraft.

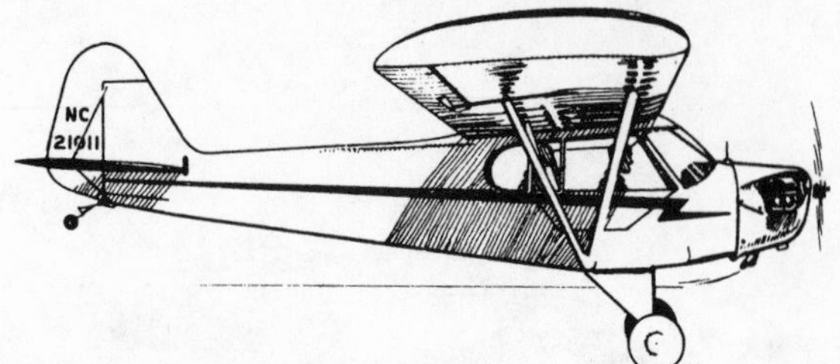

PIPER CUB The ubiquitous Cub, probably the most widely known civilian aircraft, has been buzzing around local airports for more than thirty years. Noted for its simple, safe flying qualities.

PIPER TRI-PACER 135 One of the postwar personal planes by the world's foremost producer of moderate-priced civilian aircraft.

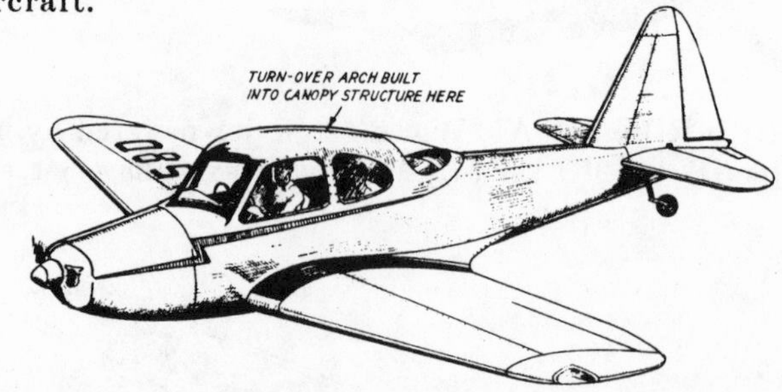

PIPER PA-6 "SKYSEDAN" Postwar 4-place all-metal personal plane abandoned in the postwar aviation slump. 165-h.p. Continental engine.

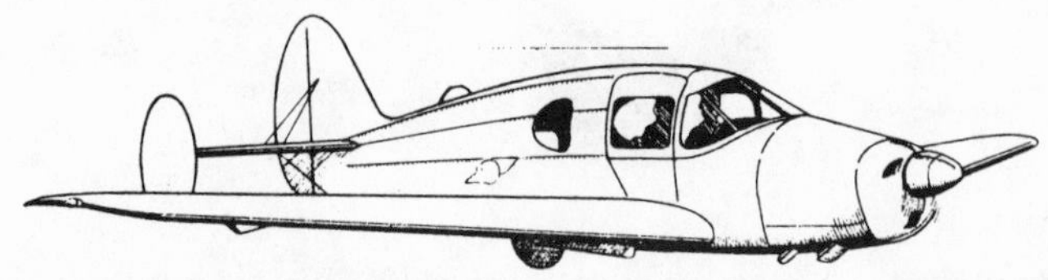

BELLANCA "CRUISAIR" Another 4-place personal plane developed after the war by a pioneer aircraft firm. 150-h.p. Franklin engine.

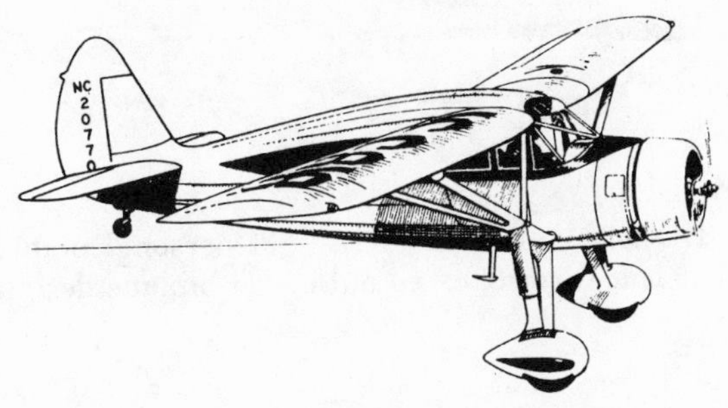

FAIRCHILD F-24 Prewar 4-place. Still in the running.

BEECHCRAFT D.17 Another prewar 5-place. Still in use.

REPUBLIC "SEA BEE" This was Republic's bid for the anticipated postwar boom in personal planes which failed to materialize. This 4-place amphibian with 212-h.p. Franklin, is still active.

S.E.C.A.T. LD.45 A postwar ultra-light personal plane, unusual in that it is a throwback to outmoded biplane design. 40-h.p. Mathis.

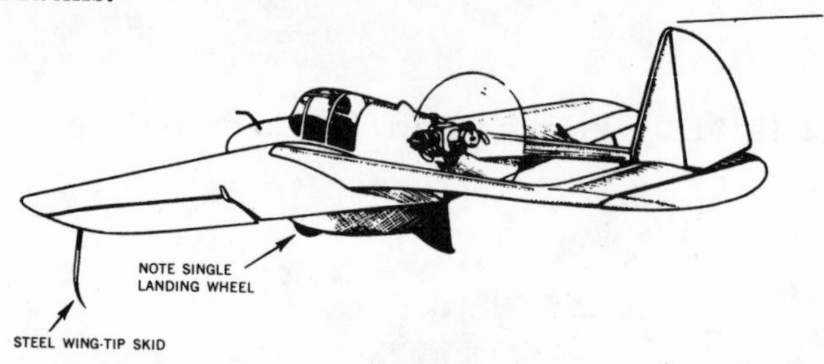

ALAPARMO TUCANO An Italian venture in the light-plane field. 38-h.p. engine.

LOCKHEED "LITTLE DIPPER" A U.S. ultra-light light plane produced by the makers of the huge Constellations. 40-h.p. Continental engine.

AERO 45 4-place, twin-engine all-metal Czech personal plane.

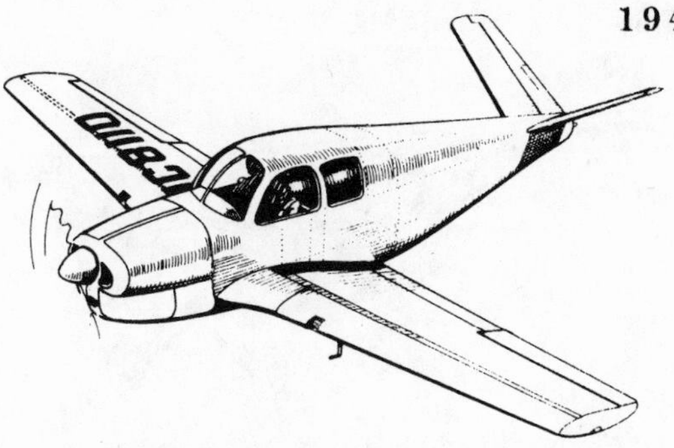

BEECHCRAFT 35 "BONANZA" One of the most interesting 4-place postwar personal planes developed in the U.S. Butterfly tail.

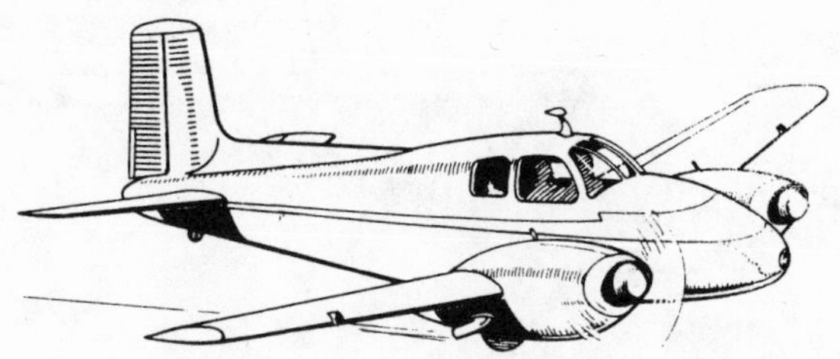

BEECHCRAFT 50 "TWIN BONANZA" Twin-engine version of the original "Bonanza" has conventional tail surfaces. One of the best light transports or personal planes in service today.

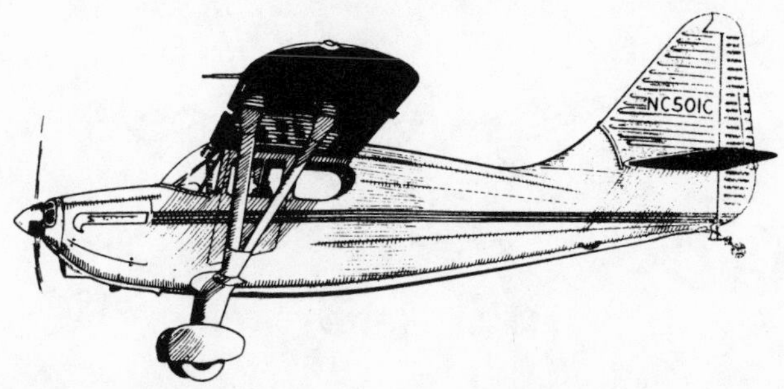

STINSON "VOYAGER" Postwar development of the Stinson Model 150 "Voyager," this 4-place personal plane is easily converted into a flying station wagon. 165-h.p. Franklin engine.

AERONCA "CHAMPION" Tandem-seat 2-place personal plane. 65/85-h.p. Continental engine.

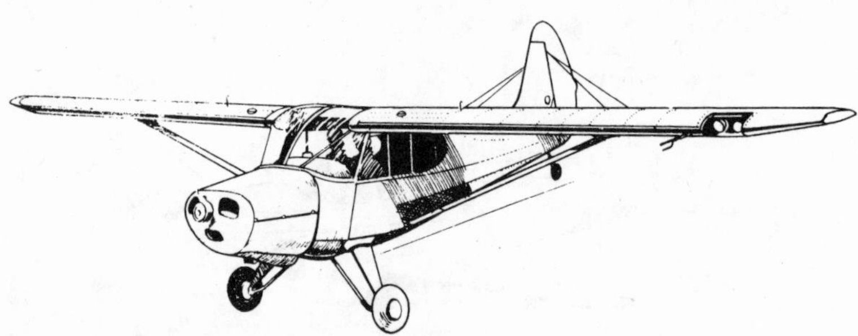

AERONCA "SEDAN" 4-place personal plane. 145-h.p. Continental engine.

WEE BEE One of the real novelties in ultra-light light plane design, the Wee Bee is a private venture. All-metal construction, prone pilot position, and tricycle landing gear.

STITS JUNIOR Also a private venture and probably the smallest airplane ever flown. Wingspread is 8 feet, 9 inches; engine an 85-h.p. Continental; and maximum speed about 170 m.p.h.

CESSNA 170 All-metal 4-place personal plane. 145-h.p. Continental engine. Cessna pioneered in high-performance personal planes.

CESSNA 190 Another 4-place personal plane by this pioneer firm. 240-h.p. Continental radial engine.

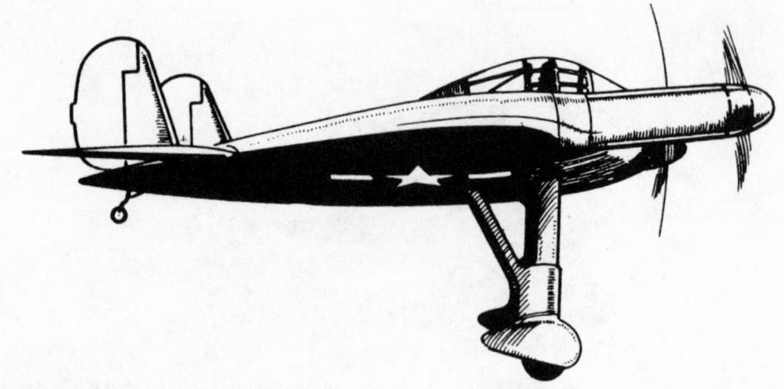

CHANCE VOUGHT 173 Prototype model of the CV-XF5U-1 with fixed landing gear.

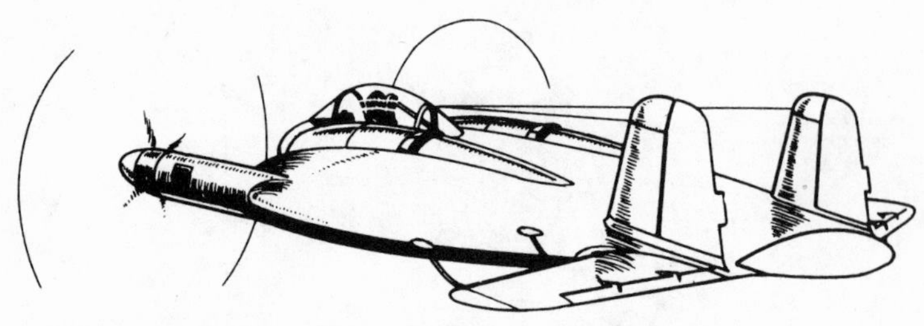

CHANCE VOUGHT CV-XF5U-1 "FLYING FLAPJACK" This experimental fighter with low-aspect-ratio wing and large-diameter articulated propellers was expected to incorporate helicopter properties with normal airplane performance.

BRISTOL "BRIGAND" Two 2,500-h.p. radial engines. Long-range attack plane, dive-bomber, torpedo-bomber, and mine layer.

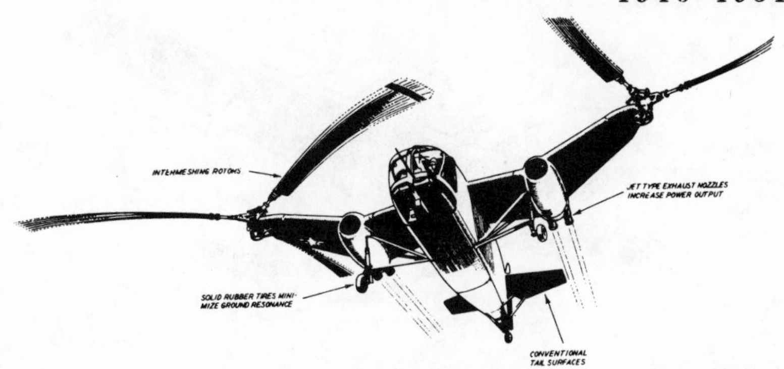

McDONNELL XHJD-1 "WHIRLAWAY" Two 450-h.p. P. & W. radials. 5-ton, 10-passenger military helicopter with laterally displaced rotors.

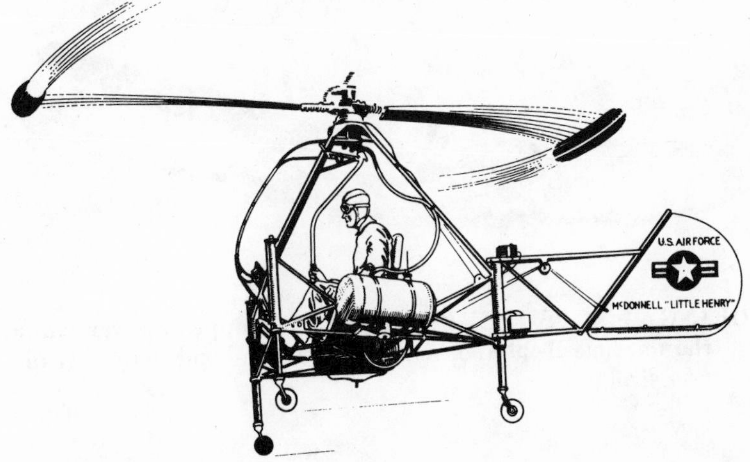

McDONNELL "LITTLE HENRY" World's first ram-jet helicopter. Self-propelled blades eliminated torque, transmision problems.

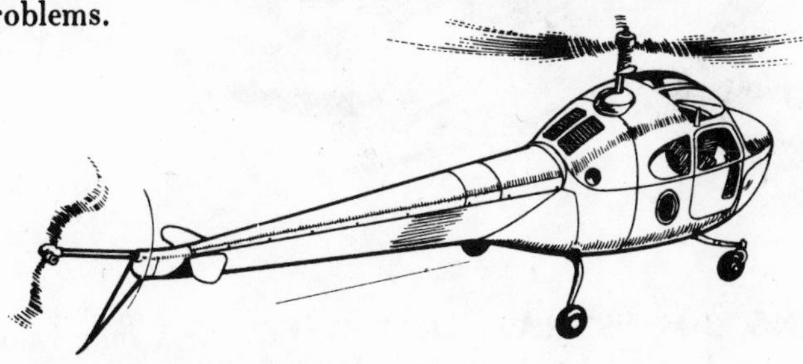

BELL 47B First U.S. helicopter to receive civil license. 175-h.p. Franklin engine.

HUGHES HK-1 "HERCULES" This king-size boat is largest all-wood aircraft ever built. Span: 300 feet; weight: 400,000 pounds. It has made short low-level flights but to date has proved an expensive white elephant.

BOEING B-50 "SUPERFORTRESS" Hopped-up version of the wartime B-29 and last piston-engine bomber by this pioneer firm.

BOEING B-47 "STRATOJET" World's first long-range jet-powered heavy bomber. It went into production in 1948 and was replaced by Boeing's B-52.

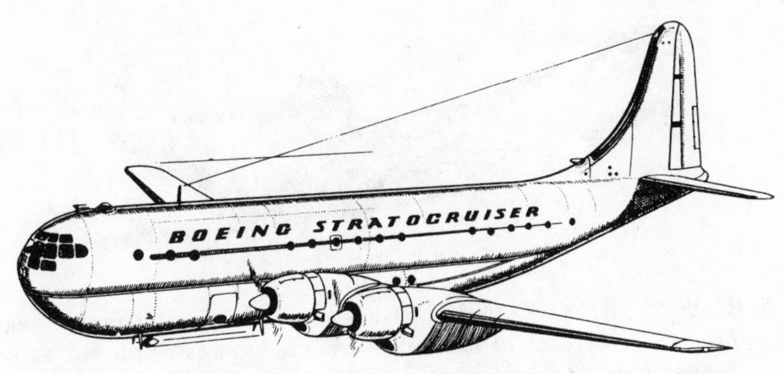

BOEING 377 "STRATOCRUISER" Four 3,500-h.p. P. & W. radials. 80-passenger double-deck air liner. In its day the fastest and most luxurious air liner in service.

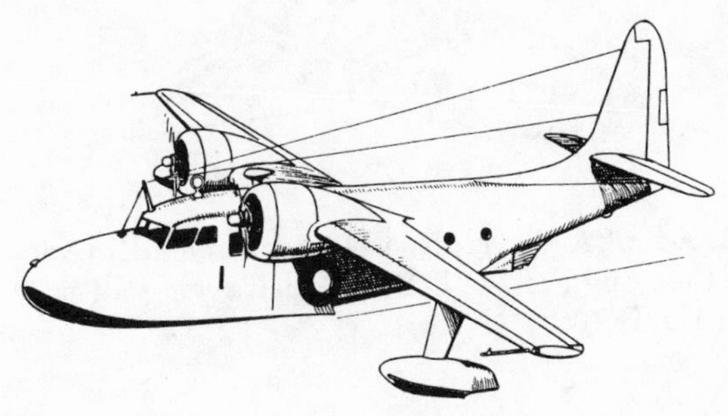

GRUMMAN "MALLARD" First postwar commercial amphibian by this noted firm.

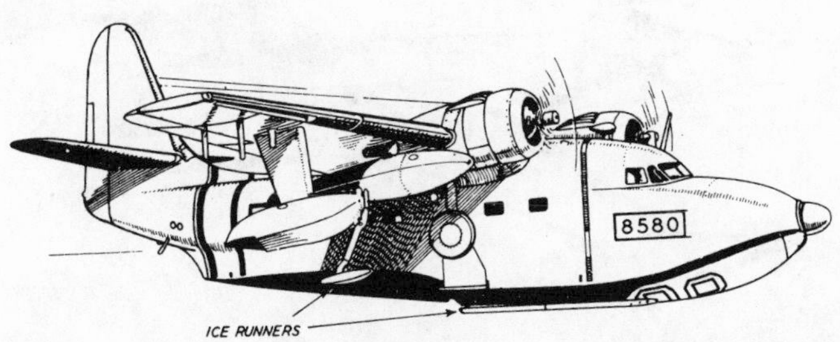

GRUMMAN SA-16A "ALBATROSS" (Navy designation:UF-1) Triphibian rescue aircraft. It can operate from land, sea, ice, or snow.

FAIREY "FIREFLY IV" Piston-engine naval reconnaissance fighter. A variant of this now-obsolete type is employed as a target tug.

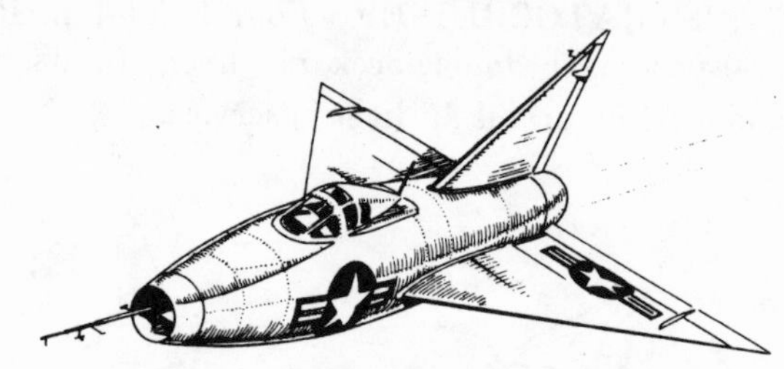

CONVAIR XF-92A A high speed research delta-wing aircraft led to the design of the U.S.A.F. delta-wing all-weather interceptor the F-102.

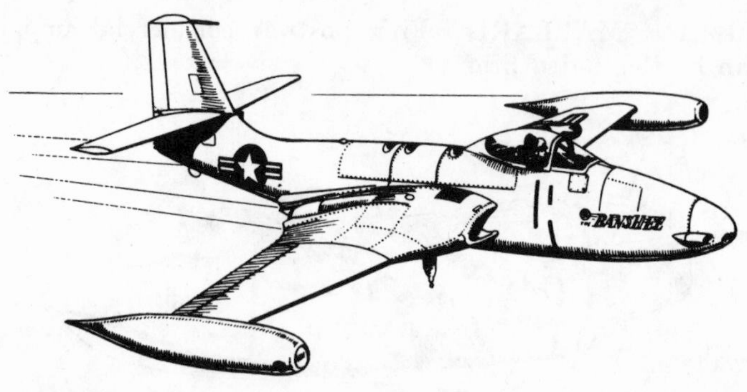

McDONNELL F2H-2 "BANSHEE" Twin-jet shipboard Navy fighter.

SIKORSKY YH-18A 245-h.p. Franklin flat-six engine. Army field forces rescue and ambulance craft. It is military version of the famed S-52/2.

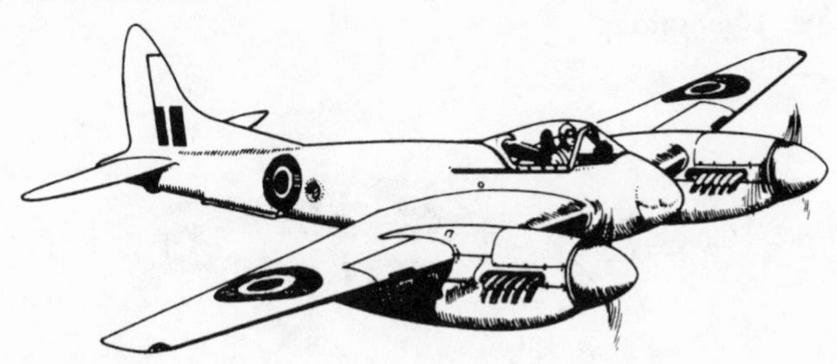

DE HAVILLAND "SEA HORNET" Carrier-based strike fighter. One of the few piston-engine fighters produced by this firm.

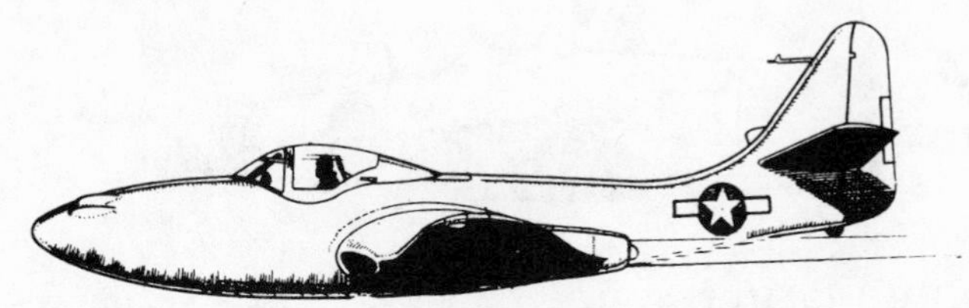

McDONNELL FH-1 "PHANTOM" First operational McDonnell jet fighter and first U.S. carrier-based jet fighter.

McDONNELL XF-88 First swept-wing McDonnell jet fighter.

AERONCA L-16A Light U.S. liaison plane. Military verson of the "Champion."

DE HAVILLAND "CHIPMUNK" Produced by the Canadian division of the De Havilland Company. All-metal military primary trainer.

HAWKER "TEMPEST II" 2,500-h.p. engine. Modification of the earlier "Tempest," it did not see service in World War II.

LOCKHEED "CONSTITUTION" Double-deck U.S. Navy transport. 189-foot span.

WESTLAND WYVERN T.F.4 Powerful turbo-prop British naval strike fighter. Contrarotating propellers.

LOCKHEED P2V-5 "NEPTUNE" Long-range radar-equipped U.S. Navy patrol bomber.

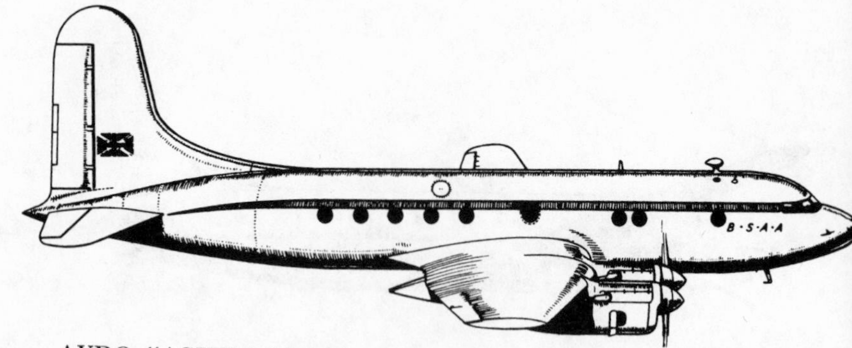

AVRO "ASHTON" This experimental aircraft was one of the few less fortunate designs produced by the pioneer Avro firm. Four 1,740-h.p. Rolls-Royce engines. A good enough looking aircraft, it was plagued with mysterious bugs.

AVRO "TUDOR 8" World's first jet air liner actually to fly, it is powered with four Rolls-Royce Nene jets mounted in pairs.

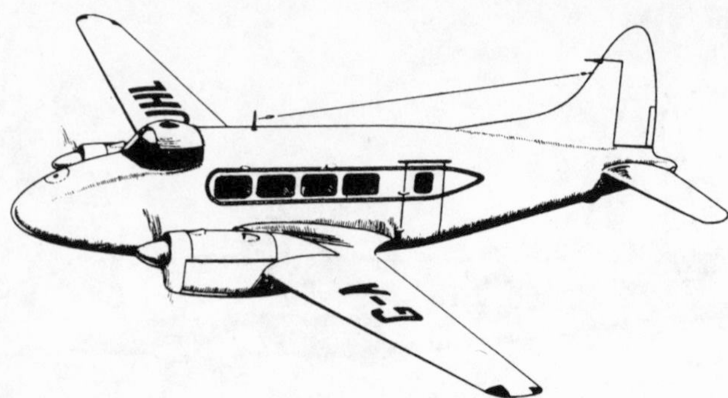

DE HAVILLAND "DOVE" 11-passenger feeder transport or executive plane. Enjoyed a vogue in the U.S.A. as a corporation or business plane due to its comparatively low cost and high efficiency.

BRISTOL "BRABAZON" One of the largest air liners ever built, the "Brabazon" had a span of 230 feet and was 177 feet long. The four 5,000-h.p. piston engines drove eight contra-rotating propellers. For reasons unknown it was never put into production despite satisfactory flight tests.

HANDLEY PAGE "HERMES V" When it appeared in 1949 the Hermes was one of the world's first turbo-prop air liners. The British have pioneered in both turbo-jet and straight-jet civil aircraft.

HANDLEY PAGE "MARATHON II" Yet another example of British progress in the field of turbo-jet aircraft.

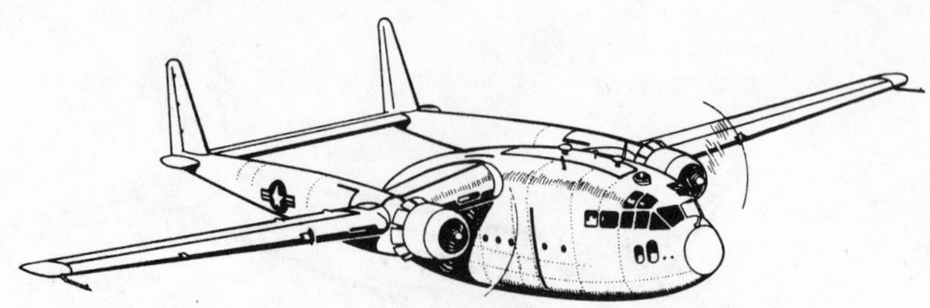

FAIRCHILD C-119 "PACKET" Standard U.S.A.A.F. freight and troop carrier. Widely employed for parachute drops of men and matériel.

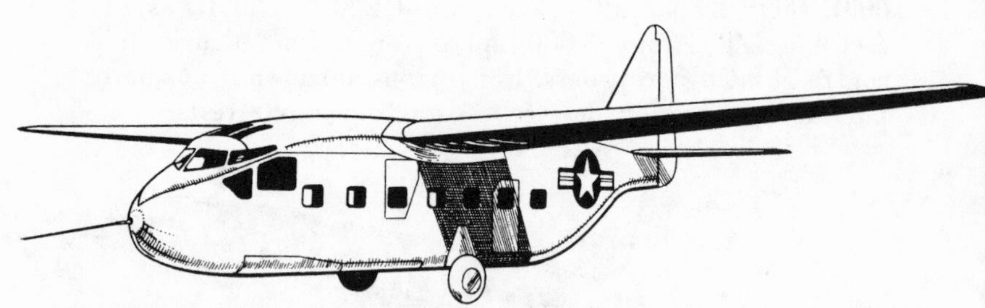

CHASE CG-18A Troop and freight glider.

CHASE C-122 Powered version of the Chase CG-18A. Versatile troop and freight transport. Two 1,250-h.p. P. & W. radials.

CHASE G-20 All-metal development of the Chase troop and cargo glider.

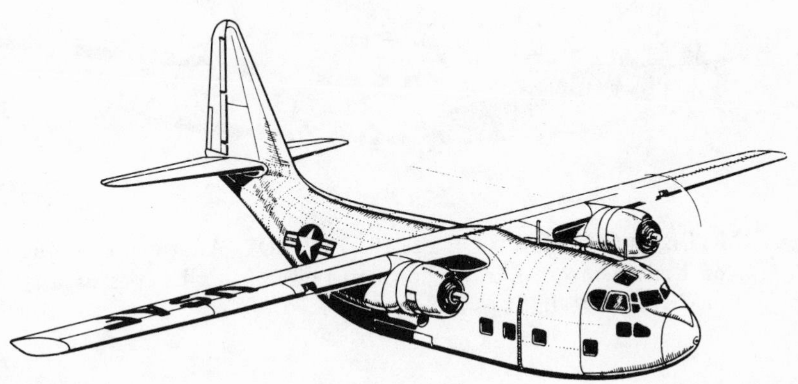

CHASE C-123 Powered version of the Chase G-20.

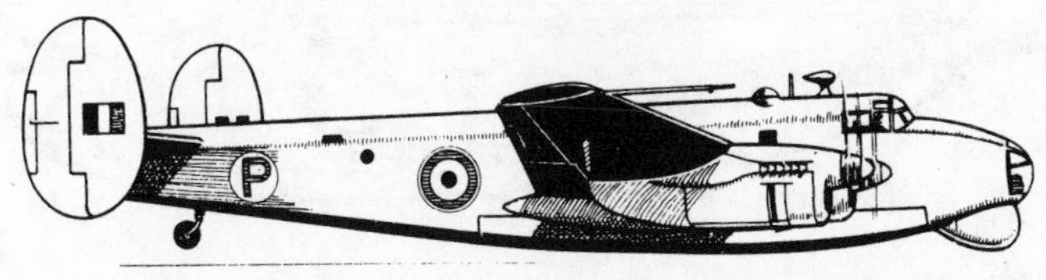

AVRO "SHACKLETON" Long-range radar-equipped anti-submarine patrol plane bears a family resemblance to the World War II Avro bombers.

MARTIN 404 40-passenger U.S. air liner.

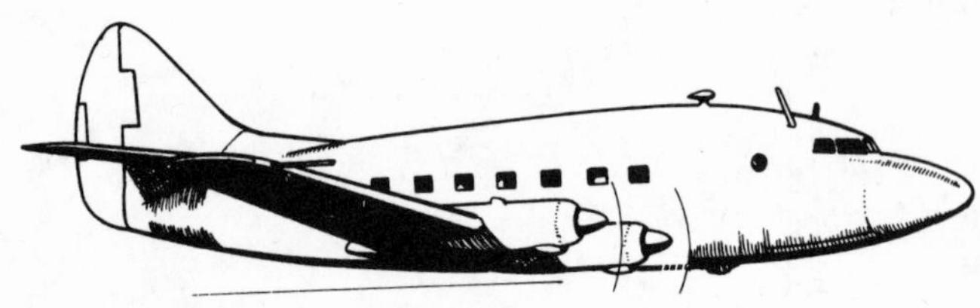

ARMSTRONG-WHITWORTH "APOLLO" Another example of British interest in turbo-prop power for all types of aircraft, this was built as a prototype.

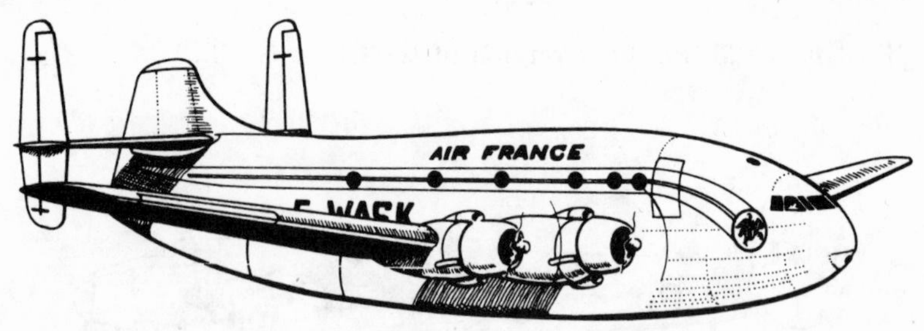

BREGUET "PROVENCE" Postwar four-engine double-deck air liner by one of the oldest aircraft companies in existence.

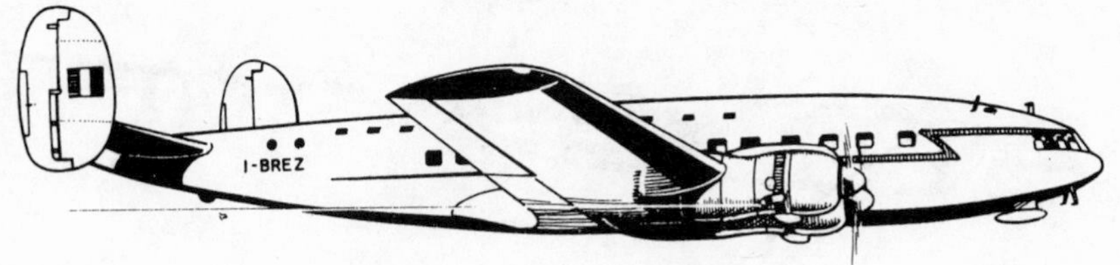

BREDA-ZAPPATA BZ-308 Large postwar Italian air liner powered with four 1,750-h.p. Bristol Centaurus radial engines.

NORTH AMERICAN RB-45 4-jet reconnaissance bomber.

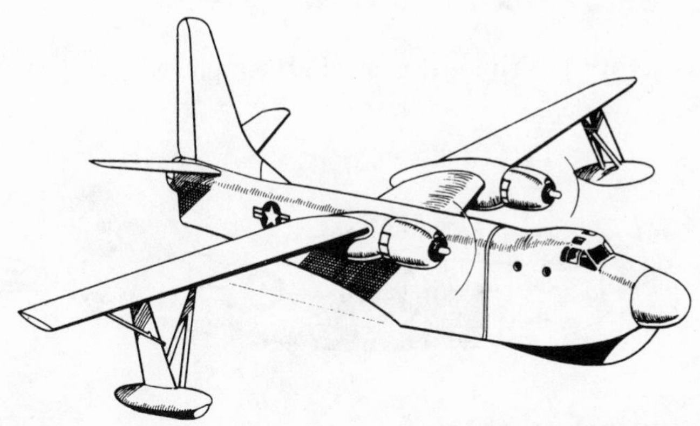

MARTIN P5M-1 "MARLIN" Radar-equipped U.S. Navy patrol boat. Compare this with earliest Martin float seaplanes.

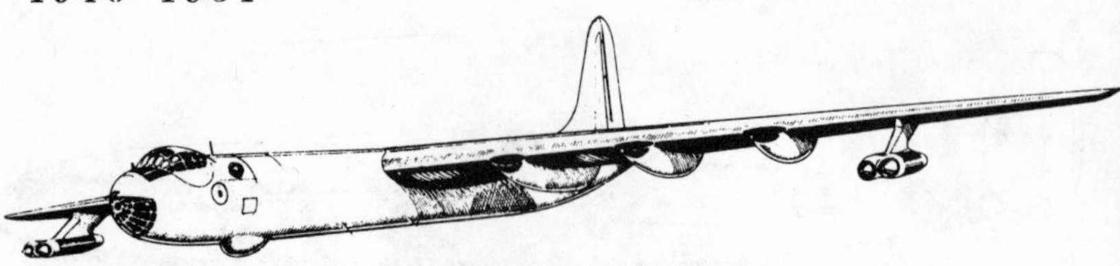

CONVAIR B-36D One of the world's largest long-range super-bombers. 6 piston engines, 4 jets. Prototype model, the XB-36, was first flight tested in 1946. Jet pods added later.

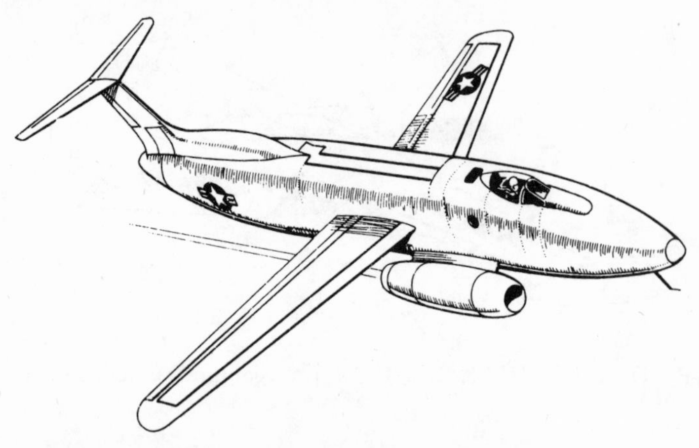

MARTIN B-51 Triple-jet ground attack plane.

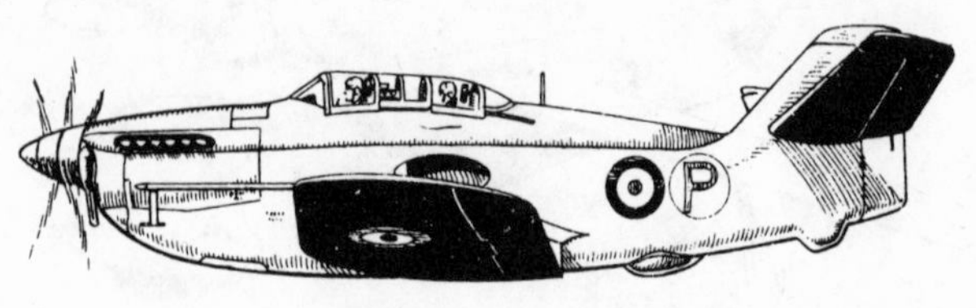

BLACKBURN Y.A.5 Prototype long-range British anti-submarine aircraft. With contrarotating props and retracting tricycle landing gear, it forms a striking contrast with the 1910 Blackburn airplanes.

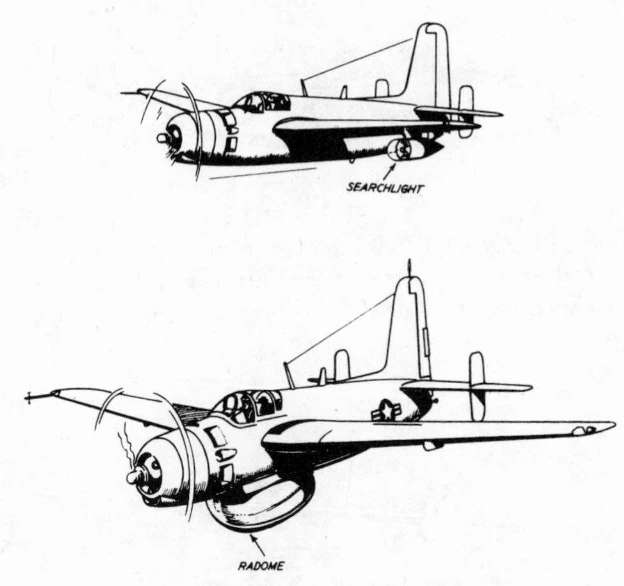

GRUMMAN "GUARDIAN" U.S. interpretation of the anti-submarine aircraft. Working in teams, the AF-2W "Hunter" version (below) is radar equipped to seek out enemy subs, which, when discovered, are destroyed by the AF-2S "Killer" version (above).

NORTH AMERICAN AJ-1 "SAVAGE" First U.S. Navy plane designed specifically to deliver the atom bomb.

AVRO "ATHENA" 1,000-h.p. turbo-prop prototype. Compare this all-metal turbine-powered aircraft with the 1914 model 504K trainer produced by this same pioneer firm.

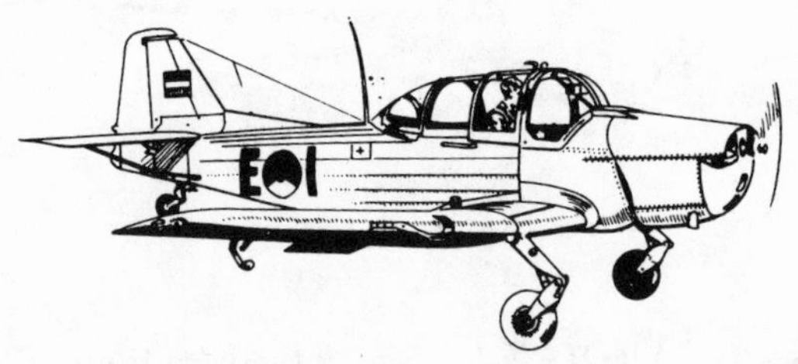

FOKKER S.11 This military and civil trainer is one of the first designs produced by the reactivated, historic Fokker Company, which shut down when the Nazis overran Holland.

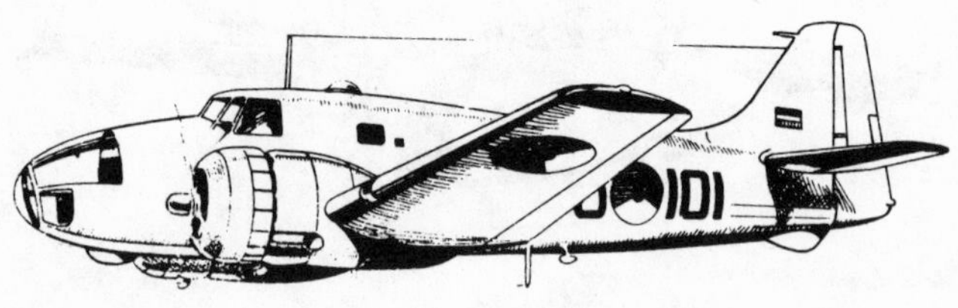

FOKKER S.13 Another postwar Fokker design. Multi-engine trainer.

GRUMMAN F9F "PANTHER" U.S. Navy and Marine Corps carrier-based fighter. First U.S. jet fighter used in actual combat (Korea).

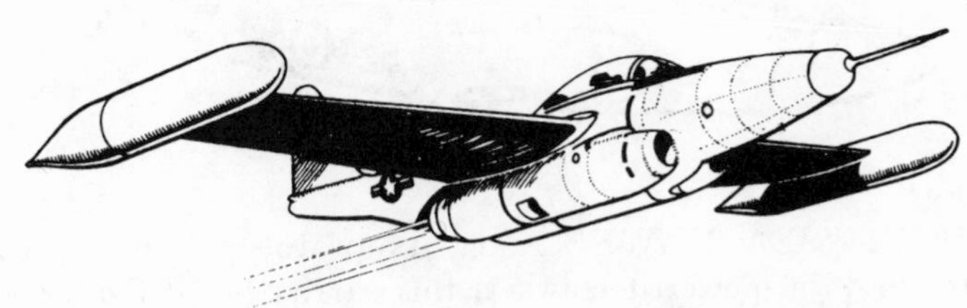

NORTHROP F-89 "SCORPION" 2-place twin-jet all-weather fighter. Shown here in later modification with extended nose.

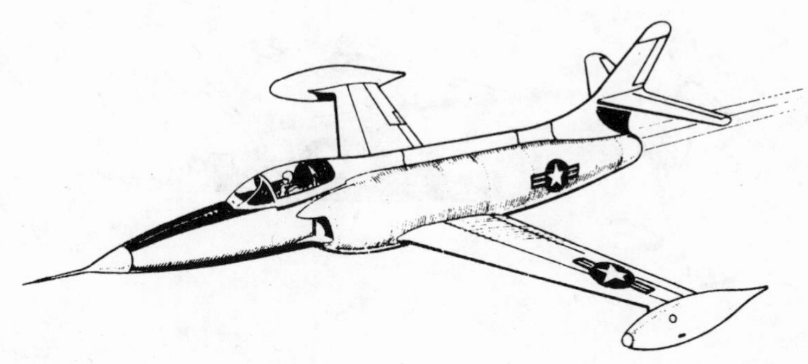

LOCKHEED XF-90 Experimental long-range penetration fighter.

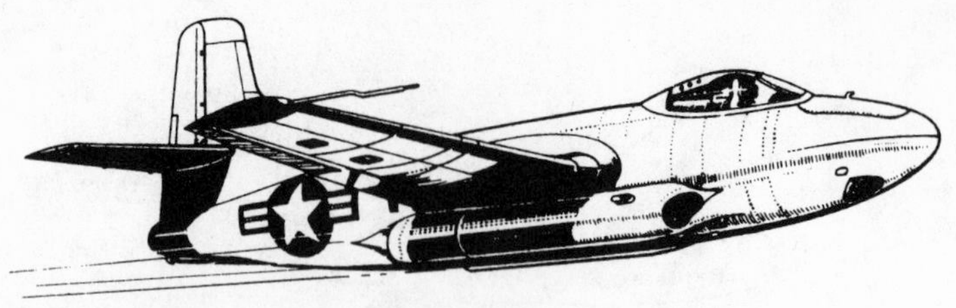

DOUGLAS F3D "SKYNIGHT" Formidable U.S. twin-jet carrier-based all-weather fighter.

HAWKER "SEA HAWK" After its prototype, the P-1040, the first jet-powered Hawker, this carrier-based fighter was powered with one Rolls-Royce Nene engine and armed with four 20-mm. cannon.

HAWKER P-1052 First swept-wing jet Hawker.

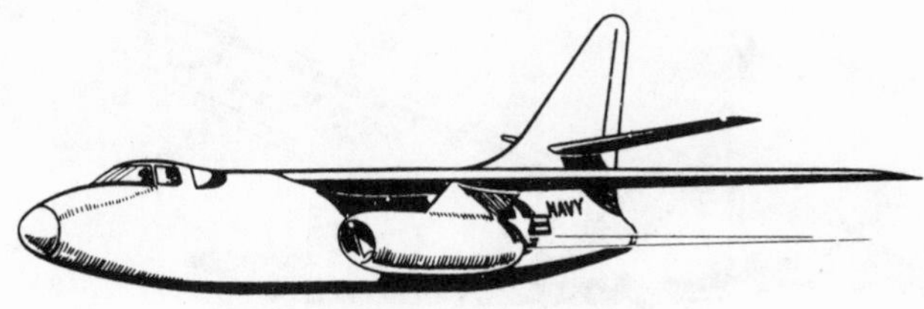

DOUGLAS XA3D and RB-66 Twin-jet reconnaissance fighter. Shoulder wing. 700 m.p.h.

REPUBLIC XF-91 U.S. jet fighter with inverse taper wings and rocket-assist unit beneath tail cone.

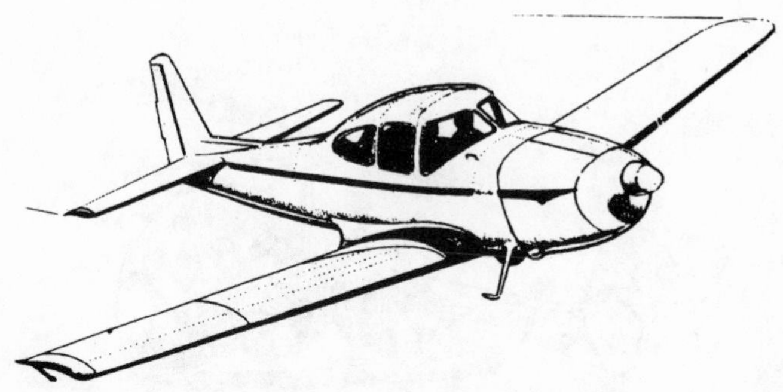

RYAN "NAVION" Postwar all-metal 4-place personal plane developed by North American but now produced by the Ryan Company.

SCHWEIZER 1-23 High-performance all-metal U.S. sailplane.

MARTIN XB-48 Only two of these large 6-jet planes were built.

BELL 47D-1 Civil and military helicopter. Top speed 98 m.p.h. Bell's patented stabilizer bar made it smoothest to date.

PART NINE

The Shrinking Sky

1952-1954

Two sets of initials were proving a shot in the arm to aviation throughout the democratic world. American funds and equipment provided by MDAP (Mutual Defense Assistance Plan) and NATO (North Atlantic Treaty Organization) for the expansion of various friendly foreign countries' military might showed up in their aircraft production. France became the first nation to produce a jet light plane, thanks to her pioneer work in "junior" jet engines. Her "Mystère" and "Vautour" jet fighters equaled the best made by the U.S. and Britain. Holland had a jet trainer by Fokker that drew interest over here, and Italy also was turning out a jet trainer, the Fiat G-80. While not a member of NATO, Sweden through her SAAB company was producing the excellent J-29 fighter and the sleek Lansen jet attack job.

England was concentrating on research in the most efficient wing shapes for sonic speed airplanes. A fertile new field seemed to be the "crescent" wing—which has a sharp sweepback beginning from the root or junction with the fuselage and then straightens out toward the wing tips. She successfully adapted the delta wing to a jet fighter, the Gloster "Javelin," and the four-jet Avro "Vulcan" bomber. But England's star achievement was to put into operation the world's first jet transports.

The four-jet De Havilland "Comet," whose cruising speed was around 475 m.p.h., began regular passenger service from London to South Africa in May of 1952. Following England, Canada also sent a jet transport into the air, the CF-102, but this plane never entered service. During the late forties when these countries were experimenting with jets for passenger travel, the United States did practically nothing to keep abreast. American airlines shied at the prohibitive operating costs for jets on short runs, and airport and traffic problems and other considerations dampened interest. In 1951 the Chase Aircraft Company fitted one of its big cargo transports with four jet engines and offered the experimental XC-123A; despite remarkable performance that allowed take-off and landing within a thousand feet, the project was not developed.

While commercial aviation was starting the slow swing-over to jets, military planes had reached the last section of the arc. The U.S. air arm was almost completely converted as 1952 drew to a close. It was radically different in both appearance and power. Keeping company with the straight jets, some planes were being equipped with jet and piston engines in combination, à la B-36. Already the B-36, last of our propeller-driven strategic bombers, was being phased out of production, to be replaced by the Boeing eight-jet B-52 "Stratofortress." The Air Force, and to a greater extent the Navy, still flew—will continue to fly—a number of piston craft. But even such old stand-bys as patrol flying boats will eventually move over for jets: with its XF2Y-1 delta-wing seaplane mounted on hydro skis, Convair demonstrated that seaplanes, too, can be supersonic.

Sport flying, in the dawning jet age, led a mixed-up life. Strangely, powerless flight had been growing in favor. France now had probably more glider activity than any other nation, and Germany once more was busy organizing clubs. Even in America, where gliding had never really caught the popular imagination, the movement was on the upswing. By 1953 the

U.S. had most of the world records—including 535 miles for distance and 42,000 feet for altitude.

But the light plane in America had fallen by the wayside. The dwindling number of light-plane manufacturers were selling "executive transports" to corporations, planes for increased agricultural and patrol purposes and the like. The private citizen, however, had become a poor prospect, with the high cost of living and plain lack of interest the causes. Now, the average person wanted to go somewhere special in a plane rather than just take a hop, and the little single-engine job's limited range and inability to cope with bad weather made long trips impractical. Without the knowledge to fly by instruments and radio—which John Q. rarely acquires—a thousand-mile jaunt to Florida can take a week, of which five days must be spent at various airports waiting for the weather to clear.

The strategic concept of the U.S.A.F., which demanded that our huge bombers have a range as great as 10,000 miles, raised the question of how protective fighters could escort them on possible intercontinental trips. Over a period of several years, improved and more widely used air-to-air refueling answered the fighter question as well as extended the range of the bombers. By taking on a fresh fuel supply from immense tanker planes like converted "Superforts" or "Stratofreighters" while in flight, short-range jet fighters now crossed the oceans. A B-47 "Stratojet" bomber refueled three times in the air, broke all distance and endurance records for jets by flying nonstop for 12,000 miles and remaining aloft for 24 hours.

And later the "Parasite fighter" idea had been revived. With an F-84F jet fighter as "parasite," a B-36 proved it could carry its own protection in its belly en route to the target and back. Logically, the smaller plane could also cut loose on its own when within striking distance of the target, drop a bomb, and return to "mother" to be secured aboard and carried home.

During 1944 the V-1 pilotless missiles of the Nazis, launched from the coast of France, killed people and wrecked buildings in the heart of London. Since then research in guided missiles has spread to most leading countries—with results for the most part secret. In 1952 the U.S. program received its first large-scale production orders, hundreds of millions of dollars being allotted for the purpose. Four basic types were under development: 1. Surface-to-surface—to be launched from the ground or naval vessels against a major ground target. 2. Surface-to-air—meaning antiaircraft weapons. 3. Air-to-air—from one warplane against another. 4. Air-to-surface—from plane to enemy below.

These complex weapons, some of which are really aircraft with wings, control surfaces, and power plants, can be guided by remote control *after* being launched. They have a mechanical brain that "thinks" for the pilot who isn't there. In their largest, most deadly form they can travel hundreds of miles. And they can carry atomic destruction. These attributes are goals partially realized and being striven for, and real attainment may be many, many years in the future. Yet, it is not inconceivable that some day the guided missile may replace the bomber and the fighter plane.

What would happen to the airplane in the immediate future? In 1954 it was the authors' belief that during the next 15 years, say, no world-shaking progress would take place. The greatest advance would be in the domain of rotary-wing craft. Already the helicopter had flown across the Atlantic, was in commercial operation carrying passengers and freight, and was growing in size. Along with the helicopter, the "convertiplane," still in a very early stage of development, offered beguiling possibilities. This hybrid flying machine that is part conventional airplane and part helicopter has the advantages of each and the bad features of neither. (See Parts 10 and 11 on VTOL development.)

Generally speaking, we believed that the shape of the airplane wing would not change drastically from the advanced forms of this era; use of the delta would be on the increase, especially in the military services. Improvements would be mostly in better and more powerful jets, in electronic equipment and safety devices, lighter weight of equipment and structure. The military plane would fly at the speed of sound in level flight, and commercial jet transports around 550 m.p.h. Come what may, it would be a long time before the civilian would hurtle across continent or ocean at sonic speed.

Even those who deal with the speed of sound in their daily lives are not yet prepared to accept it as normal, the way the airplane itself is now accepted. A story is told concerning test pilot "A" who worked for a well-known plant on Long Island manufacturing jet fighters. He was intrigued by "sonic boom," that double report like two thunderclaps coming from jet planes when they are dived from high altitudes. He knew the phenomenon was explained as the result of shock waves formed by the wings and traveling downward, and he knew about the time a "boom" was said to have broken practically every pane of glass in a greenhouse near Wright Field. But "A" had never heard the amazing thing himself! The man in the cockpit doesn't, and test pilots usually try to pick the more lonely places for the diving acts on their program. So "A" asked his friend pilot "B" for a private demonstration at the next opportunity.

"B" obliged one Saturday afternoon while "A" was on the roof of his newly bought house fixing a torn shingle. Climbing to 30,000 feet, "B" sent the fighter into a vertical dive directly over the house. The twin explosion straddled the roof ridge and knocked "A" to the ground. He was convinced . . . and more amazed than ever.

In fifty years the airplane made the fastest progress of any mechanical device ever fashioned by human hands. It was still advancing, but by 1954 the rate appeared to be slowing down. Why? We thought that the machine was waiting for man to catch up with it.

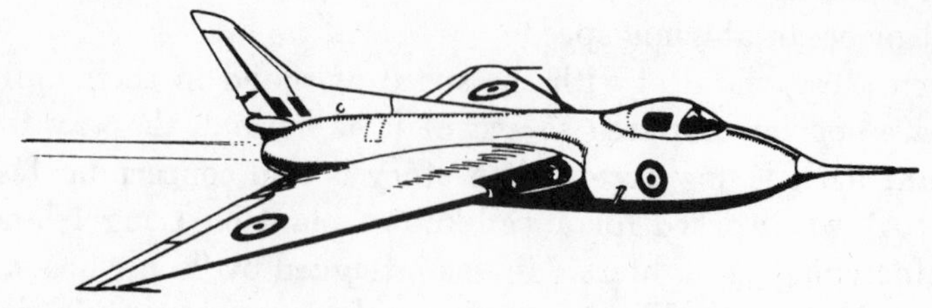

AVRO 707-A Delta-wing research aircraft. The pioneer Avro Company was among the first to investigate the possibilities of the delta wing and has produced a number of variants of the model shown, including the giant multi-jet delta-wing Vulcan super-bomber.

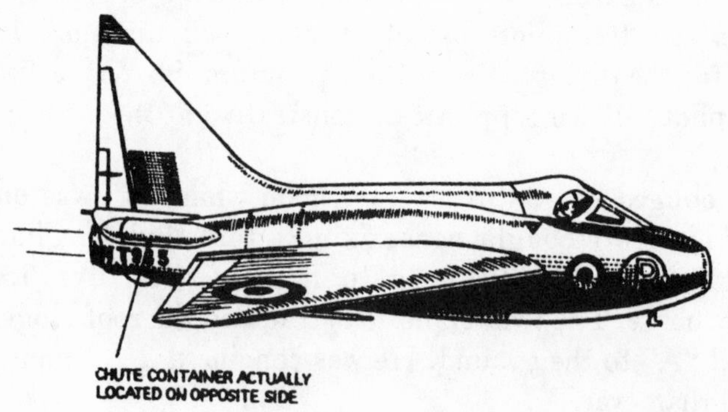

BOLTON PAUL P-III Another firm which pioneered in delta-wing aircraft and came up with this research model.

DOUGLAS F4D-1 "SKYRAY" U.S. delta-wing fighter was holder of the world's speed record for jet-powered aircraft.

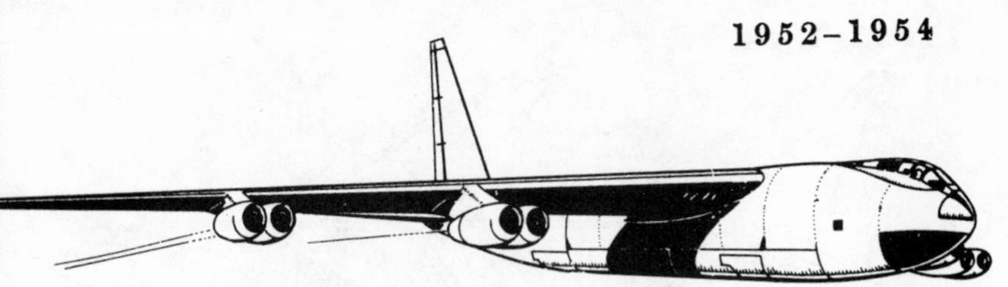

BOEING B-52 Largest of Boeing's jet-powered superbombers. The eight jet engines have a combined thrust of almost 80,000 pounds, and this huge bomber was probably as fast as most of the operational jet fighters in 1952. Compare this magnificent airplane with Boeing's first airplanes.

DOUGLAS D-558-II "SKYROCKET" First airplane in the world to double the speed of sound and (up to 1953) holder of the world's speed and altitude records. An experimental aircraft, it is airborne-launched from a mother plane, lands normally.

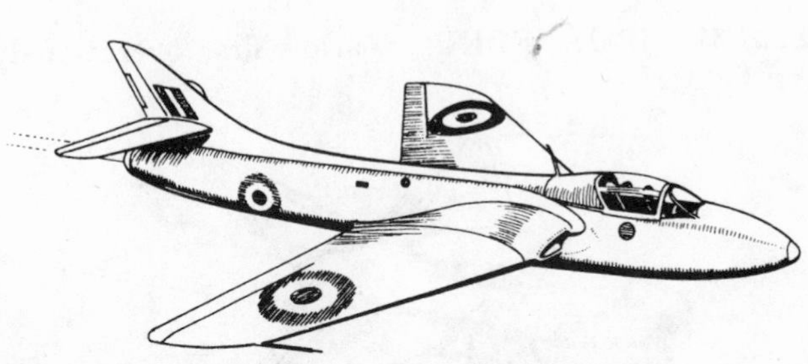

HAWKER "HUNTER" Transonic British jet fighter. Broke the world's speed record in 1953. Compare with early Sopwiths!

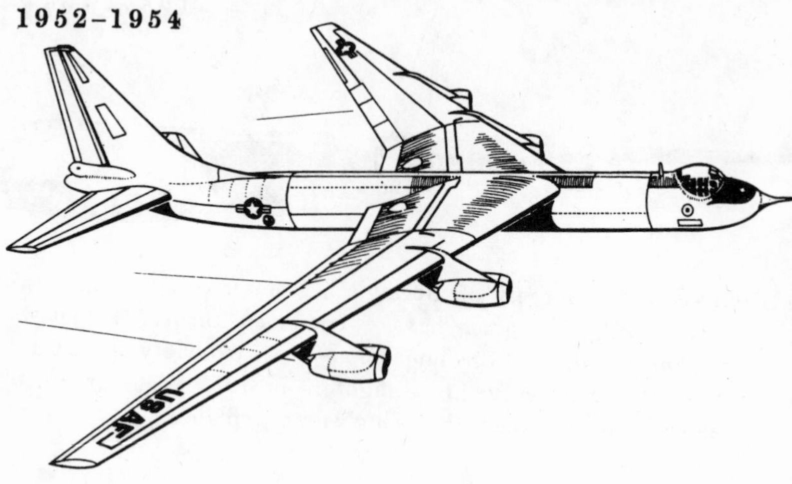

CONVAIR YB-60 Swept-wing version of the Convair B-36. Eight jets.

GLOSTER GA.5 "JAVELIN" World's first operational delta-wing fighter.

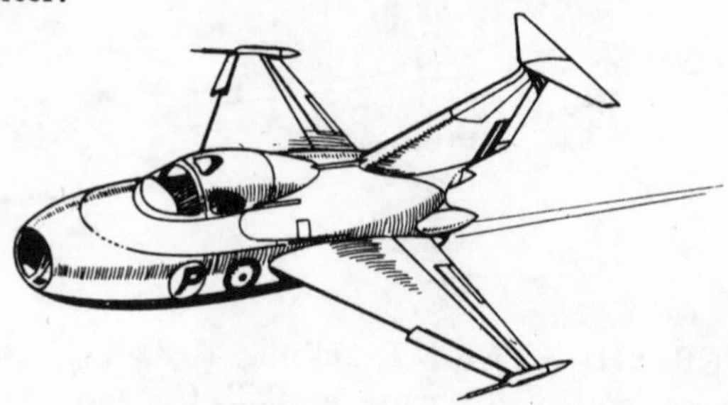

FAIREY F.D.1 Another example of British high-speed delta-wing research. The small fixed stabilizer was to be eliminated.

CHANCE VOUGHT F7U-3 "CUTLASS" Operational U.S. Navy carrier-based tailless fighter which approaches the speed of sound.

BELL X-5 High-speed research aircraft. Camber and sweep of wings can be varied in flight. Shown here with maximum sweep for speed.

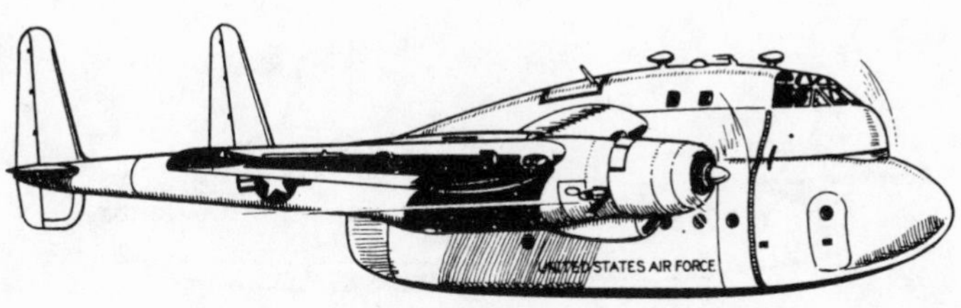

FAIRCHILD C-120 "PACKPLANE" Entire lower section of fuselage consists of a detachable pod for convenient loading. Plane may be flown with or without cargo pod.

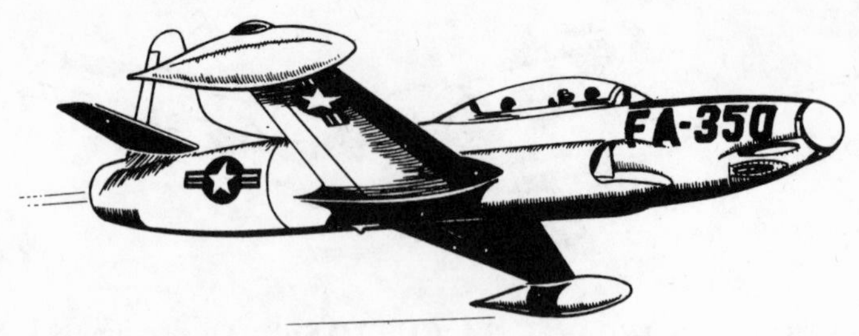

LOCKHEED F-94 "STARFIRE" U.S.A.F. all-weather, 2-place fighter.

NORTH AMERICAN F-86E "SABRE" U.S.A.F. jet fighter which won fame in Korea.

NORTH AMERICAN F-86D All-weather version of the "Sabre" with radome in nose.

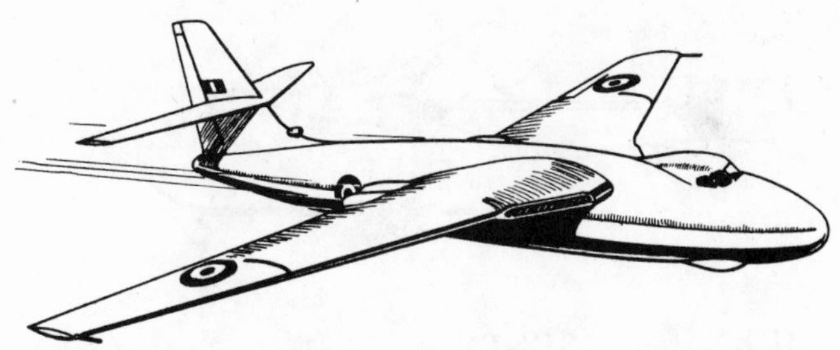

VICKERS "VALIANT" Crescent-wing 4-jet bomber for the R.A.F. Illustrates British theory of jet installation as opposed to U.S. practice of mounting jets in pods.

BREGUET "VULTUR" A French fighter with turbo-prop in nose and turbo-jet in tail. Compare with the 1909 Breguet!

GRUMMAN F9F-6 "COUGAR" Swept-wing version of the "Panther" and one of the best U.S. jet fighters.

BLACKBURN and GENERAL UNIVERSAL FREIGHT PLANE Automobile-passenger ferry plane.

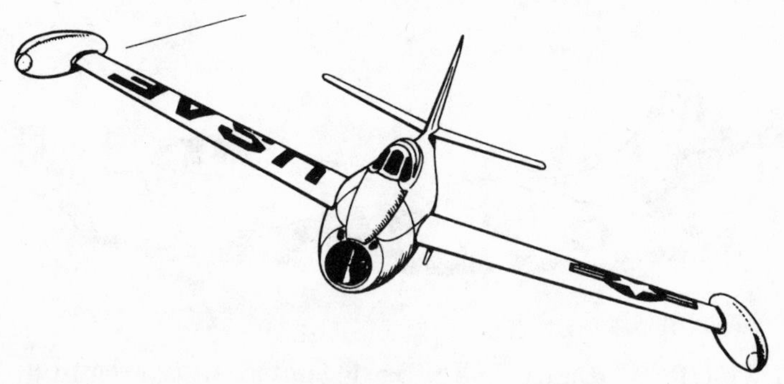

REPUBLIC F-84 "THUNDERJET" U.S.A.F. jet fighter.

McDONNELL F3H-1 "DEMON" Navy jet fighter.

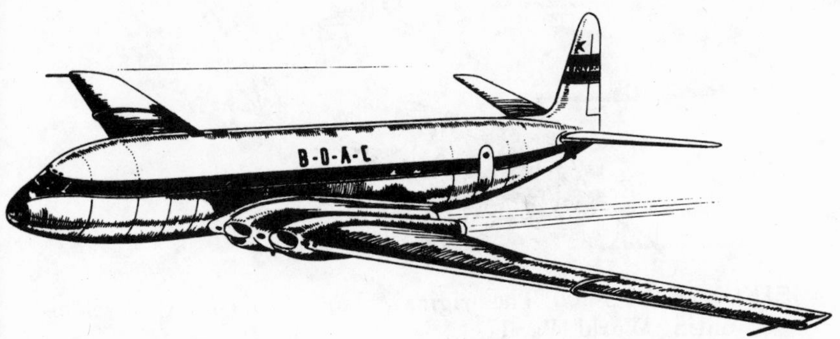

DE HAVILLAND "COMET" World's first production jet liner (1949).

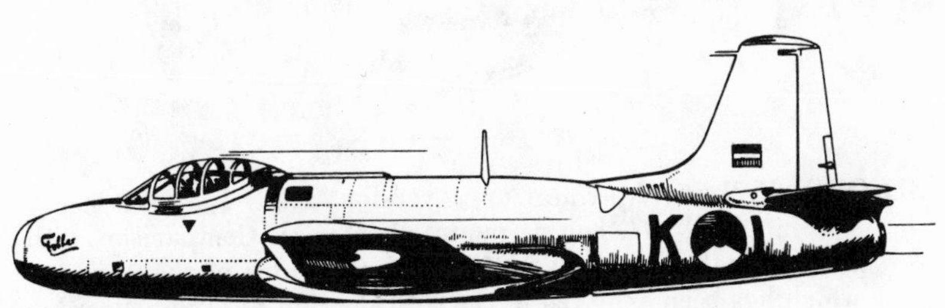

FOKKER S.14 Fighter by the firm which introduced world's first armed fighter monoplane in 1915.

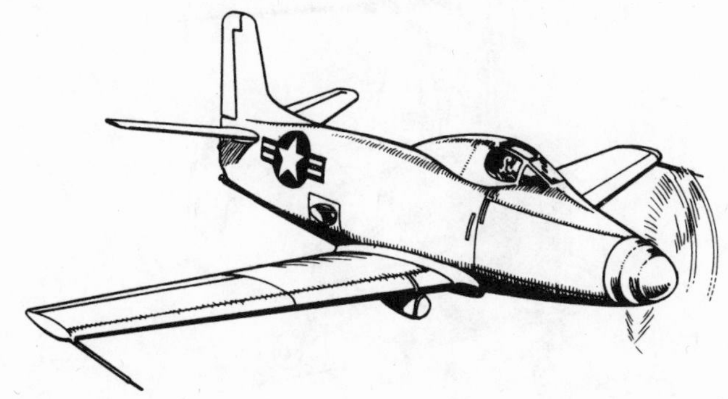

DOUGLAS A2D-1 "SKYSHARK" Turbo-prop power.

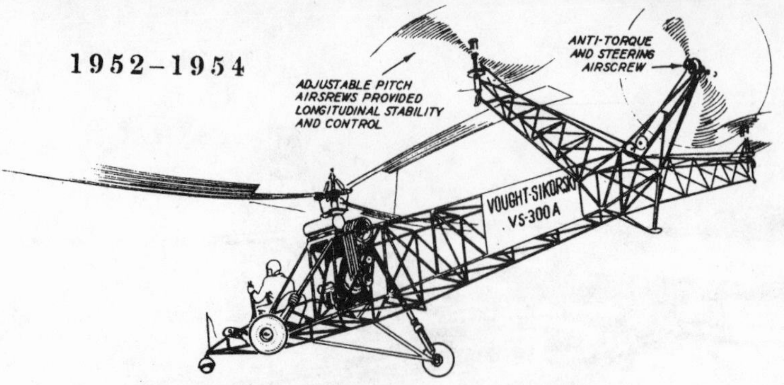

SIKORSKY VS-300 The original Sikorsky helicopter. Developed during World War II.

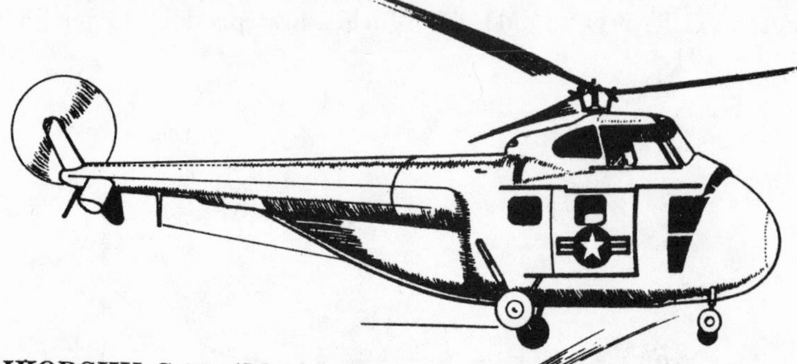

SIKORSKY S-55 (Marine Corps version, HRS-1, shown here) 600-h.p. P. & W. engine mounted in nose. Comparison with the original Sikorsky VS-300 gives some idea of the progress which has been achieved in the short period of U.S. helicopter history.

KAMAN HOK-1 One 500-h.p. Continental engine. Servo-flap rotor control makes it simple to handle.

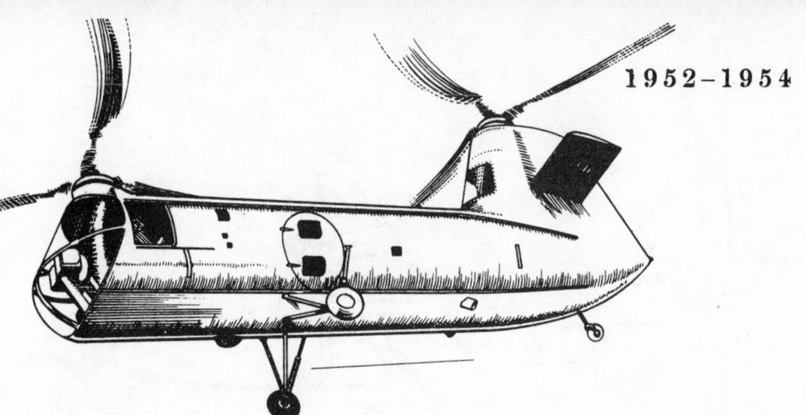

PIASECKI HUP-1 Medium-size U.S. military general-purpose helicopter.

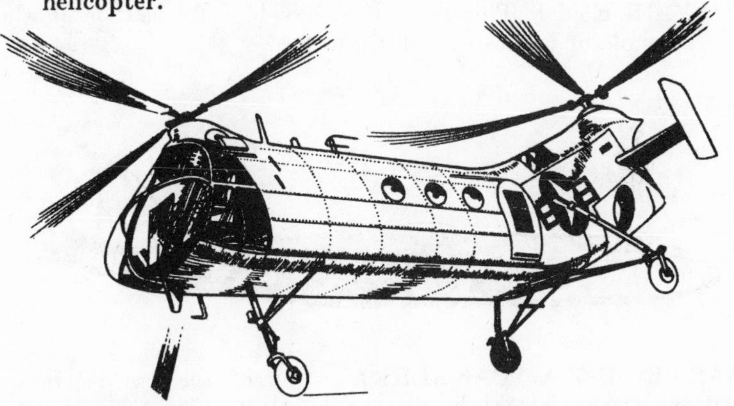

PIASECKI HRP-2 One 600-h.p. Wright. 8-place military aircraft. Maximum speed: 125 m.p.h. Folding rotors for shipboard use.

PIASECKI XH-16 Two 1,425-h.p. P. & W. engines, 25- to 40-passenger civil and military transport.

CONVAIR R3Y-1 This large U.S. naval patrol boat is another example of turbo-prop in the U.S.

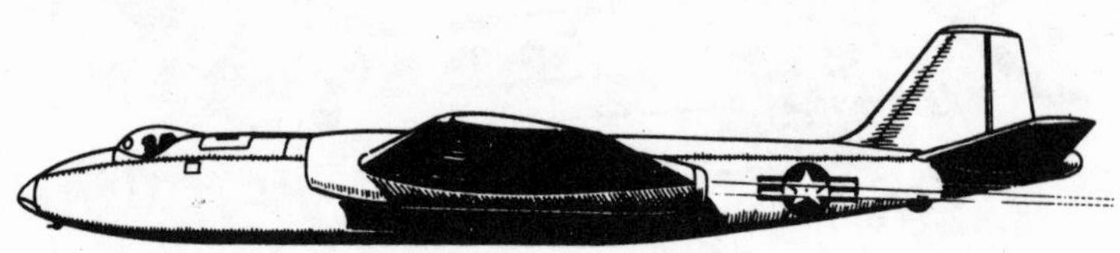

MARTIN B-57A "CANBERRA" One of the world's fastest operational attack-bombers, this is not a Martin design but was built under license from the English Electric Company, designers and manufacturers of the original "Canberra."

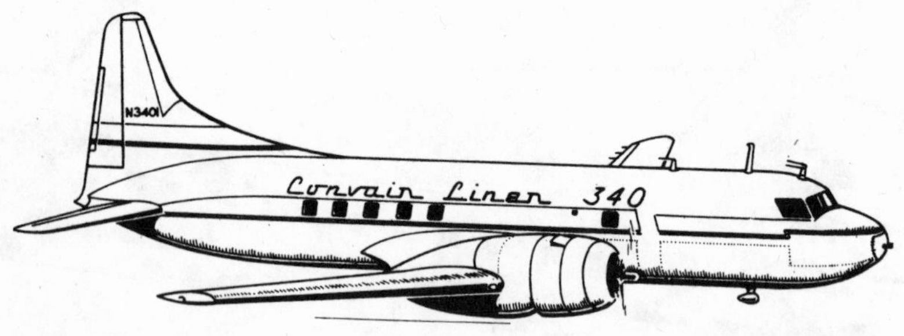

CONVAIR 340 One of the top U.S. air liners of its day.

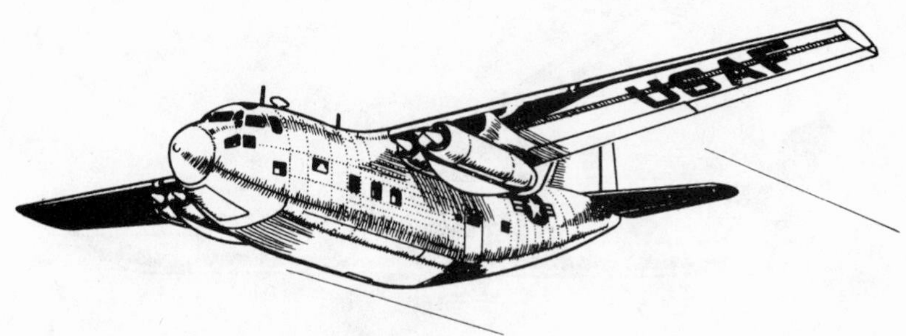

CHASE C-123A First U.S.A.F. jet-powered military transport.

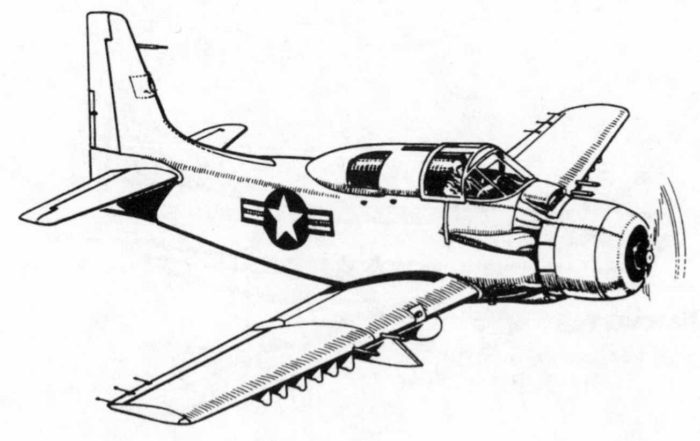

DOUGLAS AD-5 "SKYRAIDER" Standard U.S.N. carrier-based attack plane. Saw active service in the Korean war.

DOUGLAS C-124 "GLOBEMASTER" One of the largest piston-engine military transports. Clamshell doors in nose speed loading and unloading vehicles and guns.

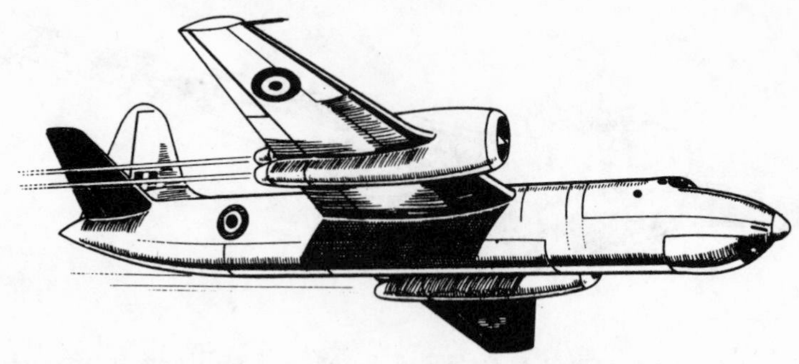

SHORT S.A./4 Prototype British 4-jet bomber with the jets stacked vertically in pairs.

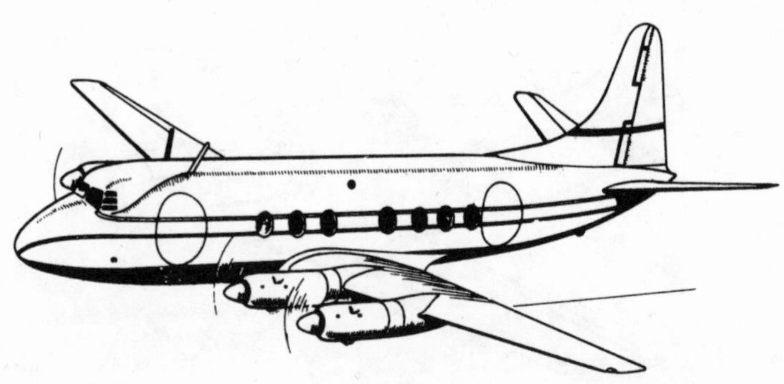

VICKERS "VISCOUNT" Fast turbo-prop British air liner popular on the Continent and with U.S. airlines.

SAAB 210 DRAKEN With an over-all span of less than 17 feet this Swedish research plane is world's smallest delta.

FAIREY F.17 "GANNET" Anti-submarine aircraft by a firm with nearly forty years of experience in the production of naval aircraft. Like so many British aircraft it is turbo-prop powered.

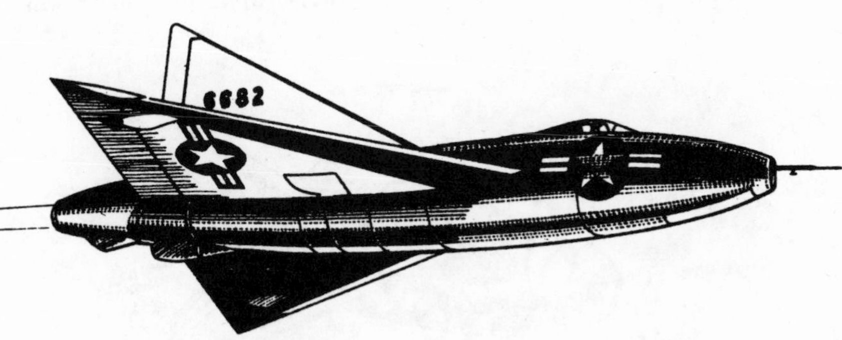

CONVAIR XF-92A Allison J-33A-29 engine with afterburner. Originally known as Model 7002, this was first U.S. jet-powered delta-wing plane.

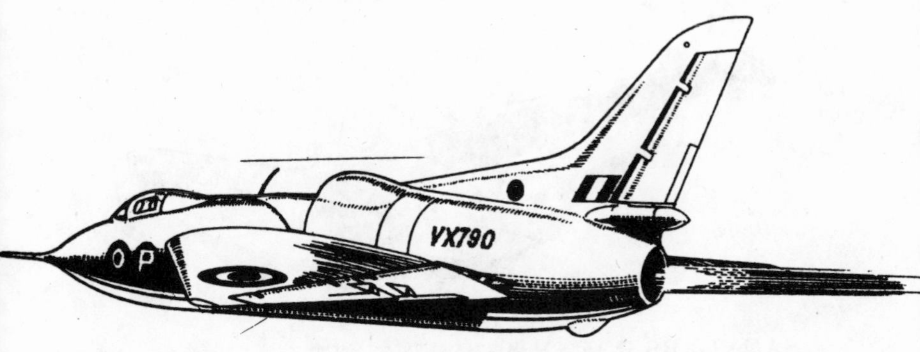

AVRO 707B Variant form of Model 707A with dorsal air-intake duct and modified controls.

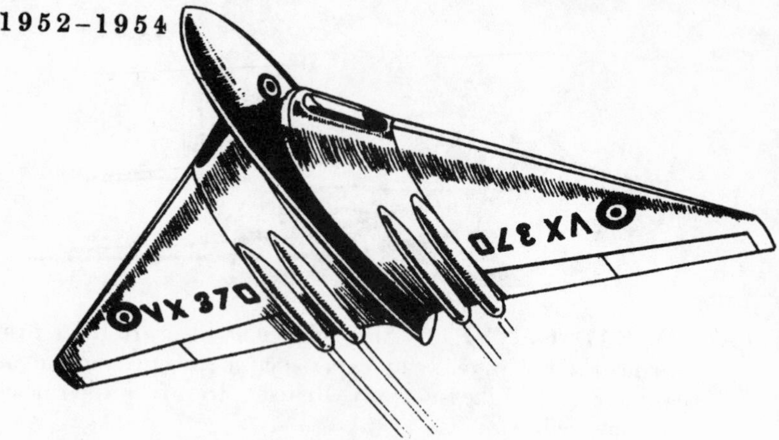

AVRO 698 "VULCAN" British delta. Span of bomber was 99 feet; length: 97 feet 1 inch.

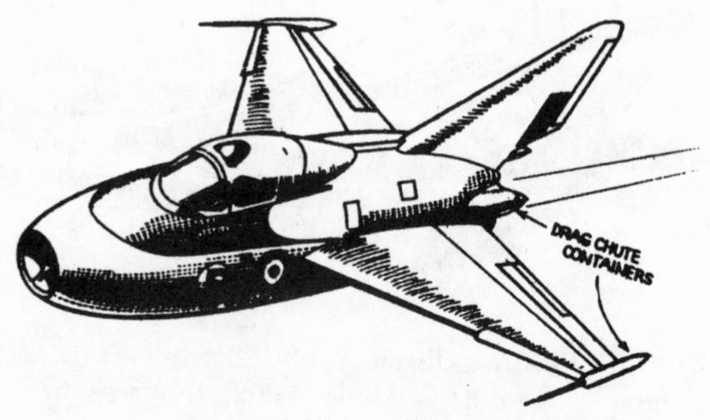

FAIREY F.D.1 Originally this plane had small stabilizer atop the rudder, but this was the intended final form.

SAUNDERS-ROE SR/45 "PRINCESS" Largest flying boat in the world. Saunders pioneered in flying-boat hull design.

PART TEN

The Aero-Space Decade

1951-1962

IN THE WORLD of flight, these ten breathless years of progress can aptly be termed "The Incredible Fifties." In retrospect, the events of the decade make patterns with implications that stagger the imagination.

Mounting pressures of international rivalry in commercial and military fields stirred fierce competitions which put national prestige, even survival, at stake. In this one decade the jet age became reality. The space age dawned.

In the beginning, the rumbling, earth-shaking, ten-engined B-36 was the marvel of its day. At the end, the airplane had flown nearly 4,000 miles per hour and hundreds of thousands of feet high. Man talked of orbital piloted flying machines to be launched by monster rockets.

What was evolution, what revolution? The two telescoped in a mid-century air world in which everything and anything became possible. If man could think of it, he seemingly could do it. And during 1951-1962 he had been happily busy with his magic wand of new-found confidence and know-how.

The fifties—and probably the sixties—are tied to the turbine. Without the limitation of reciprocating parts or the four-cycle operation of the piston engine, possessed of relatively immense power and surprising reliability, the whining turbine became the sound of the times. Turbines powered transonic and supersonic bombers and fighters and fleets of swift, giant airliners that shrunk the world. These versatile powerplants really made the helicopter a machine to be reckoned with. They power hovercraft and all manner of Short Take-off and Landing (STOL) and Vertical Take-off and Landing (VTOL) aircraft. New avenues of airplane design opened up by the turbine are changing the air world before our eyes.

A panoramic view of the air world sweeps many areas of notable activity, areas which require close-up focus—the rise of Russian air power, for instance, and its effects upon the western world. The invincible Strategic Air Command (SAC), in the early days of the intercontinental B-36's, then the B-47's, and later the B-52's, B-58's, *et al.*, made a Russian air strike patently foolhardy. The availability of the A- and then H-bomb to both nations—then to Britain and France with others to come—coupled with the American aim never to strike the first blow has created an uneasy balance of airpower in which planes (forgetting IRBM and ICBM missiles and Polaris submarines) of many types, from tiny fighters to massive bombers, can deliver nuclear and thermonuclear loads.

Whereas Britain at first conceded a whole generation of "heavies" and even used obsolescent American prop jobs before coming up with such interesting "A-bombers" as the Avro Vulcan delta-wing and the Handley-Page crescent-wing jets, and Russia once was reputed to copy old U.S. bombers that fell into her hands, all major prospective combatants today have supersonic bombers—intercontinental when necessary.

At the Tushino Air Show in 1961 Russia displayed her latest, most formidable types, including the huge delta-wing "Bounder" with supersonic dash capability and the Mach-2 "Beauty" with its twin rear-mounted turbojets. Rocket assist was much in evidence in various Russian types. Swift Mach-2-plus fighters of several makes indicated the U.S.S.R's preparation to meet attack.

In addition to her transsonic A-bombers, Britain showed her Mach-2-plus fighters in the English Electric F.Mk.1. France, from the success of her renowned "Dassault Mystère" variations of fighters, projected the Mach-2 "Dassault Mirage IV" atomic bomber.

In America, the late-model Boeing B-52's and Mach-2 Convair B-58 "Hustlers"—the latter with sustained supersonic cruise—were ceaselessly refined and honed to a razor-edge efficiency. Many U.S. fighters, Air Force and Navy, operating from heartland or overseas airfields and carriers, augmented the big bombers. West Germany, Japan, and other nations were to fly latest-model American fighters like the tiny-winged Lockheed F-104.

Throughout the decade, co-operation between many countries was seen in the operation of U.S. designed fighting machines. "Sabres" firing "Sidewinder" missiles, Chinese-flown from Formosa, shocked the Red Chinese in the mid-fifties with a supremacy that matched our own final effectiveness over the MiGs in Korea a few years before.

Electronics complicated the art of flying during the fifties. Advanced devices to fool enemy radar, measures and countermeasures, reached the point where a bomber could project a false image in the air to mislead defensive missiles. A fighter pilot could push buttons that brought his steed to a desired battle scene, practically fought it for him, then sent him on to another if he so wished. The Civil War Gatling gun had a rebirth in G.E.'s "Vulcan," a six-barreled affair firing 20-mm. shells at 6,000 rounds a minute. It was installed, for instance, in the nose of the F-104 and F-105 or the tail of the B-58. Range ceased to be the problem it had been when in-flight refueling was perfected—jet-to-jet, even fighter-to-fighter.

Air power became a chess game of move and countermove. When defensive fighters and missiles—such as "Nike" and "Bomarc" in the U.S.—threatened the bombers' ability to get through, air-to-ground missiles, blown up into ballistic, nuclear-tipped "stand-off" ALBM missiles (like "Skybolt"), were designed to be launched from afar by the bomber, which could then either turn for home or penetrate to other targets with its bomb-bay load. There was the fascinating U-2 operation, in which high-flying photoplanes sailed serene and untouched—except for the fateful one flown by Powers in 1960—

over the heads of Russian airmen, mapping missile and other sites.

The peacetime possibilities of the new age were pointed up by the global airline conversion from piston to turbine, both turbo-prop and turbo-jet. While the potential of the civil jet had been long apparent, and America risked much by letting England make an exclusive try with the "Comet" 4-jet airliner, the "Comet," unfortunately for John Bull, had serious teething troubles, evidenced in two disasters. By the time the "Comets" were debugged, in the late fifties, Boeing had stepped from her military jet bombers and tankers into the civil market, gaining worldwide ascendancy for the U.S. The Boeing 707 is one of history's most significant airplanes. Douglas followed with the DC-8, and Consolidated with its 600, 880, and 990. France scored heavily with her "Caravelle," featuring rear pod-mounted engines, and threatened to steal a march with her rush program for a Mach-2 "Super Caravelle."

Turbo-props were everywhere: long-ranged, as in the Bristol "Britannia" and the monster Russian TU-114D; and medium-ranged, as in the Vickers "Viscount" and the Lockheed "Electra" (which, like the British "Comet," ran the gamut of baffling disasters high in the sky and was then modified after a stupendous investigation and fix program). Lockheed called back well over 100 "Electras" from as far away as Australia and made changes at a cost of millions. In 1961, the "Electra" was fulfilling her brilliant promise.

As the decade closed, air cargo promised to equal passenger revenues before too long, thanks to new end-loading and swing-tail craft like the Canadair CL-44, more sensible rate structures, and development of sorely needed terminals, equipment, and ground-handling methods. Lockheed's development of a strategic air freighter for the Air Force, the 4-jet C-141 "Super Hercules," promised the updating of air logistics to match the swift pace of new air-warfare methods in general.

Peaceful air commerce and transportation required small planes, too, as attested by skyrocketing production by Piper, Cessna, Beechcraft and others of single-engine, light-twin and other business and executive types—attaining at the high end of the scale the stature of the Fairchild F-27 as well as exotic conversions of ex-airline and military heavy twins to "plush" configurations. So important had business aircraft become in the U.S. that airfields—some of them handling nothing else—were crowded with the products of Wichita, Lock Haven, and so on.

Helicopters, by the turn of the 1960-61, were in mass production, and this was only the beginning. The U.S. Army projected thousands of 'copters for close-in battlefield work, evacuation and even armed missions. In mufti, 'copters were dusting and spraying, carrying thousands of passengers on short lines networked about New York, Chicago, Los Angeles and other cities, flying pipe and power lines, landing on mountain tops and factory rooftops and making themselves useful as only rotary wings could. Choppers were carrier-based, flew from ships, hunted submarines—they were staking out a promising future.

Between the long-distance fixed-wing craft and the vertically rising helicopter lies a world of possibilities for blending their capabilities. STOL and VTOL designs of numerous and fascinating configurations—convertiplanes that tilt their wings with engines and props or just rotate their props 90 degrees for transition from vertical to forward flight—abounded in the late fifties as experimental types.

Some deflected portions of their wings to gain lift for takeoff. Some had no wings, but blasted air downward from swiveling turbines or nozzles. Some carried numerous "direct-lift" engines in nacelles and/or fuselages, plus, perhaps, other groups of jet engines to gain forward speed. Others involved huge overhead rotors and conventional engines and props. Ducted propeller platforms moved about sans wings or visible lift of any kind. In fact, man began to fly with nothing more than a rocket motor attached to his belt.

Private and sport flying was reborn during the fifties, and international interest in such things as sky diving, sailplaning, and home-built aircraft grew astoundingly by 1960-61. Delightful light aircraft, open-cockpit, cabin-enclosed, low-wing, high-wing, biplane—you name it—were built by the thousands in America in late years. Annual "fly-ins" and air shows for these amateur fliers were again a bit of Americana. The Federal Aviation Agency at long last came to understand these homemade efforts, for the overwhelming manufacturing interest in business aircraft had all but defaulted the sport and training fields.

As the decade "phased out," so to speak, promise of bigger and faster things ahead was everywhere in evidence. The in-and-out B-70 program would soon bring forth the first 2,000-m.p.h. bomber, in turn showing the way to the Mach-3 supersonic airliners America soon would need to retain her top position as airliner builder to the world. Aluminum alloys would give way to stainless steel in this fast craft. Oddly, however, man had not yet perfected the atomic-powered aircraft.

Dyna-Soar, the orbital glider in planning stage, had tie-in possibilities as a "weapons system." Perched on the nose of a Titan ICBM missile, it would loft its pilot into the wildest ride in manned-aircraft history. Later, lifted by the mighty Saturn, a booster with many times the thrust of the Atlas, Dyna-Soar could perform yet undefined missions. In such instances, at least, the question will rise: Is the man pilot or spaceman?

And, indeed, it is the proved staying powers of aviation that, as 1961 faded out, hyphenated the words "aero" and "space" to properly label the Aero-Space Age.

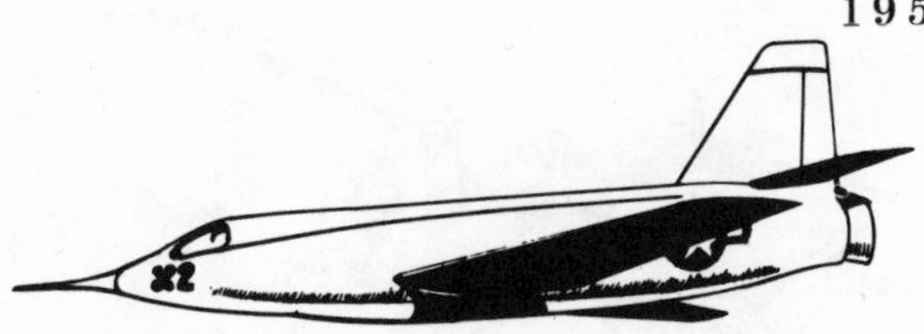

BELL X-2 American rocket plane for supersonic exploration flew 2,148 m.p.h. and 126,200 feet high on September 27, 1956. Stainless-steel and monel-metal construction.

BOEING B-52A The Strategic Air Command's primary man-carrying heavy bombardment aircraft grosses 350,000 pounds, has cross-wind landing gear and in-flight "flying-boom" refueling. Eight P. & W. J57-P9W turbo-jets.

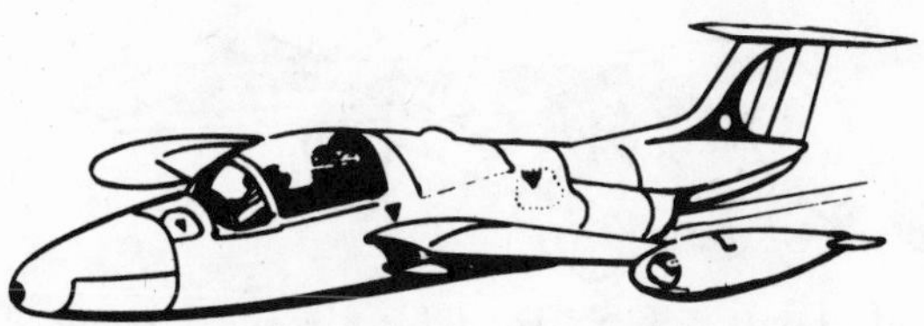

MORANE M.S. 760 "PARIS" French 4-place high-speed communications jet aircraft fitted with 2 Turbomeca Marbore 11 turbines, each 880 pounds static thrust.

FAIREY F.D.2 British delta-wing high-speed research craft powered by the Rolls-Royce Avon turbo-jet was first jet to exceed 1,300 m.p.h.

CUSTER CCW-5 Making its first flight in 1953, unique "channel wing" with two 225-h.p. Continental engines claimed ability to rise vertically and hover—flew as slow as 11 m.p.h. in tests.

McDONNELL MODEL 82 U.S. VTOL convertiplane (Air Force XV-1) had pusher prop for forward travel and rotor—driven by jet tip burners—for vertical flight. Continental 550-h.p. engine.

AEROCAR MODEL 2 U.S. roadable aircraft first used 150-h.p. Lycoming for either prop or wheel drive with prop at cabin rear. Later version shifted prop aft of tail. Clutch and brake pedals; all air and ground lights and other instruments required by vehicle codes. Towed wings and tail as trailer on ground.

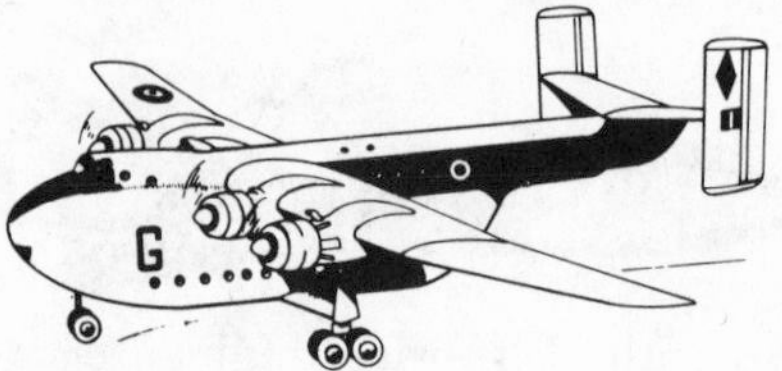

BLACKBURN "BEVERLY C" Mk. 1 R.A.F.'s heavy transport with four 18-cylinder engines rated 2,850 h.p. each at take-off, spanned 162 feet and grossed 135,000 pounds. Two to 10 rockets could assist take-off.

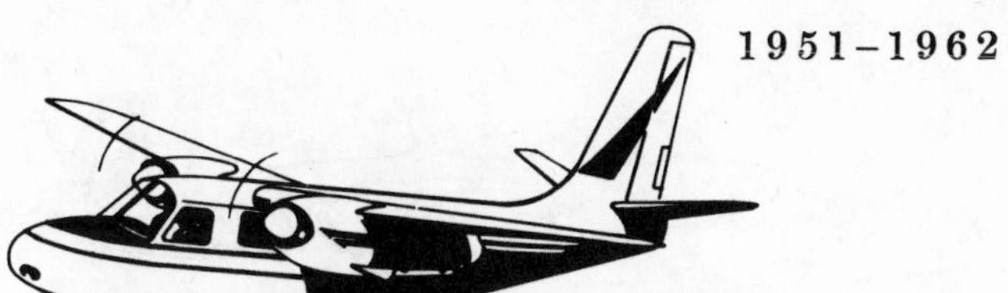

AERO COMMANDER 560 Two 270-h.p. Lycoming engines cruised this 4- to 7-place U.S. "business" plane 200 m.p.h. at 10,000 feet. Could carry freight in lieu of passengers.

LOCKHEED C-130A "HERCULES" For assault and support missions, U.S. Air Force's transport carried 64 paratroops, or 92 ground troops, or 70 stretcher cases. Four 3,750-s.h.p. Allison T56-A-1A turbo-props.

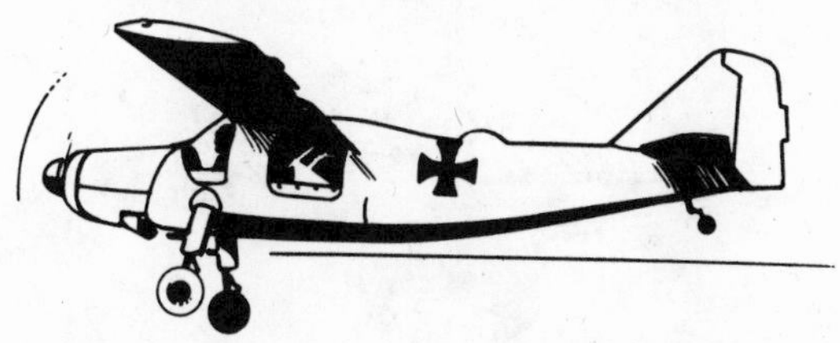

DORNIER DO.27 Designed in Spain, this STOL liaison craft was produced by Dornier of Germany. Has full-span wing slat, double slotted flaps.

CONVAIR F-106 U.S. delta-wing interceptor is a modification of the F-102B. The "Delta Dart" is powered by P. & W. J75-P-17 engine of 24,500 pounds s.t. with afterburning. Carries air-to-air missiles.

FOUGA C.M.170M "MAGISTER" Pretty French military jet trainer with 2 Turbomeca Marbore turbines was built in quantity for both French and German air forces.

BOEING KC-135 Here seen refueling a McDonnell "Voodoo" fighter, the KC-135 is military tanker version of the famed 707 jetliner and a vital cog in SAC's operations.

FOLLAND Fo.141 "GNAT" British "lightweight" fighter was one half the size and one third the weight of standard fighter. First flew in 1955.

LOCKHEED F-104 "STARFIGHTER" Knife-sharp tiny wings (span: 21 feet 11 inches; length: 54 feet 9 inches) mark Air Force's Mach. 2.2-2.3 fighter. G.E. J79 turbo-jet, 16,000 pounds s.t. with afterburner. Carries 6-barrel Vulcan 20-mm. cannon; "Sidewinder" and other air-to-air missiles.

FIAT G.91 Bristol Orpheus-powered ultralight Italian fighter, used by NATO for tactical missions, carries mixed armament of rockets, machine guns, guided missiles. Mach .91 speed.

CONVAIR B-58 "HUSTLER" SAC's delta-wing bomber attained 1,380 m.p.h. in 1957, has sustained cruise at supersonic speeds. Various military loads carried in huge detachable belly pod. Vulcan cannon in tail. Span 57 feet; grosses 160,000 pounds. Established numerous international records.

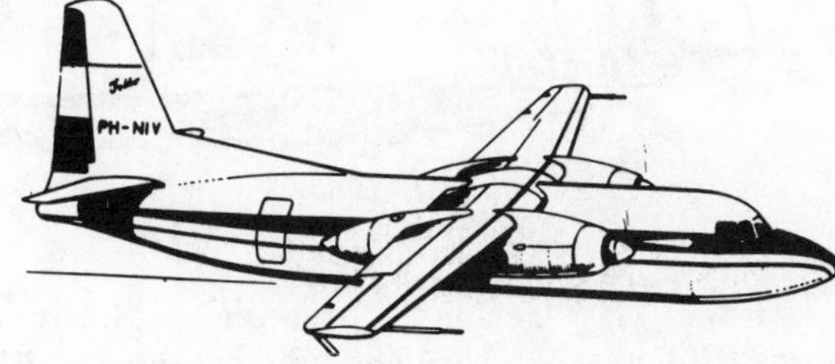

FOKKER F-27 Efficient Dutch airliner powered by 1,600-h.p. Rolls-Royce Darts is built in America by Fairchild as 40-passenger transport and as executive aircraft.

NORTH AMERICAN F-100D "SUPERSABRE" 822-m.p.h. Air Force fighter (P. & W. J57 turbo-jet) can carry 7,500-pound bomb load, has been "zero-launched" by 130,000-pound-thrust rocket. In-flight refueling of both internal and external tanks.

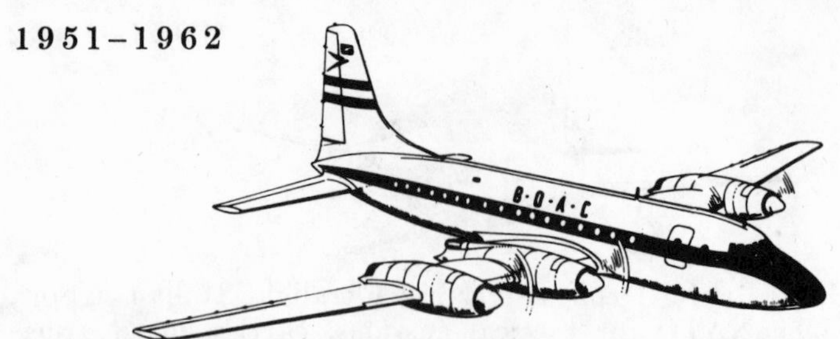

BRISTOL "BRITANNIA" Called "the whispering giant," British airliner carries 90 to 133 passengers. Has 4 Bristol Proteus 755 turbo-props of 4,120 e.h.p. Range up to 5,000 miles-plus at better than 350 m.p.h.

ILYUSHIN IL-18 "COOT" Greatly resembling the Britannia, Russian 73- to 111-passenger air liner with 4 Kuznetzov 4,000-e.h.p. turbo-props has 388–404-m.p.h. average cruise. It set 12 international records.

KLEMM KL.107B German three-place "business" aircraft. Cruises 133 m.p.h. (top 188 m.p.h.) on its 150-h.p. Lycoming engine.

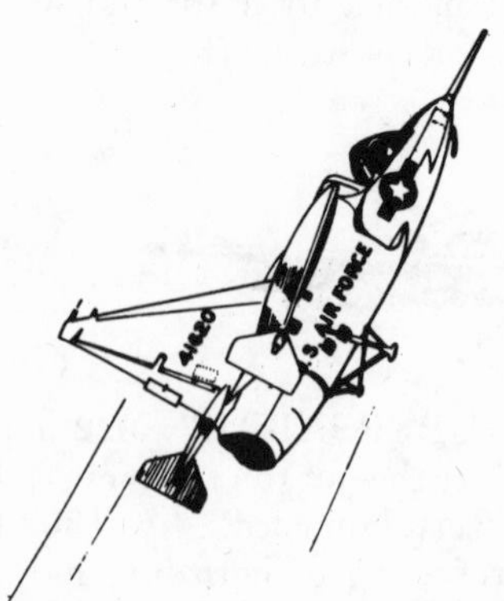

RYAN X-13 "VERTIJET" American VTOL "tail-sitting" research craft, powered by a Rolls-Royce Avon turbo-jet, takes off from and lands on mobile launcher on which it hangs suspended by under-nose hook. No conventional landing gear.

CESSNA "SKYLANE" 182 Tricycle-geared 4-place U.S. business plane cruises 158 m.p.h., has 230-h.p. Continental engine.

TUPOLEV 110 Russian jet airliner is 4-engined (Lulko turbo-jets) version of the TU-104, but has longer fuselage and 78- to 100-passenger capacity in two versions. Cruises 497 m.p.h.; range, 2,145 miles.

DOAK VZ-4DA CONVERTIPLANE U.S. experimental VTOL has ducted propellers which swivel 90 degrees to function as helicopter for take-off and hovering. Lycoming T53 840-e.h.p. turbine engine.

REPUBLIC F-105 "THUNDER-CHIEF" Air Force's single-seat fighter-bomber powered by 26,500-pounds-s.t. P. & W. J75 turbo-jet with afterburner carries heavy bomb and rocket loads long distances. Vulcan 20 mm., 6,000-round-a-minute cannon, 8,000 pounds of other weapons. Mach 2.15 at 38,000 feet, climbs 10,500 feet per minute.

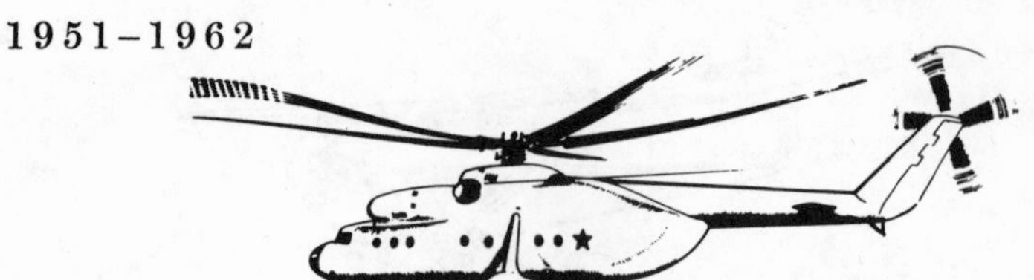

M.L. MIL-6 NATO code-named "The Hook," giant Russian 'copter can carry up to 120 passengers on its two 4,635-e.h.p. Soloviev shaft turbines. Clamshell rear-loading doors. Rotor diameter is 114 feet, 10 inches.

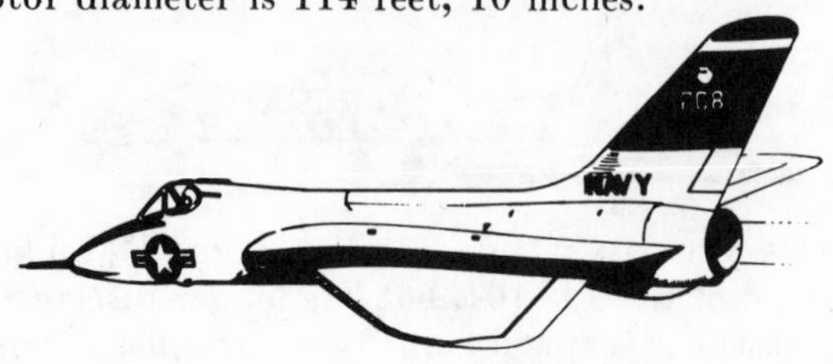

DOUGLAS F5D-1 "SKYLANCER" U.S. Navy modified-delta-wing supersonic fighter is a development of the Skyray, with thinner wing and longer fuselage. P. & W. J57 P12 turbo-jet.

LOCKHEED "ELECTRA" 4-turbo-prop airliner (3,700-e.h.p. Allisons)—handicapped by early crashes, which were followed by an extensive modification program—is in worldwide service. Spans 99 feet, carries up to 85 passengers at cruising speed of 405 m.p.h.

NORTH AMERICAN A3J "VIGILANTE" Navy's supersonic attack bomber can carry thermonuclear bombs for hundreds of miles at Mach 2 at high altitude. Ejects bomb from "linear" bay at tail. Carrier-based, also totes air-to-surface missiles. Two G.E. J79-GE-2 turbo-jets of 16,150 pounds s.t. each.

MORAVA L200A Czech light-twin business plane with two 210-h.p. M337 engines, also used by Russia's Aeroflot as air taxi.

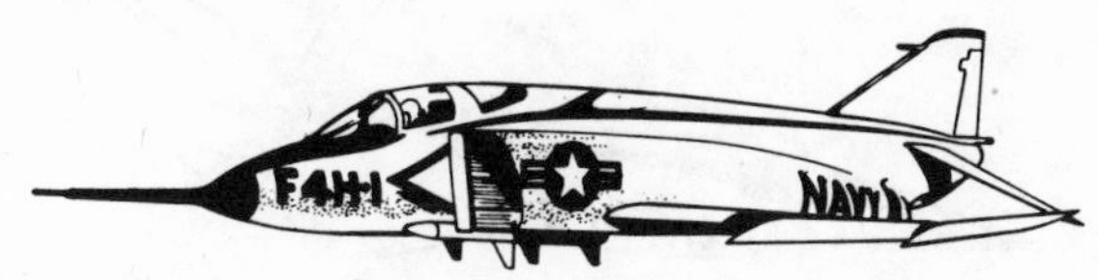

McDONNELL F4H-1 "PHANTOM II" Navy's first twin-jet two-place supersonic fighter hit Mach 2.6 in trials. Refuels in flight by "probe and drogue" or, using "buddy tank," can refuel supersonically with sister fighters.

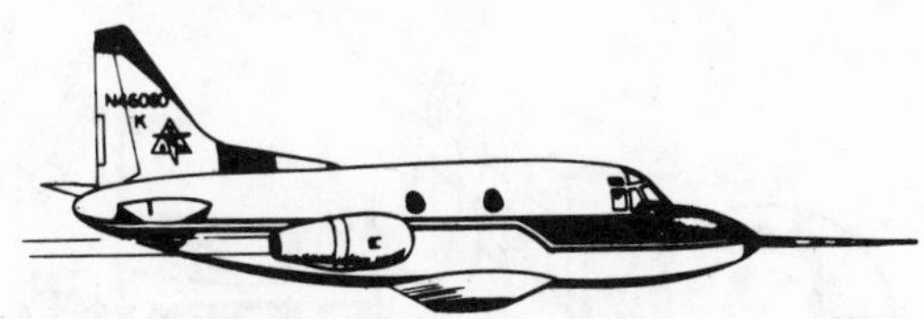

NORTH AMERICAN "SABRELINER" Executive jet and military light transport. Latter, the T-39, has a crew of 2, plus 4 to 8 passengers; P. & W. J60-P-3 turbo-jets of 3,000 s.t. each.

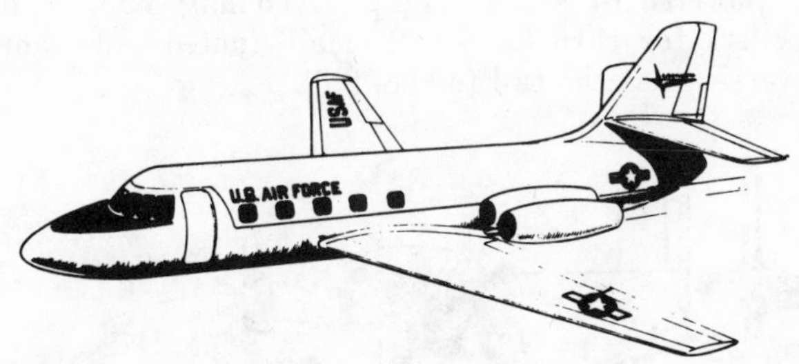

LOCKHEED "JETSTAR" Executive and military utility (C-140) jet transport with 4 rear-pod-mounted P. & W. JT12's of 3,000 s.t. each, cruises at 540 m.p.h.

PIPER PA-25 "PAWNEE" American agricultural aircraft for dusting and spraying features sturdy "rollover" cockpit structure. Lycoming 0-320 150-h.p. engine.

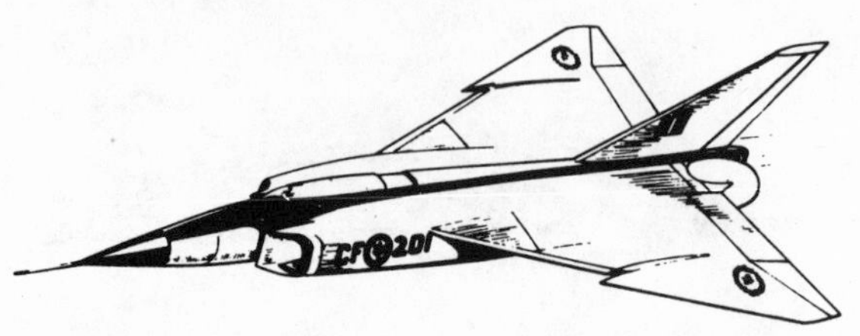

AVRO "ARROW" Canadian supersonic two-man delta-wing fighter hit 1,200 m.p.h. in level flight and climbed supersonically on its two P. & W. J75 afterburning turbo-jets. Was to fire Canadian Sparrow II air-to-air missiles. Production contract canceled.

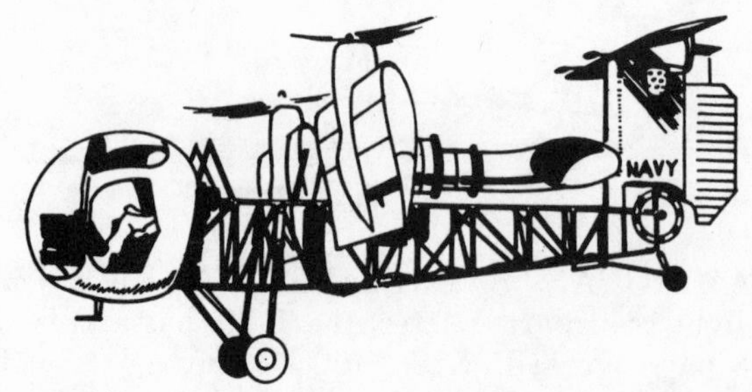

VERTOL MODEL 76 A tilt-wing U.S. experimental VTOL craft powered by a 600-e.s.h.p. Lycoming T53. Two rotor-propellers for thrust, with 2 small ducted fans, horizontal and vertical, at the tail for control.

BREGUET 940 French experimental STOL transport utilizes "deflected" wing and elevators on short take-offs. Four General Electric turbo-props.

GRUMMAN "GULFSTREAM" Executive and military transport has pressurized accommodation for 10 to 19 passengers. Two Rolls-Royce Darts of 2,105 e.s.h.p. Maximum cruising speed is 356 m.p.h.

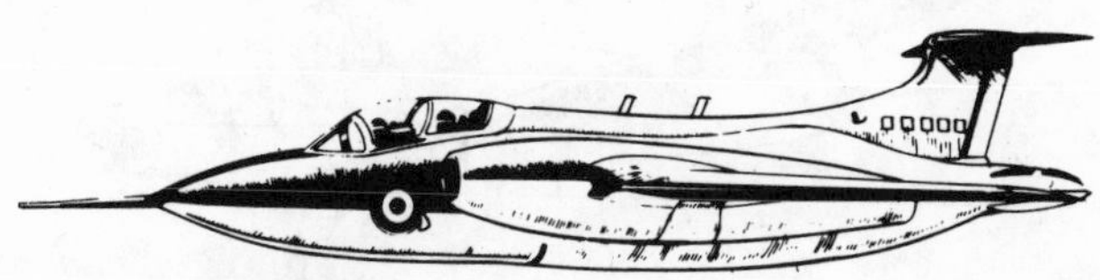

BLACKBURN NA.39 "BUCCANEER" Two De Havilland Gyron Junior turbo-jets power this British Navy transonic strike aircraft. Two sideways-hinged air brakes located in the tail cone.

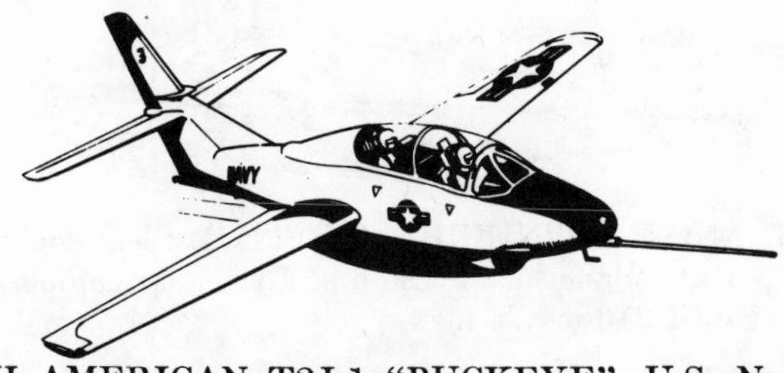

NORTH AMERICAN T2J-1 "BUCKEYE" U.S. Navy basic jet trainer is powered by a Westinghouse J34-WE-36 turbojet of 3,400 pounds s.t.

HANDLEY-PAGE DART "HERALD" British transport able to carry 44 to 50 passengers was designed for urban and "primitive" airfields. Two Rolls-Royce Darts each yield 1,910 s.h.p. plus 502 pounds s.t.

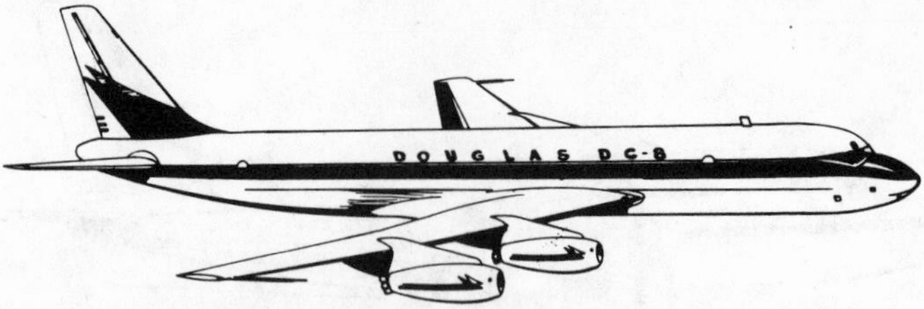

DOUGLAS DC-8 One of America's foremost long-range jetliners, the "Eight" seats from 112 first-class to 173 economy-class passengers. Version shown has four 15,800-pounds-s.t. P. & W. JT-4 turbo-jets. Cruising speed near 600 m.p.h.

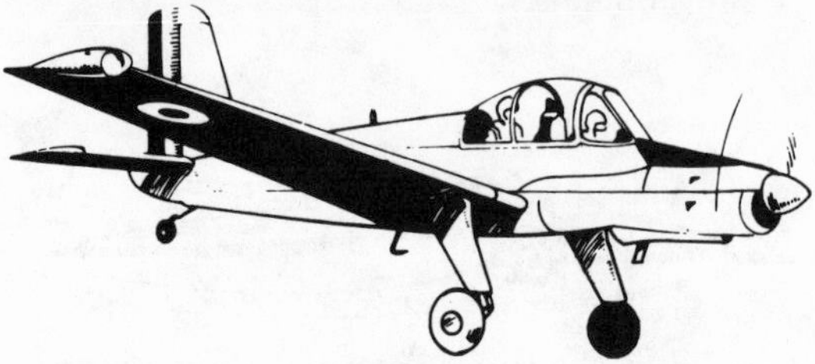

MORANE-SAULNIER "EPERVIER" French military utility craft is a two-placer powered by an 870-s.h.p. Turbomeca Basten turbo-prop. Armament includes Nord air-to-ground missiles.

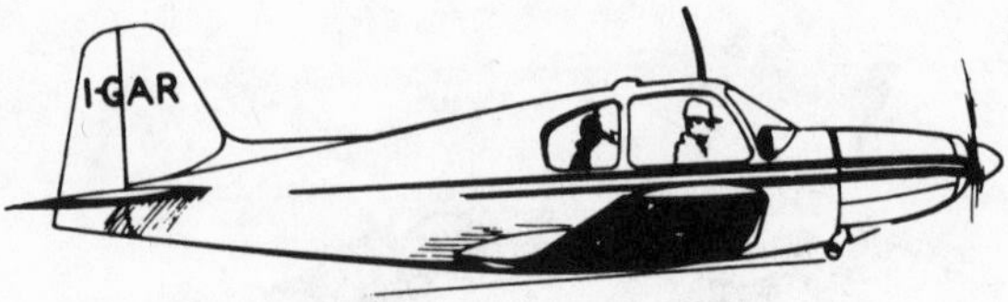

AVIAMILANO F-14 "NIBBIO" ("KITE") Clean-looking Italian private plane has a 180-h.p. Lycoming engine. This 4-seater does 210 m.p.h. max.

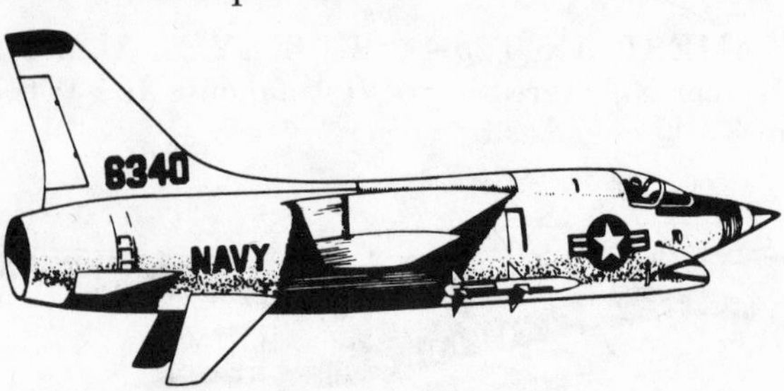

CHANCE VOUGHT F8U-3 "CRUSADER" Navy's carrier-based F8U is in the Mach-2 class. Late models have 16,000-pounds-s.t. P. & W. J-57's. Two-position variable-incidence wing and ventral fins are unusual features. Armament loads include four 20-mm. cannon, infrared "Sidewinder" missiles and thirty-two 2.75-inch rockets.

NORTHROP T-38 "TALON" A two-place supersonic trainer for the Air Force, basic design was modified into N-156F Freedom Fighter. Two 3,850-pounds-s.t. G.E. J85 (with afterburning) give Mach 1.3-plus speeds.

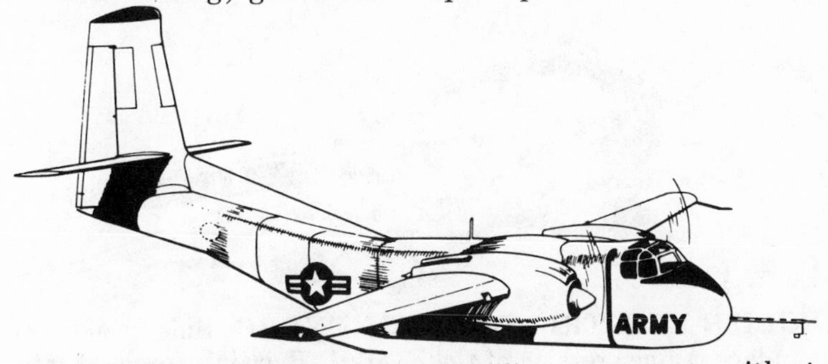

DHC-4 "CARIBOU" Canadian utility transport with two P. & W. 1,450-h.p. engines has STOL performance. Quantity ordered by U.S. Army.

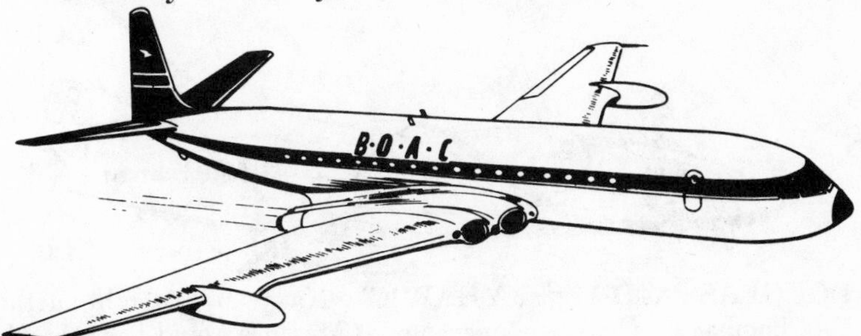

DE HAVILLAND "COMET IV" Britain's famous 4-jet airliner accommodates from 60 to 104 passengers. After modifications of "hard-luck" earlier version, the IV ran up impressive safety record. Rolls-Royce Avon (4) at 10,500 pounds s.t. each.

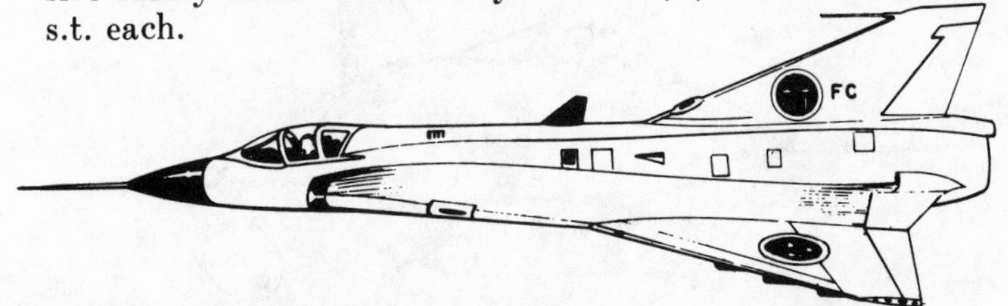

SAAB J-35 "DRAKEN" Swedish "double-delta" is a high-supersonic-speed fighter intended primarily to intercept subsonic bombers. Uses Swedish-built Rolls-Royce Avon turbo-jet of 15,200 pounds thrust with afterburning.

Z 326 TRENER Czechoslovakian 2-place trainer is renowned for aerobatic ability. Walter Minor 6-111 160-h.p. engine.

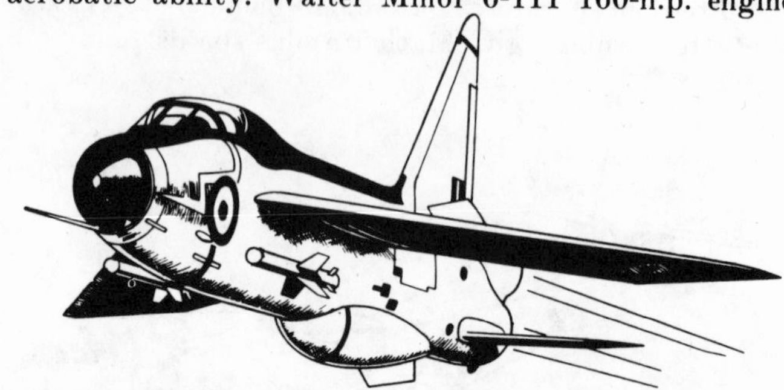

ENGLISH ELECTRIC P-11 "LIGHTNING" Side-by-side two-place trainer version of the F. Mk.1, Britain's foremost interceptor. Fighter capable of 1,500 m.p.h. on 2 Rolls-Royce Avons of 14,300 pounds s.t. each with afterburning.

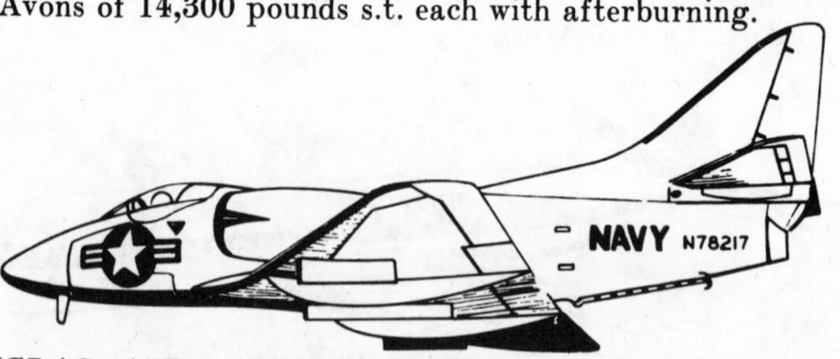

DOUGLAS A4D-1 "SKYHAWK" Navy lightweight attack bomber for carrier operation (Marines, land-based). Has Wright J65 7,800-pounds-s.t. turbo-jets; handles several hundred variations of military loads.

DASSAULT "MIRAGE 3" French delta-wing all-weather supersonic high-altitude interceptor, fighter and tactical-support craft, designed to operate from small air strips. SNECMA Atar turbo-jet of 9,900 pounds s.t.

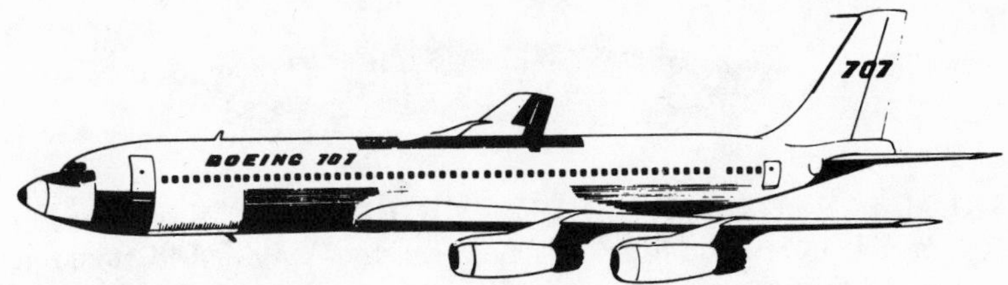

BOEING 707 Famous American jetliner used in many variations by numerous world airlines. Basic civil version, the 707-120, seats from 121 standard to 179 tourist passengers and has 4 P. & W. JT3C-6 turbo-jets of 13,000 pounds s.t. each.

PILATUS P-6 "PORTER" Swiss STOL utility 5-7-passenger aircraft also takes wheel/ski gear and twin floats. A 340-h.p. Lycoming engine.

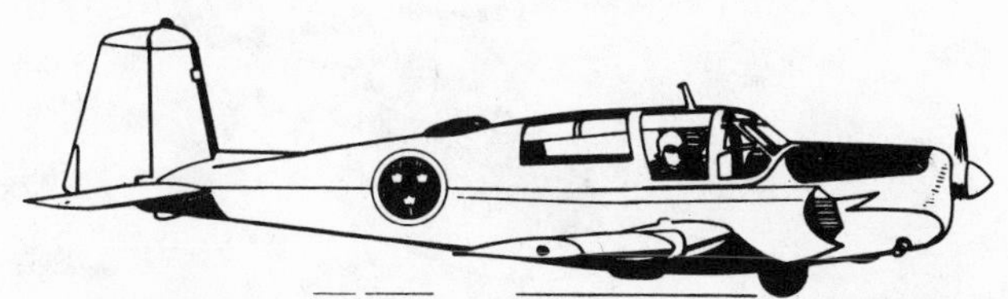

SAAB "SAFIR" Swedish four-place prop-driven trainer and business aircraft has been widely exported. Engine is 190-h.p. Lycoming.

FAIREY ROTODYNE Large British VTOL prototype passenger transport. Two 3,000-e.h.p. Napier Eland turbines drive props; rotor has tip-mounted pressure jets.

GRUMMAN F11F-1F "SUPER TIGER" U.S. Navy carrier-based supersonic fighter is powered by Wright J65 turbo-jet of 10,500 pounds s.t. with afterburning. Mach 1.12 at 35,000 feet. Four 20-mm. cannon, "Sidewinder" or air-to-ground missiles.

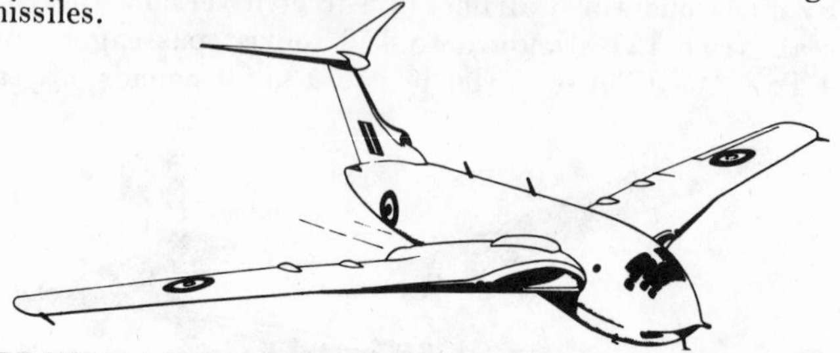

HANDLEY-PAGE "VICTOR 2" One of Great Britain's "A-bombers," the Victor is marked by its crescent-wing planform and high V-tail. Four 17,000-pound-thrust Rolls-Royce by-pass Conways.

KAMAN HU2K-1 "SEASPRITE" U.S. Navy rotary-wing aircraft is the first Kaman to employ a single rotor. General Electric T58 turbine of 1,025 s.h.p.

TUPOLEV TU-114 "CLEAT" Huge Russian airliner carrying a crew of 10 to 15 and as many as 220 passengers has 4 Kuznetsov turbines of 12,000 e.h.p. each, driving 8-bladed contrarotating props. Maximum cruise is 531 m.p.h., maximum range 6,000 miles.

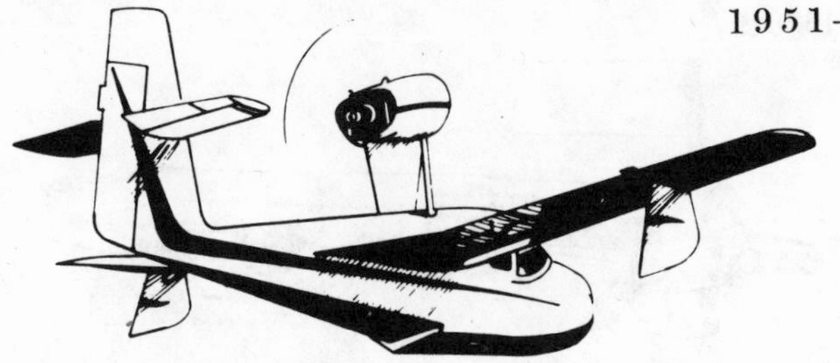

COLONIAL "SKIMMER" U.S. 4-place amphibian with 180-h.p. Lycoming, more recently manufactured by Lake Aircraft Corp. Maximum speed 130 m.p.h.

ARMSTRONG-WHITWORTH AW650 "ARGOSY" A British civil and military passenger and freight carrier, with front and rear doors for end-loading of cargo. Four Dart turbo-props with (each) 1,910 h.p. plus 505 pounds jet thrust.

MIGNET "POU DE CIEL" French "Sky Flea," grounded before World War II, was reborn during international craze for home-built planes. Later version has cabin, folding wings.

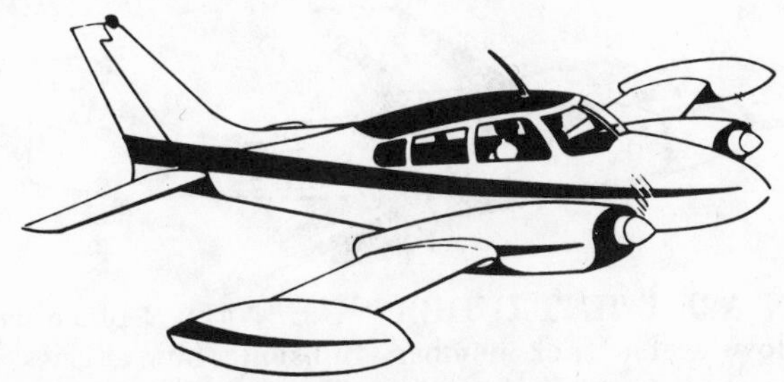

CESSNA 310F Typical U.S. business and executive light twin has two 260-h.p. Continental piston engines. Normally five-place.

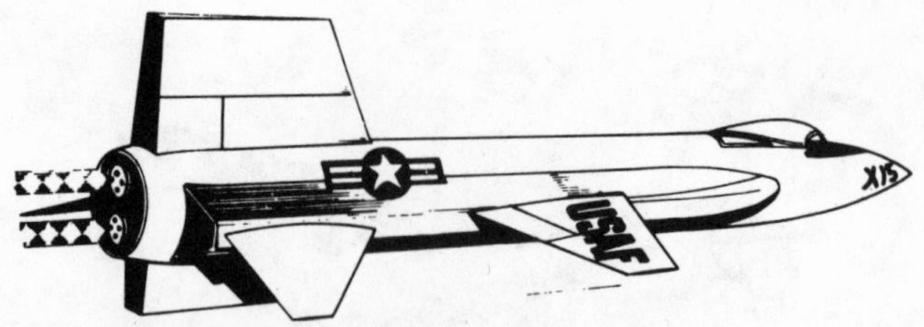

NORTH AMERICAN X-15 Designed for 4,000 m.p.h. and altitudes over 500,000 feet, famous manned craft is shown with two interim Reaction Motors rocket engines prior to installation of single 60,000-pound-thrust unit.

BELL HU-1A "IROQUOIS" Turbine-powered U.S. Army attack helicopter armed with six French Nord SS-11 solid-fuel rockets; 700-s.h.p. Lycoming T53-L-1A. Also an instrument trainer.

NIHON YS-11 Japanese 52-60-passenger "national" airliner is powered by 2 Rolls-Royce Dart turbo-props. Military version has cargo door, strengthened floor.

GRUMMAN A2F-1 "INTRUDER" U.S. Navy 2-place carrier-based low-level attack bomber. Subsonic but carries heavy load—such as two "Bullpup" missiles and three 1-ton bombs. Two 8,500-pound-thrust P. & W. turbo-jets with tilting tailpipes.

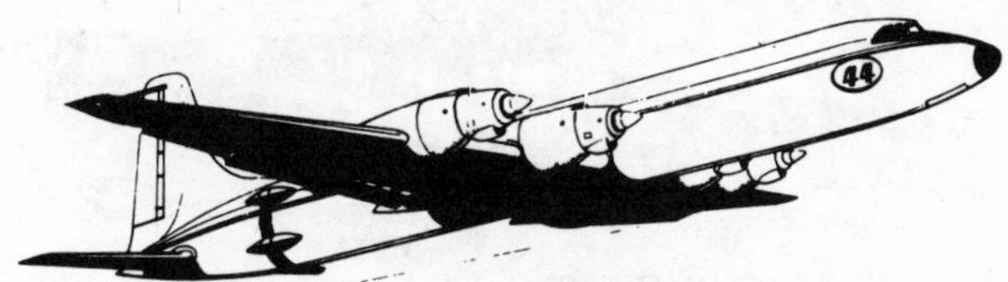

CANADAIR CL-44 Swing-tail "pure" freighter with four 5,730-e.s.h.p. Rolls-Royce Tyne turbo-props. Cargo capacity 63,272 pounds.

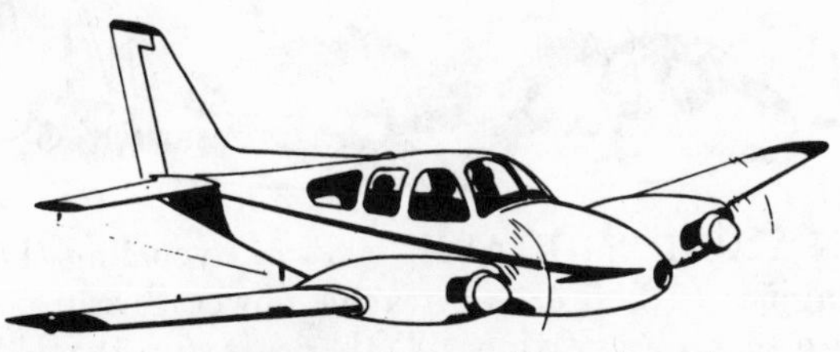

BEECHCRAFT "BARON" Five-place American executive aircraft is powered by two 260-h.p. Continental piston engines. SFERMA in France producing twin 440-h.p. turbine conversion called "Marquis."

YAKOLEV YAK-32 "MANTIS" Employed by the Soviet Aero Clubs is this neat-looking 2-place civil jet trainer.

SHORT SC-1 British experimental "flat riser" has five Rolls-Royce RB.108 turbo-jets, four for lift and one for forward propulsion. Conversion flights were feature of 1960 Farnboro display. Two prototypes built.

CESSNA "SKYMASTER" Tandem-twin business aircraft with pusher and tractor Continental engines offers single-engine handling simplicity, helpful in "engine-out" situations.

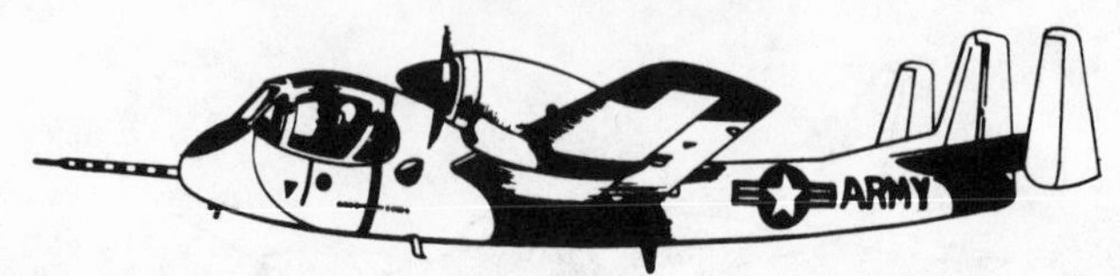

GRUMMAN YAO-1 "MOHAWK" Two Lycoming T53 turbo-prop engines (1,005 e.s.h.p. each) power this high-performance two-seat observation STOL craft for the U.S. Army. Carries many variations of electronic and other gear.

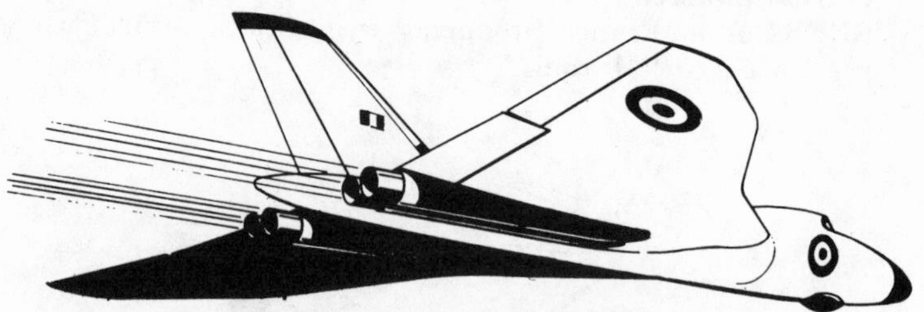

AVRO "VULCAN B-2" World's first delta-wing bomber, the British Vulcan went into squadron service in 1960. Four Bristol Olympus turbo-jets, originally 17,000-pounds-s.t., since 20,000-pounds-s.t.

BELL D-188A U.S. Mach-2 V/STOL proposed fighter with G.E. J85-5 turbo-jets—two in fuselage for forward speed, four swiveling at tips for lift and forward thrust. Drawing based on mock-up.

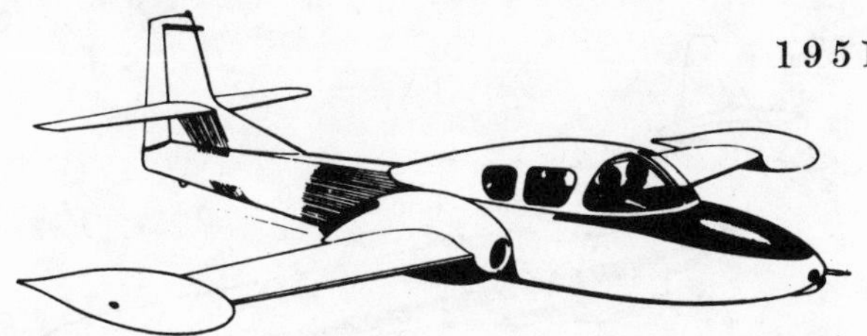

CESSNA 407 Four-seat offering of U.S.A.F. T-37A utility jet as civil possibility. Two Continental 356-9 turbo-jets of 1,400 pounds s.t. each proposed. Mock-up shown.

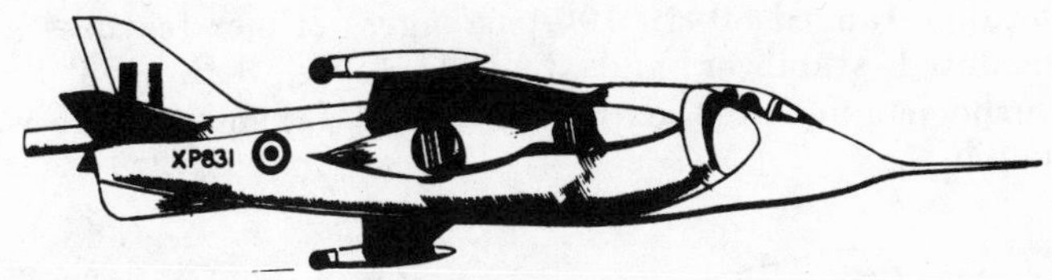

HAWKER P.1127 British V/STOL strike fighter employs Bristol Siddeley lift-thrust turbo-fan with 4 adjustable efflux nozzles for vertical or horizontal flight. First flew in March 1960.

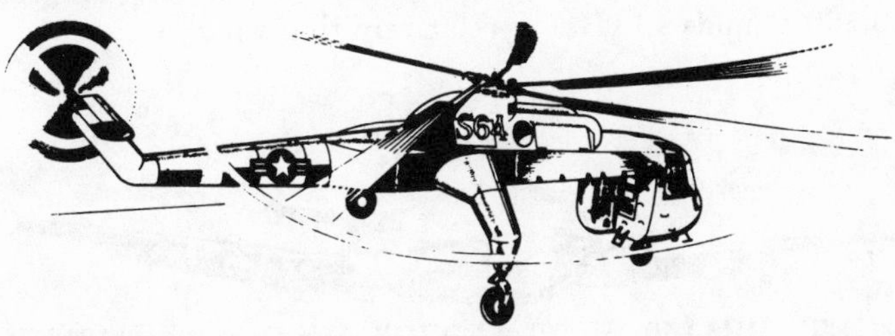

SIKORSKY S-64 "FLYING CRANE" First of a series, uses two P. & W. 4,050-s.h.p. JFTD-12 turbines. Ultimate 4-turbine craft: 12-blade rotor and 40-ton payload.

MIKOYAN MIG-21 "FISHBED" Standard Soviet interceptor is made in both day-fighter and all-weather configurations, latter with radome in nose intake. Variation shown has drogue-chute housing at base of vertical tail, JATO rockets for taking off from short, grassy fields.

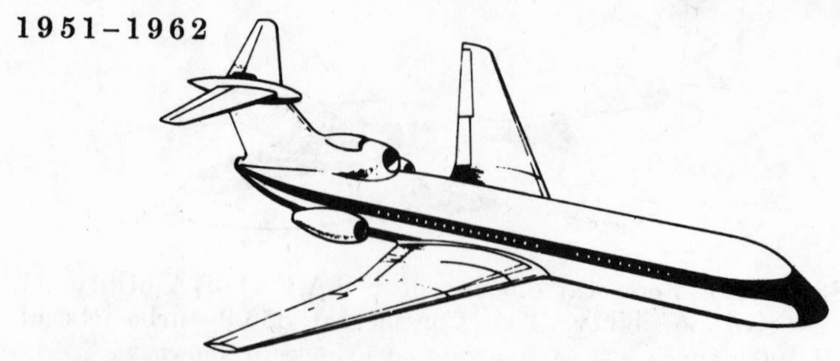

DE HAVILLAND D.H. 121 "TRIDENT" Ordered by B.E.A., medium-ranged 80- to 100-passenger jetliner features a fin-mounted stabilizer and 3 Rolls-Royce R.B. 163 bypass turbo-jets mounted aft of the wings. Maximum cruise is 606 m.p.h.

CONVAIR 990 This 96- to 121-passenger jetliner is powered by four General Electric CJ805-23 turbo-fan engines, each 16,100 pounds s.t. Has a relatively thin wing.

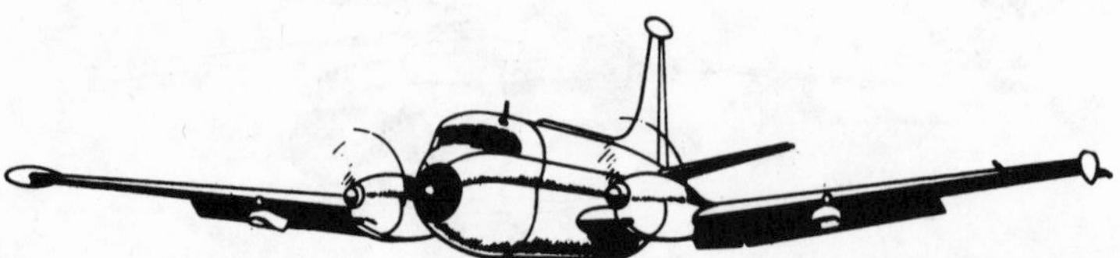

BREGUET BR1150 "ATLANTIC" French-assembled anti-submarine reconnaissance design superseded Lockheed Neptune on winning NATO competition. Two Rolls-Royce Tyne turbo-props in first prototypes.

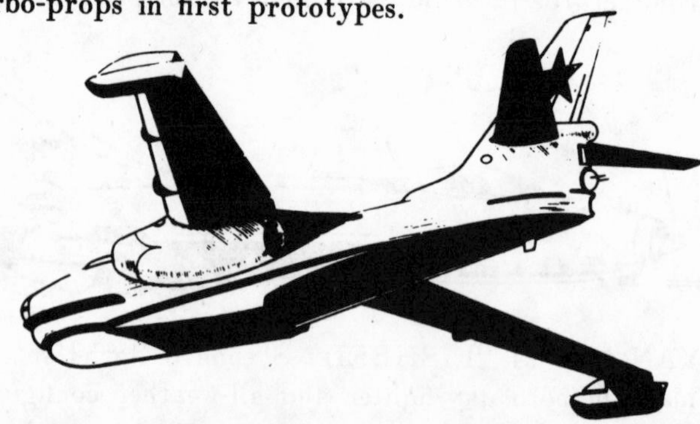

BERIEV BE-10 "MALLOW" Russian twin-jet anti-submarine flying boat. Wings have negative dihedral with tip floats.

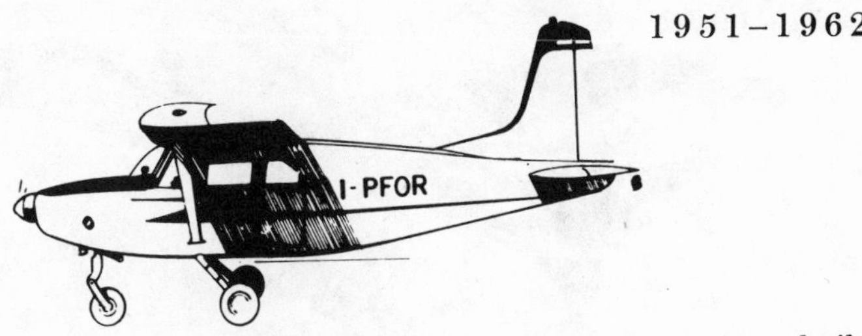

LOCKHEED LASA-60 Six-place light utility transport built by Lockheed-associated firms in Mexico, Argentina and Italy. A 260-h.p. supercharged Continental piston engine.

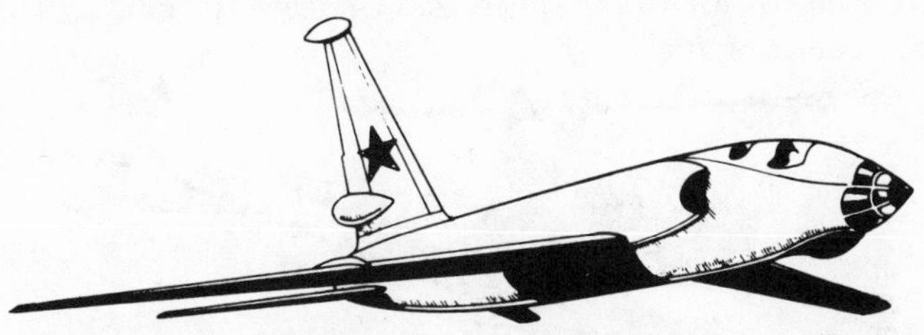

TUPOLEV "BACKFIN" Supersonic Russian medium tactical bomber has built-in booster rockets for accelerated take-offs, a crescent-wing planform, and 2 AM-3 turbo-jets of up to 22,400 pounds s.t. with afterburning.

AVIOLANDA-PRODUCED NHI "KOLIBRIE" Starkly simple Dutch 1- or 2-place ramjet 'copter is development of pilotless, electronically controlled drone. Lifts twice its empty weight.

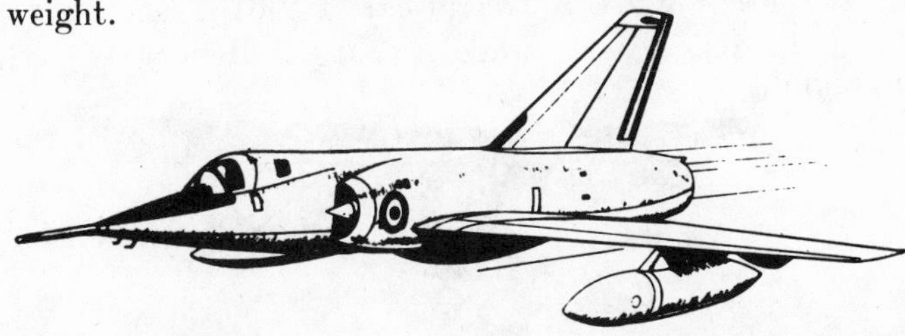

DASSAULT "MIRAGE IV" Strategic bomber, two-place delta-wing Mach-2 design to carry France's atom bomb. Two SNECMA Atar 9J turbo-jets of 16,535 pounds s.t. with afterburning.

TUPOLEV "FIDDLER" Mach-2 Russian swept-wing bomber and interceptor is believed development of the Backfin. Carries delta-winged air-to-air missiles. Underbelly package can carry radar or fuel.

BELL HUL-1M Powered by an Allison T63 250-s.h.p. turbine, this Bell "test-bed" helicopter completed initial test flights in January 1961.

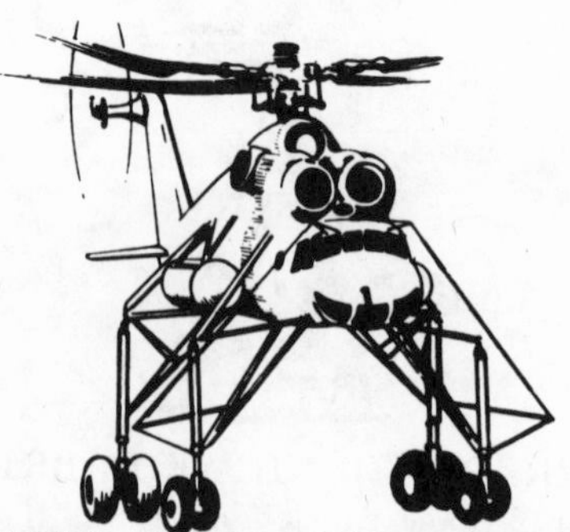

MIL MI-10 "HARKE" Russian "flying crane" lifted prefab house the size of a U.S. freight car at 1961 Tushino air show. Long landing gear straddles cargo. Reported payload: 40,000 lbs.

CHAMPION 7FC "TRI-CON" A variant of the "Tri-Traveler" with 95-h.p. Continental engine has novel "reversed" tricycle landing gear. Basic design former Aeronca Champion. Seats 2 in tandem.

DE HAVILLAND CUSTOM "DOVE 800" Two 400-h.p. Gipsy Queen piston engines power this British 8- to 11-passenger transport or executive aircraft. Also used by R.A.F. and the Royal Navy.

LOCKHEED NC-130B "BLC" One U.S. Air Force experimental test-bed item for boundary-layer control, has two additional pod-mounted turbo-jet engines (Allison YT56-A-6) under the wing to blow air over control surfaces during take-off and landing. Stall speed reduced to 60 m.p.h.

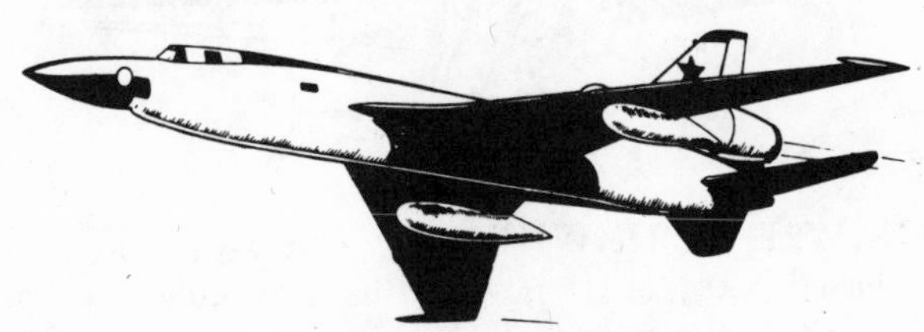

TUPOLEV "BLINDER" Russian Mach 2.5 heavy bomber is slightly larger than U.S. Hustler, has thin, highly swept wings and twin-jet powerplants mounted on either side of tail fin.

POTEZ P.840 French feeder-liner for 16 to 24 passengers is powered by 4 Turbomeca Astazou 442-e.h.p. turbo-props.

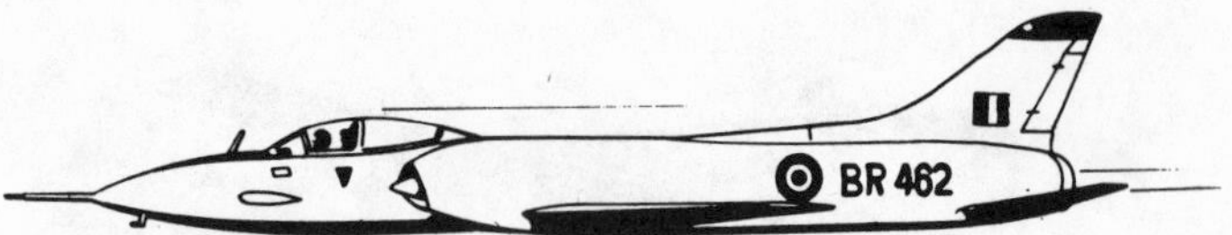

HINDUSTAN HAL HF-24 "MARUT" Indian Mach-2 all-purpose fighter was designed by Kurt Tank, creator of the Focke-Wulf 190 of World War II. Two Bristol-Siddeley Orpheus turbo-jets with afterburners.

KAMOV KA-22 "HOOP" Russian convertiplane capable of transporting 100 passengers uses modified An-10 fuselage. The 4,000-e.s.h.p. turbo-prop at each wing tip drives both propeller and rotor.

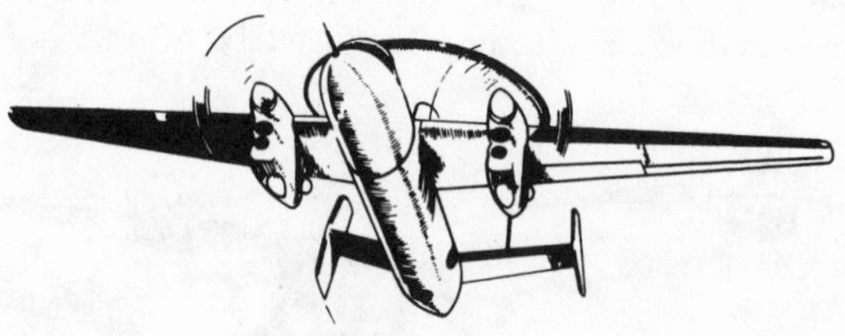

GRUMMAN W2F-1 "HAWKEYE" Early-warning; largest carrier-based Navy craft powered by two 4,050-e.s.h.p. Allison T56-A8 turbo-props. Rotating radar inside "saucer" on top.

AERO HC-3 Czech five-seat 'copter with 240-h.p. M 108H piston engine has 3-bladed rotor and 100-m.p.h. top speed.

AVIATION TRADERS ATL 98 "CARVAIR" British automobile-ferry plane has crew cabin elevated above a modified Douglas DC-4. Nose doors admit cars. Can carry 85 passengers or heavy freight.

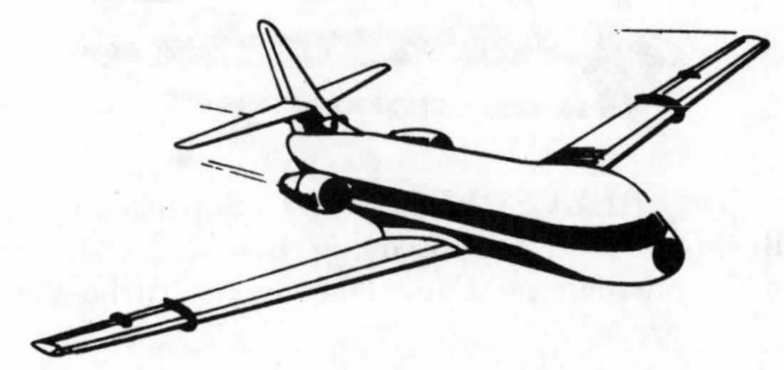

SUD "CARAVELLE" S.E. 210 French medium-range 64- to 80-passenger jetliner with pod-mounted turbo-jets behind the wings has enviable reputation. Rolls-Royce Avons of 1961 provide 12,200 pounds s.t. each.

FIAT MODEL 7002 Italian tip-drive 'copter uses "cold" jets fed from Fiat 4700 turbo-generator; combustion does not take place at the nozzles.

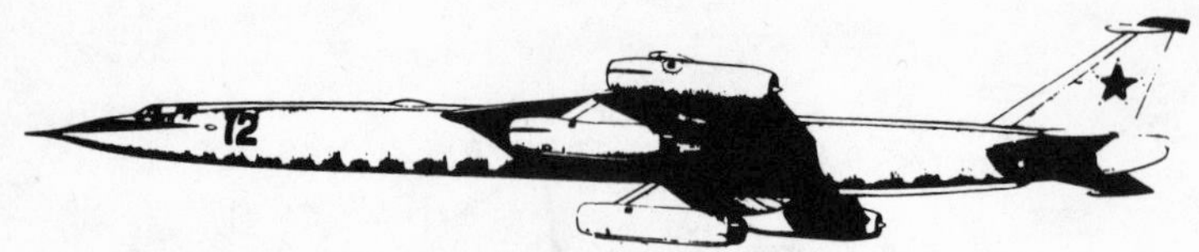

MYASISHCHEV "BOUNDER" World's largest delta-wing (with flying tail) Russian intercontinental jet bomber cruises at Mach .9, has Mach 1.4 dash capability. About 100-foot span, 200-foot length. Two 45,000-e.s.h.p. inboard turbo-jets with afterburners, plus 2 smaller outboard jets.

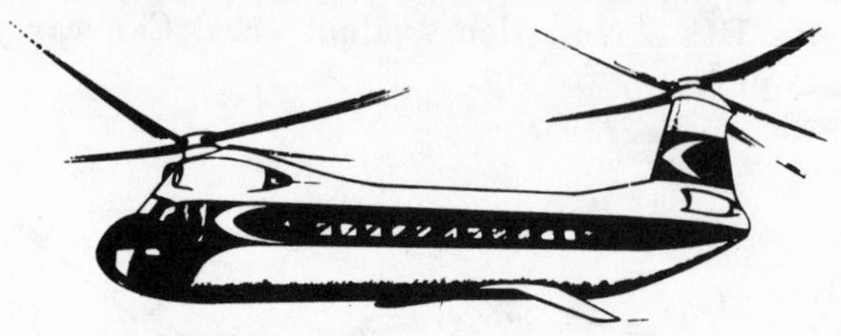

WESTLAND "BELVEDERE" 194 Superficially similar to the Boeing-Vertol, proposed big British 'copter would seat up to 60 passengers. Four DH Gnome turbo-shaft engines turn 2 rotors.

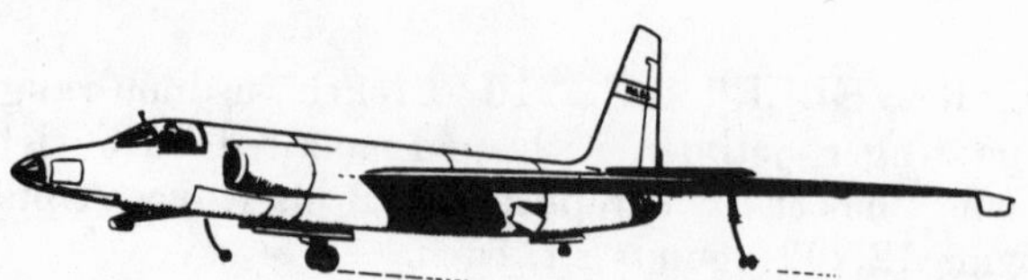

LOCKHEED U-2 One of aviation history's most famous aircraft, this ultra-high-altitude reconnaissance and research design has sailplane configuration and minimum structural weight. P. &. W. J75-P-13 turbo-jet of 11,000 pounds s.t.

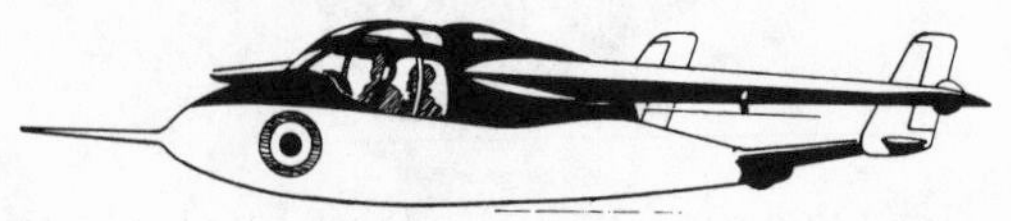

MILES STUDENT British prototype two-place jet trainer; one 880-lbs.t. Turbomeca Marbore turbo-jet.

PIPER PA-23-250 AZTEC Five-place executive aircraft developed from earlier PA-23 Apache. Speed 215 m.p.h.; range 1,400 miles; two 250-h.p. Lycoming engines.

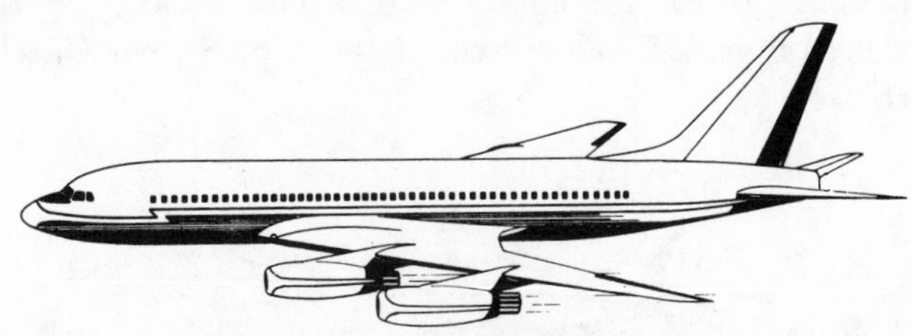

CONVAIR 880 Jet-liner transports 88 to 110 passengers; cruise speed 615 m.p.h.; range 3,995 miles; powered by four 11,200-lbs.t. General Electric CJ-805-3 turbojets.

BENSEN B-10 PROP-COPTER Experimental VTOL had pilot between tandem mounted rotors; control vanes around rotors. Uses 72-h.p. McCulloch drone engine. Top speed 60 m.p.h.

PIAGGIO P.136-L Italian 5-seat air/sea rescue amphibian assembled, marketed in the U.S. as the Trecker Gull. Speed 183 m.p.h.; range 1,056 miles; two 260-h.p. Lycoming engines.

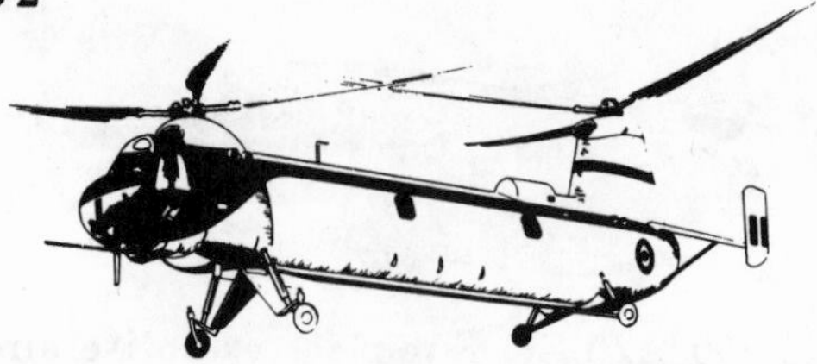

WESTLAND 192 BELVEDERE British tandem rotor military helicopter, toted 19 troops or 6,000 pounds cargo. Speed 138 m.p.h.; range 445 miles; two 1,650-s.h.p. Napier Gazelle free turbines.

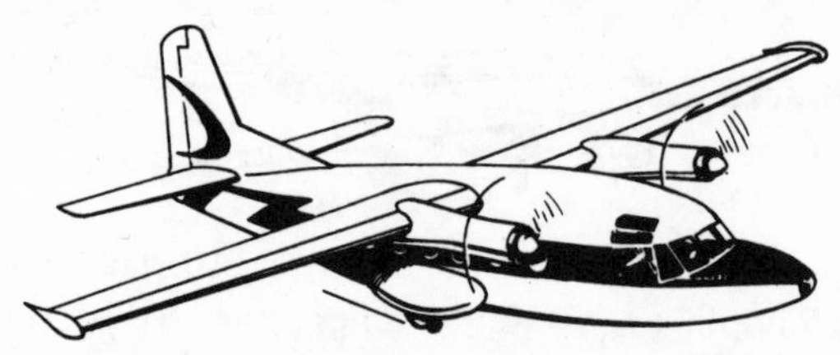

NORD 260 SUPER BROUSSARD French, 23 passenger, civil turboprop transport; cruise speed 245 m.p.h.; range 621 miles; two 960-s.h.p. Turbomeca-Bastan turboprops.

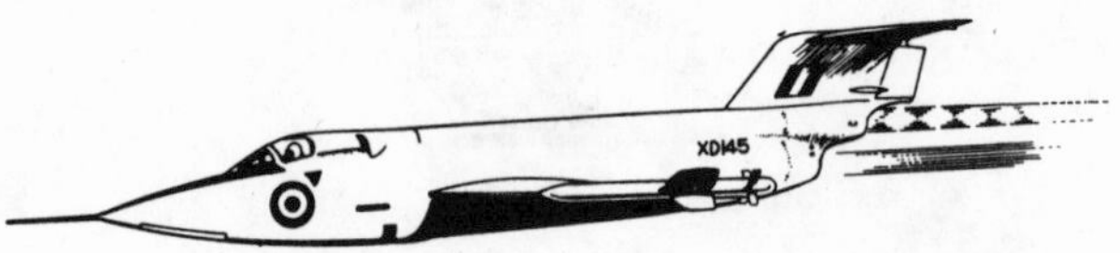

SAUNDERS-ROE SR/53 British combined rocket/jet fighter, built as a prototype, has Armstrong-Siddeley Viper turbojet plus one De Havilland Spectre rocket engine.

BEECH 95 TRAVEL AIR Five-place executive plane with 180-h.p. Lycoming flat-six engines has new fuselage married to Model 45 Mentor wings and tail. Top speed 210 m.p.h.; range 1,035 miles.

DORNIER DO.29 Experimental German single-seat V/STOL aircraft; pusher-propellers rotate downward to provide lift-thrust for takeoff and landing. Two 275-h.p. Lycoming engines.

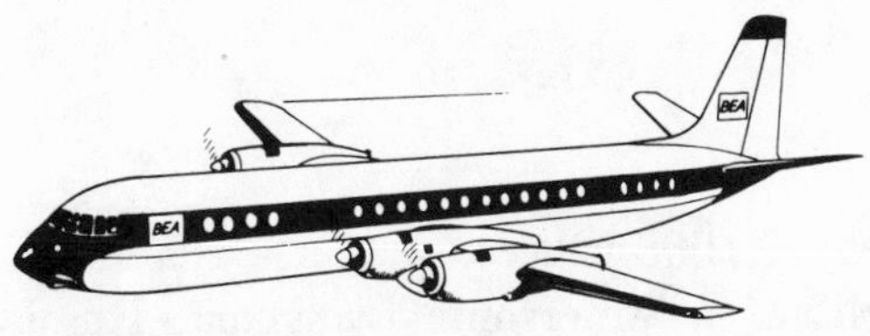

VICKERS VANGUARD 950 SRS More powerful development of the tried and trusty Vickers Viscount, transports 132 passengers. Four 4,985-lbs.t. Rolls-Royce Tyne turboprops; speed 412 m.p.h.; range 3,015 miles.

AVRO VZ-9V AVROCAR Experimental Canadian flying saucer, developed for U.S. Air Force, has 5-ft. diameter turborotor driven by exhaust of three J-69 turbojets.

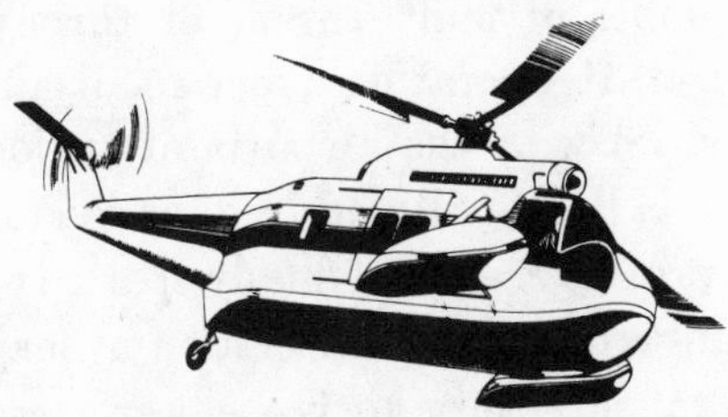

SIKORSKY S-62A Eleven passenger turbo-copter with 1,250 s.h.p. G.E. turbines, has amphibian hull for land/water operation, employs many parts from S-55. Speed 101 m.p.h.; range 255 miles.

PART ELEVEN

The Space Age

1962-1969

The last day of 1968 ushered in a new era of air travel with the first flight of a supersonic transport, Russia's Tupolev Tu-144. Capable of carrying 120 passengers at 1550 miles per hour, the Tu-144 beat the Anglo/French *Concorde* SST effort and left America's Boeing 2707-300 SST still on the drawing board. The year also saw the introduction of Boeing's 450 passenger, subsonic Jumbo Jet and Lockheed's huge C-5A Galaxy tactical transport, which was able to carry 265,000 pounds of cargo. Under construction were Douglas's DC-10 and Lockheed's L-1011, subsonic air buses, each able to carry 345 persons over transcontinental ranges. In an unprecedented short time of only seven years, air transport had moved from the 180 passenger airliner to the supersonic transport and the Jumbo Jet.

During the same period, there were almost 4,000 commercial jet transports in use by world airlines. There was also a great increase in the number of multi-engine or turbojet executive and feeder-line aircraft operating from small airfields, tying small towns and cities with the airports of major cities. The age of mass air travel had finally arrived, or so it seemed.

The vast numbers of aircraft had finally created massive, time-consuming and dangerous traffic congestion at major airports, and new solutions for inter-city air travel were needed. The answer had appeared to be the helicopter; however, cost, complexity and slow flying speeds rendered it commercially uneconomical to operate. The obvious need was for a V/STOL (vertical/

short takeoff and landing) aircraft with a much higher cruising speed that would be more economical to operate than the helicopter.

Some of the possible solutions, mostly experimental, have been the American, tilt-wing/rotor prop Curtiss-Wright X-19A, the Piasecki Pathfinder II compound helicopter, the ducted-prop Bell X-22A, Germany's vectored-thrust plus lift-jets Dornier Do.31E, and France's Breguet 941S, using deflected propeller slipstream and blown wing. Of the many V/STOL possibilities or proposals, only the Breguet 941S had been developed (with the cooperation of McDonnell Douglas) to the point where a 100 passenger, 400-m.p.h. version could be in use early in the 1970's.

In the field of military aircraft, the trend is moving in two directions: one, to the highly sophisticated Mach 3 fighter, such as the American Lockheed SR-71 and YF-12A, Sweden's Saab 37 Viggen, and Russia's Mikoyan MiG-23 Foxbat. Also to the highly complex variable-sweep or swing-wing aircraft, exemplified by General Dynamic's F-111A, France's Mirage G and Russia's Mikoyan Flogger and the experimental Sukhoi Su-7.

The other movement is to the less costly, simple to maintain, combination jet-trainer and ground-attack COIN (counter-insurgency) aircraft, for use by underdeveloped nations and in guerrilla-type wars of liberation. Typical jet-trainer/fighters are the Northrop F-5A and F-5B, Canadair CL-41G, Saab 105XT, BAC 167 and Yugoslavia's Soko Galeb. Although typically their maximum speeds are Mach 1 or less, they are extremely maneuverable at low altitudes and are able to carry heavy armament loads in their attack roles.

Another emerging trend is the VTOL (vertical takeoff and landing) jet fighter, able to operate from small, unprepared, forward battle areas. Great Britain originally developed the concept in the 1950's, with the turbojet powered, vectored-thrust P.1127 Kestrel that finally evolved into the current Harrier G.R. Mk.1, a close-support fighter. Another vectored-thrust fighter development is Russia's experimental Yakolev Freehand. However, the trend of future V/STOL fighter development appears to be the use of multiple turbojets for jet-lift only, plus a single or twin turbojets as main propulsion units, as shown by Russia's Sukhoi Flagon B and Mikoyan Faithless, Germany's VFW VAK-191B, and France's Dassault Mirage V Balzac. The development of lightweight jet-lift engines with a 20:1 thrust-to-weight ratio, and possibly higher, has provided the means whereby the V/STOL jet-fighter is feasible.

The air war in Vietnam introduced new concepts in the use of massed helicopters as tactical assault troop transports and showed the need for heavily armed escort and tactical support helicopters. Bell developed the AH-1G Huey Cobra, mounting Mini-guns, grenade launchers and rockets, into an effective escort and assault craft. Lockheed's AH-56A Cheyenne is a second-generation attack and escort compound-helicopter with a top speed of 253-m.p.h. that carries extremely heavy armament. Helicopters of all types and sizes have become the primary means of troop and cargo transports, on and off the battlefield.

Another aspect of the air war in Vietnam has been the lack of effectiveness of North Vietnam's SAM's (surface-to-air-missiles) against American aircraft due to evasive tactics and electronic countermeasures. American fighter aircraft have also been re-armed with high-speed rotary-cannon, in addition to AAM's (air-to-air-missiles), due primarily to the fact that enemy aircraft are able to out-maneuver and evade AAM's. Despite the extremely high maneuvering speeds of contending aircraft, fighter tactics have remained basically the same as in World War II, with height, maneuverability and pilot training being the determining factors.

Although the 1960's have been a period of great aeronautical advances, with supersonic bombers and airliners, huge passenger transports, Mach 3-plus fighters and Mach 8 research aircraft, the greatest achievements have been in space. On March 18, 1965, Russia's cosmonaut Alexei Leonov emerged from his Voshkod 2 spacecraft and became the first man to "walk" in space. The U.S. duplicated the feat in June, 1965, when astronaut Edward White emerged from Gemini 4 and remained outside for 21 minutes. Many additional space achievements were recorded: two-week manned space flights, photographing the surfaces of the moon and the planet Mars, and landing machines to record and send back information on the surface characteristics of the moon and the planet Venus.

Finally, space itself has been opened up to man, both in the Apollo 8 manned moon orbit and the historic manned landing on the moon, thus preparing humankind for the new age of space exploration and the logical outcome of man's attempts to fly.

DOUGLAS C-133B CARGOMASTER Military heavy freight and troop carrier has four 6,500-s.h.p. P. & W. turboprops, accommodates Atlas ICBM. Range, with 25 tons of cargo, 4,000 miles at 328 m.p.h.

HAL HOAP-27 KRISHAK Indian four-seat observation/liaison aircraft stressed for 3.8G's, also used for agricultural, ambulance and training roles. Fabric-covered metal structure. Speed 130 m.p.h.; range 500 miles; one 225-h.p. Continental engine.

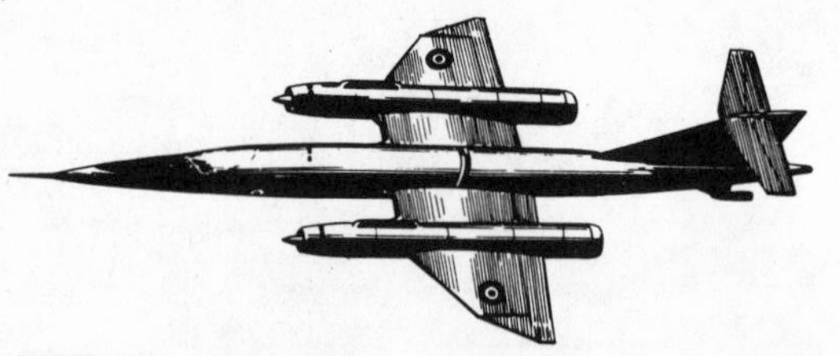

BRISTOL TYPE 188 Stainless steel research aircraft, designed to explore power plants and structures for hypersonic flight. Planned speed of 1,980 m.p.h. (Mach 3) above 36,000 feet was not achieved in practice; two 14,000-lbs. t. with reheat turbojets.

TUPOLEV TU-124 COOKPOT Commercial transport for short-field operations carries 4 crew and 56 passengers. Was first Russian transport with turbofan engines. Speed 603 m.p.h.; range 1,305 miles; two 11,905-lbs.t. turbofans in wing roots.

MEYERS 200D High performance four-place all-metal aircraft, rugged structure, highly maneuverable, used often in stock plane racing. Cruise speed 218 m.p.h.; range 1,230 miles; one 285-h.p. fuel-injection Continental engine.

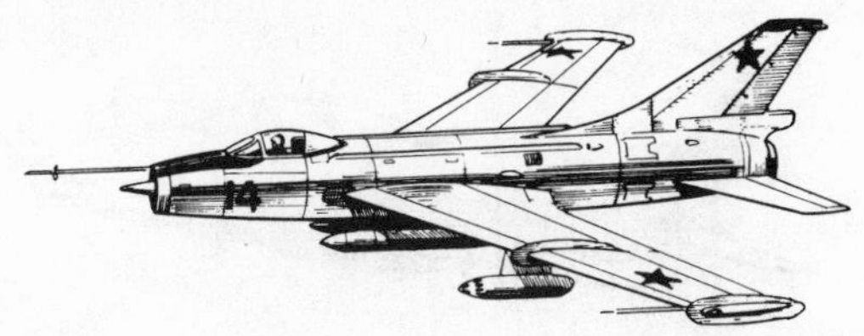

SUKHOI SU-7M FITTER Russian swept-wing single-seat ground attack fighter, mounts two 30mm cannon in wing roots, bombs, rocket pods on pylons under fuselage and wings. Speed 1,060 m.p.h. (Mach 1.6); one 22,050-lbs.t. with re-heat turbojet.

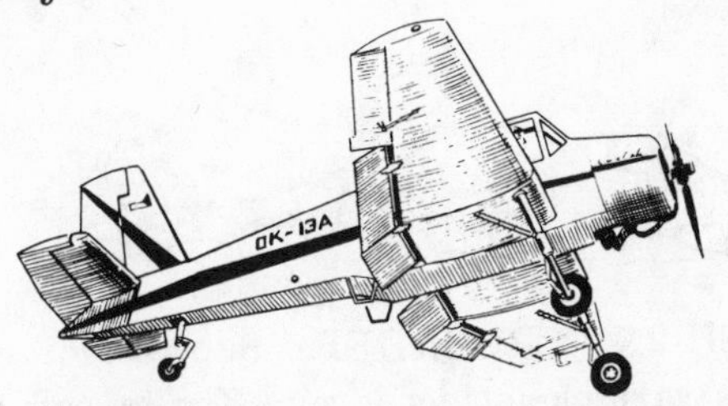

Z-37 CMELAK Czech crop-duster has sealed cabin and auxiliary underwing chemical/fuel tanks. Used during winter season as cargo and mail transport. Speed 124 m.p.h.; range 398 miles; one 9-cylinder, 315-h.p. air-cooled radial engine.

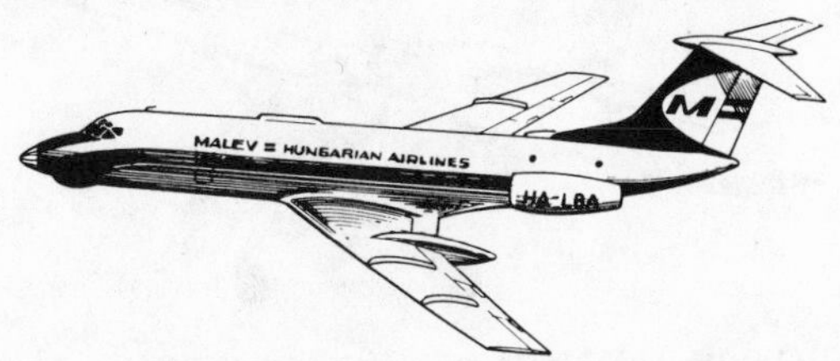

TUPOLEV TU-134A CRUSTY Russian twin-turbofan transport, derived from TU-124, operates from grass airfields with crew of 3 plus 72 passengers. Cruise speed 559 m.p.h.; range 2,175 miles; two 14,990-lbs.t. Soloviev turbofans.

CASSUTT SPECIAL II Homebuilt single-seat Formula I racing plane, with all-wood wing, steel-tube/fabric-covered fuselage and tail surfaces. Speed 235 m.p.h.; range 500 miles; one 85-h.p. Continental engine.

WING DERRINGER Compact, twin-engine two-seat aircraft has flush riveted, chemically milled, stretch-formed skins for smooth exterior surfaces. Speed 238 m.p.h.; range 1,000 miles; two 160-h.p. Lycoming engines.

VOUGHT F8U-2N CRUSADER Supersonic carrier-borne fighter, has variable-incidence wing for takeoff and landing. Powered by 18,000-lbs.t. with afterburning, P. & W. J-57 turbojet. Speed 1,300 m.p.h. (Mach 1.97) at 40,000 feet.

BOLKOW BO.208 JUNIOR Swedish/German sport aircraft has simplified all-metal airframe. In military trainer or COIN role, mounts machine gun pods or rockets under wing. Speed 145 m.p.h.; range 480 miles; 100-h.p. Rolls-Royce Continental engine.

L-29 DELFIN MAYA Czech two-seat basic jet-trainer, has indigenous 1,960-lbs.t. centrifugal turbojet. Standard trainer of Warsaw Pact nations. Speed 407 m.p.h.; range 397 miles.

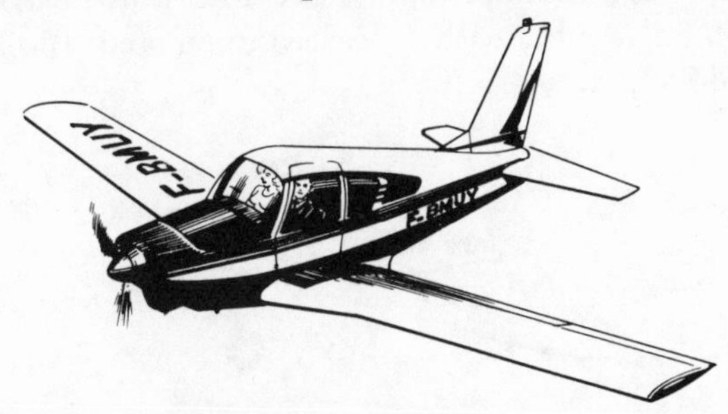

GARDAN GY-80 HORIZON All-metal French four-place aircraft has semi-retractable tri-gear and interchangeable ailerons and flaps, fin and tailplane halves. Speed 153 m.p.h.; range 777 miles; one 180-h.p. Lycoming engine.

GRUMMAN A-6A INTRUDER Carrier-borne two-seat low-level strike aircraft, electronically delivers 18,000-pound offensive load on totally obscured targets. Speed 685 m.p.h. at sea level; range 1,250 miles; two 9,300-lbs.t. P. & W. turbojets.

FALCK SPECIAL RIVETS Homebuilt T-tail single-seat Formula I racing aircraft; steel-tube/fabric-covered fuselage, all-metal wing and tail surfaces. Speed 225 m.p.h.; range 400 miles; one 85-h.p. Continental engine.

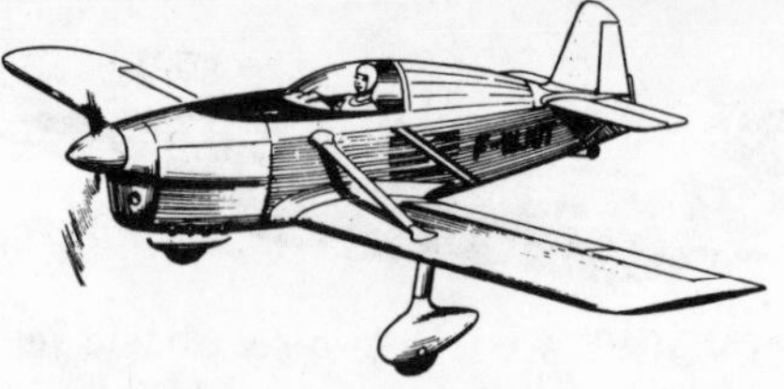

LEDUC RL-21 French homebuilt single-seat all-wood record-holder. With 135-h.p. engine, two FAI world marks were set at 195.92 m.p.h.; with increased span and 160-h.p. it did 217.086 m.p.h.

PIPER PA-25 PAWNEE C Rugged crop-duster has safety capsule cockpit and quickly removable fuselage top for inspection and cleaning. Speed 128 m.p.h.; range 290 miles; one 235-h.p. Lycoming engine.

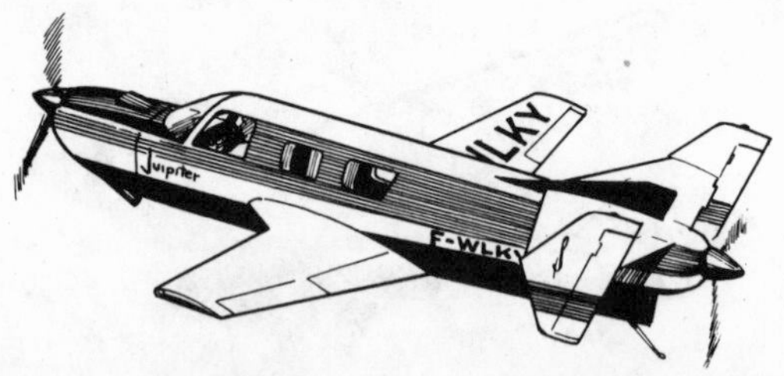

MOYNET 360-4 JUPITER Unusual five-place French aircraft employs fore-and-aft engine location eliminating asymmetric power effects. Speed 210 m.p.h.; range 1,200 miles; two 200-h.p. Lycoming engines.

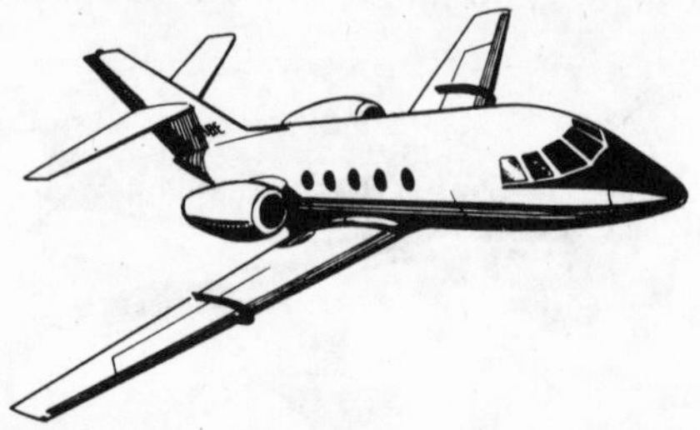

DASSAULT FAN JET FALCON French twin-jet executive transport with 2 crew and 14 passenger capacity, also serves as airline flight crew trainer. Speed 585 m.p.h. above 23,500 feet; range 2,175 miles; two 4,250-lbs.t. G.E. turbofans.

PIPER PA-30B-160 TWIN COMANCHE B Twin-engine six-place aircraft derived from single-engine PA-24 Comanche. Speed 205 m.p.h.; range, with tip tanks, 1,360 miles; two 160-h.p. Lycoming engines.

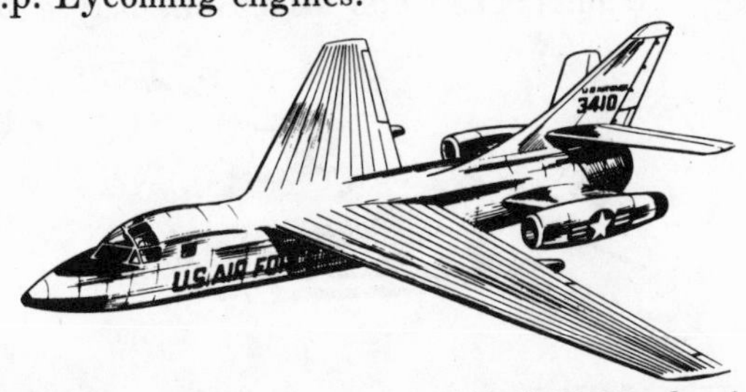

NORTHROP X-21A Twin-jet modified B-66, laminar-flow research craft has 3.2 miles of slots, 815,000 metering holes that suck turbulent boundary-layer air from top wing surface, reducing drag, increasing range. Speed 528 m.p.h. at 40,000 feet.

WITTMAN TAILWIND W-8 High performance two-seat home-built has steel-tube, wood and fabric covered structure; 250 being built or flying around the world. Speed 170 m.p.h.; range 700 miles; normally one 90-h.p. Continental engine.

SAAB 105XT Side-by-side two-seat Swedish export multi-purpose jet fighter, mounts 4,410 pounds of armament and drop tanks on external pylons. Speed 603 m.p.h.; attack radius 215 to 907 miles; two 2,850-lbs.t. G.E. turbojets.

SOKO G2-A GALEB Yugoslavian two-seat jet basic-trainer/strike aircraft, mounts two 0.50-inch machine guns in nose and bombs, rockets on wing pylons. Speed 505 m.p.h. at 2,350 feet; range 770 miles; one 2,500-lbs.t. Rolls-Royce turbojet.

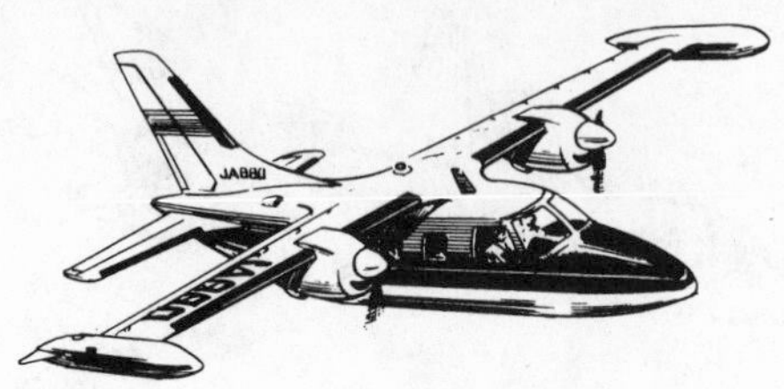

MITSUBISHI MU-2F Japanese pressurized business/utility aircraft carries pilot and 9 passengers. MU-2C used by military for tactical recon/liaison missions. Cruise speed 340 m.p.h.; range 1,550 miles; two 705-s.h.p. Garrett turboprops.

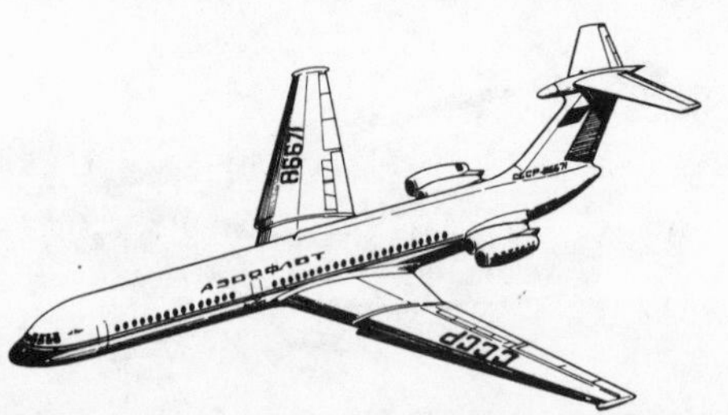

ILYUSHIN IL-62 CLASSIC Russian long-range transport has four 23,150-lbs.t. turbofans in horizontal pairs at fuselage rear, manually operated flying controls. Crew of 5 plus 186 passengers. Cruise speed 560 m.p.h.; range 5,715 miles.

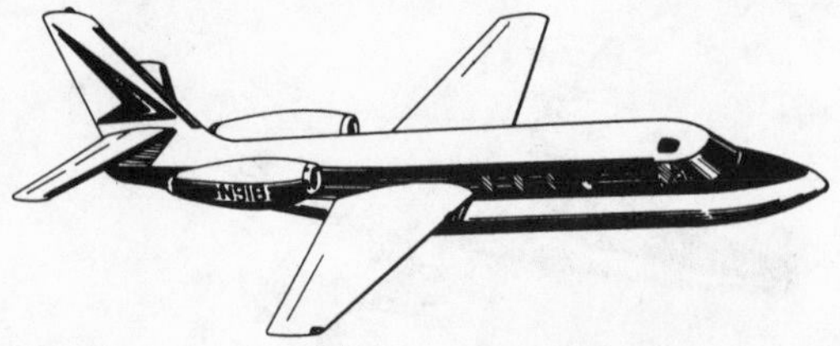

AERO COMMANDER JET COMMANDER 1121 Nine-place business aircraft for short field operations, has twin 2,850-lbs.t. G.E. turbojets. Speed 525 m.p.h. at 38,000 feet; range 1,867 miles.

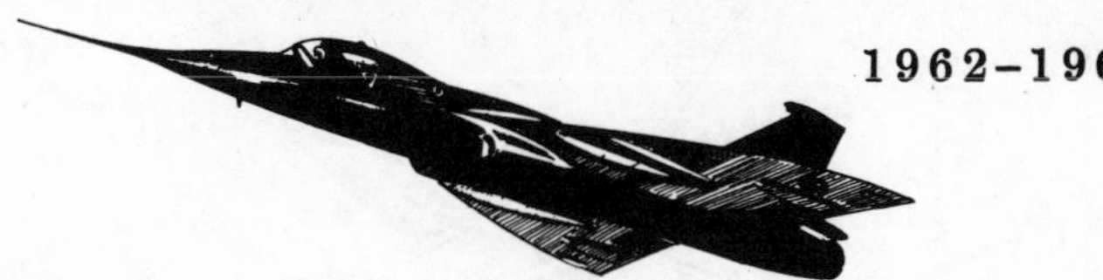

BAC TYPE 221 Supersonic single-seat aircraft had slim ogive wing mated to lengthened Fairey FD.2 fuselage, for test of Concorde Mach 2.2 airliner wing form. Speed 1,450 m.p.h. (Mach 2.2) at 50,000 feet; 10,050-lbs.t. Rolls-Royce turbojet.

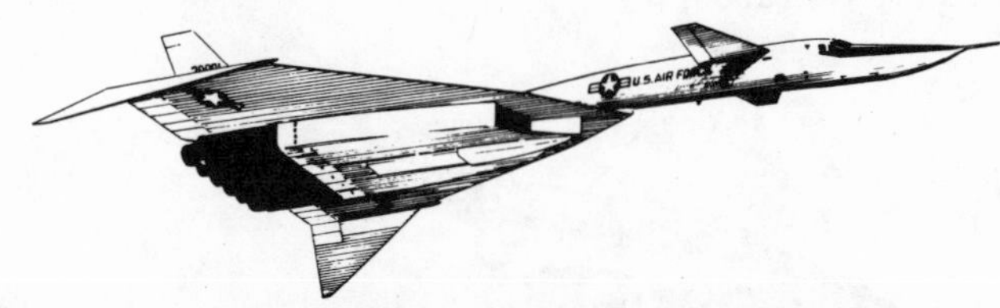

NORTH AMERICAN XB-70A VALKYRIE Huge Mach 3 six-jet research aircraft increases range by riding own shock wave for compression lift at high speeds. Drooped tips increase stability at 1,980 m.p.h. speed at 80,000 feet. Range 7,500 miles.

HFB 320 HANSA German executive/feederliner aircraft has swept-forward wings, transports 2 crew plus 15 passengers. Used as aircrew trainer by military. Cruise speed 513 m.p.h.; range 1,500 miles; two 2,950-lbs.t. G.E. turbojets.

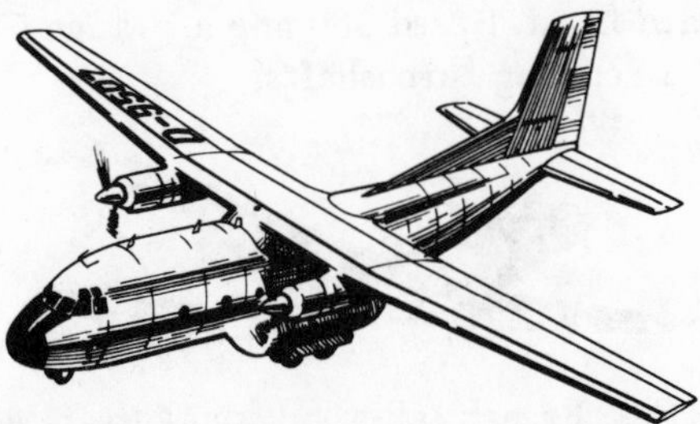

TRANSALL C.160 French/German military pressurized tactical transport, carries 4 crew plus 93 troops or 17.6 tons of military vehicles. Speed 333 m.p.h.; range 1,070 miles; two 6,100-s.h.p. Rolls-Royce turboprops.

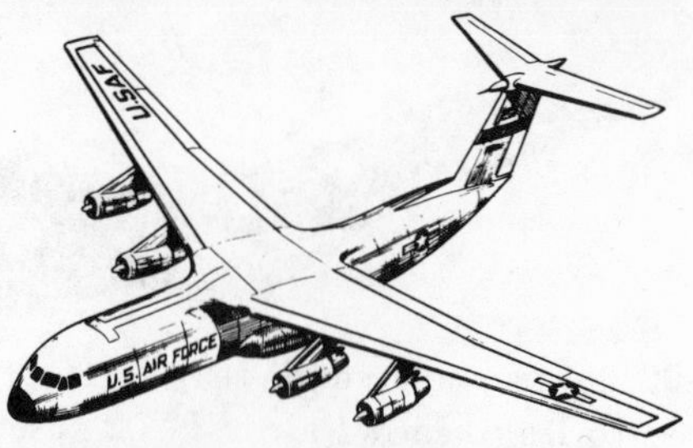

LOCKHEED C-141A STARLIFTER Cargo-troop transport airlifts 154 troops or 70,847 pounds cargo 3,975 miles. Speed 571 m.p.h.; range, with 15-ton load, 6,140 miles; four 21,000-lbs.t. P. & W. turbofans.

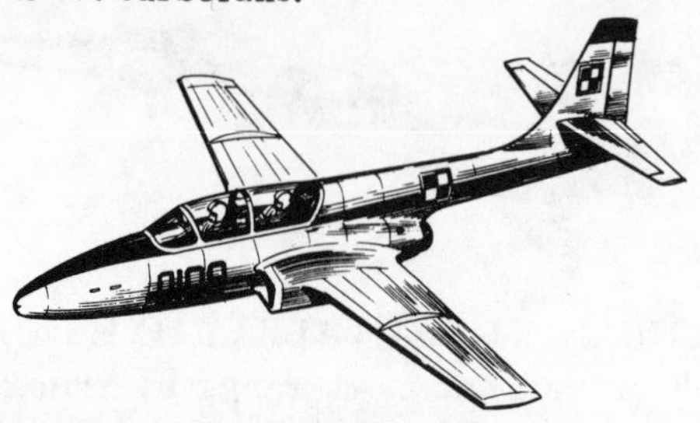

TS-11 ISKRA Polish two-seat, fully-aerobatic basic jet-trainer has single 2,205-lbs.t. SO-1 turbojet. Single-seat version established four international records for speed and distance. Speed 497 m.p.h. at 20,000 feet; range 620 miles.

CURTISS-WRIGHT X-19A Experimental VTOL utility transport with 4 tilting radial lift-force propellers that provide lift in forward flight. Speed 460 m.p.h.; range 518 miles; two 2,650-s.h.p. Lycoming turboshafts.

FOURNIER RF-4 French all-wood single-seat semi-aerobatic sport plane powered by 39-h.p. modified VW engine has clean design, sailplane performance with 18:1 glide ratio; economical flight at low power setting.

DEHAVILLAND DHC-5 BUFFALO Military tactical transport with 3 crew plus 41 troops or 24 casualty stretchers has STOL ability from battlefield airstrips. Speed 282 m.p.h.; range 1,958 miles; two 3,060-s.h.p. G.E. turboprops.

BEAGLE B.206-S British eight-place commuter/executive transport, has twin turbo-supercharged 340-h.p. Rolls-Royce Continental engines, driving three-bladed propellers. Speed 255 m.p.h. at 16,000 feet; range 1,612 miles.

LOCKHEED YF-12A All-weather two-seat interceptor, with automatic navigation system and air-to-air missile armament. Speed 2,300 m.p.h. (Mach 3.5) at 80,000+ feet; range 3,000 miles; two 32,500-lbs.t. with reheat, P. & W. turbojets.

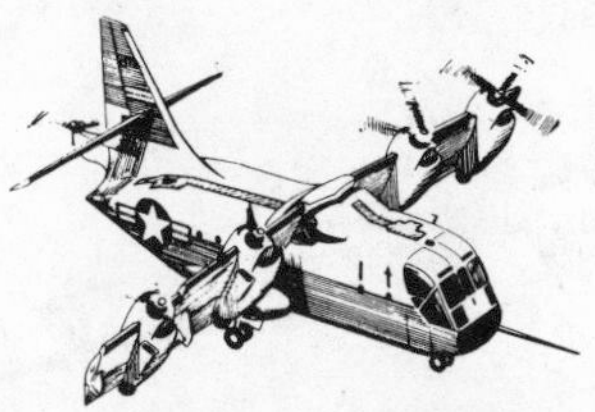

L-T-V-HILLER-RYAN XC-142A Tactical transport uses combination of tilt-wing, coupled propellers and deflected slipstream for V/STOL performance. Payload 4 tons or 32 troops. Speed 430 m.p.h.; range 345 miles; four 2,805-s.h.p. Lycoming turboshafts.

CANADAIR CL-41G Canadian two-seat basic trainer and light COIN aircraft, mounts 3,500 pounds of ordnance on wing pylons. Speed 480 m.p.h. at 28,500 feet; range 944 miles; one 2,950-lbs.t. G.E. turbojet.

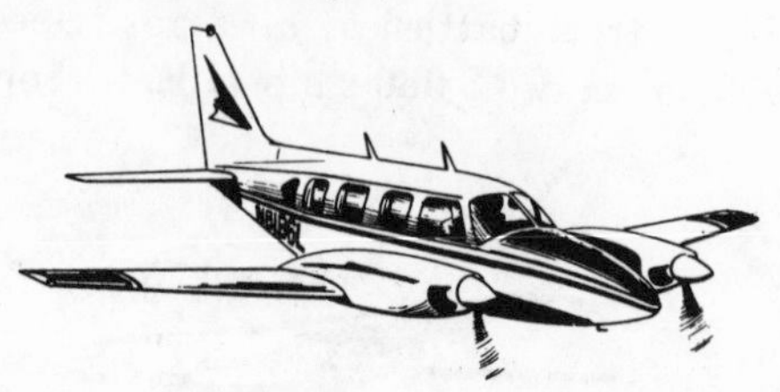

PIPER PA-31-300 NAVAJO Pressurized corporate/commuter transport for short-field operations; seats eight. Speed 224 m.p.h. at sea level; range, 75 percent power, 1,110 miles; two 300-h.p. Lycoming engines.

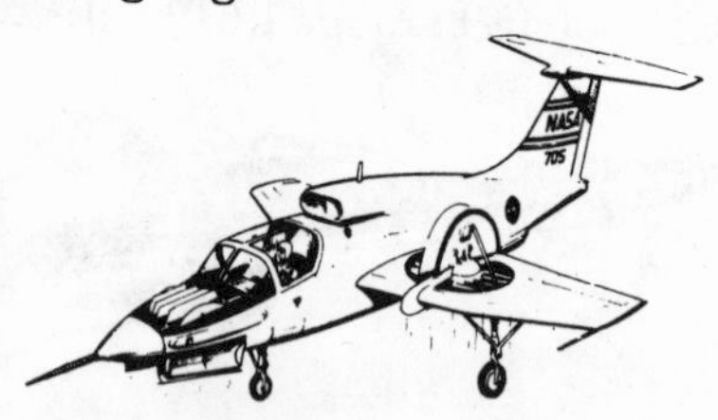

RYAN XV-5A VERTIFAN Two-seat, V/STOL research aircraft employs 5-foot diameter fans, submerged in wings for vertical lift, driven by two 2,658-lbs.t. G.E. turbojets. Fans covered in normal flight. Speed 535 m.p.h.; ferry range 730 miles.

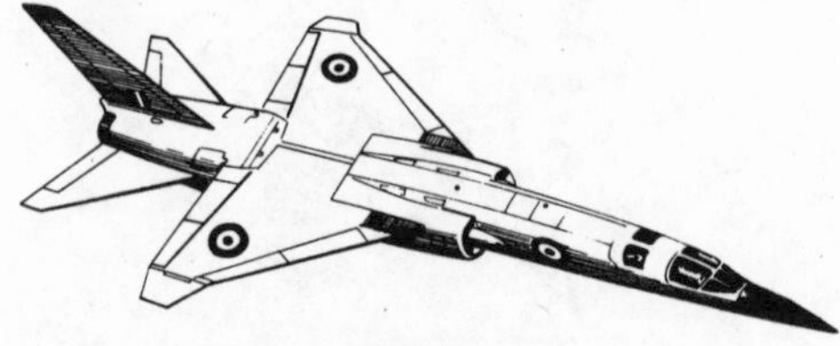

BAC TSR-2 Prototype British tandem two-seat strike and recon aircraft, carried nuclear ordnance internally plus bombs or ASM's on wing pylons. Speed 1,190 m.p.h. (Mach 1.8) at 40,000 feet; unrefueled range 4,000 miles; two 30,000-lbs.t. turbojets.

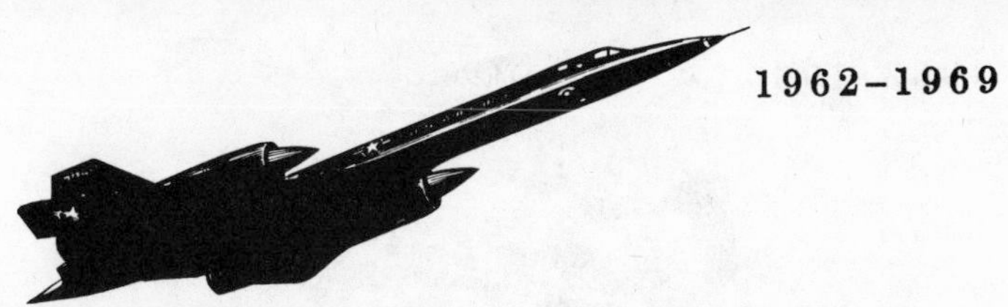

LOCKHEED SR-71 Long range strategic recon aircraft has 2,300-m.p.h. (Mach 3.5) speed at 80,000+ feet, can survey strip 30 miles wide, 2,000 miles long in one hour. Range 3,000 miles; two 32,500-lbs.t. with reheat, P. & W. turbojets.

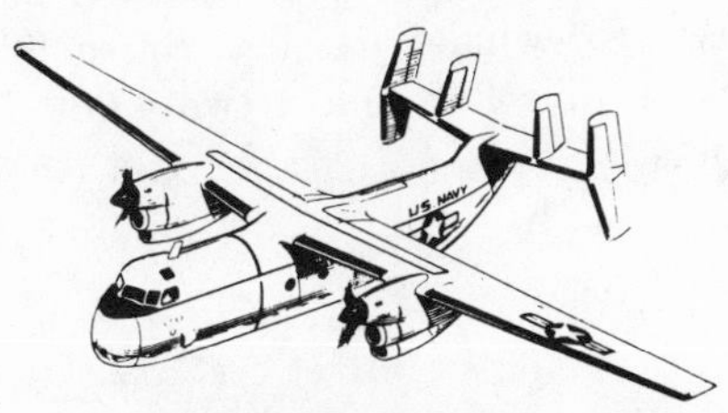

GRUMMAN C-2A GREYHOUND Carrier landing transport has pressurized cargo compartment, delivers freight, troops or stretcher casualties between land bases and carriers at sea. Speed 329 m.p.h.; range 1,520 miles; two 4,050-s.h.p. turboprops.

PZL-104 WILGA 2 Polish four-seat multi-purpose aircraft has cantilever wing, full-span fixed slots and slotted flaps. Speed 124 m.p.h.; range 435 miles; one 185-h.p. 6-cylinder horizontally-opposed engine.

BAC ONE-ELEVEN SRS.300 British medium-range 79 passenger transport has two 11,400-lbs.t. turbofans and increased fuel tankage. Speed 548 m.p.h. at 21,000 feet; range 1,350–2,130 miles.

NORTHROP F-5A Single-seat multi-purpose supersonic fighter mounts two 20mm cannon plus 6,200 pounds ordnance on pylons or two Sidewinder missiles. Speed 924 m.p.h. (Mach 1.4); combat radius 368 miles; two 4,080-lbs.t. with reheat G.E. turbojets.

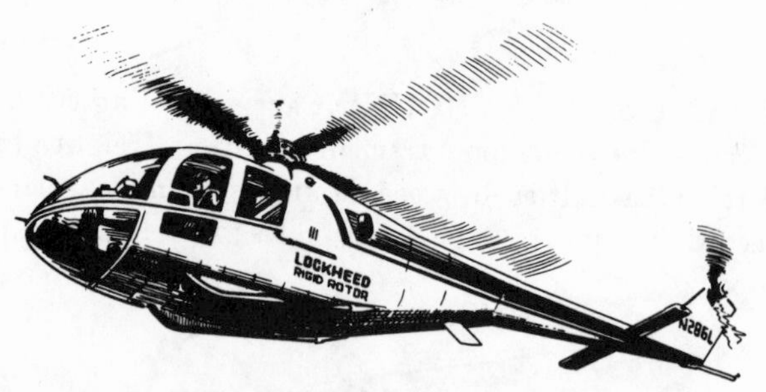

LOCKHEED XH-51A High-speed two-seat research helicopter employs 4-blade rigid-rotor system with hands-off stability. Speed 175 m.p.h.; range 240 miles; one 500-s.h.p. P. & W. turboshaft.

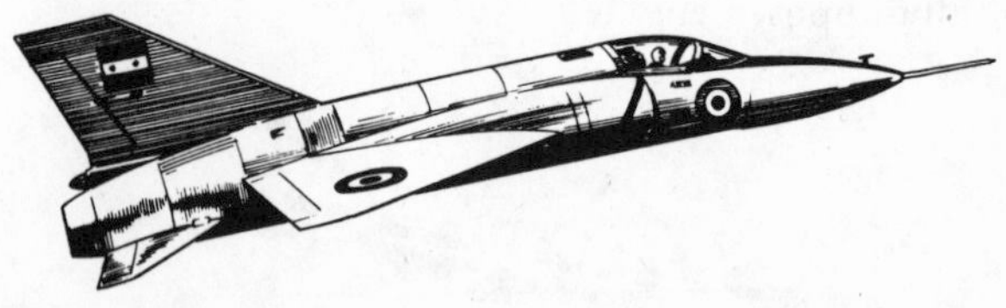

HELWAN HA-300 Egyptian lightweight supersonic single-seat fighter has delta wings plus horizontal tail surfaces, mounts single 4,850-lbs.t. turbojet. Speed 1,450 m.p.h. (Mach 2.2).

MIL MI-6 HOOK World's largest helicopter has 114.8-foot diameter 6-blade rotor, transports 65 passengers or 70 paratroops. Speed 186 m.p.h.; range 620 miles; two 5,500-s.h.p. turboshafts.

PIAGGIO-DOUGLAS PD-808 Italian business/utility transport carries 2 crew, 8 passengers. Used by military for liaison and navigational training; wing stressed for underwing loads. Speed 529 m.p.h.; range 1,270 miles; two 3,350-lbs.t. Rolls-Royce turbojets.

HAL HJT-16 KIRAN Indian side-by-side two-seat basic trainer/light attack and COIN aircraft is fully pressurized and stressed for 10G's, has zero-altitude ejection seats. Speed 446 m.p.h.; range 600 miles; one 2,500-lbs.t. Rolls-Royce turbojet.

NORTHROP F-5B Supersonic two-seat trainer/strike fighter developed from F-5, carries heavy ordnance load for COIN role. Speed 891 m.p.h. (Mach 1.34) at 36,000 feet; combat radius 380 miles; two 4,080-lbs.t. with reheat G.E. turbofans.

BRITTEN-NORMAN BN-2 ISLANDER Nine-place utility transport with short field performance for commuter and bush-type flying. Speed 168 m.p.h.; range 770 miles; two 260-h.p. Lycoming engines.

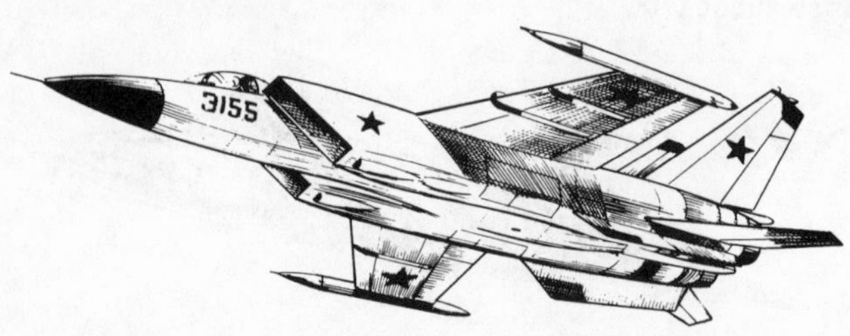

MIKOYAN MIG-23 FOXBAT Russian single-seat, all-weather interceptor/strike fighter; as E-266 set international records in payload and speed. Speed 2,110 m.p.h. (Mach 3.2) at 50,000 feet; two 24,250-lbs.t. with reheat turbojets.

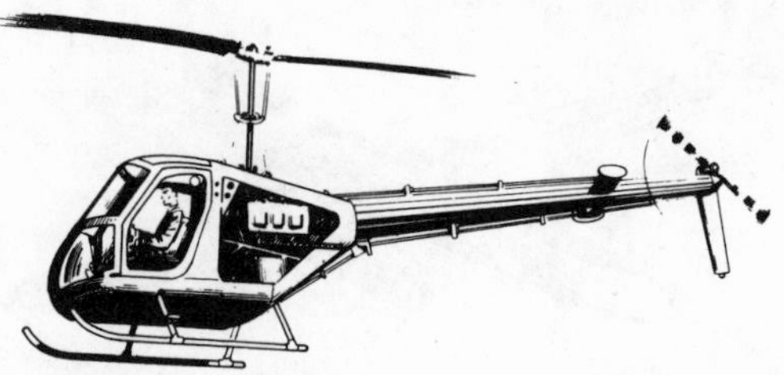

SIAI-MARCHETTI SH-4 Three-place Italian multi-purpose utility helicopter, stresses low cost, simple operation and maintenance, has 2-blade main and tail rotors. Speed 100 m.p.h.; range 186 miles; one 235-h.p. Franklin engine derated to 170 h.p.

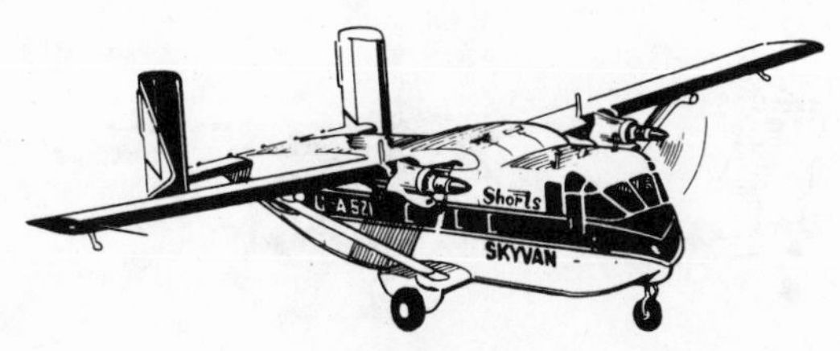

SHORT SC.7 SRS-3 SKYVAN British twin-turboprop utility transport has full-width rear loading doors, transports 2 crew plus 19 passengers or 4,600-pound cargo. Cruise speed 201 m.p.h.; range 625 miles; two 715-s.h.p. Garrett turboprops.

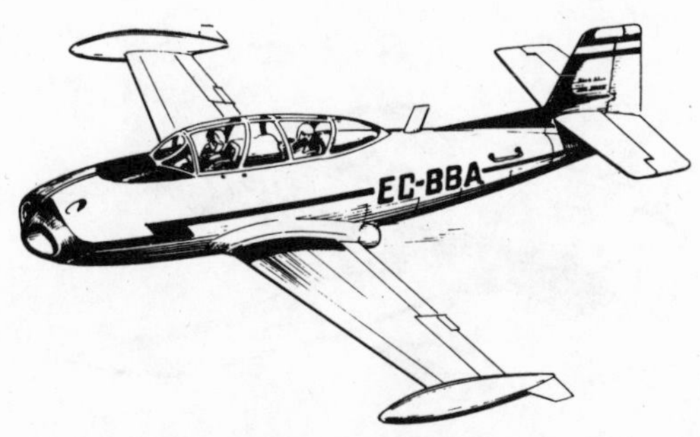

HISPANO HA-200E SUPER SAETA Spanish two-seat advanced jet trainer/COIN fighter has two nose-mounted 1,058-lbs.t. turbojets, exhausting at wing trailing edge, carries variety of weapons. Speed 429 m.p.h.; range 930 miles.

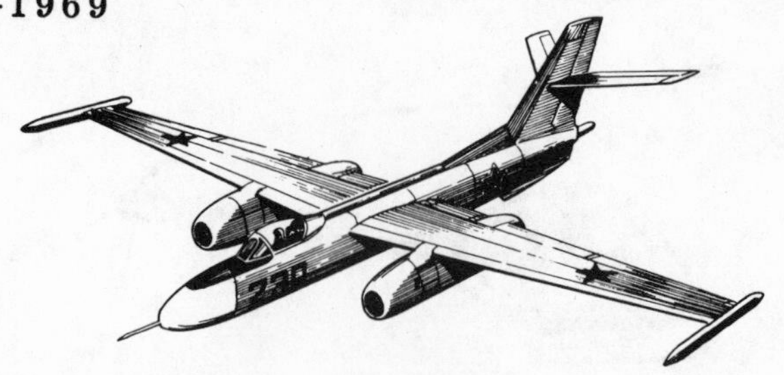

YAKOLEV MANDRAKE Russian twin-engine, single-seat, high-altitude recon aircraft, derived from Yak-25, has extended, 76-foot straight wing. Speed 560 m.p.h.; range 2,500 miles; ceiling 70,000 feet; two 6,600-lbs.t. turbojets.

PZL-104 WILGA 3 Radial engine version of Polish Wilga 2, used as glider tug, as ambulance, for parachute training and in agricultural roles. Speed 130 m.p.h.; range 435 miles; one 260-h.p. 9-cylinder radial engine.

THORP T-18 TIGER Two-seat homebuilt, high performance sport aircraft has all-metal construction without compound curves. Speed 200 m.p.h.; range 500 miles; one 180-h.p. Lycoming engine.

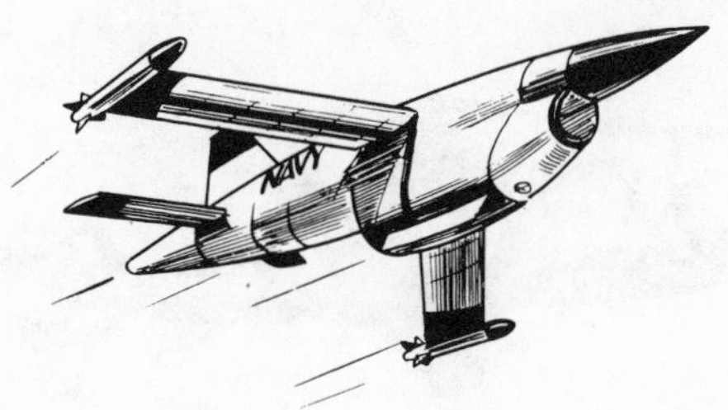

RYAN BQM-34A FIREBEE Remote controlled, jet-powered, maneuverable target drone, capable of 6G turns, trains pilots in firing missile weapons. Speed 707 m.p.h.; ceiling 60,000 feet; one 1,700-lbs.t. Continental turbojet.

BELL X-22A V/STOL research aircraft for Tri-Service multi-mission role, ducted props swivel for vertical flight, ducts provide lift in normal flight. Speed 325 m.p.h.; range 540 miles; four 1,250-s.h.p. G.E. turboshafts.

FUJI FA-200 AERO SUBARU Basic four-place Japanese sport aircraft is fully aerobatic with two persons aboard. Speed 139 m.p.h.; range 740 miles; one 160-h.p. Lycoming engine.

PIASECKI 16H-1A PATHFINDER II Eight-place compound helicopter has 1,250-s.h.p. G.E. turboshaft driving 3-blade main rotor and tail-mounted ducted propeller; vanes in duct provide directional and anti-torque control. Speed 230 m.p.h.; range 970 miles.

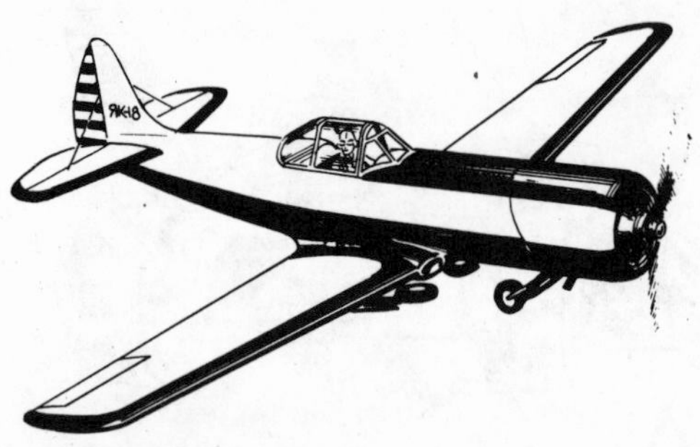

YAKOLEV YAK-18PM Russian single-seat fully-aerobatic trainer, has retractable tricycle gear, used by flying clubs in aerobatic competition events. Speed 199 m.p.h.; range 250 miles; one nine-cylinder, 300-h.p. air-cooled radial engine.

DISTRIBUTOR WING DW-1 Unique crop duster uses axial-flow fan for distribution and discharging of chemicals through wing ducts, driven by 150-h.p. Lycoming engine mounted beneath primary 350-h.p. Lycoming. Speed 150 m.p.h.; range 390 miles.

HUGHES OH-6A CAYUSE U.S. Army observation and utility helicopter transports 5-man firepower team or 1,530-pound cargo. Set twenty-three rotorcraft world records. Speed 150 m.p.h.; range 380 miles; one 317-s.h.p. (derated to 252-s.h.p.) turboshaft.

CESSNA 188 AG WAGON 300 All-metal crop duster has 1,800 pound capacity chemical hopper tank with quick dump valve. Speed 151 m.p.h.; range 320 miles; one 300-h.p. Continental engine with constant speed propeller.

CHAMPION 7KCA CITABRIA Tandem two-seat, fully aerobatic clipped-wing aircraft has 150-h.p. Lycoming engine, basic structure of wooden spars and steel tube fuselage, all fabric covered. Speed 162 m.p.h.; range 630 miles.

KAMOV KA-26 HOODLUM Russian multi-purpose helicopter has 6-passenger cabin replaced by open platform for bulk cargo. Contra-rotating co-axial three blade rotor system. Speed 106 m.p.h.; range 745 miles; two podded, 325-h.p. air-cooled radial engines.

SIAI-MARCHETTI S. 205-20F Four-place all metal Italian aircraft employs 180- to 300-h.p. engines and fixed (20F) or retractable tri-gear (20R). Honeycomb panels used widely for rigid structure. Speed 155 m.p.h.; range 830 miles; one 180-h.p. Lycoming engine.

DASSAULT MIRAGE III-V BALZAC French single-seat V/STOL strike and recon fighter has single 18,520-lbs.t. with reheat turbofan main engine plus eight vertical 3,640-lbs.t. turbojets for jet-lift. Speed 1,386 m.p.h. (Mach 2.1) at 40,000 feet; range 460 miles.

LING-TEMCO-VOUGHT A-7A CORSAIR II Single-seat carrier-borne attack bomber, carries max. 15,000 pounds bombs, rockets on wing pylons. Speed 578 m.p.h. at sea level; combat radius 715 miles; one 11,350-lbs.t. P. & W. turbofan.

DYKE JD-1 DELTA Unique three-seat homebuilt double-delta aircraft has laminated fiber glass wing skins riveted on and folding outer wing panels for towing. Speed 170 m.p.h.; range 525 miles; one 125-h.p. Lycoming engine.

PILATUS PC-6/B-H2 TURBO-PORTER Nine-place STOL utility aircraft, derived from piston-engined Porter, operates from short fields on wheels, skis or floats. Speed 174 m.p.h.; range 570 miles; one 550-s.h.p. P. & W. turboprop.

AERO SPACELINES SUPER GUPPY Extensively modified Boeing Stratocruiser, transports NASA rockets and space vehicle. Fuselage lengthened 30.8 feet, inside diameter expanded to 25 feet. Cruise speed 300 m.p.h.; payload 41,000 pounds.

LUTON GROUP BETA B-1 British all-wood ply-covered single-seat midget racing aircraft, winner of Rollason design competition. Speed 151 m.p.h.; range 280 miles; one 65-h.p. Rolls-Royce Continental engine.

ENSTROM F-28A Three-place commuter/utility helicopter, employs fully articulated main rotor of bonded alloy construction, steel tube pylon structure fuselage with alloy tail cone. Cruise speed 98 m.p.h.; range 235 miles; one 205-h.p. Lycoming engine.

TRANSAVIA AIRTRUK PL-12 Unorthodox Australian crop-duster has twin booms with separate twin-tail units, can carry 2 passengers on ferry flights. Speed 137 m.p.h.; range 380 miles; one 300-h.p. Continental engine with constant-speed prop.

SUD-AVIATION SA-321F SUPER FRELON French multi-purpose helicopter has sealed hull for emergency water landings, transports 2 crew plus 37 passengers in airliner comfort. Speed 158 m.p.h.; range 584 miles; three 1,500-s.h.p. turboshafts.

NORTH AMERICAN OV-10A BRONCO Two-seat multi-purpose COIN aircraft mounts four 7.62mm machine guns, 3,600 pounds bombs/rockets plus two Sidewinder missiles. Speed 281 m.p.h.; combat radius 228 miles; two 715-s.h.p. Air Research turboprops.

MOONEY MARK 22 MUSTANG Five-place pressurized business aircraft has PC (positive control) system that coordinates yaw/roll stability. Cruise speed 230 m.p.h. at 24,000 feet; range 1,100 miles; one 310-h.p. turbo-supercharged Lycoming engine.

BENSEN B-8M GYROCOPTER Roadable autogyro for amateur constructors has rotor spin-up for short takeoffs. Two-stroke 72-h.p. engine; speed 85 m.p.h.; range 100 miles.

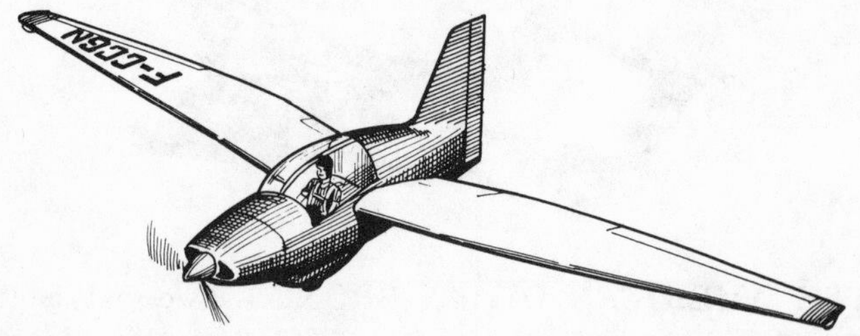

FAUVEL AV.221B French all-wood, side-by-side, two-seat flying wing sailplane powered by 50-h.p. Pygmee engine has 26:1 glide ratio at 53 m.p.h. with feathered propeller.

DINFIA I.A.53 Argentinian crop duster has provision for second person in tandem on ferry flights. Steel tube fuselage with dural panels and fiber glass/polyester plastic covering. Speed 134 m.p.h.; range 404 miles; one 235-h.p. Lycoming engine.

DOUGLAS DC-8 SUPER 61 Basic DC-8 Srs.50 aircraft with fuselage stretched 36.7 feet has 259 passenger capacity plus 2,500 cubic feet underfloor cargo space. Cruise speed 600 m.p.h.; range 3,750 miles; four 18,000-lbs.t. P. & W. turbofans.

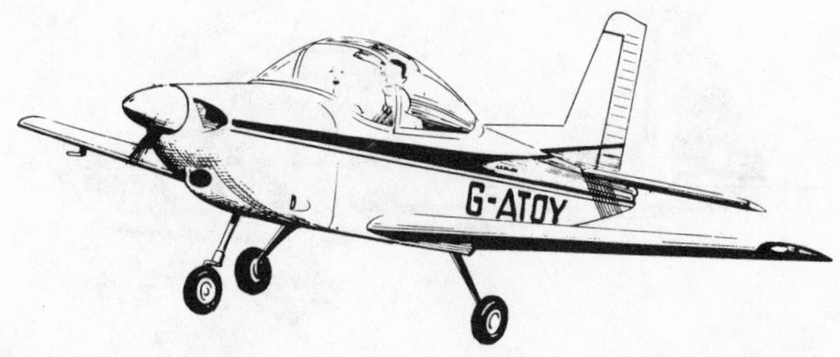

VICTA 100 AIRTOURER Two-seat Australian aerobatic sport aircraft is stressed for 6G, has center-mounted dual-control stick. All-metal construction. Speed 138 m.p.h.; range 780 miles; one 100-h.p. Rolls-Royce Continental engine.

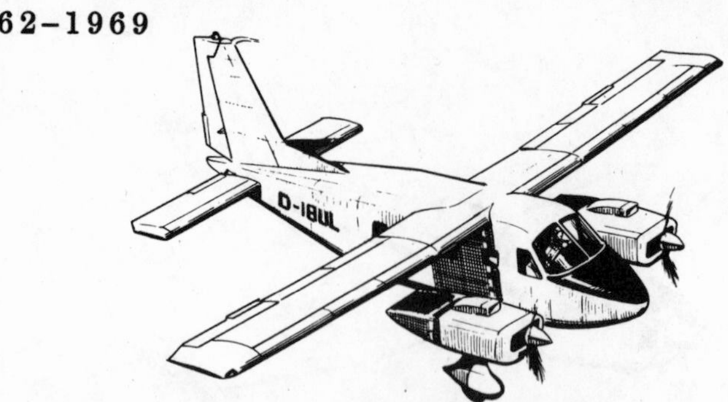

DORNIER DO-28D SKYSERVANT Feederliner and freighter has STOL performance with 14 passengers plus pilot; cabin can be stripped for cargo hauling. Speed 199 m.p.h.; range 1,141 miles; two 380-h.p. Lycoming engines.

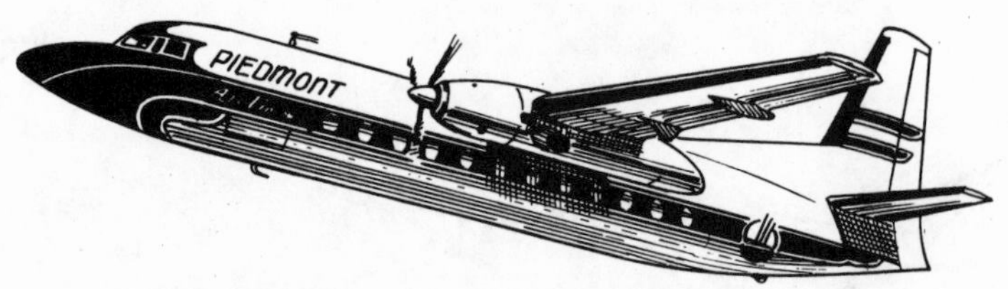

FAIRCHILD HILLER FH-227B Six-foot stretched fuselage F-27 with structural strengthening and larger 12.5-foot diameter propellers. Accommodates 3 crew plus 56 passengers. Cruise speed 294 m.p.h.; range 2,680 miles; two 2,250-s.h.p. turboprops.

AERO COMMANDER DARTER Low-priced all-metal aircraft, seats four. Steel tube cabin construction, fiber glass sprung main gear. Speed 133 m.p.h.; range 510 miles; 150-h.p. Lycoming engine.

CENTRE EST AERONAUTIQUE DR-220 Popular French 2-plus-2, all-wood sport/trainer aircraft, has smooth exterior, clean design with 130-m.p.h. cruise speed on 100-h.p. Continental engine.

AIRCRAFT HYDRO-FORMING BUSHMASTER 2000 Modernized version of Ford Tri-motor has sturdy structure, simple maintenance for bush flying. Cruise speed 140 m.p.h.; range 700 miles; three 450-h.p. P. & W. air-cooled radials. Two crew, 15 passengers.

WASSMER WA-50 French four-place aircraft with full dual-controls has airframe made entirely of fiber glass/plastic resin. Cruise speed 161 m.p.h.; range 620 miles; one 150-h.p. Lycoming engine.

AERO COMMANDER LARK Four-place aircraft has same basic airframe as Darter, but with swept fin, plush interior and 180-h.p. Lycoming engine. Speed 138 m.p.h.; range 525 miles.

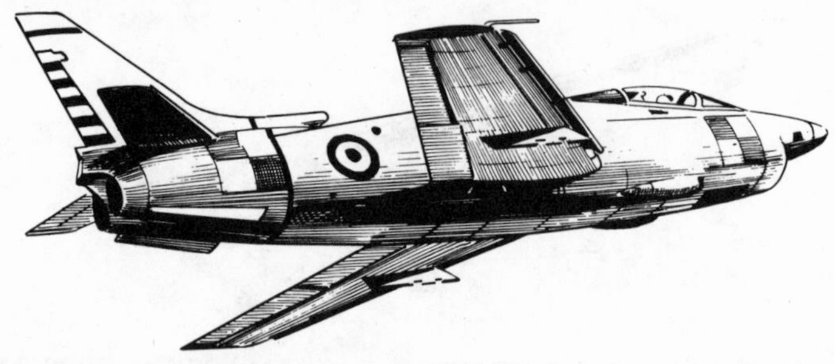

FIAT G-91Y Italian twin-engine single-seat strike/recon fighter operates from battle strips; mounts 30mm cannon and bombs, rocket pods on wing pylons. Speed 714 m.p.h.; ferry range 1,926 miles; two 4,080-lbs.t. with reheat G.E. turbojets.

BEECHCRAFT MODEL 99 Turboprop feederliner/utility transport, with 2 crew and 15 passengers, all cargo or mixed load capacity. Cruise speed 250 m.p.h.; range 975 miles; two 550-s.h.p. P. & W. turboshafts.

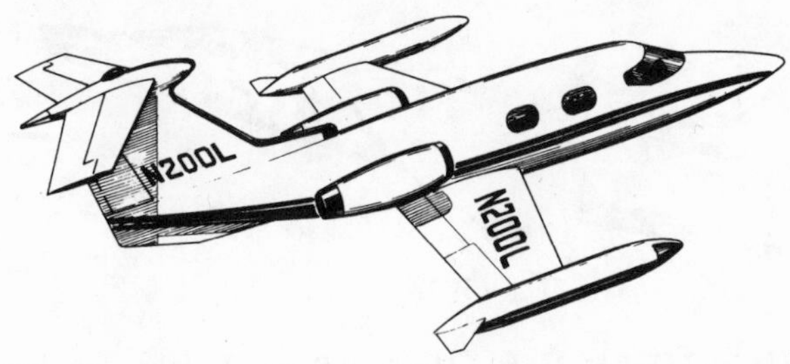

LEAR JET 23 Twin-jet pressurized eight-place executive transport has two rear-mounted 2,850-lbs.t. G.E. turbojets and high speed performance. Speed 564 m.p.h. at 24,000 feet; range 1,700 miles.

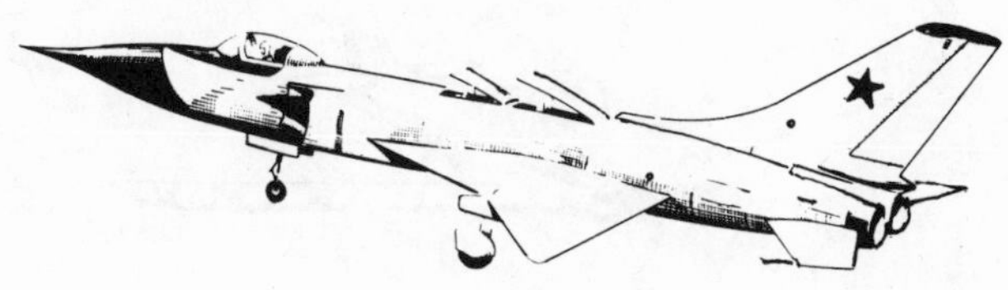

SUKHOI SU-11 FLAGON B Russian jet-lift STOL double-delta-wing version of standard Flagon A interceptor, carries two AAM's underwing. Speed 1,650 m.p.h. (Mach 2.5) at 40,000 feet; two 22,050-lbs.t. with reheat turbojets plus two direct-lift turbojets.

CESSNA 150F Stable tri-gear side-by-side two-seater, used extensively as trainer, introduced swept fin and redesigned cabin. Speed 123 m.p.h.; range 480 miles; one 100-h.p. Continental engine.

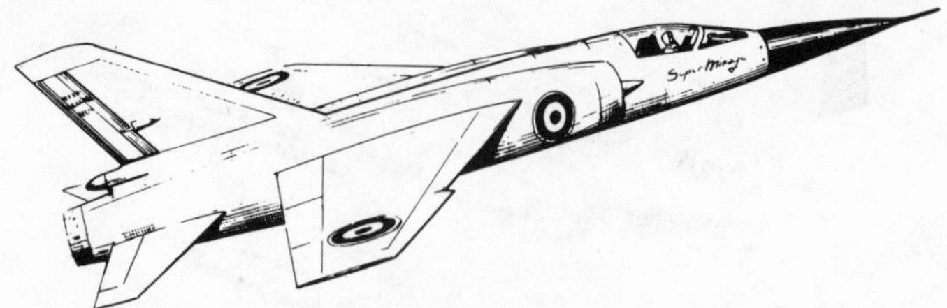

DASSAULT MIRAGE F1 Mach 2.2 single-seat swept-wing interceptor/strike fighter, evolved from Mirage III-E, mounts two 30mm cannon plus AAM's or ASM's. Speed 1,450 m.p.h. at 40,000 feet; range 2,050 miles; one 15,785-lbs.t. with reheat turbojet.

ALON A-4 Four-place, conventional three-control-system aircraft, evolutionary development of 1937 two-control Ercoupe. Speed 150 m.p.h.; range 755 miles; 150-h.p. Lycoming engine.

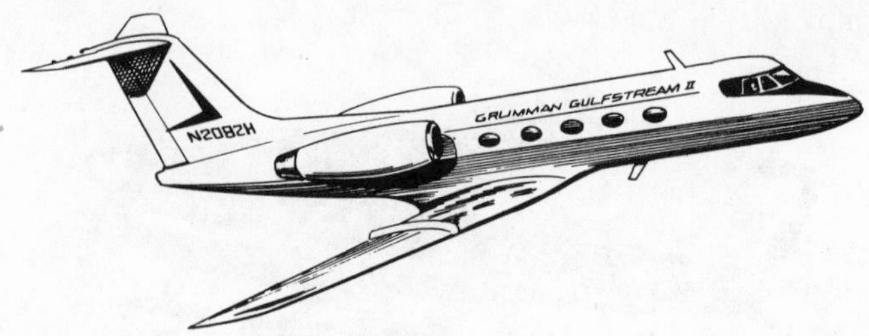

GRUMMAN G-1159 GULFSTREAM II Pressurized and air-conditioned corporate transport has short field performance, with 3 crew plus 19 passengers. Speed 585 m.p.h. at 43,000 feet; range 3,460 miles; two 11,400-lbs.t. Rolls-Royce turbofans.

DOUGLAS DC-9 SRS.20 Jet transport for short field, quick takeoff operations, combines fuselage of DC-9 Srs.10, high lift wing of Srs.30 and 14,500-lbs.t. turbofans of Srs.40. Carries 90 passengers at 561-m.p.h. cruise speed; range 1,800 miles.

BELL 206A JETRANGER Five-place turbine powered commuter/utility helicopter has extended rotor mast without stabilizing bar. Speed 150 m.p.h.; range 359 miles; one 317-s.h.p. Allison turboshaft.

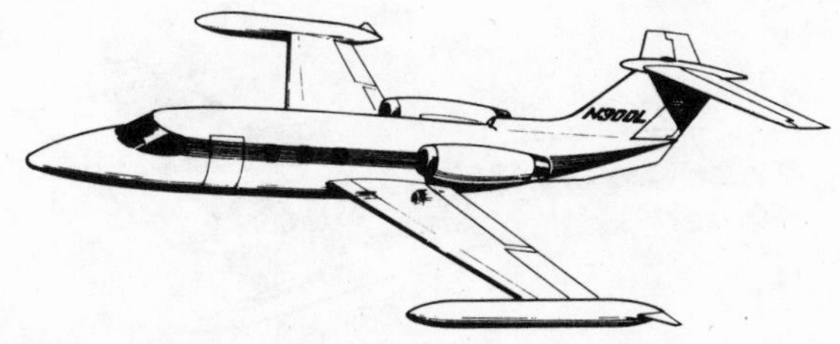

LEAR JET 25 Pressurized subsonic corporate aircraft carries 2 crew plus 8 passengers, is 50-inch stretched version of Model 23. Cruise speed 527 m.p.h. at 41,000 feet; range 1,440 miles; two 2,950-lbs.t. G.E. turbojets.

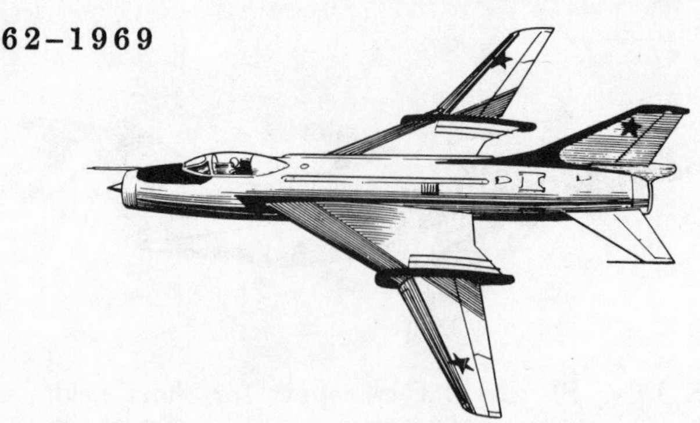

SUKHOI SU-7 SWING-WING Russian research aircraft, derived from SU-7M, has mid-span pivots providing variable-sweep to outer wing panels. Speed 990 m.p.h. (Mach 1.5) at 40,000 feet.

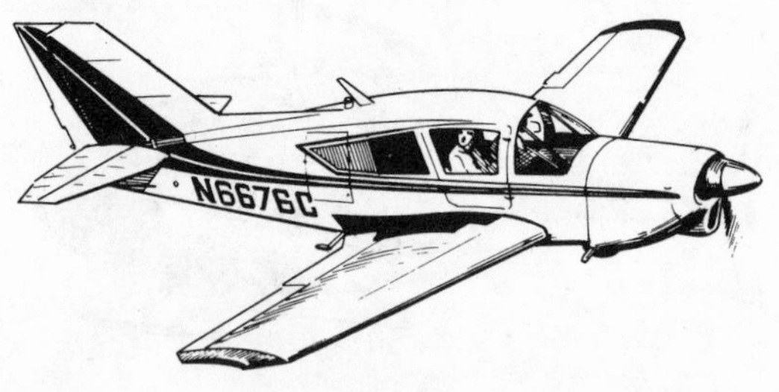

BELLANCA 300 VIKING Low-priced four-seat aircraft, has all-wood resin sealed wing, steel tube fuselage, covered with Plasticote impregnated Dacron. Speed 211 m.p.h.; range 850 miles; one 300-h.p. fuel-injected Continental engine.

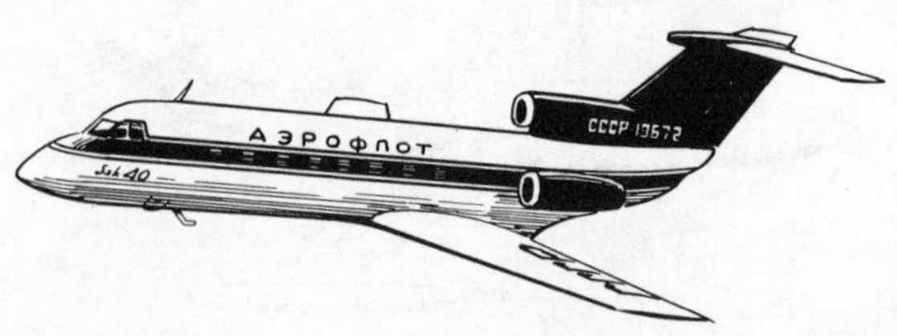

YAKOLEV YAK-40 CODLING Russian tri-jet short-haul transport, operates from short grass airfields with 2 crew and 31 passengers or 5,510-pound cargo. Speed 466 m.p.h.; range 1,025 miles; three 3,300-lbs.t. Ivchenko turbofans.

BEECHCRAFT 23 SPORT III Aerobatic all-metal two-place sport/trainer has laminar flow wing with bonded alloy skins. Speed 140 m.p.h.; range 895 miles; 150-h.p. Lycoming engine.

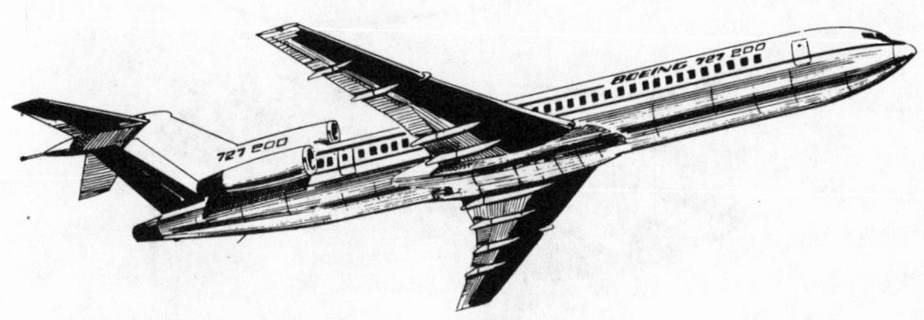

BOEING 727-200 Stretched development of basic tri-jet Model 727, for high-density tourist market, with 180 passenger capacity. Cruise speed 592 m.p.h.; range 1,400 miles; three 14,000-lbs.t. P. & W. turbofans.

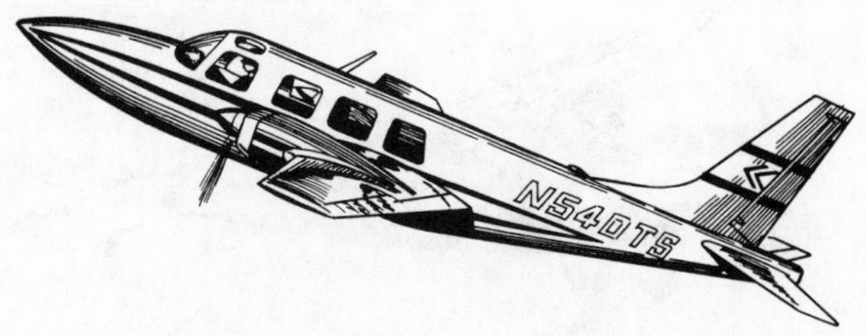

TED SMITH AEROSTAR 600 One of three twin-engine business aircraft with same basic airframe, mounting different engines, seating 6 persons. Speed 260 m.p.h.; range 1,400 miles; two 290-h.p. Lycoming engines with constant-speed propellers.

HAWKER SIDDELEY HS 125 SRS 3A-R Long-range British executive jet transport, has faired ventral tanks for increased fuel capacity and drag reduction. Two crew, 8 passengers carried. Speed 510 m.p.h.; range 1,980 miles; two 3,360-lbs.t. turbojets.

BOEING-VERTOL CH-46D SEA KNIGHT All-weather Marine Corps assault helicopter has powered blade-folding system, carries 25 troops or 4,823 pounds cargo. Speed 166 m.p.h.; combat radius 115 miles; two 1,400-s.h.p. G.E. turboshafts.

FOUND CENTENNIAL 100 Canadian six-seat utility transport has STOL performance, operates from unprepared strips on skis, floats or wheels. Speed 162 m.p.h.; range 700 miles; one 290-h.p. Lycoming engine.

KAMAN K-16B Experimental V/STOL seaplane permits vertical ascent and descent into high seas with control comparable to helicopter provided by flapping-hinge rotor-props, cyclic pitch control, tilt wing and extensible flaps.

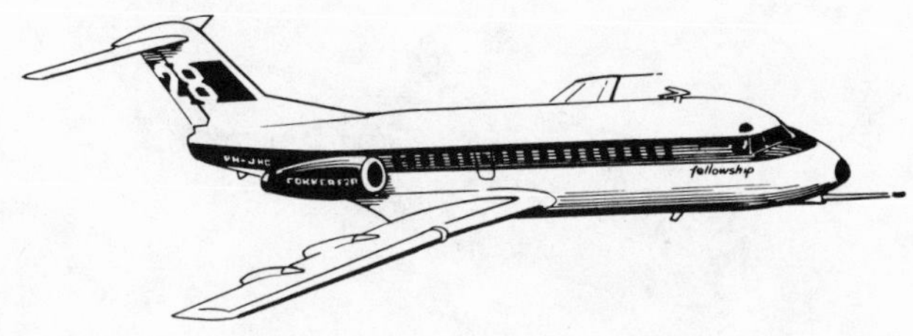

FOKKER F-28 FELLOWSHIP Short-haul commercial transport with seating for 65 passengers plus 4 crew. Two 9,850-lbs.t. Rolls-Royce turbofans provide cruise speed of 527 m.p.h. at 21,000 feet; range 637 miles.

GENERAL DYNAMIC F-111A Swing-wing two-seat strike/recon fighter, has terrain-following radar for supersonic low-level flight, mounts bombs on swiveling pylons. Speed 1,650 m.p.h. at 40,000 feet; 865 m.p.h. at sea level; range, with 8-ton combat load, 1,600 miles; two 20,000-lbs.t. with reheat turbofans.

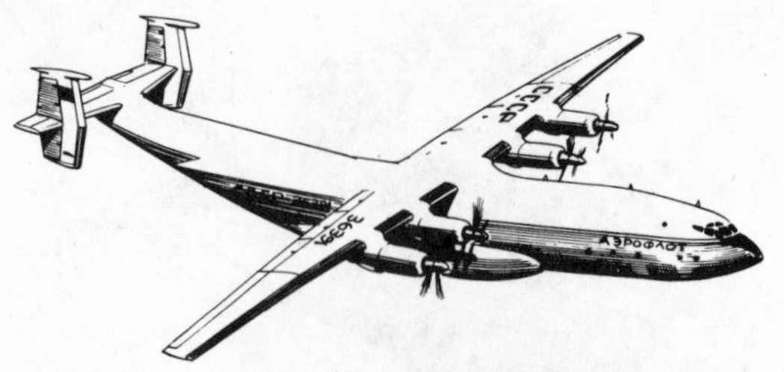

ANTONOV AN-22 ANTEI (COCK) Huge, long-range, Russian military/commercial transport with 15,000-s.h.p. turboprops carries 350 passengers, 66,140 pounds freight for 1,865-mile range. Speed 460 m.p.h.; maximum range 6,800 miles.

BELL AH-1G HUEY COBRA Two-seat attack helicopter, with 7.62mm Minigun nose turret plus rocket/Minigun pods or air-to-ground missiles on wing stubs. Speed 186 m.p.h.; range 425 miles; one 1,400-s.h.p. Lycoming turboshaft.

DASSAULT MIRAGE G French swing-wing two-place strike/recon fighter has supersonic low-level performance. Conventional or nuclear stores on external pylons. Speed 1,585 m.p.h. (Mach 2.4) at 40,000 feet; ferry range 4,000 miles; one 20,500-lbs.t. with reheat turbofan.

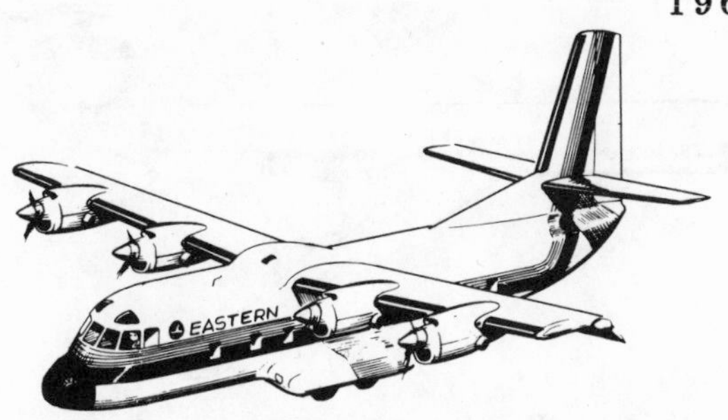

BREGUET 941S/MCDONNELL DOUGLAS 188E STOL tactical transport, carries 2 crew, 40 fully equipped troops; uses deflected propeller slipstream, trailing edge flaps for stable STOL flight. Speed 280 m.p.h.; range 1,616 miles; four 1,500-s.h.p. turboprops.

NEIVA L-42 REGENTE Brazilian four-place observation/liaison aircraft designed for rough field operation has stepped rear fuselage for improved visibility. Speed 137 m.p.h.; range 557 miles; one 180-h.p. Lycoming engine.

FILPER BETA 400 All-metal four-place helicopter employs highly stable, tandem, contra-rotating Gyroflex rigid-rotors, eliminating normally complex rotor hubs. Speed 150 m.p.h.; range 400 miles; one 285-h.p. Continental engine.

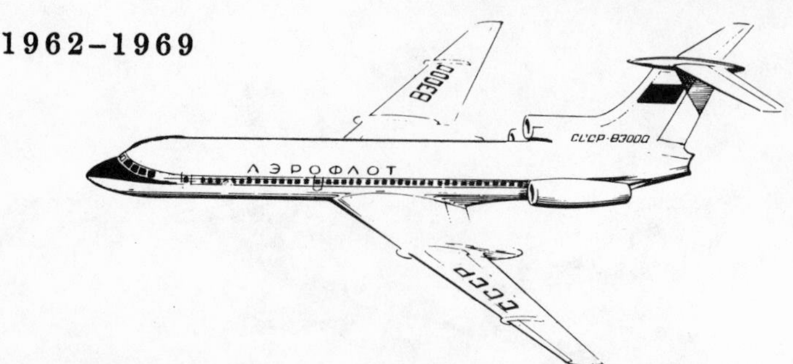

TUPOLEV TU-154 Russian tri-jet medium/long-range transport has 3 crew and 164 passenger capacity; freighter version carries 28 tons cargo. Speed 621 m.p.h. at 36,000 feet; range 3,480 miles; three 20,950-lbs.t. turbofans.

CANADAIR CL-84 DYNAVERT Tilt-wing V/STOL research aircraft for multi-mission role, with space for 2 crew and 16 passengers. Speed 330 m.p.h.; range 350 miles; two 1,400-s.h.p. turboprops.

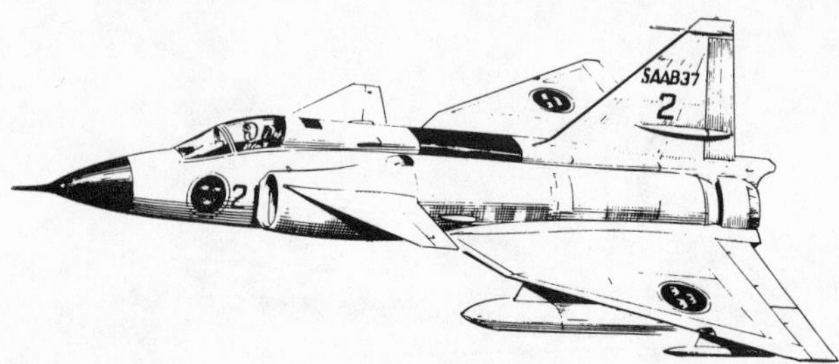

SAAB 37 VIGGEN Single-seat multi-mission Swedish supersonic fighter, employs canard-delta configuration for STOL performance. Armament carried on external pylons. Speed 1,320 m.p.h. (Mach 2); one 26,450-lbs.t. with reheat turbofan.

SIKORSKY HH-53-B U.S.A.F. heavy-lift rescue and recovery helicopter has refueling probe for almost unlimited range, transports 10-ton loads. Speed 195 m.p.h.; range 285 miles; two 3,080-s.h.p. G.E. turboshafts.

BEECHCRAFT MODEL 60 DUKE Six-place pressurized corporate/commuter aircraft, has all-weather avionics and turbo-supercharged 380-h.p. Lycoming engines. Cruise speed 260 m.p.h.; range 1,000 miles.

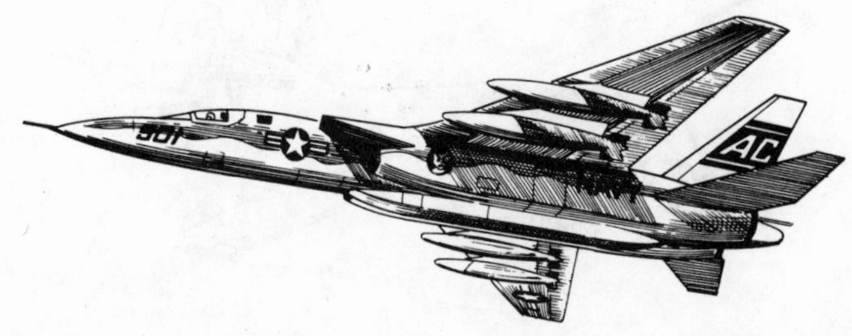

NORTH AMERICAN RA-5C VIGILANTE Carrier-based recon/attack aircraft carries camera and electronic surveillance gear plus nuclear weapons in linear bomb-bay. Speed 1,385 m.p.h. (Mach 2.1); range 2,650 miles; two 17,000-lbs.t. with reheat G.E. turbojets.

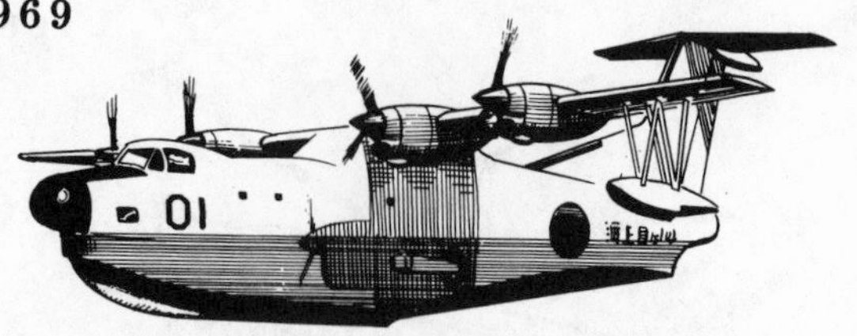

SHIN MEIWA PX-S Japanese recon/patrol flying boat has boundary layer control, deflected propeller slipstream for STOL performance. Speed 340 m.p.h.; range 2,948 miles; four 2,850-s.h.p. G.E. turboprops; one 1,250-s.h.p. G.E. turboshaft for BLC.

HANDLEY PAGE HP-137 JETSTREAM British twin-turboprop corporate/feederliner and military transport has 3 crew and 18 passenger capacity. Cruise speed 306 m.p.h.; range 1,900 miles; two 850-s.h.p. Astazou turboprops.

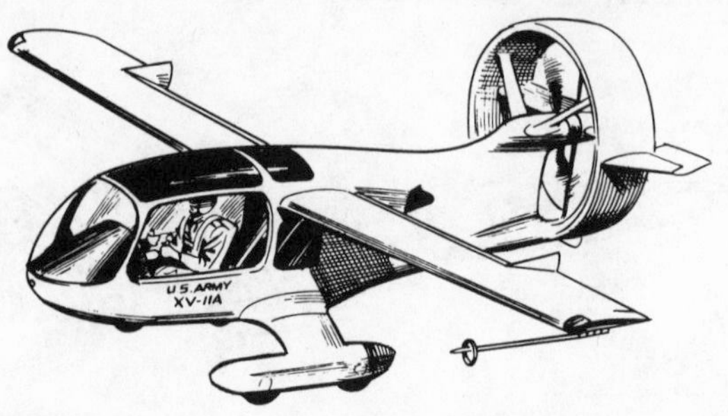

XV-11A MSU MARVEL STOL research aircraft has smooth fiber glass surfaces, employs boundary-layer control, ducted prop, wing camber change for STOL performance. Speed 225 m.p.h.; takeoff run 350 feet; one 317-s.h.p. turboprop for BLC and prop drive.

KAMOV KA-25K HORMONE Russian utility helicopter contains 12 passenger seats. Second pilot controls critical cargo handling through dual flying controls in gondola under nose. Speed 137 m.p.h.; range 250 miles; two 900-s.h.p. turboshafts.

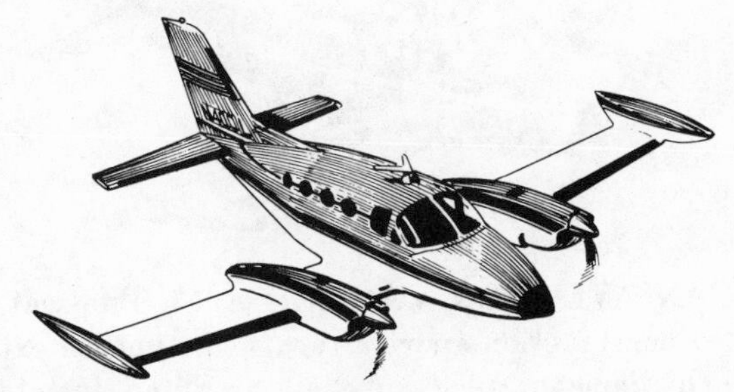

CESSNA MODEL 421 Pressurized, ten-place, business/feederliner transport has twin 375-h.p. fuel-injected, geared engines with three blade constant speed props. Speed 275 m.p.h. at 16,000 feet; range 1,174 miles.

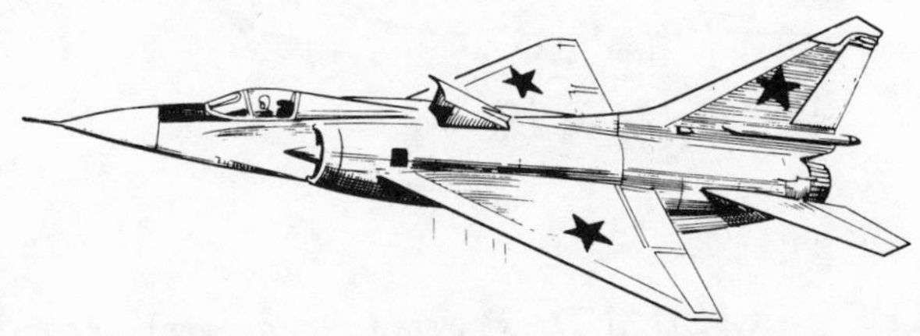

MIKOYAN FAITHLESS Russian single-seat STOL fighter, has delta-wing, swept-tail and 30,000-lbs.t. turbojet for normal flight plus two vertically mounted jet-lift turbines. Speed 1,650 m.p.h. (Mach 2.5).

CANADAIR CL-215 Canadian amphibious flying boat, scoops up 1,200 gallons of water during 80-m.p.h. takeoff run for water-bombing forest fires. Speed 219 m.p.h.; range 345–1,235 miles; two 2,100-h.p. P. & W. air-cooled radial engines.

AMERICAN AVIATION YANKEE AA-1 Two-seat, all-metal, bonded construction sport aircraft has smooth exterior, uses six-inch diameter alloy tube as spar and fuel tank. Speed 141 m.p.h.; range 512 miles; 108-h.p. Lycoming engine.

YAKOLEV FREEHAND Russian single-seat experimental tailed-delta-wing VTOL aircraft has two 9,000-lbs.t. vectored thrust turbofans for jet-lift and main propulsion. Speed 645 m.p.h.; tactical radius of VTOL 150 miles, of STOL 200 miles.

CESSNA 177 CARDINAL Four-place aircraft has cantilever wing, low-drag profile design and one-piece, all-moving, slotted stabilizer. Speed 144 m.p.h.; range 780 miles; 180-h.p. Lycoming engine.

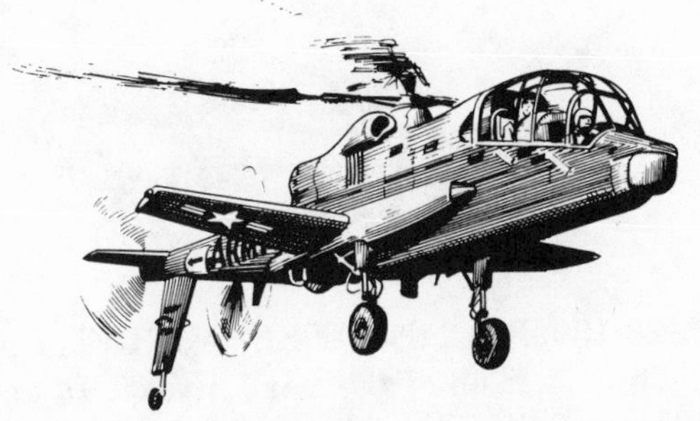

LOCKHEED AH-56A CHEYENNE Heavily armed rigid-rotor, tandem two-seat attack/escort helicopter has all-weather performance, uses tail mounted pusher prop for high speed. Speed 253 m.p.h.; range 875 miles; one 3,435-s.h.p. G.E. turboshaft.

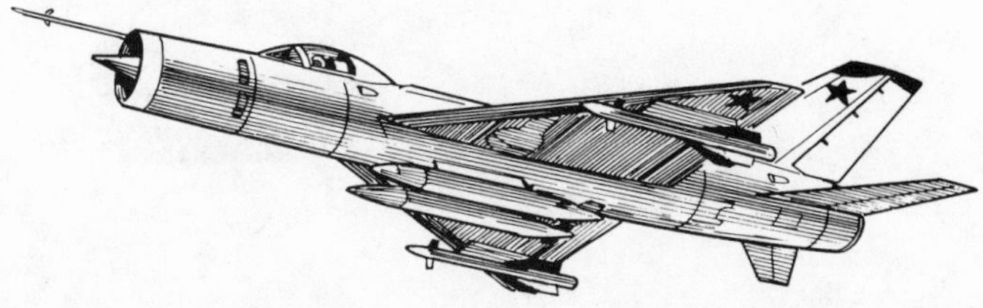

SUKHOI SU-9 FISHPOT Tailed-delta-wing single-seat Russian all-weather interceptor, mounts four radar-homing, air-to-air missiles on wing pylons plus drop-tanks under fuselage. Speed 1,190 m.p.h. (Mach 1.8); one 22,050-lbs.t. with reheat turbojet.

BOEING 737-100 Smallest aircraft of Boeing jetliner family, short-range transport has 99 passenger capacity, operates from short runways. Cruise speed 580 m.p.h.; range 680 miles; two 14,000-lbs.t. P. & W. turbofans.

PIPER PA-28-180/R CHEROKEE ARROW Four-place retractable gear version of tri-gear Cherokee D, drops landing-gear automatically with reduced power and speed below 110 m.p.h. Speed 170 m.p.h.; range 980 miles; one 180-h.p. Lycoming engine.

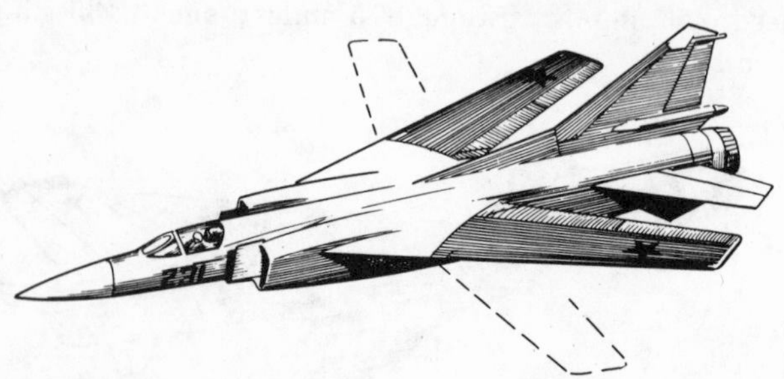

MIKOYAN FLOGGER Russian swing-wing single-seat strike/recon fighter has single 30,000-lbs.t. with reheat turbojet. Wing translates from full forward to full aft in 4 seconds. Speed 1,650 m.p.h. (Mach 2.5) at 40,000 feet, 910 m.p.h. at sea level.

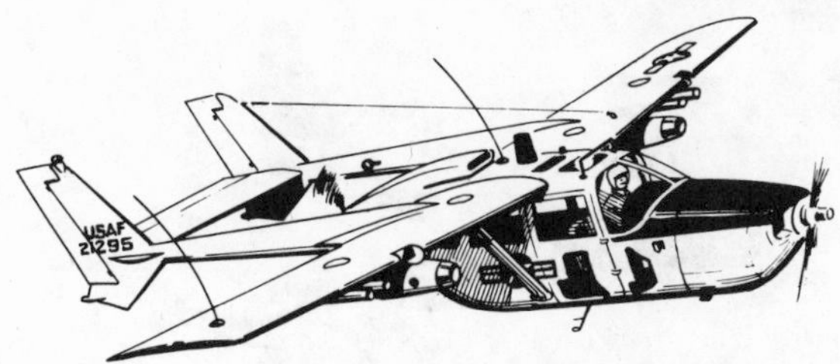

CESSNA O-2A SUPER SKYMASTER Military twin engine push-pull aircraft for observation and forward air control, mounts Minigun and rocket pods on wing pylons. Speed 200 m.p.h.; range 985 miles; two 210-h.p. Continental engines.

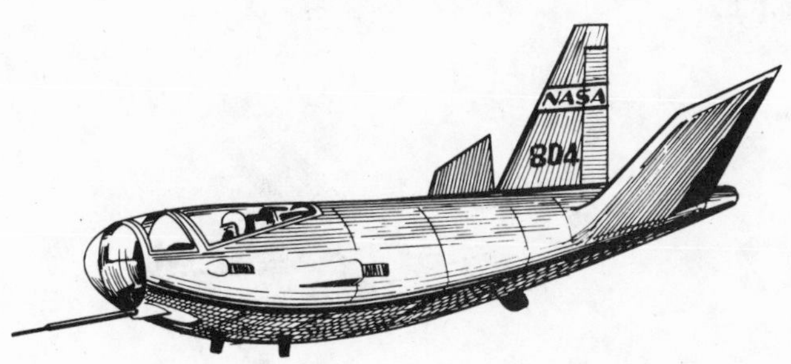

NORTHROP/NASA HL-10 Rocket-powered experimental wingless lifting body, atmospheric re-entry vehicle has flat bottom, half-cone shape, achieves aerodynamic stability and lift from body alone. Free-fall speed Mach 0.8.

BOEING-VERTOL CH-47C CHINOOK U.S. Army multi-purpose helicopter, transports 44 troops, assault weapons or recovers downed aircraft. Speed 184 m.p.h.; tactical radius 214 miles; two 3,750-s.h.p. turboshafts.

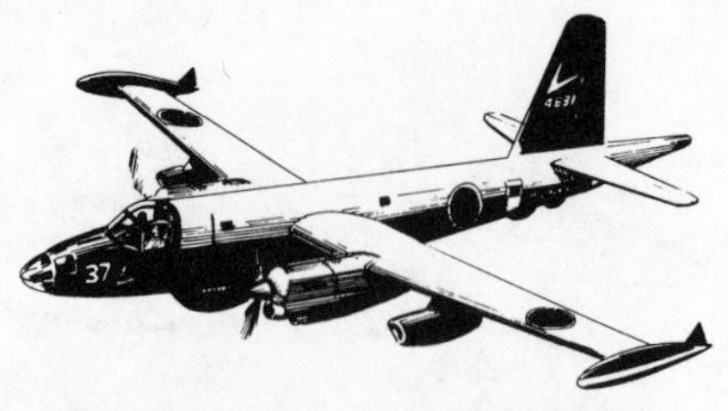

KAWASAKI GK-210 Japanese long-range maritime patrol craft, evolved from Lockheed Neptune has lengthened fuselage, piston engines replaced by two 2,850-s.h.p. turboprops plus two auxiliary 3,085-lbs.t. underwing turbojets. Speed 350 m.p.h.

HELIO H634 TWIN STALLION Ten-seat utility STOL aircraft mounts twin 317-s.h.p. turboprops on stub wings at nose. Airframe similar to single-engine Stallion. Speed 210 m.p.h.; range 965 miles.

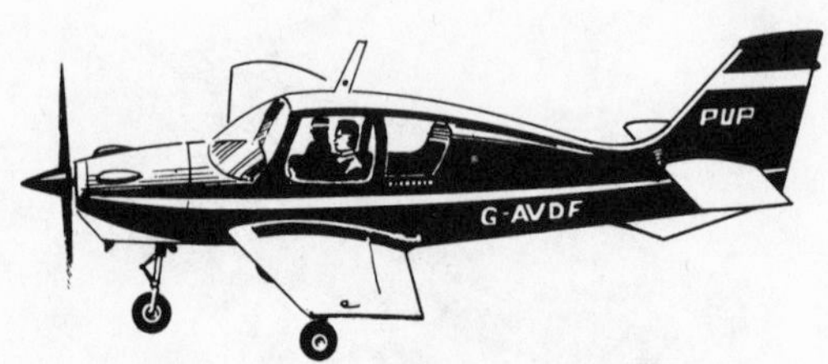

BEAGLE B.121 PUP British aerobatic two-seater, stressed for plus 4.5G's, minus 1.8G's. Flaps, dual controls standard. Speed 129 m.p.h.; range 600 miles; 100-h.p. Rolls-Royce Continental engine. Pups 150 and 180 have power increase and 2-plus-2 seating.

DORNIER DO-31E3 Tactical V/STOL transport has two 15,500-lbs.t. vectored-thrust turbofans as cruise engines plus eight 4,400-lbs.t. lift turbojets mounted vertically in wing-tip pods. Cruise speed 400 m.p.h.; range 1,118 miles.

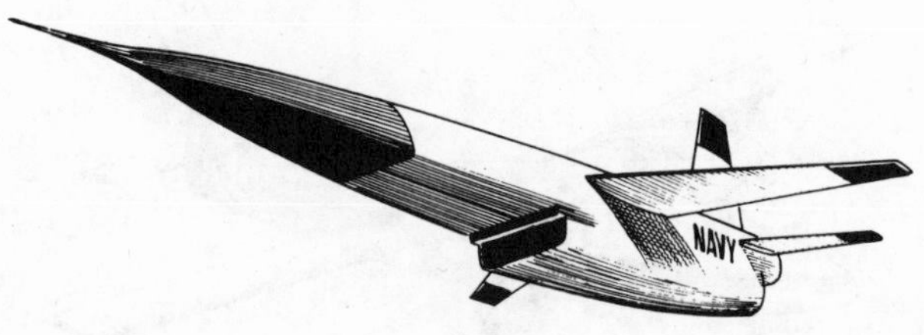

RYAN XBQM-34E FIREBEE II Supersonic, remotely controlled, highly maneuverable target drone, provides realistic fighter combat training. Speed 1,190 m.p.h. (Mach 1.8) at 50,000 feet; ceiling 70,000 feet; one 1,840 lbs.t. Continental turbojet.

CESSNA A-37B TWEETY BIRD Two-place side-by-side COIN fighter, mounts 7.62mm Minigun in nose and 4,855 pounds ordnance on wing pylons. Speed 478 m.p.h.; range 1,400 miles; two 2,850-lbs.t. G.E. turbojets.

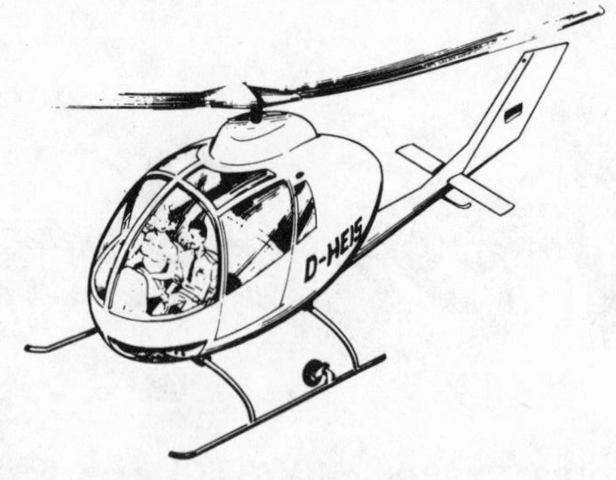

DORNIER DO-132 Four-seat helicopter, built of fiber glass/ plastic and aluminum honeycomb, uses hot gases from turbine generator ejected through rotor blade tip nozzles for torqueless rotor drive. Speed 137 m.p.h.; range 250 miles.

DEHAVILLAND DHC-6 TWIN OTTER SRS.100 Utility/ feederliner transport, has STOL performance, 2 crew plus 18 passengers and 52-cubic-feet baggage capacity. Cruise speed 182 m.p.h.; range 817 miles; two 579-s.h.p. P. & W. turboprops.

BAC 167 Two-place basic trainer and COIN aircraft, mounts two 7.62mm machine guns plus rocket pods or four 500-pound bombs for attack role. Speed 481 m.p.h.; tactical radius 253 miles; one 3,410-lbs.t. Rolls-Royce turbojet.

CHAMPION 8KCAB CITABRIA PRO Fully aerobatic, one- or two-seat aircraft designed for aerobatic competition, stressed for plus 6G's, minus 5G's. One 200-h.p. Lycoming Special engine; rate of climb 1,700 ft./min.

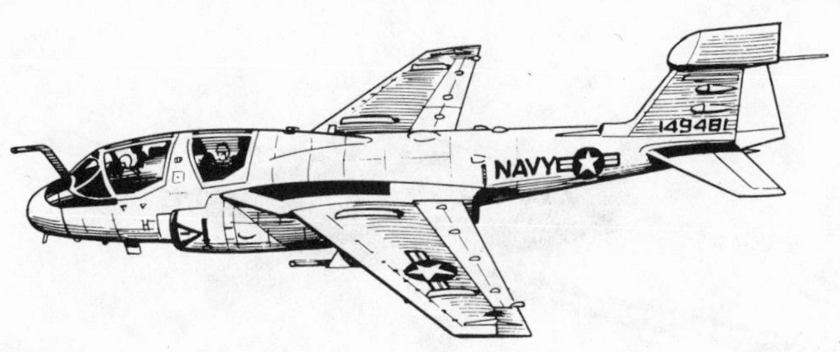

GRUMMAN EA-6B INTRUDER II Carrier-borne four-seat all-weather electronic countermeasures aircraft, mounts avionics systems pods beneath wings and fuselage. Speed 670 m.p.h.; range 1,250 miles; two 9,300-lbs.t. P. & W. turbojets.

NORD 500 Tilt-duct French VTOL research craft has two 317-s.h.p. turboshafts driving two 5-bladed connected ducted props. Control in yaw and pitch achieved by differential and collective duct tilting, roll by thrust modulation. Speed 217 m.p.h.

LOCKHEED XV-4A HUMMINGBIRD II Two-seat VTOL research craft, has six 3,015-lbs.t. turbojets, four mounted vertically for jet lift, two horizontal engines provide thrust for normal flight plus VTOL lift. Speed 402 m.p.h.

WINDECKER ACX-7 EAGLE I Four-place all-plastic aircraft has airframe built of Fibaloy, combining epoxy resins plus fiber glass and metal filaments in integrated structure. One 285-h.p. Continental engine.

THURSTON TSC-1A TEAL Economical all-metal two-seat amphibian has deep-step hull and afterbody ventilation for STOL performance. Speed 117 m.p.h.; range 380 miles; one 150-h.p. Lycoming engine.

LOCKHEED C-5A GALAXY World's largest aircraft is military logistics transport with maximum payload of 265,000 pounds or 365 persons, gross weight 728,000 pounds. Speed 571 m.p.h.; range, with 90,596-pound payload, 7,150 miles; four 41,000-lbs.t. turbofans.

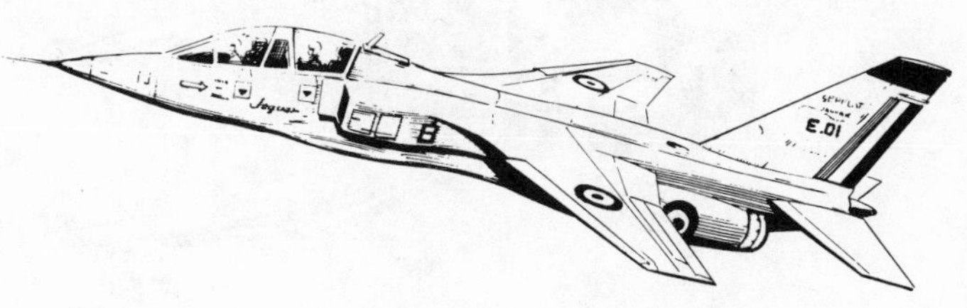

BAC-BREGUET JAGUAR Anglo-French supersonic two-seat trainer and strike aircraft has STOL performance and 10,000-pound external ordnance capacity. Speed 1,120 m.p.h. (Mach 1.7) at 36,000 feet; tactical radius 370–755 miles.

BEDE BD-4 Two-place homebuilt employs bolted angle rigid truss frame fuselage with glued-on non-stressed alloy skins; wing has fiber glass panel ribs over tubular alloy spar. Speed 156 m.p.h.; range 1,200 miles; 108-h.p. Lycoming engine.

DASSAULT MIRAGE M.5 Export version Mirage III-E, single-seat interceptor/ground attack craft has simplified avionics, greater fuel/ordnance capacity. Speed 1,386 m.p.h. at 40,000 feet; range 472 miles; one 13,624-lbs.t. with reheat turbojet.

CENTRE EST AERONAUTIQUE DR-253 REGENTE All-wood five-place aircraft, redesign of DR-250, has 8-inches wider fuselage, more headroom, metal flaps and tri-gear. Speed 177 m.p.h.; range 810 miles; one 180-h.p. Lycoming engine.

PIPER PA-35 POCONO Feederliner/cargo transport has pilot and 17 passenger capacity; large diameter fuselage provides three-abreast seating or high volume cargo loads. Speed 242 m.p.h.; range 650 miles; two 500-h.p. turbo-supercharged Lycoming engines.

TUPOLEV TU-144 SST Supersonic Russian transport of light alloy construction has conical-camber ogive delta wing, carries 3 crew and 121 passengers. Cruise speed 1,550 m.p.h. (Mach 2.3); range 4,040 miles; four 28,660-lbs.t. turbofans.

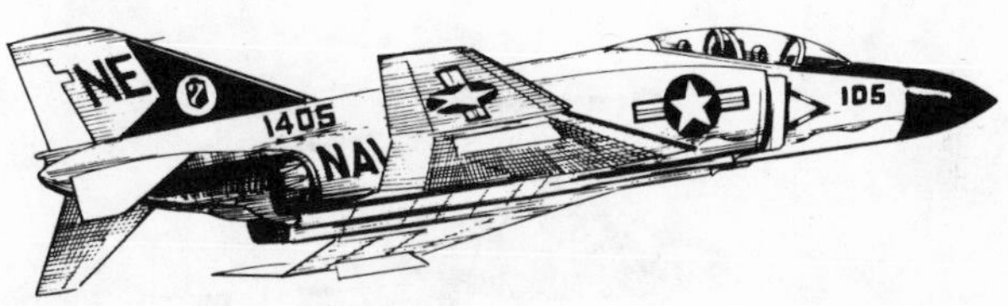

MCDONNELL F-4J PHANTOM II Navy two-seat all-weather interceptor/ground attack fighter has higher speed and combat ceiling, greater range and shorter takeoff than earlier models. Speed Mach 2-plus; combat radius 1,000 miles; two 17,900-lbs.t. with reheat G.E. turbojets.

MOONEY M-10 CADET Two-place side-by-side basic trainer, single-fin updated version of 1937 Ercoupe, has normal three control system, sliding canopy and spring-steel main gear. Speed 117 m.p.h.; range 417 miles; one 90-h.p. Continental engine.

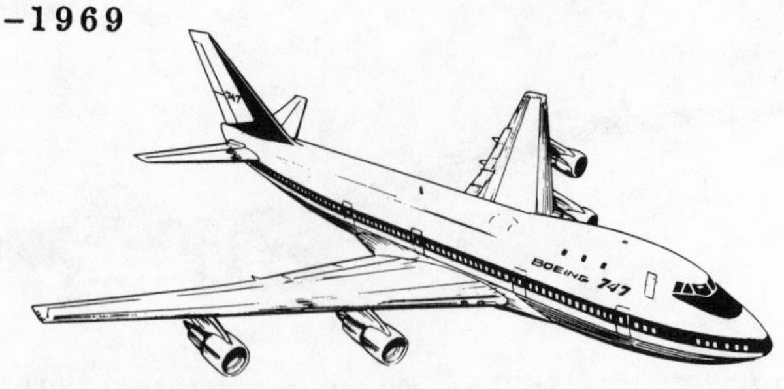

BOEING 747 JUMBO JET Giant transport for economy flights, with capacity of 490 passengers seated in 185-foot long, 20-foot wide cabin. Speed 640 m.p.h.; range 8,000 miles; four 43,500-lbs.t. P. & W. turbofans.

MCCULLOCH J-2 GYROPLANE Two-seat utility autogyro is virtually stall-proof, takes off in 40 feet, maintains full control at 30 m.p.h. Speed 120 m.p.h.; range 300 miles; one 180-h.p. Lycoming engine.

CAVALIER MUSTANG 3 Modified version of World War II fighter, has 2,185-s.h.p. Rolls-Royce turboprop for COIN role, operates from short battle strips with 2,000-pound armament load. Cruise speed 530 m.p.h.; combat range 152 miles plus 2.5 hours loiter time.

TEXTRON BELL AEROSYSTEM ACLG Research aircraft has retractable, flexible rubber bag edged with hundreds of jet-nozzles, inflated by axial fan, that provides 2-foot air-cushion for no-wheel takeoffs and landings from water, snow, ice, mud or runways.

DASSAULT MD-320-01 HIRONDELLE French turboprop utility/feederliner aircraft and military aircrew trainer, transports 3 crew and 14 passengers at 310-m.p.h. cruise speed. Range 1,245 miles; two 870-s.h.p. Astazou turboprops.

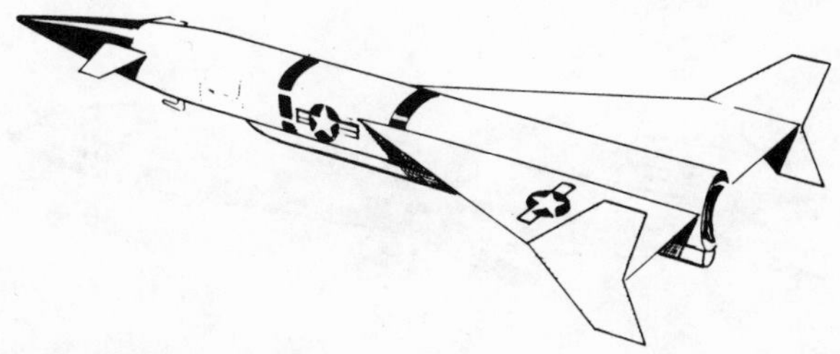

BEECHCRAFT AQM-37A Supersonic, canard-delta, target training missile, simulates enemy air-to-air and surface-to-air missiles. Pre-packaged 630-pound thrust liquid fuel rocket provides Mach 3 performance, ceiling 90,000 feet.

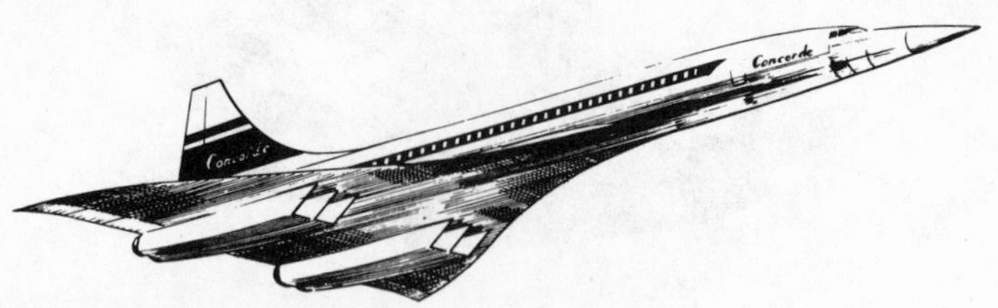

BAC-SUD-AVIATION CONCORDE Anglo-French supersonic 132 passenger transport has ogive, high lift, wing and pivoting nose for takeoff and landing. Speed 1,450 m.p.h. (Mach 2.2) at cruise altitude of 62,000 feet; range 4,155 miles; four 38,300-lbs.t. with reheat turbojets.

HAWKER SIDDELEY HARRIER T.MK 2 British two-seat V/STOL trainer and close support/recon aircraft employs single 19,200-lbs.t. vectored thrust turbofan for jet lift and main propulsion. Speed 737 m.p.h.; combat radius 500 miles; ferry range 2,000 miles.

MCDONNELL DOUGLAS DC-10 Subsonic tri-jet transport carries 334 passengers, operates from short fields over ranges from 300 to 3,200 miles. Cruise speed 600 m.p.h.; three 39,500-lbs.t. G.E. turbofans.

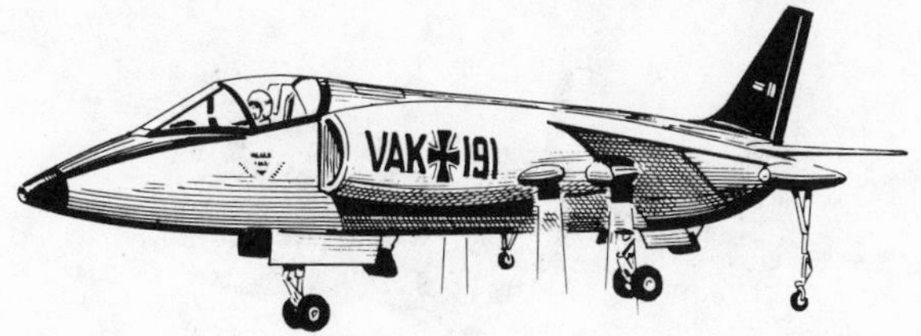

VFW VAK 191B German/Italian subsonic VTOL tactical recon fighter employs two vertical 5,990-lbs.t. turbojets for direct jet-lift plus single 10,000-lbs.t. vectored-thrust turbojet for VTOL assist and main propulsion.

LOCKHEED L-1011 Tri-jet high-density transport carries 4 crew, 345 passengers, operates from 7,000-foot runway. Cruise speed 587 m.p.h.; range 3,224 miles; three 40,600-lbs.t. Rolls-Royce turbofans.

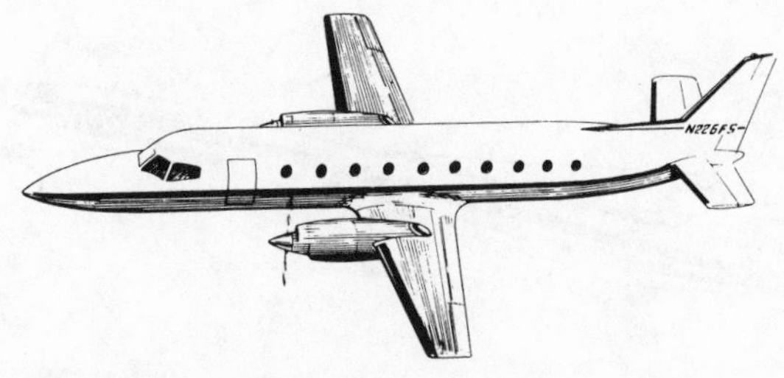

SWEARINGEN METRO Pressurized commuter and utility transport for short-field operations has STOL performance with 2 crew plus 20 passengers. Speed 300 m.p.h.; two 840-s.h.p. Garrett turboprops.

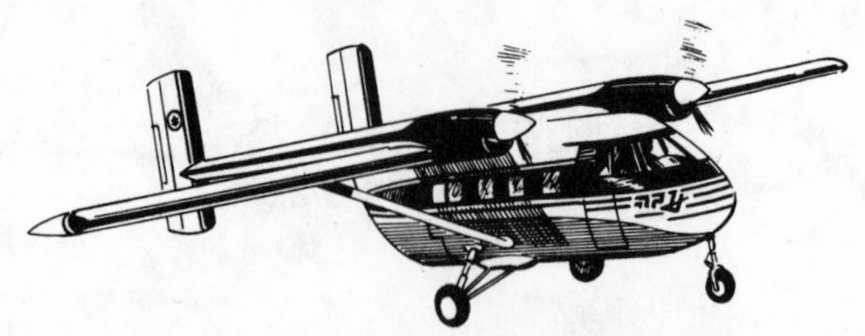

I.A.I ARAVA Israeli rough-field STOL utility transport, carries 2 crew plus 20 passengers; 12 stretcher casualties or 4,410-pound payload. Speed 217 m.p.h.; range 808 miles; two 620-s.h.p. P. & W. turboprops.

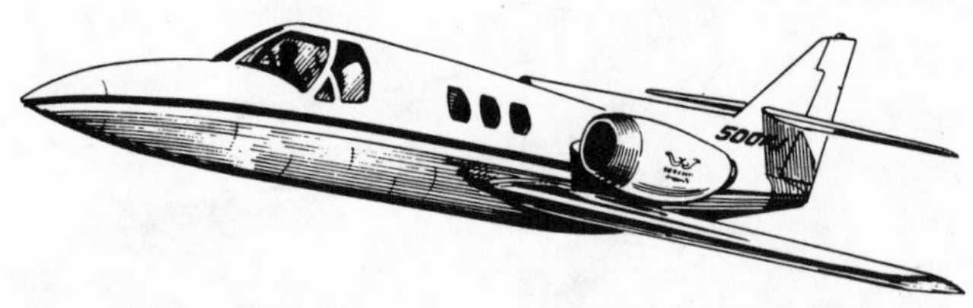

CESSNA FANJET 500 Pressurized, eight-place, twin-jet business aircraft, has straight, thick wing with slotted flaps for short field operations. Speed 413-m.p.h. at 30,000 feet; range 1,580 miles; two 2,200-lbs.t. P. & W. turbofans.

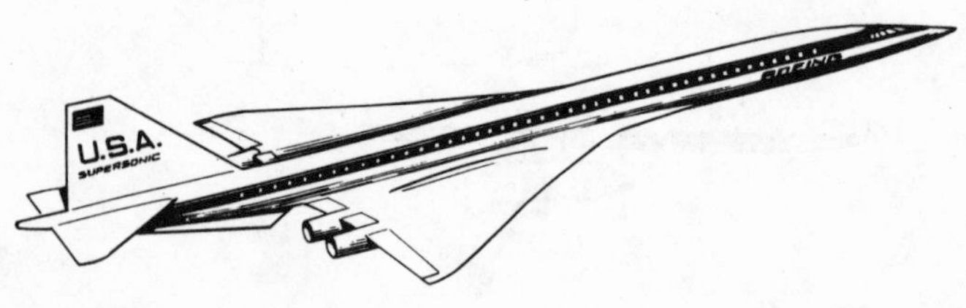

BOEING 2707-300 SST Supersonic transport has titanium airframe, seating 234 passengers, 142-foot span delta wing has inboard dihedral, outboard anhedral for stability. Speed 1,800 m.p.h. (Mach 2.7) at 60,000 feet; range 4,000 miles.

PART TWELVE

The Age of the Jumbo

1970-1976

THE MUSHROOMING COST and complexity of 1970's air and spacecraft led to increased competition in the United States and to unprecedented international cooperation in Europe during the first half of the decade.

The strong, steady growth of long-distance travel encouraged airlines to order large quantities of wide-bodied 747's, DC-10's and Tri-Stars. But then the economic slump of 1973 disrupted everyone's plans and forced very discouraging cutbacks. Still, the big American airliners showed they could move more people, at lower unit cost, than anything before them, and by 1976 the Anglo-French *Concorde* SST was routinely flying on intercontinental routes at Mach 2 with fare-paying passengers. The Soviet Tu-144 SST was still being tested on scheduled cargo runs.

New European wide-bodied airliners like the French A300 Airbus began to demonstrate even better economics as the world emerged from the massive trauma of quadrupled fuel prices. Smaller craft, like the Canadian STOL DHC-7 Dash 7 and the novel Britten-Norman Trislander, pointed the way toward improved local service, as the once-proliferating commuter air lines settled down to a few businesslike operations.

On the military side, the period was dominated by several major competitive fly-offs which led to the awarding of very lucrative contracts, and by the further merging of NATO air forces in the face of a growing Soviet offensive capability.

In the U.S.A., several new supersonic fighter planes were developed to replace those which had served well for many years but were becoming noticeably obsolescent. To supersede the venerable F-4 Phantom II, McDonnell Douglas brought out its F-15 Eagle, which offered more speed, weapons load, and sophisticated electronics. On the strictly Navy side, the Grumman American F-14 Tomcat, with its variable-sweep wings, showed a similar improvement over its predecessors.

The big competitions were between the General Dynamics F-16 and the Northrop F-17 Cobra for a standard lightweight fighter, and among transports and COIN aircraft. The F-17 was the winner of its contest and was then transformed into the McDonnell Douglas F-18 for production. The F-16 was hardly a loser, however, as it went on to capture the big NATO orders over the SAAB Viggen and Mirage F1.

The aging B-52 Stratofortress has been the mainstay of the American strategic nuclear bomber fleet for many years, and in view of its eventual retirement, Rockwell International (formerly North American Aviation) created its variable-sweep B-1 supersonic bomber, which will carry the same bomb load as a couple of squadrons of B-17 Fying Fortresses. Its main obstacle appears to be the reluctance of the Congress to appropriate the billions of dollars needed for quantity production.

The main rough-and-ready military cargo plane for well over a decade has been Lockheed's omnipresent C-130 Hercules. But it, too, is soon to be replaced by something newer and better. To decide which it will be, the U.S. Air Force is holding a competitive fly-off between two sophisticated STOL jet transports—Boeing's YC-14 and McDonnell Douglas YC-15. The resultant new Hercules could have major commercial uses as well.

On the increasingly active COIN (counter-insurgency) front, Republic-Fairchild's rear-engined A-10 came out on top and is becoming a major ground-support type. Outside the U.S.A., COIN fighter-bombers generally seem to be modified light jet trainers.

Much of the increased emphasis on new designs is the result of heightened awareness of Soviet efforts to match or exceed the West not only in numbers of aircraft but also in their performance. Mach 3 + MiG-25's (formerly called MiG-23) rocked Western intelligence experts during the 1973 Arab-Israeli war as they calmly cruised over the battlefields on reconnaissance missions, too high and too fast to be challenged by the available planes or missiles.

Business aviation—from little two-seat helicopters to air-line-equipped Gulfstream II's—suffered surprisingly little from the recession of the early 1970's. A steady stream of executive types poured from the assembly lines in Wichita and elsewhere as the transition from pistons to turbines continued without pause. As has been true for more than a quarter of a century, the American share of the world's general aviation industry continued to overshadow that of the rest of the active nations. Learjets and Citations and Jetstars and Sabreliners and their brethren still make up the bulk of the increasingly vital corporate fleet, with only the French-built Falcon providing any serious challenge to total American domination.

Private aviation—touring, training, and tooling around the patch—similarly continued to grow well, despite inflation and unemployment. Most of the new airplanes are relatively similar to those that have gone before, as the products of the American "Big Three" of Beech, Cessna, and Piper remain the world's standard. And while the American auto industry moves inexorably toward smaller, more efficient cars, its aeronautical counterpart turns out more and more of the powerful well-equipped twin-engined luxury liners, such as the Beech Super King Air 200 and the Cessna Golden Eagle. And it manages quite easily to ignore any potential threats from the high-quality but limited-production European two- and four-seaters.

One of the fastest-growing aspects of world aviation—at least in terms of numbers and enthusiasm, if not economic impact—is its sporting arm. Perhaps as a form of rebellion against the burgeoning costs and increasingly automatic and impersonal nature of much of the rest of aviation, the use of homebuilt and rebuilt airplanes is spreading around the world.

The American amateur-built airplane fleet is now more than double the number of its airliners—more than 4,000 flying and probably twice that number under construction. And while many of them are rather old-fashioned in design and structure, others like the Bede BD-5 and the Rutan Vari-Eze promise performance far beyond any factory-built airplanes, using very advanced ideas.

For the nostalgia buff, restoration of light planes of the 1930's and 1940's and warbirds from World War II brings back the intense personal feeling that accompanied their creation and original use. And it puts the "little guy" back into the air at a price he can afford.

Full-fledged competition—in the form of pylon air racing, aerobatics, and soaring—has been growing in popularity during the 1970's, with the greatest gains seen on the international front. There, specialized craft have brought with them not only the personal touch but undreamed-of performance gains.

The latest idea in aviation (and one which owes as much to the quite separate world of surfing, as it does to flying) is hang gliding. Using the triangular kitelike wings first tried for returning small manned spacecraft to earth, thousands of people in all parts of the world have learned to leap off sand dunes, hills, and even mountains and to glide down in a simulation of natural flight.

Then, at the extreme end of the aerospace spectrum from 15 m.p.h., 40-lb. hang gliders is the strange sphere of space travel, with devices that look nothing like airplanes, and have price tags as far out as their arena of action. The epoch-making series of Apollo landings on the moon was followed by the three-month flight of America's Skylab, in which daring exploration gave way to extended scientific research and pointed the way to permanent space stations.

At least as significant, though in a more political vein, was the joint U.S.A.–U.S.S.R. orbital link-up of the Apollo-Soyuz craft and the subsequent intermingling of bilingual crews of astronauts and cosmonauts. In view of the staggering costs of projected manned flights to Mars and beyond, this example of international cooperation may yet prove to have been one of the great milestones.

AERO BOERO 115 BS Three-passenger personal plane with STOL performance, produced privately in Argentina, of conventional steel, aluminum and fabric construction. Powered by 115-h.p. Lycoming 0-235 engine, cruises at 117 m.p.h. for 500 miles.

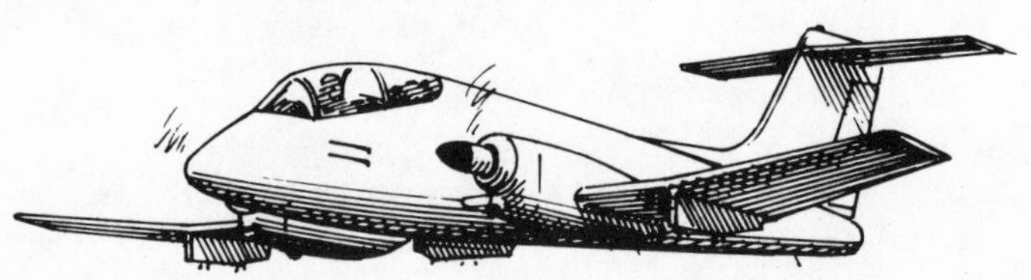

FMA IA 58 PUCARA Twin-turboprop counter-insurgency aircraft developed for Argentine Air Force and expected to see use in other South American nations. Powered by two 1,020-h.p. French Turbomeca Astazou engines, has top speed of 325 m.p.h. at 10,000 feet.

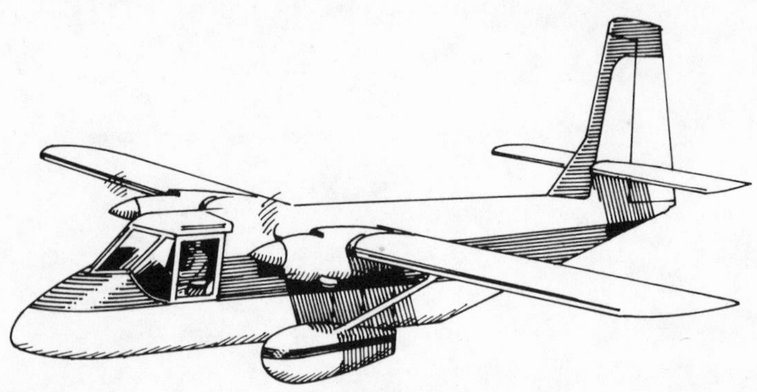

NOMAD N22 Twin-engine utility aircraft built by Australian Government Aircraft Factory for operation from short, unprepared airfields. Two 400-h.p. Allison turboprop engines give cruising speed of 195 m.p.h. with up to 12 passengers or 360 cu. ft. of cargo.

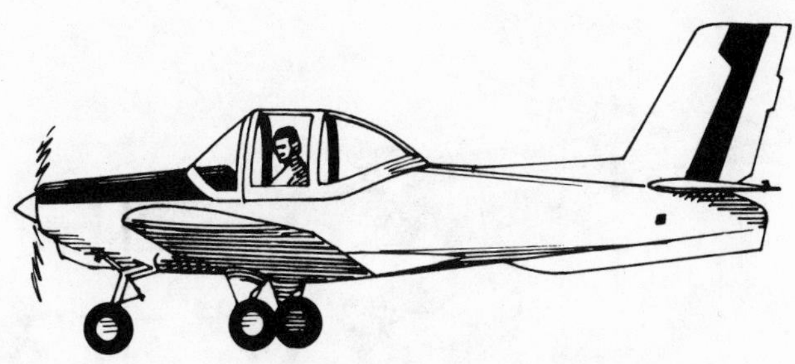

AEROTEC A122 UIRAPURU Civil prototype of Brazilian two-seat trainer, now in service with several South American air forces. All-metal airplane has 160-h.p. Lycoming 0–320 engine, cruises at 115 m.p.h. for 500 miles.

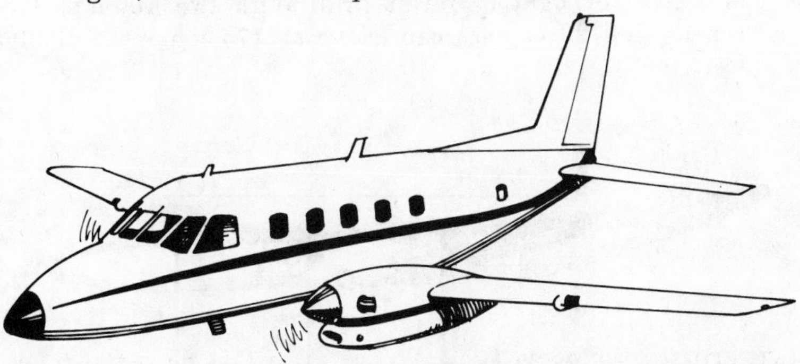

EMBRAER EMB-110 BANDEIRANTE Brazilian Air Force twin-turboprop light transport designed by French engineer Max Holste. Other versions for patrol and aerial photography. Two 680-h.p. P. & W. PT6A engines give cruise speed of 260 m.p.h. at 15,000 feet.

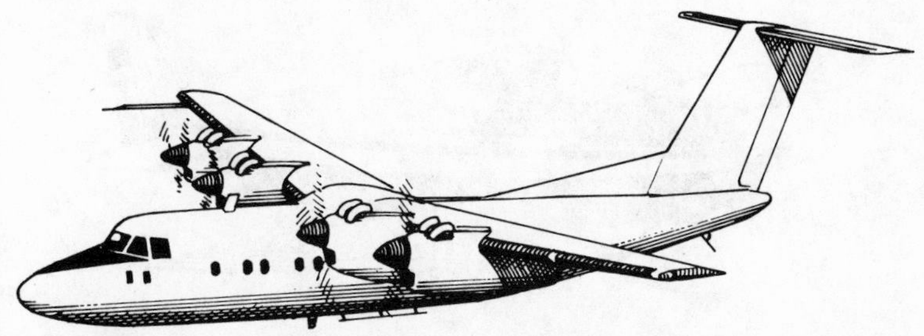

DHC-7 DASH 7 "Quiet STOL" airliner developed by De Havilland of Canada to carry up to 50 passengers from 2,000-foot airfields with minimum of noise for downtown-to-downtown service. Four P. & W. PT6A engines give range of 1,425 miles at 280 m.p.h.

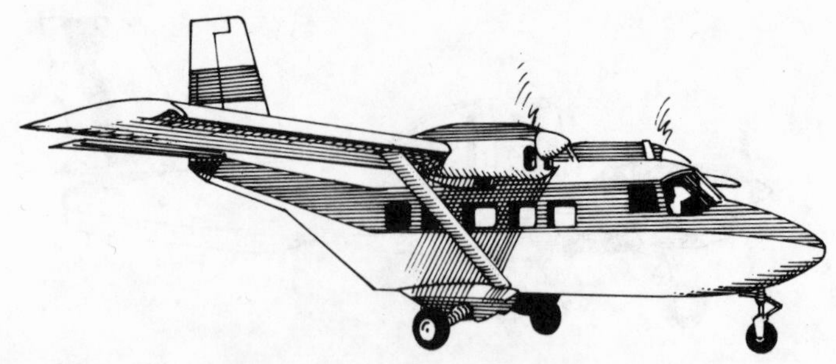

DOMINION SKYTRADER 800 Small STOL transport and general utility aircraft, designed by former Boeing engineers in Canada, can carry up to 12 passengers or 350 gallons of water for fighting forest fires. With two 400-h.p. Lycoming I0–720 engines can cruise at 175 m.p.h. at 10,000 feet.

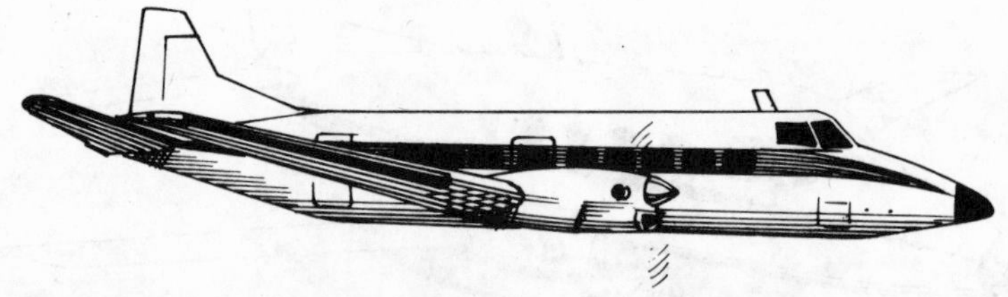

SAUNDERS ST-28 Developed from highly modified De Havilland Dove aircraft, this stretched version is built in Canada to carry 22 passengers for short distances. Powered by two P. & W. PT6A turboprop engines of 785 h.p. for 210-m.p.h. cruise.

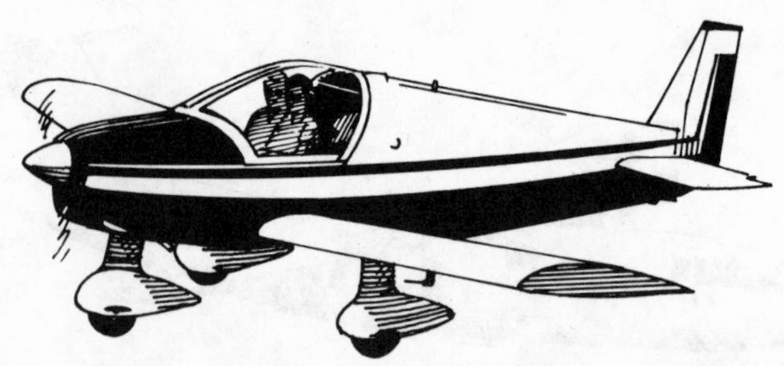

HEINTZ ZENITH Two-seat all-metal homebuilt sport airplane built in France by Chris Heintz, who then emigrated to Canada. With 100-h.p. Continental engine, has top speed of 145 m.p.h., maximum range of 500 miles. Single-seat "Mono Z" being developed.

SHENYANG F-6 Chinese-built version of Soviet MiG–19 all-weather fighter, also used by Pakistan. Powered by two Chinese-manufactured Soviet 7,200-lbs.t. turbojet engines, has top speed of 900 m.p.h. at 33,000 feet and maximum range of 1,350 miles.

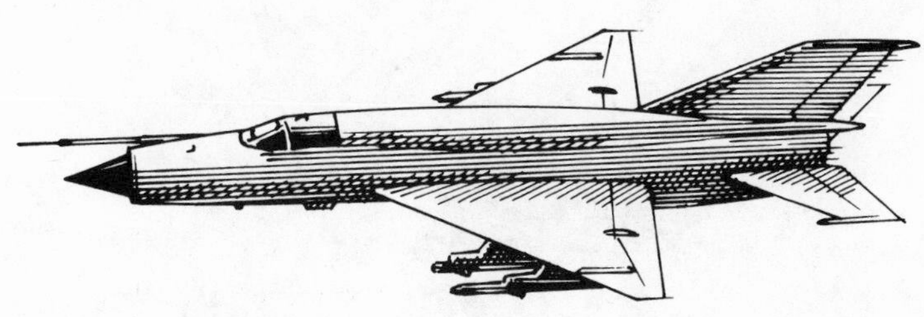

SHENYANG F-8 Copy of various versions of Soviet MiG–21 fighter, built in limited numbers in People's Republic of China for export as well as domestic use. Top speed over Mach 1.

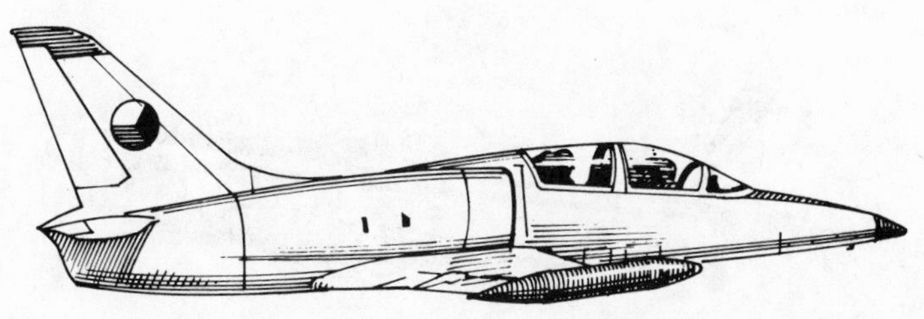

AERO L–39 ALBATROSS Czechoslovakian two-seat jet trainer can operate from rough fields with limited load of bombs and air-to-air missiles. With 3,800-lbs.t. Czech-built Soviet turbojet engine, has top speed of 465 m.p.h. at 16,000 feet.

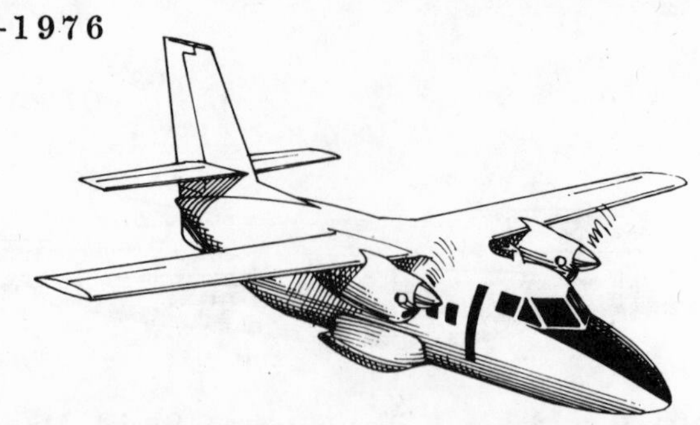

LET L-410 TURBOLET Czechoslovakian short-haul transport can be used for aerial survey and ambulance work from grass fields. Turboprop-powered by American or Soviet engines, cruises at 230 m.p.h. at 10,000 feet with up to 19 passengers.

ZLIN Z-42 Two-seat Czechoslovakian light training/touring/sport airplane is fully aerobatic and can tow gliders. Powered by 180-h.p. Avia straight-six engine, has top speed of 140 m.p.h. at 2,000 feet, can climb faster than 1,000 feet per minute.

ZLIN 526-AFS AKROBAT Ultimate version of famed Czechoslovakian competition aerobatic series which has won more European contests than any other. Has 180-h.p. Avia inline engine, giving top speed of 155 m.p.h. and 1,775-feet-per-minute climb.

ZLIN Z–50 Brand-new and much more powerful Czechoslovakian international aerobatic competition machine can do three vertical rolls. Has 260-h.p. American Lycoming engine and German Hoffmann propeller, for top speed of 180 m.p.h. and 3,000-feet-per-minute climb.

AEROSPATIALE SN601 CORVETTE French turbojet executive transport, air taxi and trainer can carry up to 14 passengers at 475 m.p.h. for 900 miles. Power is two 2,300-lbs.t. P. & W. (Canada) engines for SN601 and 2,755-lbs.t. French Turbomecas for SN602.

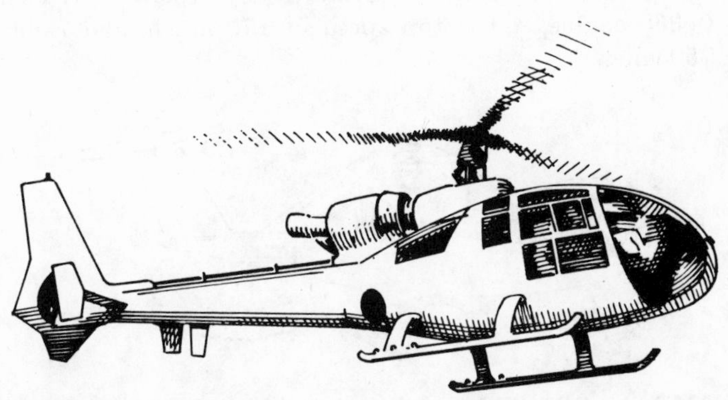

AEROSPATIALE/WESTLAND SA 341 GAZELLE General-purpose five-seat helicopter built in Great Britain and France for military and civil use. With 590-s.h.p. Astazou engine, it has top speed of 192 m.p.h. and maximum range of 415 miles.

C.A.A.R.P. CAP-20L Latest version of all-wood French competition aerobatic machine, developed from long line of Piel homebuilts. With American 260-h.p. Lycoming engine, lightweight version has much improved maneuverability and rate of climb.

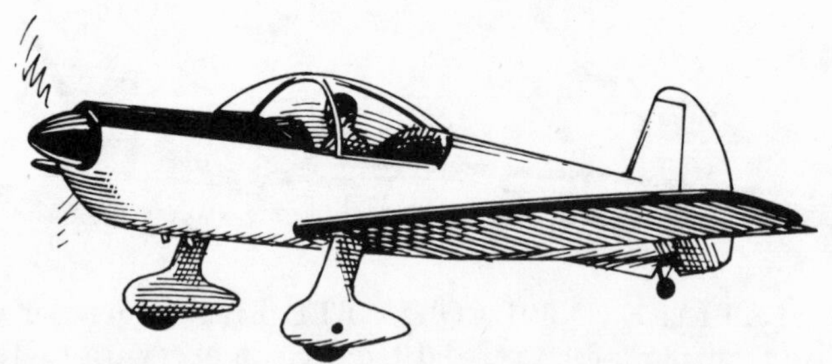

MUDRY CAP 10 Two-seat all-wood French aerobatic trainer, developed from Emeraude sport plane and used by French Air Force and schools. Powered by 180-h.p. Lycoming 0–360 engine, it has top speed of 170 m.p.h. and range of 750 miles.

COLOMBAN CRI-CRI Single-seat all-metal French ultralight homebuilt is smallest twin-engined airplane in history. Weighs 140 lbs. empty, can cruise at 100 m.p.h. with two 9-h.p. 137-cc. Rowena engines. Takes off in 525 feet and has 200-mile range.

CROSES EC-6 CRIQUET Sophisticated French two-seat development of pre–World War II Flying Flea homebuilt, with many major parts of polyester, resin and fiberglass. With 90-h.p. Continental engine, cruises at 105 m.p.h., flies as slow as 25 m.p.h., and will not stall.

DASSAULT MERCURE French wide-bodied short-haul turbofan airliner carries up to 160 passengers for 1,250 miles. Powered by two 15,000-lbs.t. P. & W. engines, cruises at 575 m.p.h. at 20,000 feet.

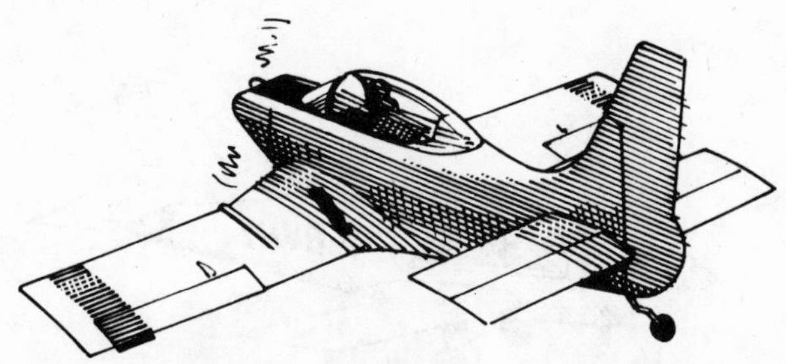

JURCA M.J. 5 SIROCCO Tandem two-seat all-wood homebuilt sport plane designed by Hungarian Marcel Jurca in France and built by amateurs in many countries. With 115-h.p. Lycoming engine, will hit 145 m.p.h., climb over 16,000 feet and take off in just 800 feet.

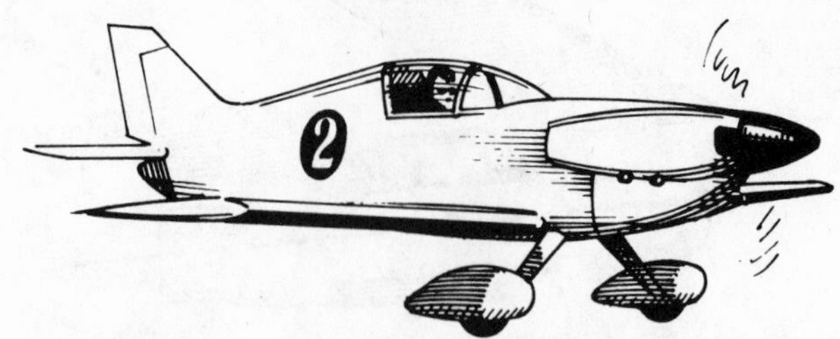

PIEL C.P. 80 First French Formula One racer can be built either of wood or laminated plastics by amateurs. With 90-h.p. Continental engine, has top speed of 200 m.p.h. and maximum rate of climb near 2,400 feet per minute.

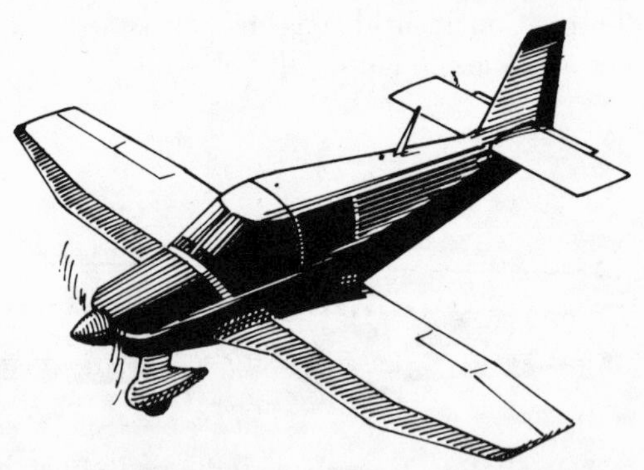

ROBIN DR 400/180 REGENT Typical of long line of French all-wood personal planes descended from late 1940's Jodel homebuilts. Seats four or five. With 180-h.p. Lycoming engine, cruises at 165 m.p.h. for more than 900 miles.

SOCATA RALLYE One of extensive series of French all-metal STOL private airplanes that are available with engines of 100 to 235 h.p. Model 235 GT will take off in less than 500 feet and cruise at better than 150 m.p.h.

HIRTH HI-27 ACROSTAR Designed in Switzerland and built in West Germany, this competition aerobatic design features interconnected controls and extensive use of fiberglass. With 220-h.p. Franklin engine, climbs at 3,000 feet per minute.

RFB/GRUMMAN AMERICAN FANLINER Joint U.S.–West German project uses parts from G–A Trainer and Traveller in unique ducted-fan design for research. With 114-h.p. Audi Wankel engine, cruises at 112 m.p.h. with two people.

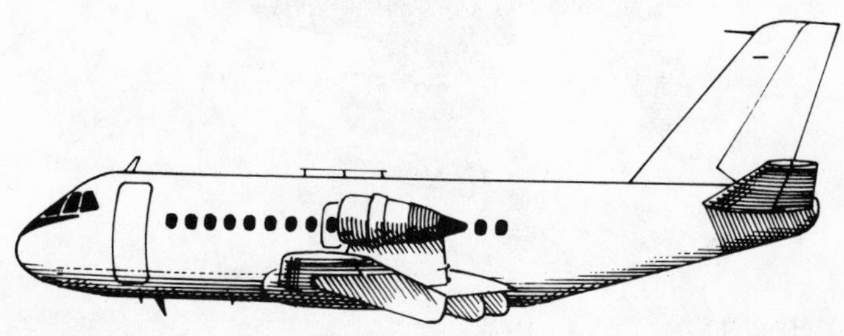

VFW–FOKKER 614 Novel twin-turbofan short-haul airliner developed for feeder airlines by firms from Germany, Belgium, Netherlands. Powered by two 7,300-lbs.t. Rolls-Royce/SNECMA engines, it will carry 44 passengers at 450 m.p.h. for 750 miles.

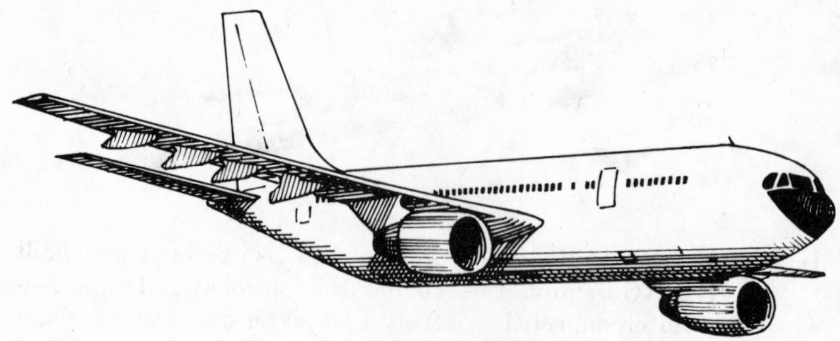

AIRBUS A300 Built by international consortium (France, Germany, Netherlands, Spain), this wide-bodied medium-range airliner is the European answer to American DC–10 and L–1011. With two 50,000-lbs.t. G.E. engines, can carry 250 passengers at 570 m.p.h.

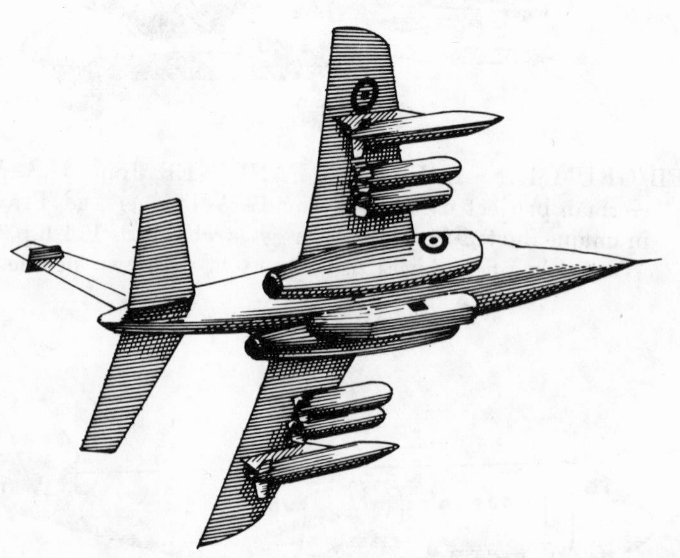

ALPHA JET Joint French-German advanced trainer and ground-support plane will become major European type. Powered by two 3,000-lbs.t. French turbojet engines, has top speed of Mach .85 and can climb to 40,000 feet in under 10 minutes.

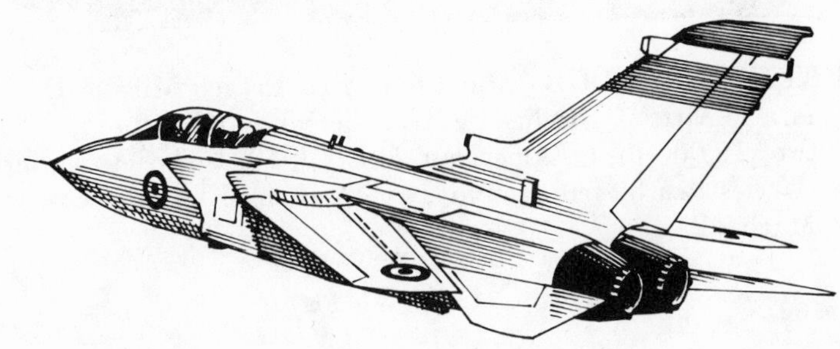

PANAVIA MRCA TORNADO Developed by and for Great Britain, France, Germany, and Italy, this variable-geometry multipurpose fighter-bomber will serve with several air forces. Has two 14,500-lbs.t. turbojet engines for top speed over Mach 2.

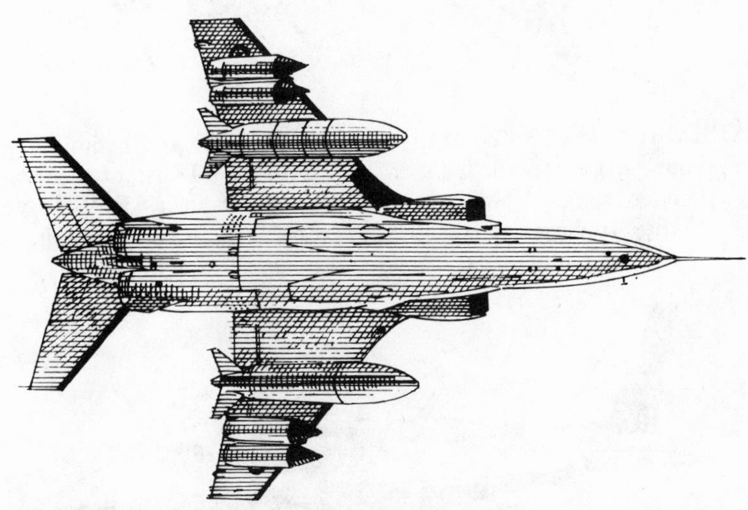

SEPECAT JAGUAR Joint Anglo-French fighter-bomber comes in single- and two-seat versions and can carry up to 7,000 lbs. of bombs and rockets. Powered by two Rolls-Royce/Turbomeca jet engines of 8,000 lbs.t., has top speed of Mach 1.5.

IAI KFIR (LION CUB) Much improved French Mirage III by Israel Aircraft Industries for defense and export, using two 18,000-lbs.t. American G.E. J–79 turbojet engines. Carries two 30-mm. cannon, air-to-air missiles, and can top Mach 2.2.

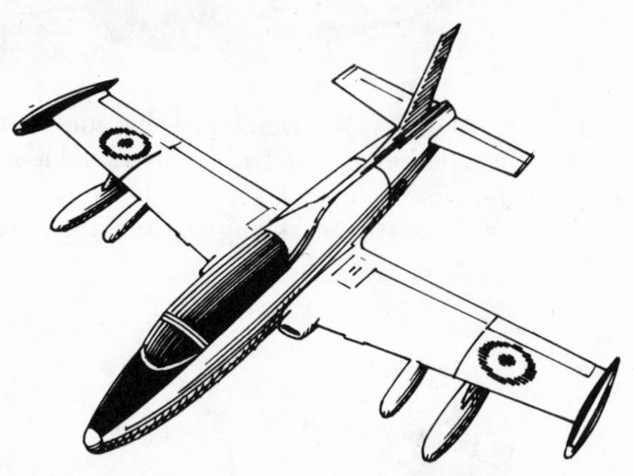

AERMACCHI MB 326 Italian two-seat trainer and ground-support attack plane can carry up to 4,000 lbs. of weapons under wings. Powered by single 4,000 lbs.t. Rolls-Royce Viper turbojet, has top speed of Mach .82 and maximum range of 1,500 miles.

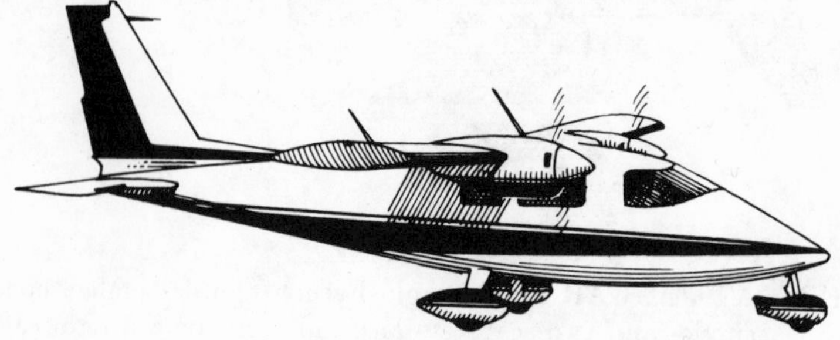

PARTENAVIA P-68 VICTOR Unusually clean fixed-landing-gear twin-engine private and business airplane built in Italy. With two 200-h.p. Lycoming engines, cruises at 190 m.p.h., takes off in 750 feet, and has range of 1,000 miles.

WSK-MIELEC M-15 Polish agricultural airplane is probably the only jet-propelled biplane ever designed. Can carry almost 5,000 lbs. of chemicals. Powered by 3,300-lbs.t. Soviet turbofan, will operate under 100 m.p.h., laying 200-foot swath.

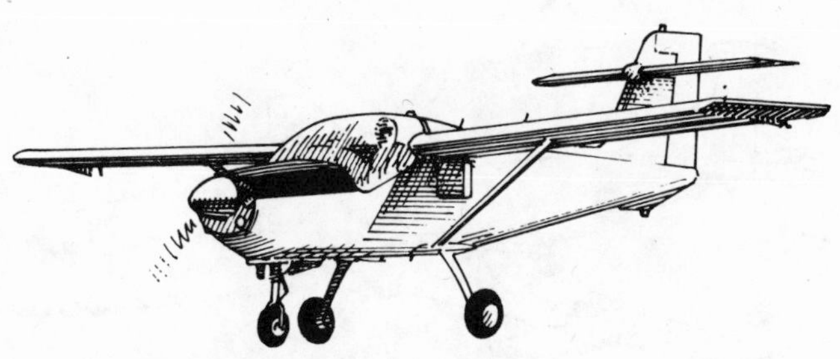

SAAB SAFARI Swedish trainer and utility airplane developed from German Bolkow Junior, which began as American home-built. Can carry 600 lbs. of droppable emergency supplies under wings. Has 200-h.p. Lycoming 0–360 engine for 130-m.p.h. cruise.

BRITTEN-NORMAN BN-2A MK III TRISLANDER Cleverly stretched Islander (see p. 368) with novel placement of third engine. Can carry 17 passengers from 1,500-foot air-strips. Powered by three 260-h.p. Lycoming 0–540 engines, cruises at 165 m.p.h. on short hauls.

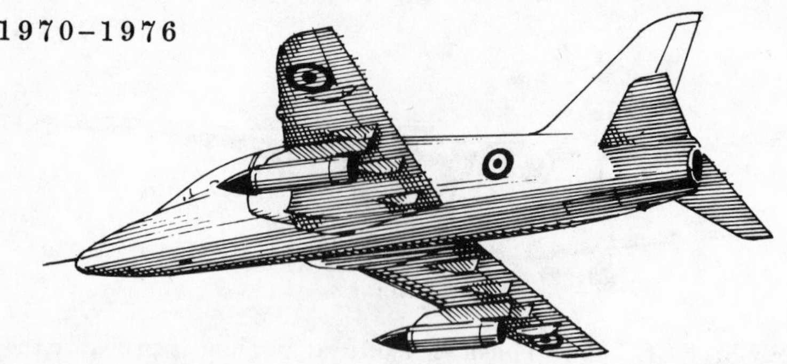

HAWKER SIDDELEY HAWK British basic and advanced military trainer with ground-support capability. Can carry 5,000 lbs. externally: bombs, rockets, long-range fuel tanks. One Rolls-Royce/Turbomeca Adour engine of 5,300 lbs.t. gives Mach .9 top speed.

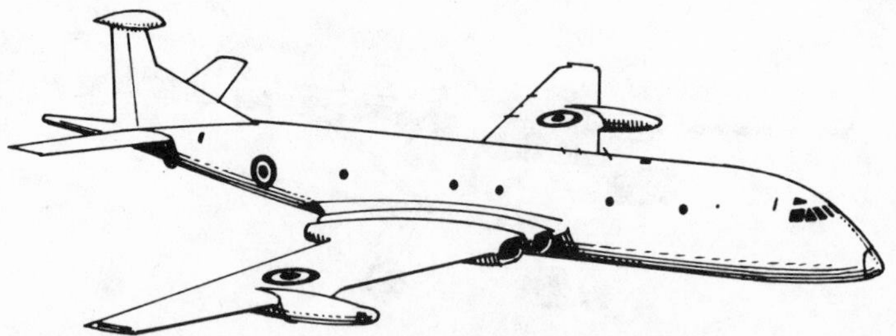

HAWKER SIDDELEY NIMROD MR MK I Long-range patrol version of pioneering British De Havilland Comet jetliner has 48-foot internal weapons bay for anti-submarine devices. Four Rolls-Royce Spey turbofans give 20-hour endurance and 5,000-mile range.

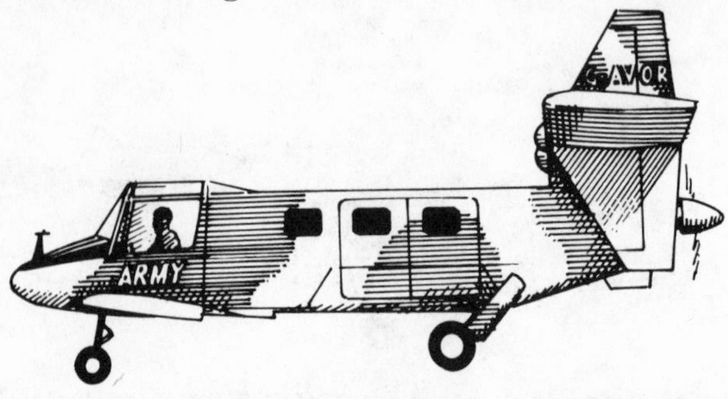

LOCKSPEISER LDA-01 Private British utility aircraft uses tandem wings for simplified loading of cargo. Has many interchangeable parts. A 7⁄10-scale prototype has 160-h.p. Lycoming engine, cruises at 105 m.p.h. and takes off in 600 feet.

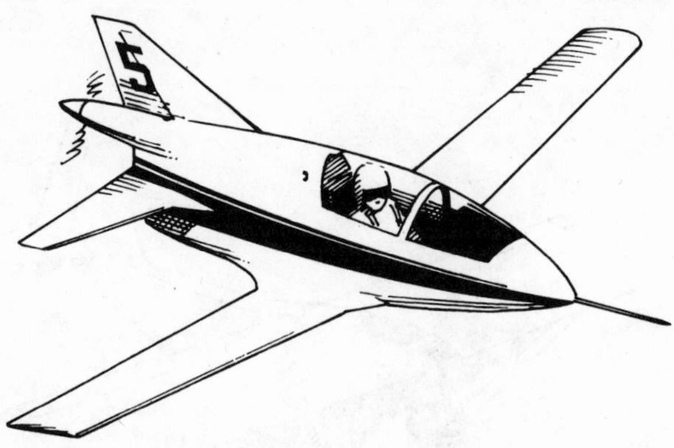

BEDE BD-5 MICRO High-performance all-metal kit-style American homebuilt is available as jet, glider or prop-driven airplane. Tiny craft weighs under 400 lbs., yet claimed to cruise near 200 m.p.h. on 70-h.p. two-cycle engine.

BEDE BD-6 Miniature single-seat version of Bede BD-4 four-place American homebuilt has simplified all-metal construction. With 70-h.p. Xenoah snowmobile engine, should cruise at 140 m.p.h.

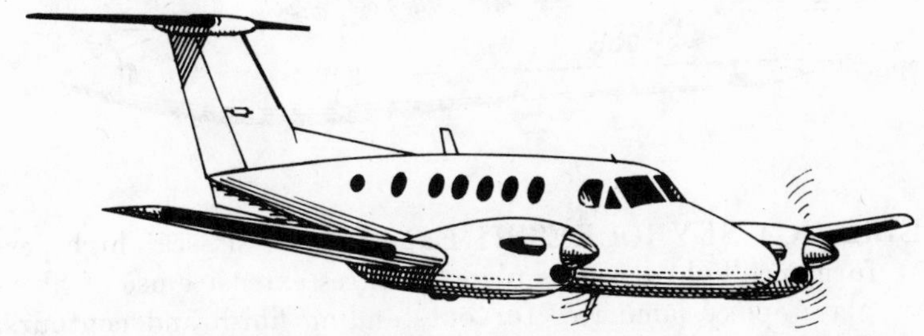

BEECH SUPER KING AIR 200 Larger, more powerful T-tailed version of popular executive transport can carry up to 13 passengers at 260 m.p.h. for 1,250 miles. Two 850-h.p. P. & W. (Canada) turboprop engines. Also U.S. Army U-21 and C-12.

BELLANCA 8KCAB DECATHLON Competition version of Citabria aerobatic trainer, descended from classic Aeronca Champion is stressed for plus 8G's, minus 5G's, has symmetrical airfoil for inverted flight. 150-h.p. Lycoming engine gives 145 m.p.h. top speed, 1,000-feet-per-minute climb.

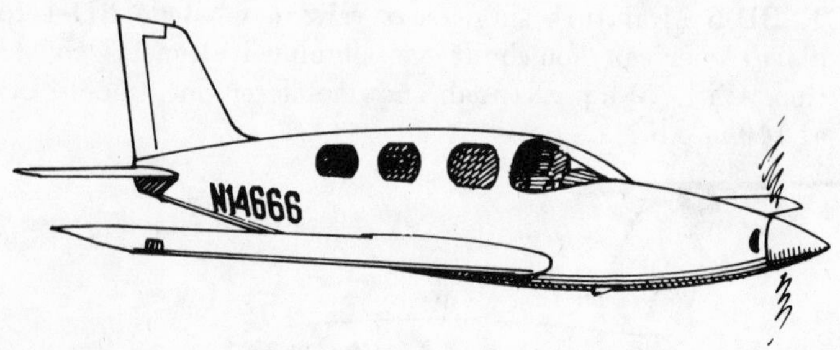

BELLANCA SKYROCKET II Experimental six-seat high-performance light business plane features extensive use of fiberglass epoxy laminates for outstanding finish and contours. With 435-h.p. Continental engine, set speed records of 327 m.p.h. for 500 km. and 302 m.p.h. for 1,000 km.

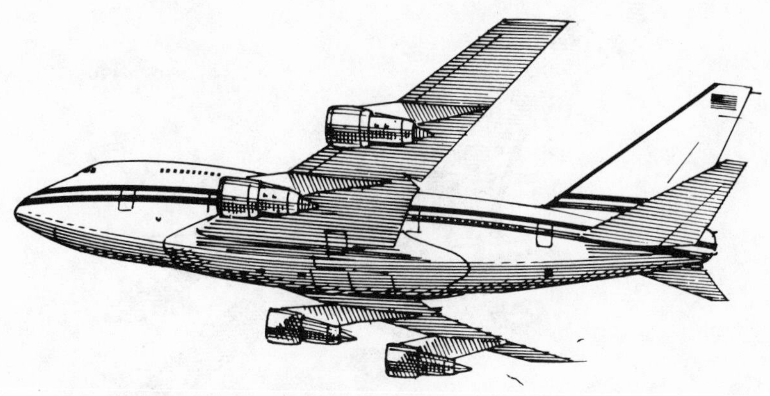

BOEING 747-SP Special-performance version is 48 feet shorter than standard giant 747 airliner. Carries maximum of 316 passengers. With four P. & W. 47,000-lbs.t. turbofans, cruises at Mach .92 for 10,000 miles.

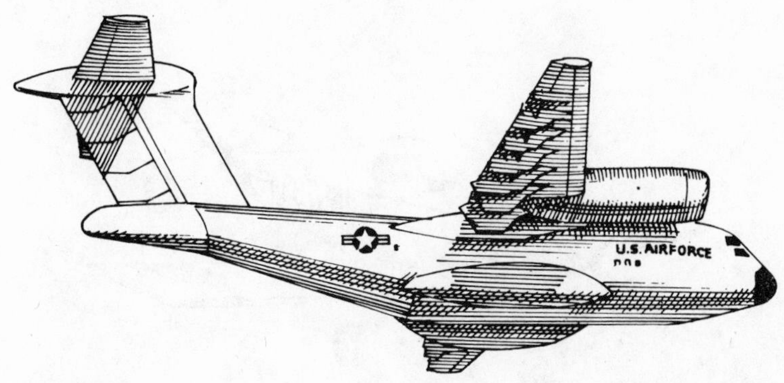

BOEING YC-14 Entrant in U.S. Air Force's STOL transport competition uses flap-blowing from over-wing engines to operate from 2,000-foot rough fields. Two 50,000-lbs.t. G.E. turbofan engines give 475 m.p.h. cruise and 1,100-mile range.

CESSNA 150 AEROBAT Special custom model of popular two-seat trainer can do all basic aerobatic maneuvers, thanks to beefed-up structure. 100-h.p. Continental engine gives top speed of 125 m.p.h. and minimum speed of 48 m.p.h.

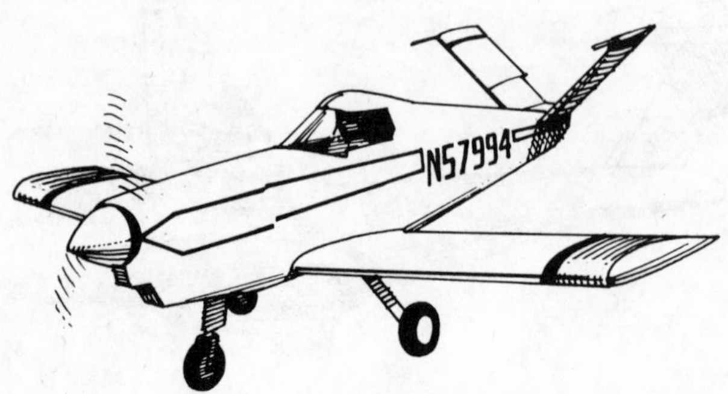

DAVIS DA-5 Single-seat all-metal homebuilt sport plane of simplified construction uses V-tail proven on earlier DA-2. With 65-h.p. Continental engine, cruises at 140 m.p.h., takes off in 600 feet, and climbs to 14,500 feet.

E.A.A. SUPER ACRO SPORT Designed by E.A.A. President Paul Poberezny for construction by high school students. Super Acro Sport is for competition aerobatics. With 180-h.p. Lycoming engine, cruises at 130 m.p.h. and climbs 1,100 feet per minute.

E.A.A. POBER PIXIE Much modernized version of 1930's Heath Parasol, by E.A.A. President Poberezny for the amateur builder. Prototype has 65-h.p. Limbach VW engine, cruises 85 m.p.h., takes off in 300 feet and lands at 30 m.p.h.

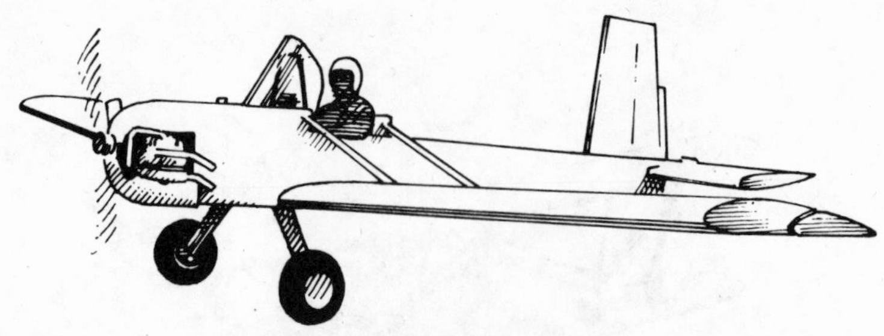

EVANS VP-1 VOLKSPLANE All-wood single-seat VW-powered ultralight homebuilt sport plane with all-flying horizontal tail. On 40 h.p., cruises at 75 m.p.h., lands in 200 feet. Can also be built as two-seat VP-2.

FAIRCHILD REPUBLIC A-10 Standard U.S. Air Force single-seat close-support aircraft, armed with 7-barrel G.E. 30-mm. cannon and up to 8 tons of external weapons. Powered by two 9,000-lbs.t. G.E. turbofan engines for top speed of 518 m.p.h., 6,000-feet-per-minute climb, and 2,900-mile range.

GARRISON OM-1 MELMOTH High-performance two-seat all-metal long-range homebuilt with full all-weather instrumentation. A 210-h.p. Continental engine and 142 gallons of fuel give range of over 2,000 miles at 170 m.p.h.

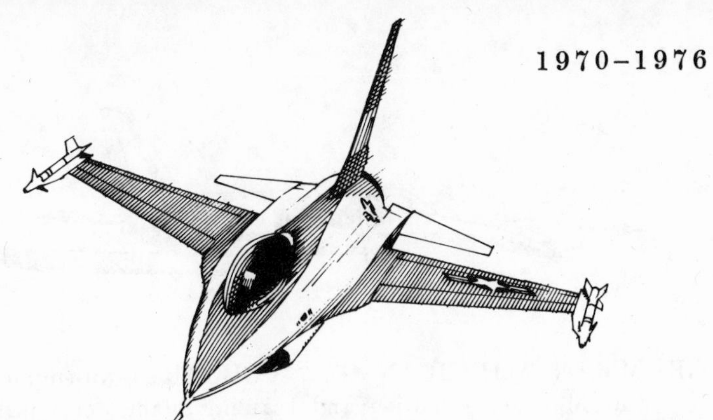

GENERAL DYNAMICS F-16 Lightweight single-seat air combat fighter and two-seat trainer. More than 1,000 ordered by U.S. Air Force and NATO after winning design competition. One P. & W. F100 turbofan of 25,000 lbs.t. gives top speed over Mach 2, and 2,300-mile range.

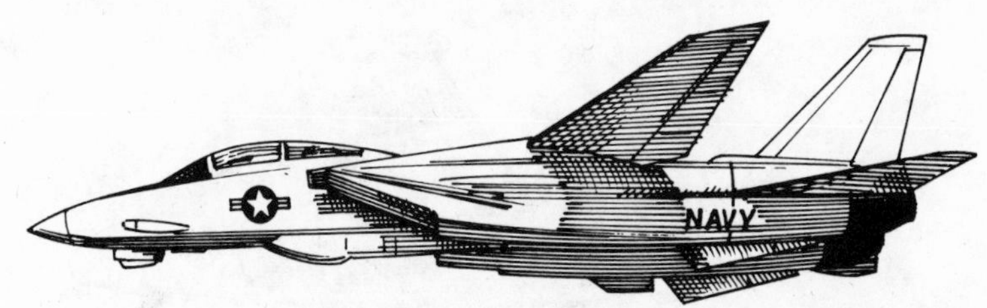

GRUMMAN AMERICAN F-14 TOMCAT Variable-geometry carrier-based U.S. Navy multi-mission fighter carries 20-mm. Vulcan cannon and 14,500 lbs. of bombs and missiles. Two 21,000-lbs.t. P. & W. engines give top speed of Mach 2.3+ and ceiling over 56,000 feet.

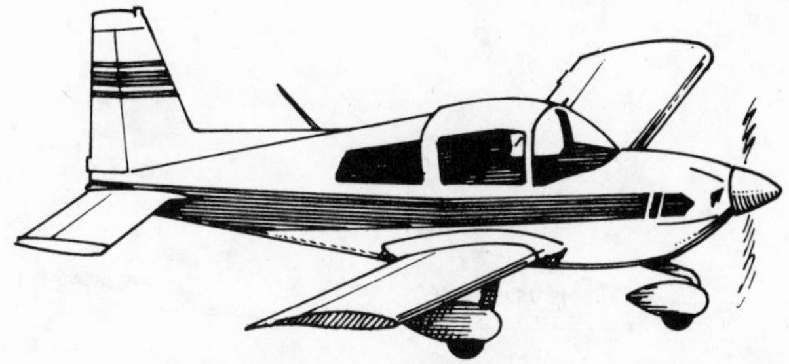

GRUMMAN AMERICAN TIGER Four-seat improved-performance version of AA-5 has much structural use of aluminum honeycomb. A 180-h.p. Lycoming engine gives top speed of 170 m.p.h., cruise of 160 m.p.h. and take-off run of 875 feet.

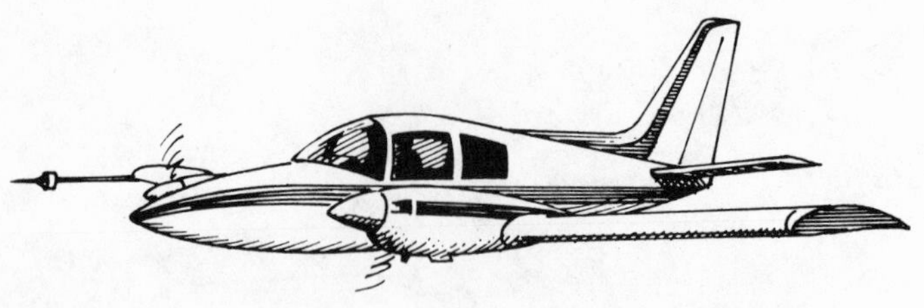

GRUMMAN AMERICAN GA-7 COUGAR Twin-engine four-seat low-cost executive and training plane developed from American Yankee line. Two 160-h.p. Lycoming engines give cruise speed of 190 m.p.h.

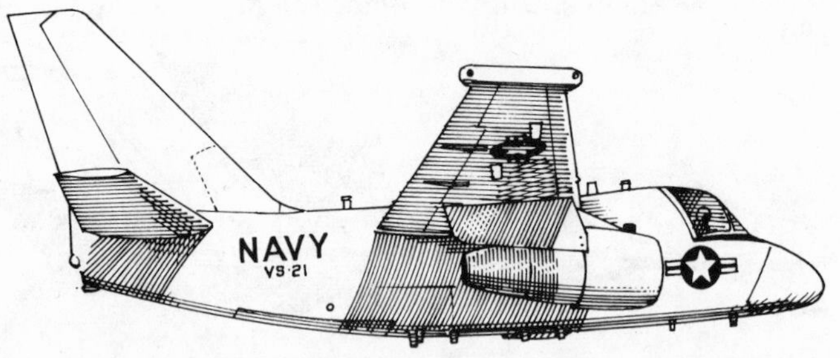

LOCKHEED S-3 VIKING Carrier-based anti-submarine patrol bomber for U.S. Navy carries mass of advanced electronic gear and variety of bombs and missiles. Two G.E. TF34 turbofan engines of 9,300 lbs.t. give 425-m.p.h. cruise speed, 2,300-mile range.

MARTIN X-24 Wedge-shaped lifting-body vehicle for re-entry research leading to spacecraft which can be landed like airplane is 19 feet wide, 37½ feet long, weighs 13,000 lbs. at takeoff. One 8,000-lbs.t. rocket motor gives top speed of 1,200 m.p.h. after air launch from B-52 carrier plane.

MAULE M-5 LUNAR ROCKET Four-place V STOL personal plane has 210-h.p. Continental or 220-h.p. Franklin engine. Takes off and lands in 400 feet, cruises over 165 m.p.h. for 1,000 miles. Four-foot door for bulky cargo.

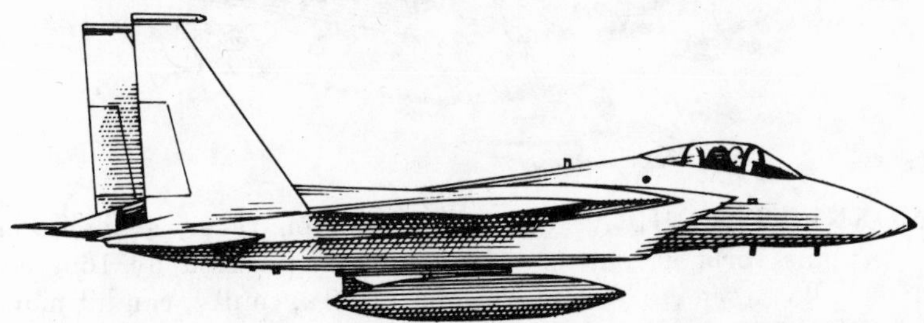

MCDONNELL DOUGLAS F-15 EAGLE U.S. Air Force air-superiority fighter has two-seat trainer version. Has climbed to 94,000 feet in 4+ minutes, and carries 15,000 lbs. of weapons. Two P. & W. F100 turbofan engines of 25,000 lbs. t. give top speed of Mach 2.5+, ceiling of 100,000 feet.

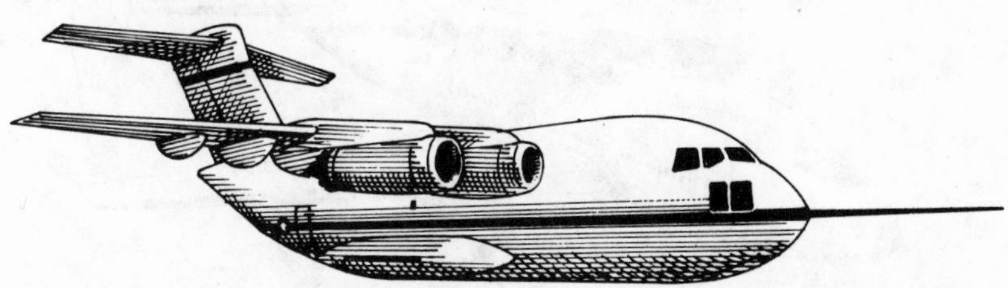

MCDONNELL DOUGLAS YC-15 Entrant in U.S. Air Force competition for STOL jet cargo plane to replace C-130 Hercules can carry 150 troops. Four P. & W. turbofan engines permit loaded takeoff in 2,000 feet, 500 m.p.h. cruise speed, range of 3,000 miles.

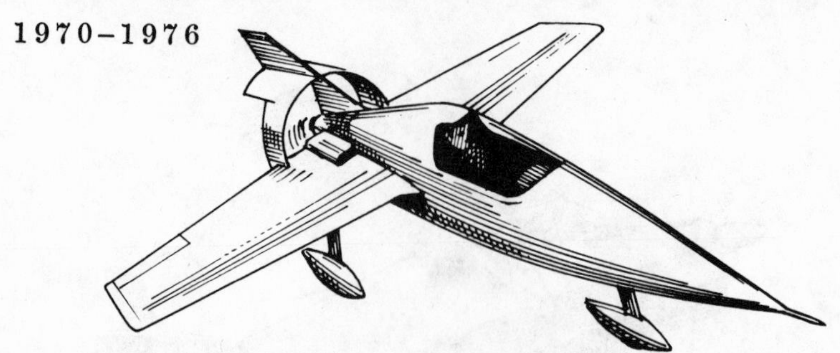

MILLER JM-2 TEXAS GEM Prototype radical Formula One racer built of honeycomb-reinforced vacuum-molded fiberglass. Original canard surface and propeller shroud removed after tests. A 100-h.p. Continental engine gives 230 m.p.h. top speed.

MONNETT SONERAI Formula Vee pylon racer, available in plans form as one- or two-seater, is powered by 1600-cc. Volkswagen car engine. Weighs 475 lbs, empty, can hit more than 160 m.p.h. and cruise at 125 m.p.h. for 2½ hours.

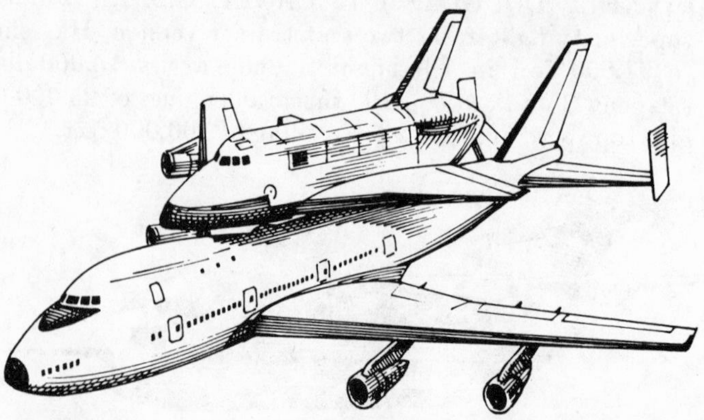

SPACE SHUTTLE First airplanelike reuseable manned spacecraft with multiple orbital missions. Orbiter resembles delta-winged airplane, has three 375,000-lbs.t. rocket motors, weighs over 4.4 million pounds with boosters, and can put 65,000 lbs. in earth orbit.

MCDONNELL DOUGLAS F-18 Advanced U.S. Navy combat fighter developed from Northrop F-17 Cobra is powered by two 16,000-lbs.t. G.E. turbojets. Has top speed of Mach 1.8+, range of 2,300 miles and can carry 13,000 lbs. of weapons.

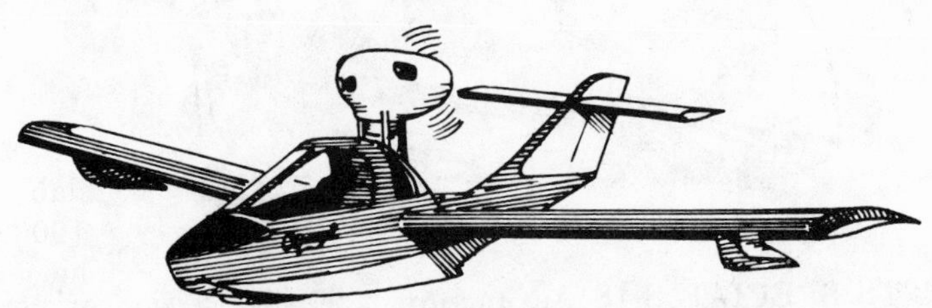

PEREIRA GP3 OSPREY II Two-seat homebuilt amphibian with 150-h.p. Lycoming engine cruises at 120 m.p.h., stalls at 55 m.p.h., and will take off from water in 520 feet. Developed from earlier single-seat Osprey I.

PAZMANY PL-4 Single-seat all-metal sport plane intended for amateur builders features 1600-cc. Volkswagen engine with V-belt reduction drive. Cruises at 98 m.p.h. for 340 miles at 30 miles per gallon and stalls under 50 m.p.h.

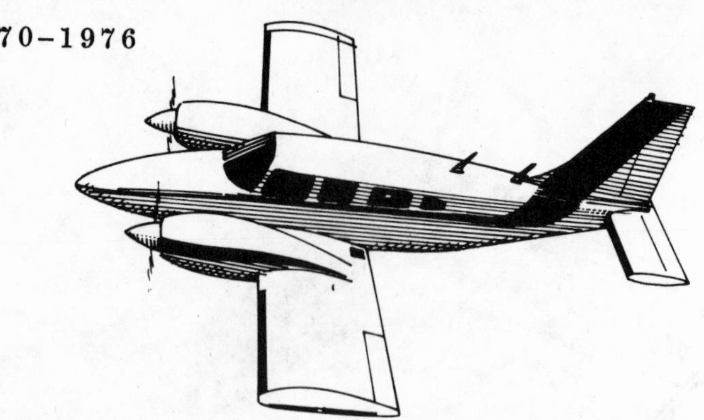

PIPER PA-34 SENECA Six-passenger light business and personal plane with two 200-h.p. Continental engines driving opposite-rotating propellers. Cruises at 218 m.p.h. at 20,000 feet for 650 miles.

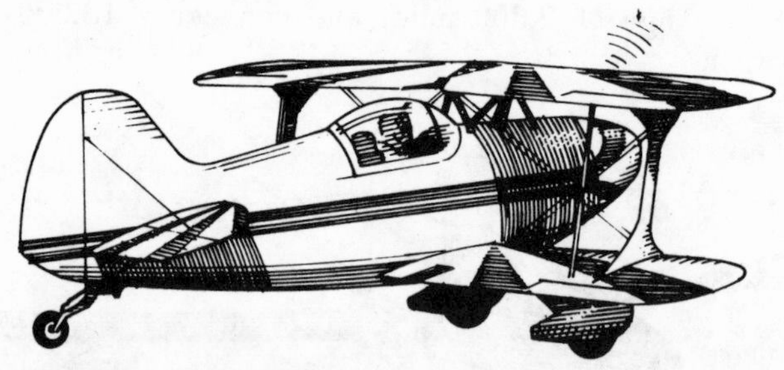

PITTS SPECIAL S-1S Advanced-competition version of popular homebuilt aerobatic plane is available in plans or from factory. Features 180-h.p. Lycoming engine, symmetrical airfoils, four ailerons. Cruises at 150 m.p.h., climbs 3,000 feet per minute.

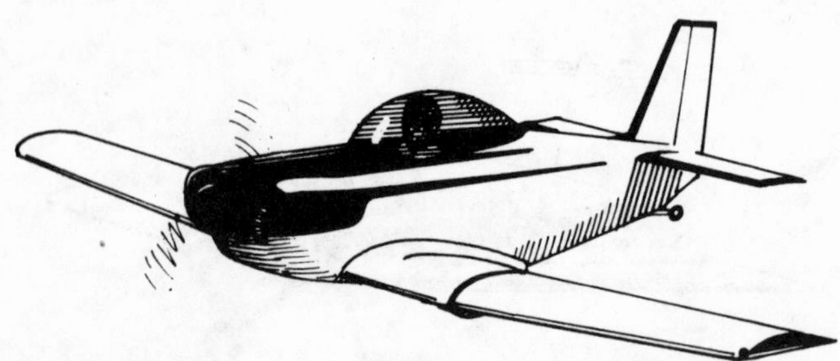

RAND KR-1 Single-seat ultralight homebuilt sport plane features simplified construction of polystyrene foam covered with Dynal epoxy fabric. With 1200-cc. Volkswagen engine, cruises at 140 m.p.h. for 750 miles. Also two-seat KR-2 version.

OWL RACER OR-70 Series of sophisticated and successful Formula One racers from designer George Owl feature 20-foot-high aspect ratio wings. With 100-h.p. Continental engine, can reach 250 m.p.h.

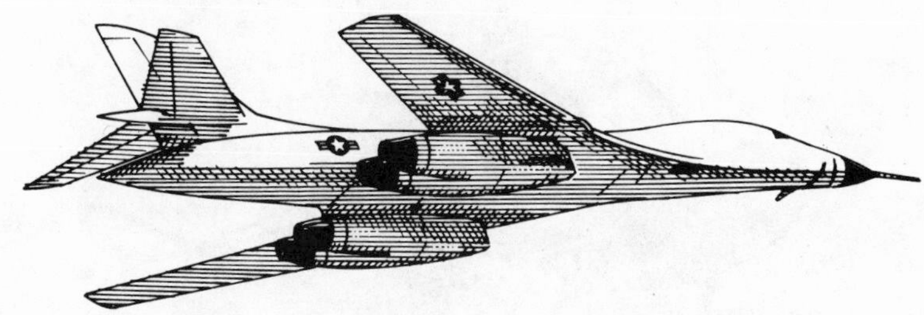

ROCKWELL B-1 Advanced supersonic heavy bomber for U.S. Air Force replaces aging B-52. Variable-geometry wings and four 30,000-lbs.t. G.E. turbofan engines give Mach 2 speed, 650-m.p.h. cruise speed and 6,000-mile range with up to 115,000 lbs. of nuclear weapons.

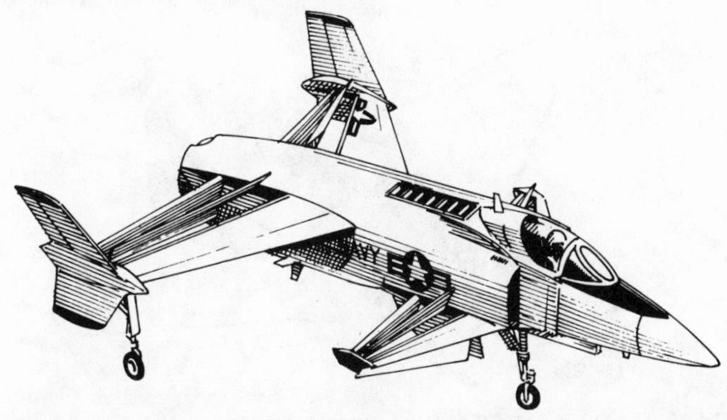

ROCKWELL XFV12A Single-seat carrier-based V/STOL attack fighter for U.S. Navy features delta-canard layout and augmentor wing which ducts power of 30,000-lbs.t. turbofan for speed range of 0 to Mach 2+.

ROCKWELL COMMANDER 112 Advanced all-metal four-seat light personal plane has 200-h.p. Lycoming engine for cruise of 160 m.p.h. at 7,500 feet. Takes off in 1,200 feet, has range of 975 miles.

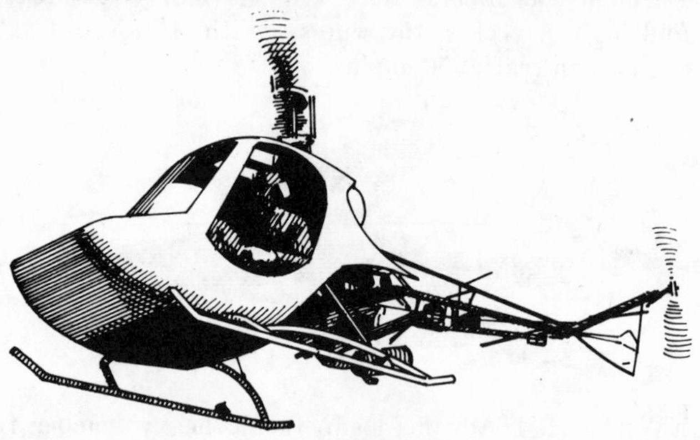

ROTORWAY SCORPION TOO Two-seat amateur-built true helicopter powered by 140-h.p. Vulcan water-cooled marine engine cruises at over 75 m.p.h., can hover at 9,500 feet, weighs 690 lbs. empty.

RUTAN VARI-VIGGEN Two-seat delta-canard homebuilt flying test-bed for extreme low-speed control and safety ideas. With 150-h.p. Lycoming engine, cruises at 150 m.p.h., tops 180 m.p.h., and lands at 50 m.p.h. in 600 feet.

RUTAN VARI-EZE Two-seat tandem ultralight homebuilt canard featuring NASA-designed winglets for wingtip vortex control. Very-easy construction of fiberglass-covered urethane foam. Prototype hit 180 m.p.h. with 63-h.p. Volkswagen engine; later version has 100-h.p. Continental.

STEEN SKYBOLT Two-seat fully aerobatic biplane for amateur builders resembles larger Pitts Special. With 180-h.p. Lycoming engine, cruises at 130 m.p.h., climbs 2,500 feet per minute; stressed to plus 12G's, minus 10G's.

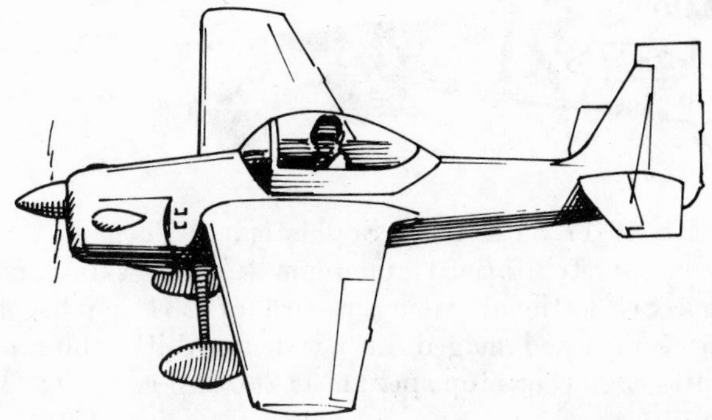

STEPHENS AKRO Single-seat competition aerobatic craft varies from usual American biplane practice. As modified by Leo Loudenslager, won 1975 U.S. Championships. With 200-h.p. Lycoming engine, cruises at 150 m.p.h., lands at 55 m.p.h., climbs 4,000 feet per minute.

STOLP SA-300 STARDUSTER TOO Very popular two-seat version of homebuilt Starduster can use engines from 150 to 260 h.p. Cruises at 120 m.p.h., lands at 60 m.p.h. and can fly three hours on normal fuel load.

WILLIAMS W-17 STINGER Sophisticated Formula One racer features stretch-formed aluminum fuselage skins and wood wings. Set national racing record of 234 m.p.h. prior to being severely damaged in accident. With 100-h.p. Continental engine, has top speed near 260 m.p.h.

MAHONEY SORCERESS Advanced all-metal Sport Biplane Class racer designed by Lee Mahoney set many racing records. Powered by 135-h.p. Lycoming engine, has top speed of 220 m.p.h., range of 1,500 miles on 45 gallons internal fuel.

VAN'S RV-3 All-metal single-seat amateur-built sport plane features speed range of 48 to 220 m.p.h. using flaps and drooping ailerons. Can be powered by engines from 100 h.p. to 180 h.p. for sport and aerobatic flying.

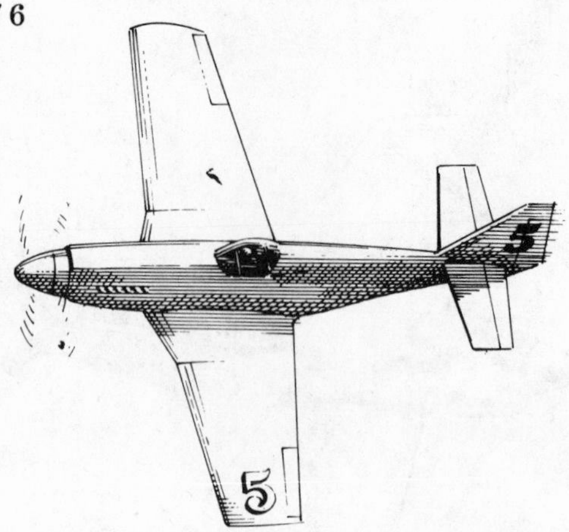

RED BARON RB-51 Highly modified North American P-51D Mustang used for Unlimited Class pylon racing has Rolls-Royce Griffon engine and contra-rotating props from Avro Shackleton patrol bomber. Top speed near 500 m.p.h. required much enlarged tail.

RLU BREEZY Novel two- or three-seat homebuilt sport plane features uncovered fuselage for antique look; can use engines from 90 h.p. up. Cruises 70 to 75 m.p.h., takes off in less than 500 feet, is easy to fly.

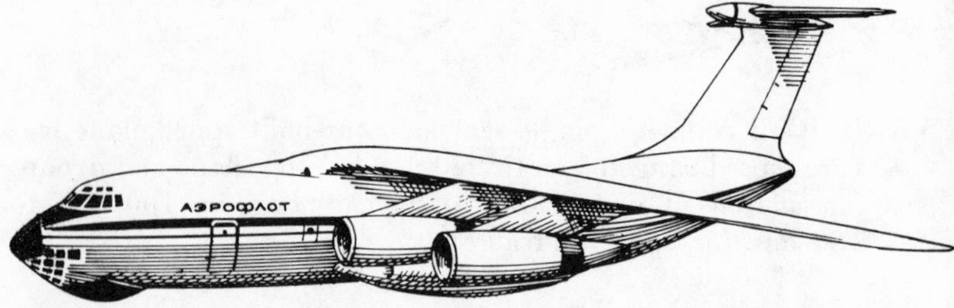

ILYUSHIN IL-76 Wide-bodied turbofan heavy-logistics transport in service with Soviet Air Force. Powered by four 26,000-lbs.t. engines, can carry 80,000 lbs. of cargo from short, rough fields for 3,000 miles.

MIL V-12 Enormous general-purpose heavy-lift helicopter of Soviet Air Force has four 6,500-lbs.t. engines driving two 115-foot rotors. Has lifted record 88,000 lbs. of cargo. Can cruise at 150 m.p.h.

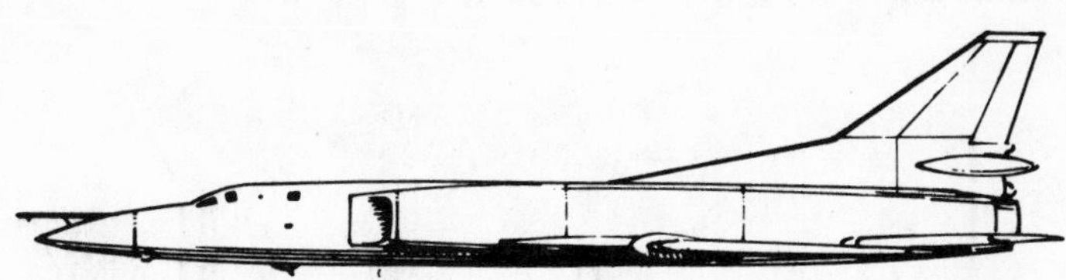

TUPOLEV BACKFIRE Twin-jet strategic patrol bomber of Soviet Air Force has variable-geometry wings, can reach Mach 2 at 48,000 feet. Carries two large stand-off missiles at Mach 1.5 or 17,500 lbs. of bombs. Powered by two 45,000-lbs.t. turbofans.

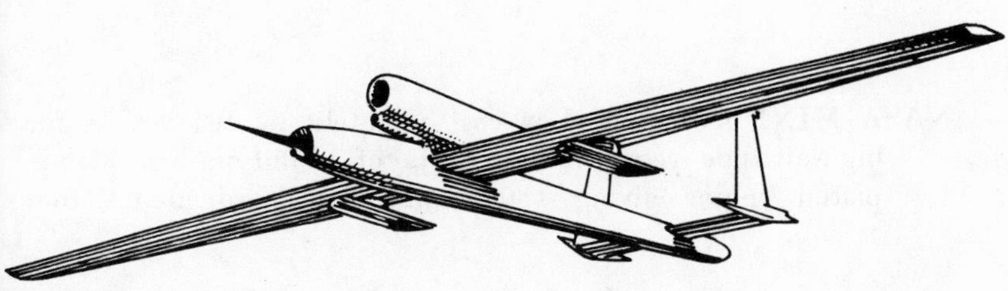

BOEING B-GULL YQM-94A Remotely piloted vehicle (RPV) to be used for long-range reconnaissance missions with TV cameras and other secret equipment by U.S. Air Force. A 5,300-lbs.t. turbojet engine gives 300-m.p.h. cruise speed at 50,000+ feet for up to 30 hours.

E-SYSTEMS L450F Turboprop-powered long-range high-altitude reconnaissance drone first tested with pilot. Developed from Schweizer 2–32 sailplane, can fly at 100 m.p.h. for more than 24 hours above 50,000 feet.

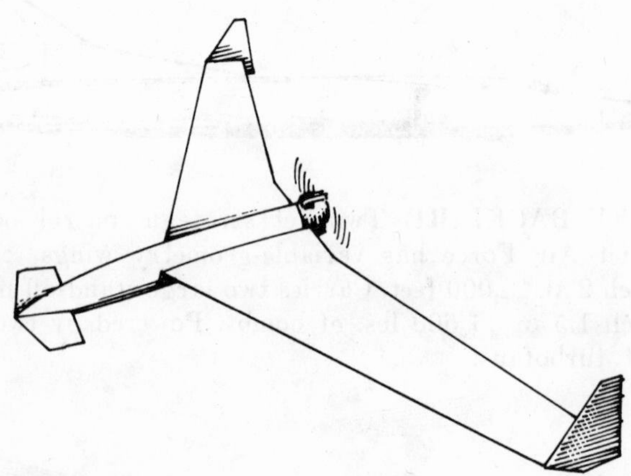

NASA MINI-SNIFFER Low-cost remotely piloted vehicle for high-altitude research on effects of pollution has 15-h.p. piston engine giving 180 m.p.h. top speed, 90,000-foot ceiling.

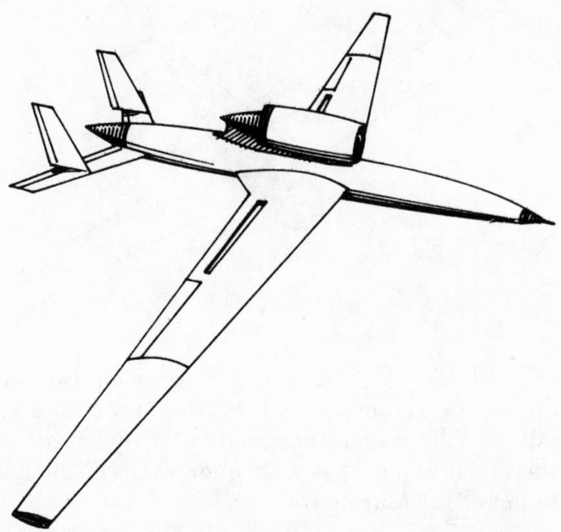

RYAN YQM-98A R-TERN Remotely piloted vehicle for U.S. Air Force's Compass Cope project can cruise at 70,000 feet for 30 hours at Mach .6. Has 81-foot wingspan and can carry extensive sophisticated electronic gear.

MILITKY MB-E1 World's first electric airplane, developed in West Germany from Austrian-powered sailplane. Has battery-driven 10-kw. motor giving 56 m.p.h. and more than 12 minutes duration.

SCHEIBE SF-25 SUPER FALKE German two-seat powered sailplane for training and touring uses 65-h.p. Limbach-modified Volkswagen car engine. Cruises at 100 m.p.h., stalls at 43 m.p.h., has best glide ratio of 29:1 and can fly with power for four hours.

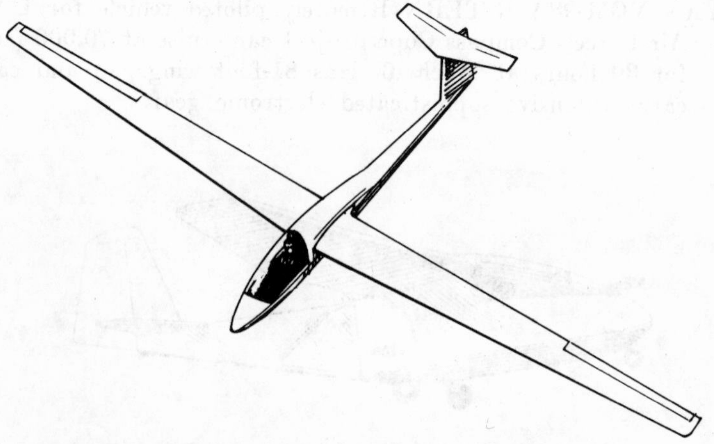

SCHEMPP-HIRTH STANDARD CIRRUS Highly successful German competitive sailplane in 15-meter class is built entirely of fiberglass/foam sandwich and stressed to 10G's. Weighs 445 lbs., has 38:1 glide ratio and can be flown 135 m.p.h. in rough air.

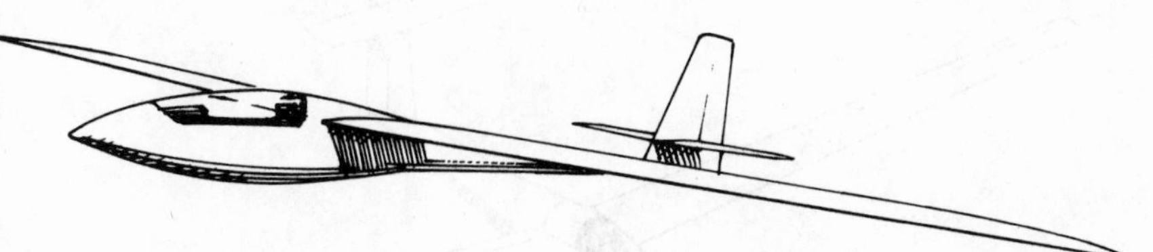

SCHLEICHER ASW-17 World Championship caliber German Open Class sailplane with 66-foot wingspan is built of fiberglass, sandwiched with aluminum and plastic foam. Glide ratio is 48½ :1, and maximum speed is 150 m.p.h.

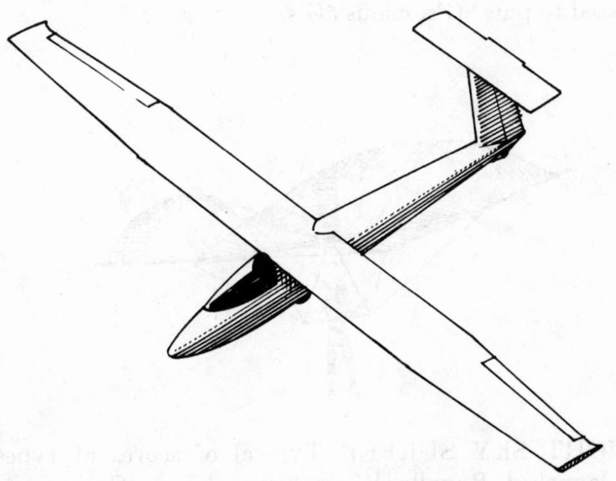

SZD-30A PIRAT Single-seat Polish 15-meter Standard Class sailplane for competition, training and aerobatics is built mainly of wood with fiberglass fairings. Has 33:1 glide ratio and 155 m.p.h. top speed.

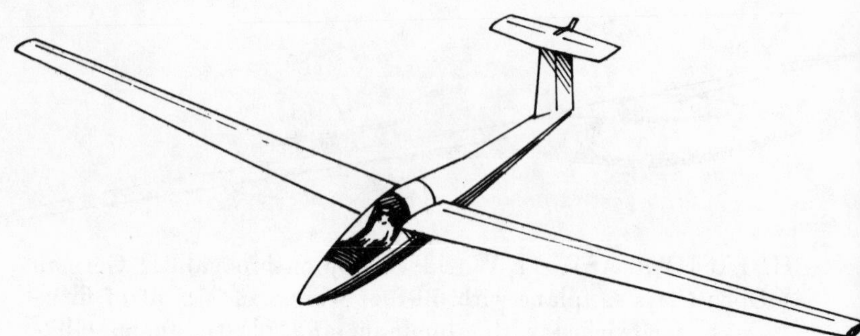

SCHWEIZER SGS 1-35 Latest in long line of popular American sailplanes is all-metal Standard Class craft with 38:1 glide ratio. Weighs 400 lbs., carries 325 lbs. of water ballast and is stressed to plus 8G's, minus 5G's.

MANFLIGHT SKY SURFER Typical of scores of types of foot-launched Rogallo Wing hang gliders. Cruises at 22 m.p.h., stalls at 16½ m.p.h., has 4½:1 glide ratio. Weighs 40 lbs. and can be folded for ease of transport.

INDEX

[The page numbers in italic type indicate illustrations; all other numbers indicate text references.]